The drama of the English Middle Ages is perennially popular with students and theatre audiences alike. *The Cambridge Companion to Medieval English Theatre* provides an authoritative introduction and an up-to-date, illustrated guide to the mystery cycles, morality drama and saints' plays which flourished from the late fourteenth to the mid-sixteenth centuries. The book emphasises regional diversity in the period and engages with the literary and particularly the theatrical values of the plays.

After a general introduction there are chapters devoted to the York, Chester, Towneley (Wakefield) and N-Town cycles of biblical plays, together with an account of the less well-known Cornish drama of the period. Attention to the contribution of different regions is developed in a chapter on East Anglia, and continued in essays on the morality drama and the saints' plays. Two illustrated chapters are devoted to the performance of medieval plays, both in their own time and in recent modern revivals. A full reference section includes a guide to scholarship and criticism, an extensive classified bibliography and a chronological table.

THE CAMBRIDGE
COMPANION TO
MEDIEVAL
ENGLISH
THEATRE

Cambridge Companions to Literature

The Cambridge Companion to Old English Literature
edited by Malcolm Godden and Michael Lapidge

The Cambridge Companion to Dante
edited by Rachel Jacoff

The Cambridge Chaucer Companion
edited by Piero Boitani and Jill Mann

The Cambridge Companion to Shakespeare Studies
edited by Stanley Wells

The Cambridge Companion to English Renaissance Drama
edited by A. R. Braunmuller and Michael Hattaway

The Cambridge Companion to English Poetry, Donne to Marvell
edited by Thomas N. Corns

The Cambridge Companion to Milton
edited by Dennis Danielson

The Cambridge Companion to British Romanticism
edited by Stuart Curran

The Cambridge Companion to James Joyce
edited by Derek Attridge

The Cambridge Companion to Ibsen
edited by James McFarlane

The Cambridge Companion to Brecht
edited by Peter Thomson and Glendyr Sacks

The Cambridge Companion to Beckett
edited by John Pilling

THE CAMBRIDGE
COMPANION TO
MEDIEVAL
ENGLISH
THEATRE

EDITED BY
RICHARD BEADLE

CAMBRIDGE
UNIVERSITY PRESS

Published by the Press Syndicate of the University of Cambridge
The Pitt Building, Trumpington Street, Cambridge CB2 1RP
40 West 20th Street, New York, NY 10011–4211, USA
10 Stamford Road, Oakleigh, Melbourne 3166, Australia

First published 1994

Printed in Great Britain at the University Press, Cambridge

A catalogue record for this book is available from the British Library

Library of Congress cataloguing in publication data

The Cambridge Companion to Medieval English Theatre / edited by
Richard Beadle.
p.   cm. – (Cambridge Companions to Literature)
Includes bibliographical references and index.
ISBN 0 521 36670 4 (hardback) – ISBN 0 521 45916 8 (paperback)
1. Theatre – England – History – Medieval, 500–1500. 2. Theatre –
England – Production and direction – History. 3. English drama – To
1500 – History and criticism. 4. Mysteries and miracle plays,
English – History and criticism. I. Beadle, Richard. II. Series.
PN2587.C36 1994
792'.0942'0902 – dc20   93–4397 CIP

ISBN 0 521 36670 4 hardback
ISBN 0 521 45916 8 hardback

CE

CONTENTS

CONTENTS

ILLUSTRATIONS

ACKNOWLEDGEMENTS

Illustrations 21, 23–29, 31 and 32 are from photographs taken by Richard Axton, reproduced with his kind permission; 2–4, 11, 12, 14–16 are reproduced by permission of the British Library Board.

CONTRIBUTORS

RICHARD BEADLE, University of Cambridge

JOHN C. COLDEWEY, University of Washington, Seattle

ALAN J. FLETCHER, University College, Dublin

DARRYLL GRANTLEY, University of Kent, Canterbury

PETER HAPPÉ, *formerly* Barton Peveril College, Eastleigh

PAMELA M. KING, University of London

JOHN MARSHALL, University of Bristol

PETER MEREDITH, University of Leeds

DAVID MILLS, University of Liverpool

BRIAN O. MURDOCH, University of Stirling

MEG TWYCROSS, University of Lancaster

WILLIAM TYDEMAN, University of Wales, Bangor

PREFACE

'Medieval English theatre' is an expression which possesses more the virtues of custom and convenience than those of strict descriptive accuracy. Of its three components, the least satisfactory is undoubtedly the first, and it is with good justification that many prefer to speak of 'early' English theatre, since the major genres of dramatic composition that came into being during the later medieval period – cycles of biblical drama (or 'mystery plays'), moralities and saints' plays – all sustained a vigorous life until well into the sixteenth century, often into its latter half. 'Medieval' drama, then, continued as a potent cultural force through many decades of what historians tend to call the 'early modern period', and literary scholars 'the Renaissance'. The term 'English', whether understood geographically or linguistically, also has serious limitations, since we have plays from both Scotland and Ireland that follow this banner, as well as a substantial body of texts in the Cornish language which have a natural claim to be regarded as 'English' drama of the period. The most significant word in the title, however, is 'theatre', for it is intended to convey the sense that, more than in any subsequent era, the plays composed in that time were intended to be seen and heard, not read. As 'quick [living] books', they were designed for a general audience which was more accustomed to hearing its literature than to reading it silently, and it is essential to grasp that both the conceptual substance and the imaginative qualities of such plays are inseparable from their theatricality. This is something we may seek to recover partly through traditional means, by a combinative study of texts, documentary records, music and iconography, but it may equally be sought by re-creating performances, in a spirit of authenticity, as best we can across the gap of four or five centuries. Much of what will be found in the chapters that follow is informed by this new spirit of practical enquiry into medieval stagecraft, and two are devoted specifically to it.

A Companion to Medieval English Theatre, at the present time, must content itself with being something of an interim report on a field of knowledge and interpretation which has changed out of all recognition over the last two decades or so, but yet continues to develop. The major shifts and expansions have been taking place in three areas: editorial and textual activity, the accumulation of reliable documentary information about early plays and playing, and the completely new insights furnished by modern attempts to perform the plays in the light of what has thus become known of early theatrical conditions. Accretions in each of these areas are coming in at different rates and at different levels, and it is likely to be some years before a convincing new synthesis emerges to replace the traditional (and easily taught) but flawed 'evolutionary' picture of the early drama (see chapters 1 and 12 below). In the meantime, one of the main lessons of the book is that critics of medieval literature and historians of the drama, and likewise their students, will need to find means to respond intellectually and imaginatively to circumstances of far greater complexity than prevailed less than a generation ago.

Editorial activity in relation to the familiar body of medieval English dramatic texts has recently been more intense than at any time since the manuscripts and early prints were first discovered in the nineteenth cen-turry, and there has been a substantial yield of often difficult bibliographical and textual evidence, some of which must of necessity be taken into account by those who wish to study the plays from the point of view of their literary interpretation and their theatrical values. Chapters 3 to 6 below, devoted severally to the four major cycles, are as much intended to convey a solid idea of these new responsibilities as to impart a sense of the fresh interpreta-tive possibilities that they open up. Part of a responsible critical approach to these texts relies upon the possession of some knowledge of their modes of transmission, each of which differs radically from the others. Newly-published ancillary sources of a kind often unfamiliar to students, such as facsimiles of the manuscripts, are invoked here with some frequency, for they prove to have a role which is integral with, rather than prior to, evalua-tive processes.

Re-editing of the textual corpus has gone hand-in-hand with a vigorous and now well-established campaign of renewed research into the nature and extent of the documentary evidence for late medieval and early modern theatrical activities of all kinds. These 'records' of early English drama have given their name to a series of publications, cited frequently in the following pages, which provide authoritative scholarly accounts of crucial materials that, prior to the late 1970s, were sometimes only haphazardly available, if at all, in early antiquarian or amateur publications. Though here, too, demanding problems of context and interpretation have emerged, the posi-tive yield has been a strong impression of very marked local and regional differentiations in theatrical practice across the country, once again displacing convenient but reductive pedagogic generalisations of the kind found in older textbooks on the early drama. Illustrations of the complex interplay between textual and local documentary information in the study of the drama in York and in Chester will be found in chapters 3 and 4 below. Chapter 7 is given over to the most striking new development of a regional sense in medieval dramatic activity, focusing on East Anglia as a case-study in the assimilation of textual and documentary evidence to a broader social, cultural and economic picture. Chapter 8, for the first time in a book of this scope, places the Cornish drama on an equal footing with the better-known English-language plays.

The most innovatory aspect of current research on the early drama has taken the form of modern productions of some of the plays themselves, usually under academic auspices, aimed at recovering at least some of the authentic sense of the original theatrical occasion in terms of *mise-en-scène*, acting styles, costume, properties, special effects and so forth. The journal *Medieval English Theatre* (1979–) was founded partly as a forum for those most intimately concerned in this kind of work, and it is probably cited with greater frequency than any other periodical in this book. As well as textual and documentary sources, iconographic information has begun to contribute more significantly than hitherto, and most of those now studying the early drama do so with the sense that it was as much a visual as a literary art of the period. Nearly all medieval plays involved music, and some included dance, the theatrical impacts of which can only properly be assessed in the context of performance. Modern revivals aimed at authentic production values, so far as they can be reliably recovered from textual, documentary and iconographic sources, propose a variety of delights, insights, questions and problems which previous studies of the early drama have seldom sought to address in any systematic way, even where they have been aware of them. A number are taken up specifically in several of the chapters below, and the entire project is placed under critical review in chapter 11.

The accumulated bibliography of secondary material relating to early theatre now in print is very large, and reference to it in a book of this kind must necessarily be selective. Chapter 12 outlines how scholarship and criticism of the subject have developed, and where current contributions fit into this existing framework. The select bibliography towards the end of the book provides for references made within the texts of the chapters, but it has also been arranged in such a way as to be of use as an instrument of study and research in its own right. A guide to the arrangement of the bibliography will be found at the beginning.

I am indebted to all of the contributors to this book for their patient cooperation, and in particular to Peter Happé for his bibliographical expertise, and for wise counsel at several stages in its preparation. Meg Twycross was kind enough to bring her unrivalled knowledge of the connections between the visual arts and the early theatre to bear in the choice of illustrations and gave substantial assistance towards obtaining many of them. It is properly considered superfluous to acknowledge the good grace and efficiency with which the Cambridge University Press goes about its business, but thanks are especially due to Sarah Stanton and Kathryn Puffett for their keen interest in the book's progress, and their invaluable advice in matters of presentation. Others whom I have consulted with profit in matters great and small involving early drama include Sandy Johnston, Del Kolve, Alan Nelson and the late Arthur Cawley, but it is above all a Cambridge colleague, Richard Axton, whom I must thank for constant advice, stimulation and encouragement in thinking about how best to present what has been going on in the study of medieval English theatre over the last twenty years or so. Scholars, critics and performers of early English plays currently constitute a singularly congenial and fertile group amongst those devoted to medieval studies, and if this book conveys something of the significance of their cooperative findings and their corporate enthusiasm to those newer to the subject, it will have begun to succeed in its task.

Richard Beadle
St John's College, Cambridge

ABBREVIATIONS FOR JOURNALS AND SERIES

CD	*Comparative Drama*
EDAM	*Early Drama, Art and Music*
EETS	Early English Text Society
	ES Extra Series
	OS Original Series
	SS Special Series
ELH	*English Literary History*
ELN	*English Language Notes*
JEGP	*Journal of English and Germanic Philology*
LSE	*Leeds Studies in English*
MÆ	*Medium Ævum*
METh	*Medieval English Theatre*
MLN	*Modern Language Notes*
MLQ	*Modern Language Quarterly*
MLR	*Modern Language Review*
MP	*Modern Philology*
NM	*Neuphilologische Mitteilungen*
N&Q	*Notes and Queries*
PMLA	*Publications of the Modern Language Association of America*
PQ	*Philological Quarterly*
REED	*Records of Early English Drama*
RES	*Review of English Studies*
RORD	*Research Opportunities in Renaissance Drama*
SATF	Société des Anciens Textes Français
SP	*Studies in Philology*
TN	*Theatre Notebook*

Documentary sources and secondary works, cited by bracketed italicised numerals within the text and in the endnotes to the chapters – for example (*314*) – are keyed to the serial numbers in the select bibliography.

Quotations from plays within the text are from the following editions, full details of which are given under the respective serial numbers in the bibliography:

The York Plays, edited by Richard Beadle (*70*)

The Chester Mystery Cycle, edited by R. M. Lumiansky and David Mills (*73*)

The Towneley Plays, edited by George England and Alfred W. Pollard (*75*)

The N-Town Play, edited by Stephen Spector (*78*)

Two Coventry Corpus Christi Plays, edited by Hardin Craig (*82*)

The Macro Plays [*The Castle of Perseverance, Wisdom, Mankind*], edited by Mark Eccles (*83*)

The Late Medieval Religious Plays of Bodleian MSS Digby 133 [*The Conversion of St Paul, Mary Magdalen, Killing of the Children*], edited by Donald C. Baker and others (*84*)

Non-cycle Plays and Fragments [including *The Pride of Life*, the Croxton *Play of the Sacrament*, the Norwich Grocers' *Creation and Fall*, the Newcastle Shipwrights' *Noah's Ark* and the Northampton and Brome plays of *Abraham and Isaac*], edited by Norman Davis (*85*)

Everyman, edited by A. C. Cawley (*87*)

The Plays of Henry Medwall [*Fulgens and Lucres, Nature*], edited by Alan H. Nelson (*88*)

Youth and *Hick Scorner* in *Two Tudor Interludes*, edited by Ian Lancashire (*89*)

John Skelton, *Magnyfycence*, edited by Paula Neuss (*90*)

The Cornish *Ordinalia: The Ancient Cornish Drama* [*Origo Mundi* (OM), *Passio Christi* (PC), *Resurrexio Domini* (RD)], edited by Edwin Norris (*97*)

The Cornish *Creacion of the World* [*Gwreans an Bys* (CW)], edited by Paula Neuss (*98*)

The Cornish *St Meriasek* [*Beunans Meriasek* (BM)], edited by Whitley Stokes (*100*)

Most of the dates given in the following table cannot be expressed precisely. This is usually because, in the absence of specific records or firmly established facts, they are based on scholarly judgements as to various kinds of evidence (palæographic, linguistic, internal, etc.). Current opinions about the dates of texts will be found in the editions cited.

c. 970	*Visitatio Sepulchri* (The Visit to the Sepulchre), in the *Regularis Concordia* of Æthelwold
c. 1160–70	*Le Mystère* (or *Jeu*) *d'Adam*
c. 1180	*La Seinte Resureccion*
c. 1275	MS of *Dame Sirith*
c. 1300	MS of *Interludium de Clerico et Puella* (The Interlude of the Clerk and the Girl)
	MS of 'The Cambridge Prologue'
	MS of 'The Rickinghall (Bury St Edmunds) Fragment'
c. 1350	Composition of *The Pride of Life* (extant text first half of the fifteenth century)
	Barking Abbey liturgical *Visitatio Sepulchri* and *Harrowing of Hell*
c. 1375?	Composition of Cornish *Ordinalia* (extant text mid-fifteenth century)
1376	First mention of York Corpus Christi pageants (extant text 1463–77)
1377	First mention of Beverley Corpus Christi pageants (no text extant)
1392	First mention of Coventry Corpus Christi play (extant texts early sixteenth century)
c. 1400–25	Composition of *The Castle of Perseverance* (extant text mid-fifteenth century)
	MS of *Dux Moraud*

c. 1400–25	MS of Cornish 'Charter Fragment'
	MS of 'The Shrewsbury Fragments'
	MS of 'The Durham Prologue'
	MS of *The Pride of Life*
1415	The York *Ordo Paginarum*
1421	Chester Corpus Christi play first mentioned; no text extant
1424–30	John Lydgate's mummings
1427	Newcastle Corpus Christi play first mentioned; extant text of Noah pageant only, probably sixteenth century
mid 15th century	MS of the Cornish *Ordinalia*
	MS of the 'The Winchester Dialogues', including *Occupation and Idleness*, an early interlude
c. 1460–70	Composition of *Wisdom*? (extant Macro text late-fifteenth century, Digby fragment early sixteenth century)
c. 1461	Composition of the *Play of the Sacrament*? (extant text *c.* 1520)
	MS of the Northampton *Abraham and Isaac*
1463–77	Compilation of Register (MS) of York Corpus Christi play
c. 1464	Composition of *Mankind* (extant text later fifteenth century)
1468	Date mentioned in N-Town MS; extant text of whole collection late fifteenth century
mid–late 15th century	Composition of Wakefield pageants in Towneley cycle (extant text early sixteenth century)
	MS of the Brome *Abraham and Isaac*
late 15th century	MS of the N-Town plays
	Macro MSS of *Wisdom* and *Mankind*
	Cornish *Beunans Meriasek* (Life of Meriasek; extant MS dated 1504)
	MS of 'The Reynes Extracts'
	MS of 'The Ashmole Fragment'
	Robin Hood plays
c. 1490–1500	Composition of Henry Medwall's *Nature* (printed 1530–4?)
1496–7	Composition of Henry Medwall's *Fulgens and Lucres* (printed 1512–16?)
c. 1500?	Composition of Digby *Mary Magdalen* and *St Paul*
c. 1507–8	Composition of *Mundus et Infans* (The World and the Child) (printed 1522)
1512	Date given in MS of Digby *Killing of the Children*; other Digby plays (*Mary Magdalen*, *The Conversion of St Paul*, *Wisdom* fragment) from about this date or somewhat later
1515–16?	*Hick Scorner* printed (composed *c.* 1514?)

1510–19?	*Everyman* printed
c. 1520	MS of the *Play of the Sacrament*
from *c.* 1521	Chester Whitsun plays (i.e. the Chester cycle, possibly based on the earlier Corpus Christi play; extant texts late sixteenth – early seventeenth century)
1530?	John Skelton's *Magnyfycence* printed (composed *c.* 1519–20?) Norwich pageants and plays in Pentecost week, including extant text of the Grocers' *Adam and Eve*
1532–3	*Youth* printed (composed *c.* 1513?)
c. 1535	Extant texts of two Coventry Corpus Christi plays
1562	Chelmsford records suggest possible revival of Digby plays
1575	Last performance of the Chester Whitsun plays
1576	Plays at Wakefield banned
1580	Last (unsuccessful) attempt to stage the York Corpus Christi play

I

WILLIAM TYDEMAN

An introduction to medieval English theatre

> You that love England, who have an ear for her music . . .
> Listen. Can you not hear the entry of a new theme?

During the last few decades, the 'new theme' of medieval English theatre may be said to have swelled beyond all expectation. In the place of the modest harmonious arias of a few soloists we now confront a mighty but not totally co-ordinated anthem issuing from a many-throated chorus. In the past thirty years the status of medieval plays has been transformed, not merely through the advocacy of academics, but by the enthusiastic response of students and, even more remarkably, spectators. Much of the main repertory is accessible on the shelves of libraries and bookshops; civic and county archives are being scrutinised for practical details of local organisation and presentation. Periodicals and volumes replete with competing theories are announced frequently; live performances of medieval plays now seem as predictable a feature of the British summer as rain-threatened stagings of *A Midsummer Night's Dream*. Today there is probably greater awareness of the existence, nature and appeal of fourteenth- and fifteenth-century English drama than at any time since its creation.

The haphazard survival of early dramatic texts and documents makes it difficult to offer anything like a complete picture of what must once have existed. Medieval plays were not designed as reading matter, and the physical form in which they were recorded was manuscript, so it is not surprising that very few of them have come down to us from the time in which they were performed. It is as if we have inherited a small number of pieces, some few of which connect with one another, from a huge but lost jig-saw puzzle. The chronological table occupying the preceding pages gives a fractional idea of its temporal, and to some extent its spatial, dimensions, in terms of these surviving texts. The documentary evidence, which is rather more abundant, but altogether shadowier and more difficult of interpretation, is still in the process of being gathered.[1] It is therefore largely the texts of the major English vernacular plays which form the focus of what follows, and, though sherds of earlier dramatic traditions have survived, the chronological table discloses the obvious starting-point with the hazy origins of the mystery cycles and morality plays during the latter half of the fourteenth century. In the broadest sense, these powerful didactic genres took their rise as one element in a systematic campaign on the part of the Church to instruct the laity, in their own language rather than the Latin of the clergy or the Anglo-Norman French of the nobility, as to the essential features of their faith. These included the submerged narrative of the spiritual relationship between God and mankind, revealed by patristic exegetes in the articulation of the New to the Old Testament, which found compelling expression in the Fall–Redemption–Doomsday structure of the mystery cycles. Equally arresting was the perpetual struggle between the forces of good and evil for possession of the individual soul, naturally coupled with the urgent imperatives implied in the facts of death and an imminent eternal afterlife in heaven or hell, which give shape to the morality plays. Plays associated with these subjects, and on the exemplary lives of saints, seem first to have become common in the later years of the fourteenth century, but it is generally not until the mid-fifteenth century or later that the texts as we now have them appear as manuscripts, whilst at the same time documentary evidence about how they were staged and financed becomes reasonably abundant in a few places. The extraordinary longevity of the plays is attested in records of performance stretching forwards until the last quarter of the sixteenth century, by which time the ideological shifts begun at the Reformation, combined with changes in literary taste and new theatrical possibilities, finally put paid to the old genres.

The chronological table is also important in suggesting geographical and other dimensions to the study of the medieval English theatre, such as patterns of staging across time and place. For example, it implies an interesting map of dramatic activity expressed in terms of the surviving texts, though it has to be said that another map drawn on the basis of the documentary evidence would look rather different. Traditionally, the main geographical emphasis has been placed on the great civic enterprises of the craft guilds in the north of England, where the surviving cycles from York and Chester, and the plays associated with Wakefield in the Towneley manuscript, can confidently be located. But urban drama, and the intricate social and economic infrastructure that supported it, though documented in sometimes remarkable detail, is not the whole story. More recently, attention has also been focused on the steadfastly rural region of East Anglia, which bibliographical and linguistic research has shown to be the home of a significant group of texts: the N-Town plays, the morality plays of the Macro manuscript, the saints' plays of the Digby manuscript, and other 'non-cycle plays and fragments'. Nothing in this repertoire can be connected with urban craft guilds, and it is probable that religious guilds and other rural parish organisations supported productions of at least some of the East Anglian plays. The central midlands, by contrast, are sparsely represented by parts of the Coventry cycle and a single play from Northampton, whilst great areas of the west midlands and the south (including, rather surprisingly, London), yield no surviving texts at all. This is true until we reach the Celtic-speaking areas of the extreme south west, which boasts the extensive body of Cornish drama, still not well known, and as interesting for its differences from as its similarities to that of the remainder of England. Staging patterns to some extent reflect the geographical distribution of the plays that have survived. Processional performances using pageant wagons paid for by craft guilds were certainly a conspicuous feature in some northern towns, though not exclusive to that region, whilst 'place-and-scaffold' (or, more loosely, 'in the round') productions, sometimes in purpose-built earthenwork 'amphitheatres', are clearly detectable in Cornwall and East Anglia, but were not the only way that plays were presented in either region. A good many of the surviving scripts evidently reflect outdoor performances, and it is interesting to note that texts of plays designed for the typical type of indoor production ('great hall'), such as the interludes, do not come down to us in any quantity until around the turn of the fifteenth century, when they appear as printed books, rather than manuscripts. Finally, one may note that almost nothing from the repertoire of popular itinerant entertainers or the nascent professional acting troupes has survived in written form from any period before the end of the fifteenth century. Though broad generalisations of this kind, for what they are worth, are reasonably safe, closer acquaintance with the material soon acts to replace them with a more precise impression of an underlying complexity – generic, chronological and regional – which it is not the business of this book to simplify or shirk.

Because of the relative paucity of play texts, our knowledge of English medieval drama must rely in larger measure than in other eras on information gleaned from ecclesiastical injunctions, parish registers, legal depositions, civic accounts, family papers and so forth. The task of collecting and interpreting such documents is now being systematically undertaken, yet such are the limitations of terminology employed in the Middle Ages to designate the several branches of entertainment offering themselves, that too often we can never be certain as to what extent drama is the principal feature of what documents refer to, nor indeed whether at times we are dealing with drama at all. Were, for example, those popular 'ludi' objected to by outraged prelates 'plays' in our sense of the term, since the Latin word 'ludus' can be used to denote a sport or a pastime as well as a drama? Does a reference to a 'game' in Middle English parlance indicate a dramatic performance or a communal activity of another kind? How far should certain parts of the Roman Catholic church's schedule of divine worship – the church services known collectively as the liturgy – be accorded the title of 'drama', given that their originators probably saw them as no such thing? What should the familiar term 'pageant' convey to us, granted its several meanings for a medieval spectator? Which term – 'mystery', 'miracle', 'craft cycle', 'Corpus Christi play' – most appropriately describes the great sequences of biblical episodes presented annually in medieval cities, since all these labels can mislead, and some 'Corpus Christi plays' were manifestly not presented as part of the Church's feast of Corpus Christi at all? These and similar semantic niceties have a more prominent role in today's discussions of medieval English drama than yesterday's innocent explorer would readily credit.

Recent increases in knowledge have rarely produced greater certitude: the new emphases not only challenge old assertions, but complicate the current picture, so that it is not merely novices in the field who are bewildered by the implications of newly-available data or the contentious claims of rival experts. Scholarly discoveries and critical heterodoxy are here to stay, and the present *Companion* is not designed to reduce the study of this dynamic phase in Britain's theatrical history to an undesirable state of drab conformity and limp consensus. Rather it seeks to guide readers, spectators, performers and directors through the profusion and diversity of accumulated evidence and interpretative opinion, in the hope of making it a little less formidable to grasp.

THE DRAMA OF DEVOTION

Almost all medieval drama inevitably has to be scrutinised through the lens supplied by the Church. Much of what survives is religious in character, but even our knowledge of secular dramatics is chiefly obtained from admonishments and embargoes emanating from a clerical establishment horrorstruck by the unrestrained vigour of the common people's pleasures. Much of what we glean of the nature of popular diversions must be treated as reflecting the viewpoint of prejudiced censors rather than detached observers, yet the Church did not disapprove of all forms of playmaking, and its eventual acceptance of drama as a means of instructing the laity may well represent an attempt to compete with less decorous amusements, by harnessing the methods of profane presentation to lure the worldly away from what was deemed to be imperilling their immortal souls.

At what point in its long history the Christian faith began to assimilate acts of apparent theatre into its modes of worship has not been universally agreed, but though some do not accept that the most commonly cited ceremony (found in a Latin manual of English provenance) offers valid evidence for the presence of acted drama in the liturgy by c. 970 AD, its nature and appearance warrant serious consideration. For many scholars the so-called *Visitatio Sepulchri* (Visit to the Sepulchre) testifies to a 'second birth' for Western dramatic art, following the dispersal of the heritage of Greece and Rome occasioned by the barbarian invasions of the occidental empire. Whether Christianity manifested theatrical tendencies at some earlier date is fiercely debated; several pseudo-dramatic passages, one from the seventh Advent lyric of the Old English *Exeter Book* and another in Latin from the so-called *Book of Cerne*, have been canvassed as constituting evidence of 'drama in the service of religion' as early as the ninth century,[2] but while these pieces superficially resemble play texts, there is not the slightest hint that they were ever presented before an audience, and their claim on our attention must be marginal.

Indeed, the whole question of whether material closely associated with the Roman Catholic liturgy (like the Easter practice already cited) can legitimately be annexed for the theatre involves the whole issue of medieval dramatic perception. Much hinges on the significance attached to any religious activity that consists of or incorporates imitative action, for many observers a key feature in drama. Clearly the priest celebrating Mass is not play-acting when he repeats certain of Christ's reported words at the Last Supper or utilises gesture in blessing the bread and pouring the wine, but advocates argue that if participation in a religious ceremony calls for one to display the presumed behaviour or to repeat the imagined actions of another without acknowledging the fact, then one may be said to be engaging in a form of impersonation, and this activity may be reckoned dramatic.

Others, notably O. B. Hardison Jr (29), claim that to insist on imitation or impersonation as essential to medieval drama (whether staged inside or outside a church) is to invoke an outdated principle of naturalistic theatre where a play is expected to present spectators with an experience intended to convey the illusion of actuality passing before their eyes. Such a concept of theatre has in recent years been complemented by a revival of the notion that the essence of drama is not to imitate life, but rather to present a heightened sensation whose aesthetic premise lies in *transcending* strict verisimilitude, 'piercing the veil' of actuality so that what is done intensifies what we see or feel (43). It is said that no early performer would have been conscious of the need to identify with another human being, although late antique or medieval mime artists (such as Vitalis, whose epitaph alludes to his powers of mimicry) specialised in a form of illusionism (22, pp. 17–18). Some feel, however, that just as the priest at the altar does not 'play the part' of Christ when celebrating Mass, so a medieval player would not be required to impersonate the figure he was called on to represent or stand in for, and that elementary histrionics involved a different process. Others maintain that while medieval performance may have involved a more limited form of self-camouflage, when a participant in church ceremony is instructed to change his customary vestments or to conduct himself in an unwonted manner, we encounter what most of us would recognise as true drama.

Another objection to the standard account of the genesis of medieval church-theatre is that it is invidious to single out a single ceremony as being dramatic, since to the contemporary mind all worship could be deemed dramatic in character, not least the rite of the Mass, which was written of in terms of a divine drama by Amalarius of Metz prior to 850 (29, pp. 35–79). Furthermore, it is clear that the *Visitatio* has been made to appear more like an embryonic play than it truly is by such editors as Karl Young (69), through the use of typographical devices which misrepresent the original context, and therefore preempt our response to it. Moreover, can a combination of a sung text and a series of ritual actions be truly regarded as forming a play, when it is nowhere alluded to us as constituting one and we possess no evidence to suggest that at its inception it was perceived as something separable from the remainder of the liturgy? Perhaps not, yet the dominant belief among scholars still remains that by bringing together within the framework of Christian worship a pre-created literary and musical text and the adaptation of pre-existing ceremonial actions, clerics created the first piece of medieval religious theatre.

That the earliest surviving example of a so-called liturgical drama is British in origin is no more than accidental, since the Easter routine was almost certainly developed originally on the continent, and imported to England. Its first appearance in an English document results from the initiative of the saintly Bishop of Winchester, Æthelwold, in attempting to bring a degree of conformity to the practices and conduct of members of the Benedictine order in about 965–75. A group of senior ecclesiastics, by drawing up a consuetudinary, a manual of customs and usages to be observed in monastic houses, entitled the *Regularis Concordia* or, more fully, *The Monastic Agreement of the Monks and Nuns of the English Nation*, laid down a code of observances and regulations in order to standardise such matters.[3] The ceremony to which so much attention has been devoted was one of many projected, but because of its theatrical significance the *Visitatio Sepulchri* has too often been discussed out of context, arguably weakening its position as a proto-drama.

Among its many instructions the *Regularis Concordia* recommends that the proposed ritual, no doubt already in use in many churches, could be presented if so desired in the course of the Nocturn or Matins service held on Easter morning immediately after the first Mass of Easter Day. Its chanted text, adopted from a common liturgical embellishment or decoration known as a trope, was conceived in this instance as a short exchange of dialogue between a monk representing the angel at the empty tomb on Easter Day and three other monastic brethren standing in for the three Maries arriving at dawn to anoint Christ's dead body. The brothers enacting the roles of the women were instructed to wear copes (not customarily worn at this service) and to carry incense thuribles to represent the precious ointments. They were also advised to advance down the nave of the church 'in a hesitant manner as if seeking something'; as they neared the altar, the angel was to accost them and enquire what it was they sought, by chanting the Latin words 'Quem quaeritis in sepulchro, o Christicolae?' (Who are you seeking in the tomb, o dwellers in Christ?). The ensuing sung dialogue between angels and Maries taken from the trope revealed the fact that Christ had risen from the dead, and that the news should be shared with his followers. General rejoicing among the brethren was to culminate in the ringing of the abbey bells and the resumption of the regular office of Easter Matins.

Admittedly, the 'dramatic' portion of this service is not differentiated from the residue, and there is nothing in the *Regularis Concordia* to indicate that those sanctioning the celebration of the *Visitatio* were aware that they were consciously pioneering a new mode of stimulating devotional piety, apart from a rubric that speaks of the ceremony being introduced for the purpose of 'strengthening the faith of the neophytes [novices to the order]'. Yet sufficient indications of a limited concept of performance appear for many to feel that the *Visitatio* must be seen as a prototype religious play, albeit concealed in a document primarily addressed to issues other than the encouragement of dramatics in the monastic churches of the Benedictine order.

Whatever label we attach to the *Visitatio*, its blend of sung words and ceremonial actions initiated a period of artistic inventiveness in the eleventh and twelfth centuries which saw the creation of a vast repertoire of liturgical pieces, the majority of which are reproduced in Young (69). Ceremonies linked with Christmas and Epiphany came to join the Easter play, whose action was often extended backwards to form a Passion sequence; this involved the introduction of fresh characters and the elaboration of its dialogue. Gospel material was supplemented with the treatment of Old Testament matter: one of the finest of the liturgical plays is the *Ludus Danielis*

(The Play of Daniel), composed and performed at the cathedral choir school in Beauvais in about 1180.

Although the best of such Latin plays with music are now mainly associated with continental centres, they range from Sicily to Dublin to Poland, and Britain once possessed a store of such pieces intended for church performance on feast days. Records confirm that Durham, York, Beverley, Lincoln, Lichfield, Norwich, Salisbury and Wells all had their liturgical repertoires: in 1150 Laurentius, Prior of Durham, composed a *Peregrinus*, now lost, commemorating, like many kindred pieces, Christ's post-Resurrection encounter with two disciples on the road to Emmaus. The most important texts from England to survive are the so-called 'Shrewsbury Fragments', actually originating in the Lichfield diocese and consisting of extracts from three scriptural plays. The 'fragments' are in fact copies of the lines assigned to the Third Shepherd, the Third Mary and the disciple Cleophas, in a Nativity, a Resurrection and a *Peregrinus* respectively, with appropriate cues and some music (85). The language is sometimes Latin, sometimes English, and the Shepherds' Play or *Pastores* bears some relationship to the comparable English play in the vernacular York cycle. Though these texts are of late date, during the episcopate of Hugh of Nonant (1188–98) Lichfield was (perhaps coincidentally) the venue for presentations on the three themes covered by the 'fragments'.

Such dramas of devotion were conceived of as aids to worship, not as vehicles of evangelism. A preface to one of the liturgical ceremonies devised by Lady Katherine of Sutton for use in the Essex nunnery of Barking in the mid-fourteenth century confirms that the aim was to strengthen and stimulate faith among those already initiated into the mysteries, Lady Katherine being spoken of as wishing to eradicate spiritual torpor and 'to excite the ardour of the faithful more intensely' towards the Easter celebrations (69, vol. 1, pp. 165–7). Her invention was clearly slanted towards the dramatic: of one ceremony we learn that she and her nuns had themselves shut into their chapel to assume the role of the Old Testament patriarchs confined to hell while awaiting delivery from Satan's bondage by Christ; a priest striking the doors with the words 'Lift up your heads, o ye gates!' represented the figure of the Messiah releasing the captive souls and leading them forth in triumph bearing palms and candles. It is hard to deny such graphic symbolism the status of theatre.

These and other rituals suggest that the Church frequently found the drama latent in the faith it professed so compelling as to require its realisation in action, but it must be emphasised that this was a form of theatre designed to confirm the devout in their beliefs and intended as an occasional augmentation of the functions of the divine offices, rather than as carrying the Church's doctrinal message to the people. Earlier in their history scholars were happy to accept that the liturgical music-dramas served as the precursors and progenitors of those religious plays in the European vernaculars that emerged in the twelfth century, and that they shared with them a common aesthetic and didactic purpose. In the last few decades many (though not all) commentators have come to believe that the spirit and conventions of the two styles of drama differed so profoundly that the genesis and development of the vernacular plays owed little debt to the Church's presentations. The Latin performances that surfaced from the divine offices were governed by the conventions of their place of origin; the vernacular plays were broader and more populist in their appeal, more daring in their assumptions and techniques for attracting attention from those more easily distracted by worldly concerns than monks and nuns. Indeed, the 'new wave' of religious playmaking was probably more dependent on the prevailing forms and traditions of secular drama than on the stiffer, more restrained and esoteric conventions of the Latin church dramas it came to complement. At the same time Rosemary Woolf (*138*) may be correct in saying that the liturgical plays remained 'an abiding authoritative model' for the authors of the great sequences of scriptural dramas which are such a dominating feature of the theatrical literature of late medieval France, Germany and Britain.

THE DRAMA OF PASTIME AND PROFIT

The extant corpus of medieval drama in English is not extensive, particularly when measured against the volume of European play texts surviving from the same period. It is roughly two centuries after the emergence of Latin liturgical dramas around 970 AD that vernacular pieces in the Anglo-Norman dialect of French begin to appear, and virtually two centuries after that before texts in English itself make their mark on the English scene (see the chronological table above). However, valuable documentary evidence makes it clear that, as one might expect, the enjoyment of and participation in live entertainment of a dramatic kind was common among all classes both before and after the composition of those plays of Christian instruction and celebration that constitute the major part of the salvaged repertoire of the English stage of the Middle Ages.

Outside a handful of texts, our knowledge depends almost entirely on sources inimical to the theatre, or at least to those unhallowed forms of it indicted in frequent denouncements and prohibitions issued down the centuries by outraged prelates and despairing patriarchs. In strikingly similar phraseology church councils and individual clerics fulminate against a plethora of popular pastimes which include not only singing, dancing and merrymaking, but also what are referred to as *spectacula* or *ludi*, both of which terms may refer to drama in performance. However, the frequently-encountered Latin term *ludus* poses a problem, since it can signify both a game and a stage play, an ambivalence still reflected in such English words as the verb 'to play' and the verbal noun 'playing'. *Spectaculum* too may indicate no more than something to look at, such as a sporting contest, though a staged play is not ruled out; conversely the English term 'game' can often signify performed drama rather than sport or some other diversion. This lack of semantic precision makes the task of distinguishing between raucous and ribald recreations and scandalous play performances more complicated, the Church strongly disapproving of both, especially since churchyards were favoured venues for games-playing and riotously convivial junketings, as well as for watching plays. However, even this ambiguity can at least remind us that firm differences between playing games, competing at sports, 'partying' and acting drama might not have occurred so readily to the medieval mind as they do to ours.

One potent source of annoyance was clearly the performance of drama for profit by troupes of professional entertainers whose activities until late in the Middle Ages remain distinctly shadowy. Their repertoire is only scantily represented by surviving texts in English, but what may be the most ancient native play script to come down to us points a way. Composed in the West Midland dialect and dating from 1275–1300, it is entitled *Dame Sirith* and consists of a mixture of narrative and dialogue, capable of mimed recitation by a soloist or presentation by a small team complete with performing dog. An anecdotal sketch in which an elderly crone tricks a reluctant girl into sleeping with her lover, its plot is probably the same as that of a fragment in northern dialect of *c.* 1300, entirely in dialogue, and known as the *Interludium de Clerico et Puella* (The Interlude of the Clerk and the Girl).[4] Both pieces seem to have little other purpose than libidinal titillation and the provocation of laughter at the girl's naivety, the crone's cunning and the lover's success. A fragment in Cornish from *c.* 1400 (see below, chapter 8) was possibly created for similar purposes, though here potential marital discord appears to be the subject. One can scarcely doubt that pieces blending bawdry, guile and comic discomfiture would have proved popular on every social level. Continental analogues include the lively French comedy of *Courtois d'Arras* (*c.* 1200–25), which ostensibly tells the story of the Prodigal Son but with a wealth of secular detail and 'low' business, and the curt black sketch from Tournai, *Le garçon et l'aveugle* (*c.* 1280), a two-man routine depending on roguery, mimicry and disguise.[5] It is paralleled in a large collection of later French farces based on the frauds, upsets and reversals of everyday life, the supreme example of which is the celebrated *Maître Pierre Pathelin* (*c.* 1465). From Austria come the early *Neidhart-spiele*, which satirise the pretensions of the upwardly-aspiring peasantry and again specialise in the humiliation of the central figures, with excremental humour a prominent feature.

Some of this material presumably reflects the influence of those professional bands of entertainers who traced their lineage back to performers who regaled the citizens of Rome with their various skills up to the time of the barbarian invasions of the fourth and fifth centuries. The Church's hostility to those classed variously in documents as *mimi*, *histriones*, *joculatores*, *lusores*, and so forth[6] is amply testified to, partly on the grounds of their low moral reputation, partly for their corrupting effect on clerics who might be diverted from more solemn duties by witnessing their skills and antics. Countless injunctions sourly exhort the clergy to distance themselves from minstrels and mime artists, and so avoid the stigma associated with them. In 679 the Council of Rome ordered English bishops and other clerics not to keep musicians in their households and not to permit 'jocos et ludos' to be presented in their presence. In 823–4 Agobard of Lyons castigated clergymen who gave lavish hospitality to mimes, players and buffoons while the poor were left to perish of hunger.

Whether such advice was taken to heart may be doubted from the frequency with which these warnings were repeated throughout the Middle Ages; as late as 1511 John Colet was complaining in a sermon that priests were devoting themselves to 'sportes and playes', and in 1520 Cardinal Wolsey's statutes for monasteries of regular Augustinian canons insisted that they should not become involved in 'ludis ... inhonestis', though whether these refer to professional performances or the pastimes of the people is unclear (4, pp. 60, 61). On the other hand, those in secular authority at an earlier period certainly found it politic, if not pleasant, to allow entertainers to divert them: Attila, feasting a Byzantine embassage in 448, provided a cabaret which included a Moorish and a Scythian clown; Theodoric II of Gaul (*c.* 460) allowed after-dinner performances so long as the participants did not insult his guests. Emperor Louis the Pious (778–840) did not debar musicians, jesters, clowns and players from appearing before him, though his biographer Theganus records that their efforts never persuaded Louis to laugh aloud. Disapproval also seems to characterise the remarks of Edgar, ruler of England from 959 to 975, who deplored the activities of the *mimi* in lampooning his clergy for their decadence by mocking them with song and dance in the market-places of his kingdom.

The precise repertoire of the professionals must remain conjectural, but probably most of the traditional skills were represented – acrobatics, clowning, mimicry, miming, dancing, music-making, singing, jesting, along with specialised arts such as conjuring, sword-swallowing, fire-eating and juggling. It is impossible to be certain that acted drama in the form of sketches or monologues (such as the French *Dit de l'herberie* (The Herbalist's Yarn), of which there are several versions) formed part of the medieval entertainer's stock in trade, but it seems highly probable.

The Church's antipathy to the less regularised forms of drama enjoyed by the medieval populace may have resulted from their pagan associations. It is of course impossible to say how drama first came into existence, its origins being obscured in those proverbial mists of time which have often proved a blessing in disguise. Yet on few issues has dispute raged more furiously than on the troubled question of whether or not secular dramatic activity had its beginnings in pre-Christian rites and ceremonies. Even if the centuries down to the European Renaissance were richer in theatrical allusions than they are, it would still prove impossible to advance a convincing theory as to the true genesis of medieval profane theatre, and in view of the many gaps in the pattern of information, attempts to piece together all we know of early and primitive drama and link it to such sporadic medieval evidence as exists must end in frustration. Most venturers into this fitfully charted sea have now ceased to search for continuities between the drama of the Middle Ages and its pre-Christian past.

Yet curiously theatre historians have been the last group to abandon the old fixations as to where a satisfactory conclusion to the quest might be located. Under the potent influence of Sir James Frazer (1854–1941) and the 'Cambridge School' of anthropologists, the origins of drama have been detected in what have been taken to be quasi-universal communal rites linked to the cyclic rhythm of the seasons and the preservation of fertility in the natural world and within human society.[7] For Frazer the unifying factor was supplied in the useful myth of the slain god (or his royal substitute or his scapegoat), put to death and then reborn either literally or symbolically in order to mirror and so maintain the seasonal pattern of growth and decay. To early rituals embodying this phenomenon in multiple forms were attributed the rise and development of drama, and to ceremonies, customs, games and plays as practised in communities both ancient and medieval a common source in archetypal fertility worship was assigned. This in turn led to much scanning of medieval and post-medieval material in search of any traces of the elemental struggle between the forces of light and darkness or Winter and Summer, or of signs of the death and rebirth of a vegetation-spirit, which would bolster the notion of 'ritual origins'. One favourite subject for this type of analysis has been the celebrated English mumming play of St George with its Hero Combat and quack doctor with his miraculous powers of revival, but sadly the earliest textual examples of the form date from the eighteenth century, and while there may well have been 'death and resurrection' plays of this type in medieval England, we cannot trace the ancestry of routines whose precursors have disappeared.

Moreover, as A. E. Green points out in *The Cambridge Guide to World Theatre* (1988), drama and ritual are not synonymous but analogous, and we cannot assume that the former develops directly or automatically from the latter. Frazer's armchair anthropology is now highly suspect, in deriving its assumptions from evolutionary genetics and its illustrative examples from eclectic sources. Today Frazer's theory of sacrificial god-substitutes and fertility cults has ceased to convince objective investigators; Joseph Fontenrose, for instance, has established authoritatively the lack of evidence for the ritual slaughter of any reigning sovereign from the time of ancient Egypt onwards.[8] *The Golden Bough* has encouraged the abandonment of strict historicity and firm topology:

> evidence from any culture, past or contemporary, might be used to reconstruct a kind of ur-process whereby the emergence of theatre anywhere can be explained ... what is known to be true at one time and place might be assumed to be true at another time and place where evidence is lacking
>
> (43, p. 8).

The same faulty technique has been used in a similar way to create a spuriously homogeneous portrait of medieval literary drama: an increased awareness of local and temporal distinctions makes it less likely to occur in the future.

The danger of the tendency to focus on 'pagan origins' for early theatre is that such an exclusive emphasis can distract scholars from making a truly objective appraisal of what confronts them. While pre-Christian culture may well have contributed to the development of popular medieval customs and practices, it no longer offers the master key to the origins of dramatic activity. What now receives more stress is the notion that drama has always been a crucial force for encouraging communal integration and for expressing a sense of corporate identity; medieval society maintained numerous traditional celebrations and usages whose social function was doubtless to foster a spirit of mutual dependence and collaboration, as well as to provide the solace of pleasure and diversion amid the harshness of daily life. Such an approach may ultimately take us closer to the heart of medieval theatre than an abortive search after pagan beginnings.

Nevertheless, the Church did undoubtedly view many common pastimes as tainted with heathen excess and lewdness: a Council of Rome held in 826 castigates women who attend church festivals, not to participate in worship, but to dance and sing shameless words in chorus, 'behaving just like pagans'. A lusty choric song of $c.$ 1050[9] incorporating dialogue and mime turns on sexual invitation and imitation, and in the Church's eyes such uninhibited sensuality compounded the evils of singing and dancing, especially when church precincts were often selected for such wanton displays. Small wonder that in $c.$ 1005–7 Archbishop Wulfstan required his secular clergy to abstain from 'heathen songs' and other devilish games on feast days.[10] Evidently dance-songs could include dramatic action, though (as with the liturgical ceremonies) it is hard to decide where mere participation ends and true play-acting begins. Clerics may have had dramatics in mind when they abhorred the existence of 'inhonesti ludi', but these, as Alexandra Johnston has recently claimed, may have amounted to no more than raucous singing, seductive dancing and rowdy fun, three traditional targets for disapproval by the more sedate members of every generation. To be certain that it was drama itself which aroused ecclesiastical ire we need to turn to a handful of well-known thirteenth-century references, which illustrate the nature of contemporary secular plays as far as it can be established.

In 1240 Bishop Walter Cantilupe of Worcester charged his clergy not to support the setting-forth of plays 'de rege et regina' (King and Queen plays) along with 'ram-raisings, or wrestling-contests or illicit guild-ales'; a few years later Bishop Robert Grosseteste of Lincoln protested against clerical participation in plays 'which they call miracles' as well as in 'other plays which they call the Bringing-forth of May or Autumn'. Almost twenty years later a Scottish record speaks of 'comedies and tragedies' which celebrate 'Robert Hode' and Little John and their fellows, though games or plays featuring the famous outlaw are only recorded again some centuries later, one of the most famous allusions stemming from Sir John Paston in 1473 while deploring the loss of a servant who in Paston's jaundiced view had spent most of his time playing St George and in *Robin Hood and the Sheriff of Nottingham*; the play text in which the errant retainer appeared may well be one that has been preserved in fragmentary form.[11]

If these instances refer to play performances, they share the clerical opprobrium reserved for such popular diversions as raising funds for guild or parish purposes by putting drink on sale at 'ales', and the money-making aspect is certainly a feature of the Robin Hood plays that formed the core of a *quête* or foray to collect cash for a variety of local causes, presumably with a drama at its centre. If some of the activities referred to also come under the heading of 'summer games', condemnation of these seems widespread (374). Robert Mannyng in *Handlyng Synne* ($c.$ 1303) associates such games with 'daunces' and 'karols' (choric round dances) from which 'many shames' derive, and in *Piers Plowman* significantly it is Sloth who prefers 'a somer game of souteres' (cobblers) to the gospels, causing one to wonder if the medieval craft guilds mounted 'summer games' as they did the civic cycle plays at roughly the same period. Chaucer's Wife of Bath recounts a cautionary tale of the Roman who abandoned his wife because she attended 'a someres game' unsupervised: if such games were linked to Grosseteste's 'Bringing-forth of May' and Cantilupe's 'King and Queen plays' and involved the suggestive mime and dialogue of the Latin song of *c.* 1050, clerical and masculine disapproval are more readily accounted for.

More exclusively and better documented are the clerks' plays 'which they call miracles', mentioned by Bishop Grosseteste; these appear to have been popular but unauthorised scriptural plays publicly staged by those in minor orders, and hence deplored by those in authority because of their un-officially-sanctioned mode of presentation. However, one early example, a play on the life of St Katherine, 'which in common speech we call a "Miracula"', was produced by Geoffrey of Le Mans, perhaps in the presence of King Henry I, at Dunstable between 1100 and 1119 and does not sound to have been of the type castigated later; when William Fitzstephen (*c.* 1170–82) praises the sacred dramas presented in London – 'representations of miracles performed by holy confessors, or of the sufferings by which martyrs demonstrated their constancy' – there is also no hint of reproof. However, a document of *c.* 1220 may hint at the type of piece that aroused the episcopacy to indignation: it alludes to the performance of a Resurrection play given on the north side of the churchyard at Beverley in Yorkshire and presented not at Easter but in the summer, with masked players taking part. We are told that 'a large crowd of both sexes gathered together, led there by differing motives, some by nothing more than pleasure and curiosity, but others for the holy purpose of stimulating pious sensations'. However, masked performance seems synonymous with the disreputable side of *miracula*: William of Wadington in the *Manuel des Pechiez* (*c.* 1300) writes of 'fols clercs' who stage 'miracles' disguising their faces with 'visers'; in his *Summa predicantium* of 1325–50 John Bromyard observes that 'players in the play which is commonly called a *Miracle* use masks, beneath which the persons of the actors are concealed'. Bromyard also contrasts people's reluctance to attend divine service with their readiness to be present at 'novis spectaculis' (the latest shows) 'as in plays which they call "Miracles". Why are they not prevented from attending the Miracles of foolish clerics?'[12]

Another form of secular theatre that often involved donning a mask was the so-called disguising or mumming, whose customary setting was the royal court or the household of some nobleman. Certainly the early Plantagenet kings were no strangers to theatrical entertainments, Edward II being censured for (among other things) mixing with 'harlottes [clowns] . . . syngeres and . . . gestoures' and for preferring to the See of Canterbury a prelate who had excelled 'in ludis theatralibus' (4, p. 51). Under Edward III lavish tournaments involved disguises of varying degrees of exoticism: in 1331 the king and his courtiers dressed as Tartars in masks were led in golden chains by their ladies; twelve years later knights attending 'solemne justs' dressed up as the Pope and twelve of his cardinals. Jousts at Reading and Canterbury between 1347 and 1349 also featured masked figures; a costumed procession before a joust held in Smithfield in 1374 starred the king's mistress Alice Perrers wearing a gorgeous costume 'as Lady of the Sunne'. Such public parades remind us that the Middle Ages pioneered profane as well as sacred street theatre (41, pp. 70–9, 87–95).

Not only the nobility adopted disguise in order to create entertainment; as early as 1335 and again in 1352 official orders were issued to restrain the citizens of London from going about the streets wearing 'false faces' or a 'fause visage' while proceeding from house to house to engage in dice-play with the occupants. Before the century's end this custom seems to have been turned into a form of royal tribute, the clearest description emanating from the Elizabethan chronicler John Stowe, who recounts how in 1377 the future Richard II received at Kennington Palace a company of citizens 'disguizedly aparailed' (some of them 'arrayed and with black vizardes like devils') who played at dice with the boy-prince in total silence before feasting, dancing and departing.

It may well be that the bourgeois custom of complimenting their noble betters with a silent masked 'disguising' led to less improvised amusements being devised for the aristocracy of the fifteenth century. The dance of bare-breasted girls before the horrified young Henry VI, which again Stowe records, may have been one such diversion, but the only texts to survive are seven mummings or 'momeries' by the eminent poet John Lydgate (c. 1370–1450) (308, pp. 237–44, 305, 103–4). Staged at various palaces, castles and halls in the 1420s, Lydgate's entertainments required the construction of quite elaborate scenic devices, but their most curious feature is that they are *scripted* mummings, an apparent contradiction until one perceives that usually only a single speaker (perhaps the author) was required to recite lines, while the other participants merely mimed before finally presenting the guest of honour with a gift. Most of Lydgate's mummings abound in allegorical symbolism in which classical and biblical personages intermingle, but in his liveliest offering, 'a disguysing of the rude upplandisshe people [yokels] compleynyng on hir wyves, with the boystous [forceful] aunswere of hir wyves', we break new ground. This *Mumming at Hertford* (c. 1425) dispenses with allegory and presents the rival sexes as speaking protagonists in the action. At least, the wives who enter armed with distaffs have their spokesperson, but it may be that only the conventional commentator spoke for the henpecked husbands. Some real dramatic tension is certainly engendered, and performed in a banqueting hall during Christmas revels, the Hertford mumming anticipates Henry Medwall's debate drama *Fulgens and Lucres* of 1497. What links such aristocratic amusements had with the rustic mumming play must be a matter for speculation, but such indigenous dramas could well have begun as silent mimes.

Lydgate also composed several of the sterile pageants in aureate verse employed ceaselessly to grace such ceremonies as the entry of a monarch into one of his principal cities, the civic welcome accorded to a foreign potentate, a coronation or a royal wedding. Too little literary evidence remains to facilitate confident comment on this more official aspect of medieval drama, but although the stiff ornate verses deployed were dwarfed by scenic marvels, their creation was by no means entrusted to hacks. The pageantry exhibited has more interest for us today since it is frequently related to the iconography of the cycle play performances in England's major towns and cities; indeed, in the area of street performances, sacred and profane imagery were often closely allied.

By comparison with the secular drama of France, Germany and the Netherlands, the British repertoire is modest enough. England possesses nothing like the superbly funny farces that survive in France, nor the *sotties*, which are usually plotless comic routines performed by *sots* or fools in the traditional cap and bells. Nor can one point to plays equating with the German Shrovetide or Carnival play known as the *Fastnachtspiel*, a frequently exuberant and bawdy genre presented as a pre-Lenten indulgence by members of such town guilds as that of Nürnberg, although Tom Pettitt has recently proposed that the English religious morality *Mankind* might be placed within this Carnival play convention (*335*). Nor can Britain match the four serious secular plays known in Dutch as the *Abele Spelen* dating from the fifteenth century, the plots of three being drawn from epic and romance, the fourth being a debate drama. Their quality helps to remind us that unfortunately a great deal of medieval secular drama in English must be regarded as lost for ever.

THE DRAMA OF SALVATION

By far the great majority of plays in the existing medieval repertoire are devoted to religious purposes and primarily brought into being to render the salient truths of the Christian faith graphic and compelling for those unable to read the scriptures for themselves, even if the better-educated were not excluded from attending. It has become traditional to characterise the principal types of plays as Corpus Christi or craft cycles, moralities and moral interludes, saint plays, miracle plays and so on, but recent studies stress that such classifications are in many respects arbitrary, and can obscure interrelations of theme and character, or the wide range of elements within a single piece, and similarities of staging that cut across generic boundaries (*305*, pp. 1–14). For example, both *The Castle of Perseverance* and *Everyman* are styled moralities, yet one is built on an epic scale, the other almost frugally. Techniques employed in the so-called 'saint play' of *Mary Magdalen* have much in common with those employed in the cycles, yet the strong infusion of allegorical types aligns it with the morality form. Like many labels attached to literary genres for convenience's sake, those applied to the main forms of medieval play constitute no more than a set of rough-and-ready divisions. The plays' shared evangelising purposes should never be ignored: their authors' primary business was to instruct the populace in those truths essential for their salvation by rendering them accessible, and to alert men and women to the cosmic battles being waged over the fate of their own immortal and individual souls.

No single explanation can account for the rise and development of drama in the chief European vernaculars from the middle of the twelfth century onwards. The earliest text to use a popular tongue systematically is the *Sponsus* (*c.* 1150), a mainly Latin liturgical drama treating of the five wise and five foolish virgins of Matthew's Gospel, which employs the Provençal *langue d'oc* for certain portions of its sung dialogue. The inclusion of the demotic strand doubtless stems from an aesthetic desire for stylistic variation rather than a wish to enlighten the laity, since it is only the foolish virgins who sing lines in the vernacular. Similarly, the Latin Passion play from Benediktbeuern (*c.* 1250) has a striking sequence in German in which Mary Magdalene leads a dancing chorus of girls on a shopping expedition to buy rouge and other allurements, a sequence which may owe something to secular convention (*69*).

However, the existence of French versions of certain stanzas in an Easter play from Origny-Saint-Benoîte (*c.* 1284) may reflect a different spirit, and an evangelising motive may well have underlain the composition of what appears to be the first religious drama entirely in a vernacular tongue, a unique but probably incomplete Old Castilian text entitled the *Auto de los Reyes Magos* (The Play of the Magi Kings), dating from *c.* 1155. Apparently standing independent of the liturgy, this *auto* was probably written for presentation in Toledo Cathedral during Epiphany. Almost contemporary with it is an astonishingly accomplished play in Norman French, the *Ordo representationis Ade* or *Le jeu d'Adam*, made up of a sequence of several

Old Testament episodes, consisting of the creation and fall, the murder of Abel and the Messianic prophecies, an integrated vernacular sequence interspersed with liturgical chants taken from the office of Matins for Septuagesima and from other sacred texts including the Vulgate.[13] Much interest has been generated by this most sophisticated piece, and its sequential development has led to speculation as to the origins of the accretive tendencies in medieval religious playmaking. Its inventive characterisations, and its psychological and theatrical deftness are undeniable, and suggest an established tradition of vernacular composition in existence by *c.* 1170. The fact that *Adam* is couched in Norman French postulates the presence of a lay rather than a clerical audience, for whose benefit the French scenes were devised to gloss the chanted readings and responses from the Latin. Its exact venue is keenly disputed, but performance for the benefit of the laity would suggest an open space outside a place of worship, though indoor presentation also has its strong advocates. Certainly *Adam* anticipates much of the energetic demotic appeal of the later cyclic drama, and its techniques are assured; associated with it is an unfinished and less remarkable Anglo-Norman piece of roughly comparable date, *La Seinte Resureccion*, which focuses on Christ's burial and restoration from the dead, and contains an interesting prologue on the suggested manner of staging the action, possibly at set locations established inside a church building, although its liturgical links are few.

The emergence of such pieces in the main European tongues precedes a great upsurge in the composition of religious drama in French, German, Italian, English, Dutch and Spanish during succeeding centuries, a phenomenon which has sent theatre historians in pursuit of a common explanation for it, but without complete success. Undoubtedly, the rise of vernacular drama could scarcely have taken place without that vital shift in spiritual sensibility that gave prominence to Christ's assumption of human form, an emphasis found as early as St Anselm's treatise on the Incarnation, *Cur Deus Homo?* (Why did God become Man?) of *c.* 1097. It sems unquestionable that the theological and devotional implications of this fresh assertion of Christ's significance as the type of vulnerable and suffering humanity acted as a powerful stimulant to religious thought and artistic creativity during the twelfth century. But it has also become customary in recent years to place equal emphasis on the emergence, from the conflicts besetting the twelfth-century Church, of the fraternal Orders of St Francis and St Dominic, in 1210 and 1215 respectively, and the missionary zeal of their members in expounding the message of personal salvation to the lay individual may well hold the key to the production of religious plays written in tongues accessible to the illiterate. By going out into the community and preaching the gospel of salvation though Christ to ordinary men and women, the Dominicans and Franciscans were perhaps establishing unawares a potential audience for popular Christian dramas in the vernacular.

Most scholars accept that these plays were inspired by different factors from those governing the growth of drama created from the ceremonies and discourse of church worship. Intended to divert as well as edify and instruct the laity, vernacular religious drama adopted many techniques associated with profane theatre in order to win acceptance for its doctrinal content. Characterisation had to be broad and arresting, dialogue racy, earthy and often declamatory, comedy prominent and often scabrous, though its didactic potential was also recognised, and frequently exploited. Such plays were not conceived as regulated aids to devotion or as serving the ulterior aims of formal worship, but rather as vehicles designed to bring home to the people their spiritual potentialities and responsibilities, and there is general agreement that the vernacular plays display a separate and distinct mode of aesthetic perception from that enshrined in the Latin music-dramas. There now seems little justification for the long-promoted view that the Church's dramas were expelled into the street and the market-place because of their disreputable populist tendencies. The impulse and spirit behind the two forms of medieval scriptural play seem too dissimilar to sustain the notion that the sacred material became 'secularised' and hence downgraded to become a popular form of entertainment of which the Church disapproved. Indeed, it is possible that the plays came into being in England to combat those unauthorised *miracula* to which the ecclesiastical hierarchy objected: rather than have sacred truths set forth by junior clerics in masks, the Church may have agreed to encourage worthier representations, and so have inspired the cycle plays for which it may have shared responsibility with the trade guilds.

It has been common to attach a good deal of importance to the institution of the feast of Corpus Christi during the fourteenth century as stimulating the growth of popular religious theatre. This festival, inaugurated as a thanksgiving for Christ's gift of his body on the cross and in the Eucharist for the benefit of humankind, was introduced into the Church calendar in 1311; its observance rapidly became a highpoint in the religious year, being celebrated in early summer with a street procession of clergy and lay dignitaries behind the Communion Host. At some centres, particularly in Spain, it became the custom for the townsfolk to dress in biblical costume as they accompanied the parade through the city, and then to organise a series of static tableaux on floats to form an integral part of the procession. It is at least plausible that these tableaux or pageants formed the excuse for the development of short dialogues which suitably expanded became the cycle, mystery or miracle plays associated in many countries with the Feast of Corpus Christi (41, pp. 97–102).

However, this explanation of the evolution of the genre must be treated cautiously, since it cannot account for the genesis of every scriptural sequence known to us. *Le jeu d'Adam* clearly pre-dates the establishment of Corpus Christi and was a winter play; the lengthy series of Creation and Passion performances by the clerks of London, recorded between 1390 and 1411, do not appear to be associated with the feast day either. At some centres Corpus Christi was not celebrated with a *sequence* of plays but with merely a single episode, nor was every sequence presented a scriptural one: Alexandra Johnston has recently argued that the plays performed at Coventry (of which two now remain) probably formed a work based on the Apostolic Creed rather than on the Old and New Testaments (52, p. 11); even at York, where we know a Corpus Christi cycle took place, a Creed play was substituted every tenth year. Nor can we be certain, even where records state that a 'play' was presented, that it implies more than a series of tableaux touring the town streets with no human involvement by way of actors and dialogue. Not every acted sequence was performed at Corpus Christi either: the Chester cycle, for example, was played on the three days following Whitsunday. However, its origins doubtless lie in a Corpus Christi presentation, though at first this may have been set forth at a single site, rather than in processional form.

It is also interesting that none of the extant English cycles places conspicuous emphasis on the inauguration of the Mass at the Last Supper, as one might have expected if the Corpus Christi celebrations alone had stimulated the creation of dramatic pageants asociated with the feast.[14] Of course we do not need to seek one exclusive explanation for the cyclic impulse, but since in many European centres the form is closely akin to the British type, the method of serial accretion of episodes must be felt to transcend any pattern developed solely in association with the Corpus Christi parades. Moreover, the progress from Creation to Doomsday peculiarly characteristic of the English cycles is not reproduced abroad. Some continental offerings consist of a multiplicity of scenes with a staggering overall impact, but they nevertheless fail to embrace the whole of humanity's spiritual history as the English plays do.[15]

In France and Germany the harvest is particularly rich: in Spain vernacular religious drama developed late, and even in the fifteenth and sixteenth centuries Easter and Christmas plays relied heavily on liturgical tradition. The earliest dramatic text dates from Mallorca in 1442, and a codex of forty-nine plays is associated with staging in Palma Cathedral. However, the largest group of biblical plays derives from pageants associated with Corpus Christi and involving the trade guilds of various cities including Valencia, Madrid, Salamanca, Seville and Toledo, though whether they presented stage plays or merely mounted tableaux and dumb-shows is often unclear. In Italy the roots of vernacular drama can be traced to the *laudi* first created by the flagellants of Umbria in the latter half of the thirteenth century, such hymns of adoration often assuming a semi-dramatic form. Costumed impersonation led on to drama proper, and by 1400 spoken plays were common, paving the way to the splendidly spectacular *sacre rappresentazioni* of the fifteenth century, some hundred texts of which survive, all originating in Florence, home of the most elaborate performances. In 1454 a cycle of Old and New Testament plays required the erection of twenty-two *edifizi*, each representing a separate location; processional dramas on floats featured in the annual Feast of St John the Baptist. Passion plays were also popular, one being staged annually in Rome's Coliseum from 1460 to 1539, another at Revello in the Italian Alps in 1494.

The Passion play was also a favourite form in German-speaking countries, along with the Corpus Christi plays or *Fronleichnamspiele*, the earliest of which dates from 1391 and comes from Innsbruck. Another from Künzelsau in Württemberg was presented at least between 1479 and 1522, and other examples occur at Freiburg and Ingolstadt. These plays, like the Chester and York cycles, were presented processionally along a defined route, although tableaux probably alternated with staged scenes. By contrast, Passion plays seem to have been mounted within a confined area, as at Alsfeld in 1501, at Frankfurt and Villingen later in the century, and, above all, at Lucerne as late as 1583 and 1597, where detailed stage plans of the local Weinmarkt given over to the performances have proved an invaluable source of information on the principles of late medieval place-and-scaffold staging.

But pride of place must go to France, where Jean Bodel's early thirteenth-century *Jeu de St Nicolas* and Rutebeuf's *Miracle de Théophile* (*c.* 1260) anticipate the creation of forty miracle plays presented by the Parisian guild of Goldsmiths in the mid-fourteenth century and known as the *Miracles de Nostre Dame par personnages*, in which sensational incidents and effects serve the ends of salvationist doctrine. Equally lurid in many cases are the *mystères* drawn from the lives of eminent saints, which in many instances involve the depiction of grisly tortures inflicted on martyrs and offer a gloss on William Fitzstephen's commendation of London's religious drama in around 1170. The vogue in France for hagiographic plays endured into the sixteenth century, one of the best-known being the *Mystère des trois doms*, a large-scale production of which was staged at Romans in 1509 as a civic thank-offering for delivery from the plague.

Some of France's scriptural dramas are monumental in their scope, and although their ostensible subject matter is Christ's Passion, they in fact incorporate not only scenes from Christ's earlier life but incidents from the Old Testament, too. The earliest specimens of the form are the *Passion du Palatinus* and the Ste Geneviève *Passion de Nostre Seigneur*, relatively modest texts of 2,000 and 4,500 lines respectively, but in 1420–30 appears Eustache Marcadé's somewhat sombre and prolix *Passion d'Angers*, some 25,000 lines long, and around 1450 appears its more inventive and versatile successor, Arnoul Gréban's *Mystère de la Passion*, containing roughly 35,000 lines. Indebted in large measure to Gréban is Jean Michel's *Passion* played at Angers around 1486, and on later occasions compilations were assembled which combined the best of Gréban and Michel with material from *Le Mystère du Viel Testament*, one particularly well-documented production being recorded at Mons in 1501. Other mammoth sequences included *Les Actes des Apôtres*, an immense epic by Simon Gréban of almost 62,000 lines, which interweaves apostolic activity with a vast tapestry of world events; mounted in a former Roman amphitheatre at Bourges in 1536, its presentation lasted a marathon forty days. By comparison, even the forty-eight pageants of the York cycle or the three-day spectacle presented at Chester seem modest ventures; if Britain saw similar stagings of the martyrdoms of the saints or the acts of the apostles, no traces survive.

Fragments of prologues to two lost plays form the prelude to religious drama in the English language. One, the so-called 'Cambridge Prologue' (*c.* 1300) portrays the messenger of a pagan emperor calling for silence so that the action can begin; the passage appears first in Anglo-Norman and then in English couplets. In the slightly later 'Rickinghall Fragment' from the Bury St Edmunds area, a pagan king summons his barons and vassals to his presence, also in two languages. The bilingual versions of both prologues have suggested a mixed audience of *hoi polloi* and governing class, but Lynette Muir has recently argued that they are a writer's trial-runs for alternative renderings of the speeches, the Frenchified version intended to characterise an exotic court, much as the Chester cycle creates an alien environment for Herod and the Emperor of Rome. The prologues may form part therefore of early religious plays, possibly ones blessed by the Church, but perhaps the unauthorised *miracula* generally deplored (85; 33, pp. 59–60).

Similar circumstances may have attended performances of the earliest English Christian drama to survive in more than fragmentary form; although *The Pride of Life* (*c.* 1350) is incomplete, its prologue and text characterise the action fully enough for us to perceive that its main strength lies in the vividness with which its doctrinal impact is realised (85). The boastful King Life (Rex Vivus) challenging Death in single combat is a powerful personification, and the play has some claim to be the forerunner of those notable fifteenth-century morality pieces that emphasise the effects of yielding to sinful temptation in a context of graphically delineated allegorical creations. *The Pride of Life* appears to have clear affinities with the later French *moralités*, of which some seventy survive, but the intervention of the Virgin to intercede for Rex Vivus recalls rather the *Miracles de Nostre Dame*. Relevant in this context are the plays of the Dutch Rhetoricians or *Rederijkers*, the *Spele van sinnen*, whose didactic function is also complemented by lively theatricality, and of which *Elckerlijc*, from which the English *Everyman* derives, is only one (albeit the best) example. In Rex Vivus too we find yet another instance of the arrogant stage tyrant, a figure whose discomfiture anticipates the fate of countless subsequent dramatic monarchs, not excluding the Herods, Pharaohs and Pilates of the cycle dramas.

Much of what requires to be said of the vibrant and impressive sequences of scriptural dramas least ambiguously referred to as the cycle plays will be found in later chapters of this volume: all that will be attempted here is a brief indication of their place in the overall development of English medieval theatre. The first of the great panoramic surveys of biblical and eschatological events appears in Britain in about 1375, and is cast in the Cornish tongue. We cannot be certain at what point during the fourteenth century episodes ultimately to be incorporated into the cycle sequences began to be dramatised at other centres, but the Cornish *Ordinalia* probably includes the most ancient scripts to survive from a British source, although some would argue that the *Jeu d'Adam* should be regarded as a proto-sequence, and that its birthplace may well be somewhere in the south of England rather than in Northern France. However, it is irrefutable that documentary evidence for the preparation of biblical 'pageants' (whatever these involved, and their existence does not imply that they featured human elements) appears from about 1375 onwards in many English and Scottish cities and towns. For example, a 'pagine' is alluded to at York in 1376, and another at Beverley in the following year, though in neither case dare we deduce that the presence of 'pageants' means that acted dramas or mimed or static tableaux were being mounted on or within them, or that they were necessarily paraded through the streets, though this is the obvious inference. Certainly far fewer texts of plays survive than records of their performance, and many of our deductions concerning the cycles in general have to rely on scripts which may unfortunately be atypical of the genre as a whole. The greater part of the cyclic repertoire that survives in written form consists therefore of virtually complete works from the cities of York and Chester, a full sequence from the town of Wakefield (though not every scholar is happy with the ascription) and a composite text, somewhat imperfectly co-ordinated, associated with Bury St Edmunds or perhaps some other East Anglian locale (Thetford is suggested by Alan Fletcher below) and generally known by most scholars as the N-Town plays. This curious title stems from a reference in its trailer or 'banns' attached to the text, which indicates that a peripatetic company presented the play or more probably parts of it at sites of their choice within a finite region. Although it is the four major sequences which, along with the Cornish cycle, have received the lion's share of recent critical attention, the existence of isolated plays and fragments of pieces from Coventry, Norwich, Newcastle-on-Tyne, Northampton, and Brome in Suffolk indicates the widespread distribution of a popular type of dramatic offering.

At what point in their development the cycle texts came to take the form that they manifest today is difficult to establish, given the lack of sufficient intermediary versions, but there seems to have been a general increase in situational and verbal elaboration. Composition was of course continuous and spread over perhaps decades, involving constant revisions from radical re-writing to a process of minor modifications. Although major alterations were carried out on specific occasions – the distinctive contributions of the so-called 'Wakefield Master' must have considerably transmuted the flavour of that particular sequence – in general change was less drastic, and individual authors did not stamp their literary personalities too indelibly on the dramatic totality. It is impossible to gauge exactly what factors loomed largest in the minds of the revisers when changes were executed, but with increasing popularity and more regular presentation, those responsible for the plays' contents would have needed to adapt and develop their artistry in order to set forth the truths of Sacred Writ in pleasing, worthy and illuminating ways. Shifts in religious tastes and doctrinal preoccupations, organisational changes within the administrative structure of a particular community, public demand, the desire for novelty, even competition with other centres, may all have played a role in determining textual extensions or excisions. Sadly, the extant texts offer the scholar little assistance in determining the processes by which they came to read as they do today.

The plays' authorship has recently come under renewed scrutiny. That the anonymous dramatists were clerks in at least minor orders and more probably fully-fledged ecclesiastics has for a long time been regarded as virtually axiomatic. It is certainly clear that within broad limits the religious authorities of the late Middle Ages bestowed their blessing on the artistic aspirations of the various guilds and craft associations sponsoring the performance of Christian drama. Indeed, if the Church endorsed the cycle presentations in order to combat the less reputable *miracula*, its cooperation in providing scripts which contained nothing inimical to the transmission of God's message of salvation would seem a natural corollary. But Lawrence Clopper has pointed out (128) that documentary support for clerical involvement in the cycles, as either authors or participants, has so far not been forthcoming, and that in our present state of knowledge the most likely creators of the sequences appear to be the laity. Nevertheless, it is reasonable to ask whether the needful literary skills and exegetical know-how were to be readily discovered within the secular community. The question will remain profoundly significant for future investigators.

Whatever the circumstances of their composition, whoever ultimately prove to be their creators, what must come as something of a shock initially is the nature of the cycle texts. Despite their subject matter and their scriptural and liturgical heritage, the plays in general demonstrate few of those qualities we might anticipate would be the hallmarks of reverential authorship. Whoever wrote the cycles (and we must be discussing the work of scores of writers) certainly appear to have been subject to few restraints when it came to devising methods of appealing to a broad spectrum of the medieval public. While the didactic task is not shirked and the implantation of doctrinal enlightenment not resisted, these texts should be regarded as essentially exercises in popularising what the medieval mind perceived as constituting the truths necessary for human survival in this world and the next, and no literary or theatrical strategies are deemed too downmarket in their associations to be rejected. Even where the faint patterns of liturgical discourse are still detectable, there is a demotic orientation which overrides the routines of organised worship. Elsewhere characterisation is forceful and immediate in its effect, even the virtuous being endowed with a welcome robustness of utterance, which though occasionally strident in its own defence, has the effect of rendering goodness palatable. The vicious may lack subtlety, but their overt defiance of God's will renders them comic as well as sinister, and they stand out as graphic emblems of the human perversions of which evil is capable. There is little hesitation shown in deriding those authoritarian figures – emperors, kings, prelates, governors – who set themselves up in opposition to the Supreme Being or who seek to resist its mandate: the period's predisposition towards civic and social dissension is latent in the merciless satirisation of those whose conduct fails to match their status.

Similarly the dialogue, almost exclusively cast in rhymed stanzaic verse, is frequently concrete, pithy and colloquial, with no concessions made to a fallacious concept of decorum. These were plays for the public forum; they had to declare both openly and tacitly their affinities with the life of the market-place, the backstreet, the farmyard, and the language, both verbal and visual, had to convince onlookers that the men and women of the Bible looked, and, even more importantly, spoke as they did themselves. The admixture of popular saws and common images, of oaths and obscenities, of references to bodily functions, was not introduced as a colourful insertion of realism: they were part of the deliberate tactics employed to command not merely attention, but assent.

The manner in which the plays of the period exploit and transcend their conditions of presentation must never be taken for granted. What many recent analyses confirm is that their staging techniques, like their literary tactics, are consciously geared to the problems of attracting a mass audience and retaining its interest. Their authors' understanding of what popular taste will accept is usually, though not invariably, impeccable, and the unsentimental and unhectoring presentation of the Christian account of history can still command respect, even from those who do not endorse its doctrines.

At the same time we must be aware of treating the whole of this rich yet diverse material as if it constituted a homogeneous mass. Despite the clear affinities of purpose, method and impact of all the cyclic dramas, each has its own individual nature, and recent scholarship and criticism have combined to demonstrate beyond all question that each sequence has its own individualising traits which stand out by contrast with what is current elsewhere. Whether this tendency results from editorial activity late in the cycles' evolution (as would seem to be the case with the Chester plays), or whether the idiosyncrasies are inherent in the materials of which the sequences are made or in the approach adopted (which may be the case with N-Town), it is vital to remember that local differences are essential to the understanding of each individual series and must be respected in any future research into its textual and theatrical character.

Of those plays that lie outside the major cycles of York, Wakefield, Chester and N-Town the most interesting are perhaps the two remnants of the series associated with Coventry (82), the Newcastle play on Noah and the Northampton and Brome versions of Abraham's projected sacrifice of Isaac (85). The fact that each turns on a theme or subject embraced elsewhere reminds us that the cycles were not simply ragbags of miscellaneous episodes, but carefully orchestrated sequences whose component parts were selected to reinforce a point of exegetical interest or doctrinal importance. Thus Noah's survival in the waters of the Flood prefigured Christian baptism; the selection of Isaac as potential sacrificial victim and the substitution for him of the lamb foreshadowed the symbolism of Christ as Lamb of God giving his life on the cross for the redemption of humanity.

The two plays that survive from the original series of at least eleven presented at Coventry indicate that this cycle must once have constituted a very notable literary achievement: the Shearmen and Tailors' pageant of a two-part Nativity sequence is highly charged with tension, not least on account of a memorably maniacal Herod, subject of one of the most graphic of all medieval stage directions – 'Here Erode ragis in the pagond [pageant wagon] and in the strete also' – which helps us to visualise the close nexus between actor and audience at this period in theatre history. The Coventry play also contains the enchanting 'Coventry Carol', sung by the mothers of the Innocents prior to the slaughter of their offspring by Herod's soldiery: here too we have direct evidence of the central role played by sung music in realising the full potential of the medieval cycle sequences, but instrument-alists also made a major contribution to the proceedings.

By contrast with the Nativity pageant the Weavers' composite *Prophets*, *Presentation of Christ in the Temple* and *Doctors* has received less critical attention, yet it is a pleasing treatment of a subject which often bridges the gap in a cycle series between Christ's birth and the beginning of the ministry. It has three main elements: a purely descriptive account from 'three prophets' of the appearance of the star in the east, and the journey of the Magi; a lengthy dramatisation of the encounter between Simeon and the infant Jesus; and a final selection which treats of Christ's encounter with the learned doctors at Jerusalem and their consternation at his spiritual erudi-tion. It is by its very nature episodic, but within its limits it is skilfully wrought, and extracts not a little drama from material ostensibly unpromising.

Perhaps the most interesting point about the Coventry survivals has been recently made by Alexandra Johnston in arguing that the two pageants may be relics of a Creed play (i.e. one illustrating the principal clauses of the Apostles' Creed) rather than a scriptural sequence (52, p. 11). Seeking to extend the term 'Corpus Christi play' to cover a wider variety of dramas than merely biblical pageants, she argues that the absence of Old Testament episodes at Coventry may indicate that a different type of drama was pre-sented there from that which dominated at York and Chester; moreover, an allusion in a work of 1526 to satisfying one's curiosity concerning the tenets of the Creed by visiting Coventry notes 'there ye shall se them all played in Corpus Christi playe'. But which sections of the Creed the two surviving plays illustrate is not easy to demonstrate.

The Newcastle play of Noah seems part of a similar pageant series of perhaps a dozen plays, but one which apparently made provision for Old Testament incidents, unlike that of Coventry. The limited nature of the series is quite interesting, in that Newcastle was a prosperous medieval town with a well-developed guild system, yet not all the individual associations presented plays, and others came to the task late in the history of the civic performances (47, 85). It was the Shipwrights who presented, appropriately enough, the Noah episode, but its text is badly corrupted, existing only in a poor eighteenth-century reprint. The Newcastle version is, however, notable in one respect: the Devil is introduced as a character, bemoaning the fact that Noah and his family will escape the flood and hence his diabolic clutches. He resolves to seduce Noah's wife as he beguiled Eve, and comedy ensues when she seeks to undermine her husband's labours. But the ending is inconclusive, and one must assume that corruption rather than dramatic ineptitude causes the action to peter out as it does.

The Northampton and the Brome versions of the story of Abraham's sacrifice are much more finished and accomplished productions (85). The incident was a popular one, and occurs in all the major series; indeed, much interest attaches to the fact that considerable portions of the Brome text closely echo the Chester cycle's version of the same episode. Most recently scholarly opinion favours the view that Brome's is the superior handling, but whatever the ultimate decision reached, the relationship between the versions raises the intriguing question of the nature of the physical and textual contacts between the play-producing centres of medieval England. Clearly a number of resemblances can easily be accounted for by reference to a common source in scriptural, apocryphal or liturgical material, but on numerous occasions this cannot account for a piece of verbal parallelism, or shared features of characterisation or plot development. We know, for example, that at some point in its evolution the Wakefield play cycle acquired six episodes from York, episodes which were later elaborated by authors at work in the cathedral city (see below, chapter 5). Much more work remains to be done on the interrelationships between one sequence and another. What is clear already is that regional distinctions were a major force in the related but distinctive developments of the cycle plays at different centres.

The Northampton and Brome plays of Abraham and Isaac illustrate this diversity quite neatly; while both versions rely on simple homely colloquial speech and unadorned domestic sentiments to emphasise the poignancy of the situation, the Northampton text prefaces the main action with a dialogue between God and an angel cast in a more elevated register, which renders the ensuing action something of a controlled experiment, while Brome conveys a greater sense of dramatic excitement as God's injunction disturbs the contented musings of the patriarch. Furthermore, the Northampton play dissipates something of the familial bond between Abraham and son by introducing Isaac's mother Sarah into the action, even though the effect of this is to complicate Abraham's feelings of guilt and remorse at the task laid upon him, by forcing him to dissemble. Although there is a touching reunion scene in this case, Brome's is a more streamlined treatment, though the author felt it needful to introduce a learned sage to point the moral in a slightly otiose epilogue. Northampton also employs two non-essential characters in the form of two of Abraham's men, suggesting that human resources may have been more plentiful in the midlands piece, though neither play calls for the immense investment of cash and personnel frequently called for in the major centres.

Equally varied in their demands are the other dramas of the fifteenth century, the earliest to survive being the epic-scale morality play of sin and repentance known as *The Castle of Perserverance* (*c.* 1400–25), whose origin may have been in the Lincoln area, though the extant manuscript containing it (the Macro manuscript) circulated in East Anglia (83). Immensely ambitious in its spatial and histrionic requirements, *The Castle* is typical of a theatre full of self-confidence and bravado, and of an acting company eager and talented enough to respond to the challenge of a lengthy, verbally showy but rewarding script. One of the chief excitements of the text is that it is complemented by a unique sketch plan of its realisation within and around an enclosed circular space analogous to a Roman amphitheatre or a modern circus ring (see illustration 8). Much discussion has been devoted to the correct interpretation of this drawing (42, pp. 78–83), but at all events, the setting obviously supplied the cast with ample opportunities for spectacular stage movement, not least when Belial, the play's principal devil, led his forces in an exuberant assault on the castle of the title with smoke streaming from pipes concealed in his hands, his ears and his hind-quarters. The piece is celebrated for its coverage in allegorical terms of the entire span of human life from cradle to grave, and indeed, beyond, since the final third of the action pivots on the fate of Humankind's soul as it hangs suspended between the rival claims of Justice and Mercy. The vast cosmic implications of individual virtue or vice are forcefully dramatised in an impressive blend of sounding oratory and dynamic stage activity.

Modest and even homely are other plays centred on sin and salvation, although another East Anglian play, the Digby *Mary Magdalen* (84), rivals *The Castle* here and there in its striking scenic effects. The play is a slightly uncomfortable amalgam of genres and moods, but it has immense panache as befits a narrative that contemporises Mary Magdalene's descent into deadly sin and her recovery of grace, and in the process blends elements from the scriptural cycles, the epic morality and sentimental romance in a farrago of crowd-pulling devices. Rather less of a *mélange* is *The Conversion of St Paul* from the same manuscript (Oxford, Bodleian, Digby 133), which also capitalises on the opportunities to introduce pyrotechnics and low comedy (84). Much interest has been engendered by the possibility that this was an early 'promenade' production, presented at three separate sites within easy reach of each other, and that spectators followed the action from 'station to station'. Others argue that the stations were no more than moveable pageant wagons wheeled into place as needed (see below, chapters 10 and 11).

Dux Moraud, or *Duk Morawd* (c. 1425), which exists only in the form of the lines allocated to the player of its leading role, has lurid features akin to those of a group of French texts celebrating the miracles wrought by the Virgin, the *Miracles de Nostre Dame (85, 254)*. Its sensational theme, which originates in an incestuous relationship between the 'Duke' of the title and his daughter, culminates in multiple murder, but these sordid events are a prelude to redemptive penitence, and serve to demonstrate that spiritual indoctrination was not viewed as incompatible with theatrical *frisson*. More cerebral and restrained is *Wisdom Who is Christ* or *Mind, Will and Understanding* (c. 1460), which warns of the perils attendant on the human soul when diabolic forces corrupt the faculties of spiritual awareness, determination and devotion to God (the trio of virtues covers many aspects of righteousness), which can only be restored by the intervention of Wisdom (83). The tone is sombre and didactic, unlike that of any other extant English play of the period, and W. A. Davenport has suggested that its poetic, intellectual and academic qualities indicate its provenance to be that of a noble household, a university or lawyers' hall, or a monastery school. Certainly its masque-like formality contrasts strongly with the earthy realism and sprightly grotesqueness of most morality drama of the time. Not that *Wisdom* is a drab tract: its costume requirements, its need for a cast that can sing and dance, its strong emphasis on religious iconography, make it the most balletic or operatic of medieval plays (305, 329).

In marked contrast, despite its presence in the same manuscript as *Wisdom*, is *Mankind* (c. 1464), a racy and scatological piece which has only recently been accorded its true importance as a piece of excellent didactic drama (83). Its strategy is to lure its audiences into an unholy alliance with a set of vicious figures, the 'Vices' of the piece, whose efforts to seduce the virtuous but vulnerable hero from the ways of truth are backed by diabolic agents. Probably composed as a Shrovetide entertainment in anticipation of the Lenten season of self-denial and self-examination, *Mankind* has attracted much recent attention, by virtue of both its lively stagecraft and its deployment of excremental humour and obscene diction to ensnare the unwary spectator, much as the eponymous hero is trapped by his own human credulousness. Once its dramatic strategy is perceived, *Mankind* may be recognised as an outstanding feat of popular dramatics.

Mankind is an East Anglian play, and so too is the only extant example in English of a genuine *miracle* on French lines, the *Play of the Sacrament* (*c.* 1461) which is associated with Croxton, a village near Thetford in Norfolk (*85*). This piece combines true popular appeal with what seems an attempt to reassert the doctrine of the Real Presence in the face of Lollard refutation, dramatising a widely-known anecdote with a shrewd eye for its psychological possibilities as well as its theatrical sensationalism. In refashioning the story of the Jewish merchant who subjected a stolen Mass wafer to torments, the author skilfully parallels the central features of Christ's Passion up to the point where literal and symbolic action interfuse, and Christ appears in person to reproach the Jew and his followers for their sceptical cruelty, so converting them to the true faith. The physical energy generated by the aliens is much in evidence, but their comic-grotesque allure is countered by an apparent lack of anti-Semitism in their portrayal, and the ingenuity with which the scenes of violence are made to echo Christ's own persecution. One point of interest lies in the possibility that the final sequence of the play took place inside a church building, and that the audience was required to leave its places in order to witness the baptism of the Jews at the font. If permission for this were granted, it would serve to demonstrate yet again the close identification of church and stage at even the latter end of the Middle Ages.

THE STATE OF PLAY

On one level at least it is hard to fathom the appeal that the English medieval theatre appears to have for today's readers and spectators. Religious if not devotional in essence, most of what survives was written to serve the doctrinal and propagandist aims of a faith which ceased to be that of the majority of the British people over four centuries ago. Even among practising Christians now, the theological premises on which most medieval dramas rest are unlikely to command total assent. Yet all the evidence suggests that the repertoire can still stimulate a measure of interest and response that transcends the dutiful reactions of classroom and lecture hall, and meets some contemporary need which other stimuli fail to reach.

Several explanations for this phenomenon deserve consideration (*472*, pp. 142–3). Despite the heterodoxy and even the unbelief of the public at large, a vaguely Christian heritage is still something the majority of us share, if reluctantly, even if it amounts to no more than observing Christmas and Easter and being conscious of the rich legacy of churches and cathedrals which impinges on us at salient moments in our national and domestic existences. As we contemplate medieval plays on stage it may be that 'an age more spiritual than ours' is fleetingly restored to us, and a sense of shared confidence in a caring God and mutual values is briefly ours once again. Moreover, since the Second World War and the blurring of cultural distinctions not only between countries but between continents as the concept of the 'global village' takes hold, the British have become fiercely possessive of their national past as successive phases of the Coca-Cola culture have threatened to overwhelm them. Despite their close links with analogous continental dramas, ironically it is frequently the 'Englishness' of the cycle plays in particular which has been extolled as part of our legendary historical distinction, and which has in turn contributed to the effort to recover some awareness of a lost national identity.

In addition, one cannot fail to be aware of the role played in all this by a lost sense of *local* identity. It becomes clearer year by year that the regional affinities of the major medieval dramas are a central aspect of their success, both in their terms as well as in our own. If there has been one contemporary contribution to a fuller appreciation of medieval drama which deserves special commendation, it is the increasing realisation that for a true understanding of the texts and staging of the cycles and moralities, consideration of all those factors peculiar to a particular dramatic locality is paramount. Here the *REED* project is of major significance, providing as it will all the evidence available to modern systematic researchers, in order to assist our efforts to perceive how local conditions, resources, influences, preferences and prejudices helped to shape the dramatic experiences of which the extant scripts can provide us with only pallid reflections.

In this context a number of recent publications possess considerable importance, not least the recent crop of freshly-edited texts of the main items in the medieval repertoire, which have increased awareness of the physical nature of the various manuscripts and their contents. For example, the Chester play manuscripts, once felt to preserve the earliest forms of the cycle sequences, have now been shown to contain a very late version of the cycle, because of, rather than in spite of, its direct diction, the regularity and simplicity of its metrical patterns, its placid, even inhibited register. Its most recent editors have demonstrated that Chester's tightly-organised unity probably results from the editorial labours of a single redactor (182). A similar figure appears to have been responsible for the textual complexities of the N-Town pageants, in that he was attempting to create a composite group of plays from a number of disparate texts. Into a sequence of a traditional scriptural type he wove episodes from a play on the life of the Virgin and an independent two-part Passion sequence. Here again local conditions may have been a factor in initiating this attempt to create a new whole from pre-existing parts. The latest edition of the York plays has also added considerably to our appreciation of medieval methods of dramatic composition and selection; unlike the Chester cycle, the York plays cannot be discussed as examples of cohesive wholes created according to conscious artistic principles, nor yet have they been assembled from heterogeneous sources as is the case with N-Town. What their modern editor suggests is that, while a whole series of episodes may have been transcribed into the master-copy (the Register), not every single piece was necessarily presented on each annual occasion on which performances were called for. Moreover, the plays' texts could clearly undergo considerable modification from one year's presentation to the next: the script should not be regarded as a static, unvariable specimen pinned to the page for all time, a point reinforced by recent textual scholarship in the Shakespearean field (143). The fluidity of early dramatic texts is something that the late twentieth century is only now starting to take into account.

Some of the major work on the genesis and evolution of texts has been devoted to the Wakefield or Towneley plays (Towneley being the name of the family in whose possession the manuscript resided for many years). Part of the reason for this is that the most distinguished dramatic achievements among all the cycle plays are arguably those of the so-called 'Wakefield Master', though here John Gardner (206) has probably erred in his helpful book on the construction of the sequence by trying to demonstrate that this charismatic figure sought to impose unity on the cycle as a totality. The quality of the Master's acknowledged work has made it the subject of frequent critical scrutiny, and the praise now bestowed on the general level of artistry and sophistication exhibited by medieval playwrights is in large measure an extension of the admiration rarely withheld from the author of *The Second Shepherds' Play*.

A welcome feature of modern scholarship in this area is that staging is no longer viewed as an irrelevant or distracting aspect of the serious study of medieval dramatic literature. Regarding both Chester and York, much attention has been devoted to processional staging, which may have developed at the former centre with the transfer of the annual performances from Corpus Christi to Whitsun week. Here discussion has focused in part on Archdeacon Rogers's early seventeenth-century accounts of the plays, and the degree of reliance that can be placed on them. The York records too have generated a long and sadly inconclusive controversy relating to the feasibility of staging the lengthy series of civic pageants at a number of fixed stations along a processional route within the compass of even the longest summer's day. Various solutions have been propounded, but despite the exercise of much ingenuity and the discovery and dissemination of much valuable data, an agreed picture has so far not emerged, though most would now accept that the York performances were processional, that plays were acted at all twelve stations. Whether every play available for presentation was seen at every station on every occasion is another matter. Even here regional diversity must be stressed: the Wakefield plays may well have been staged at a single location using place-and-scaffold methods, and the same mode may well have been the norm for the N-Town sequence, even in its peripatetic form.

Certainly in stage terms techniques employed by medieval playwrights no longer seem as alien to us as would have been the case when the naturalistic methods perfected in the late nineteenth century governed assumptions concerning the proper social milieux, narrative content, scenic backgrounds, character psychology and linguistic register appropriate to drama. Successive waves of revolutionary change in the modern theatre, ranging from poetic symbolism and expressionism to concepts of 'the epic' and 'the absurd', have eroded the bulwarks of illusionism, and pre-Renaissance theatre with its unconscious but manifest rejection of naturalistic stage practices has in recent decades seemed so often to be at the forefront of the *avant garde* that we feel more at home with bare stages and token or makeshift scenery than in the ballrooms and sitting-rooms and waiting-rooms of Ibsen or Wilde or Shaw. The apparent processes of democratisation in British society over the last fifty years have also played a part by making us feel obliged to identify more readily with workmen and peasants than with duchesses or mill owners, though the empathetic procedures may in reality be equally spurious.

Finally, we live in an age increasingly attuned to the visual and preferably the pictorial. One of the most significant advances in medieval theatre research since the 1950s has been the exploration of the multiple relationships to be traced between Gothic iconography of every kind and the *mise-en-scène* of dramatic entertainments (453). While being careful to treat questions of chronological priority with caution, thus avoiding the notion that artists merely copied what they saw mounted on pageant wagons or that devisers of pageants could only imitate existing art works, the leading investigators have alerted us to the undeniable fact that drama and the graphic and plastic arts were constantly drawing on a common cultural and iconographical pool while sharing countless basic assumptions about the function, interpretation and value of the visual image. To be reminded that in stained-glass window and misericord, in roof boss and richly-embroidered vestments medieval playwrights had ready access to a remarkable source of pictorial analogies to what they were seeking to bring to life on stage, is to recall once more that the drama they created was an integral part of the vibrant life of its times (253).

NOTES

1 Publications in the REED series to date are listed in the 'Documentary materials' section of the Select Bibliography below (items 47–61). See also Ian Lancashire's *Dramatic Texts and Records of Britain. A Chronological Topography* (4).

2 David N. Dumville, 'Liturgical Drama and Panegyric Responsory from the Eighth Century?', *Journal of Theological Studies*, NS 23 (1972), 374–406; Neil D. Isaacs, 'Who Says What in "Advent Lyric VII"? (*Christ*, lines 164–213)', *Papers on Language and Literature* 2(1966), 162–6.

3 See Dom Thomas Symons (ed.), *The Monastic Agreement of the Monks and Nuns of the English Nation* (London: Thomas Nelson, 1953), esp. the *Visitatio Sepulchri*, pp. 49–50.

4 Texts in J. A. W. Bennett and G. V. Smithers (eds.), *Early Middle English Verse and Prose*, 2nd edn (Oxford: Clarendon Press, 1968), pp. 80–95, 196–200.

5 Texts (in English translation) in Richard Axton and John Stevens (eds.), *Medieval French Plays* (Oxford: Basil Blackwell, 1971).

6 See further J. D. A. Ogilvy, '*Mimi, Scurrae, Histriones*: Entertainers of the Early Middle Ages', *Speculum* 38 (1963), 603–19.

7 Frazer's *Golden Bough* was published between 1890 and 1915. The chief writers on the drama influenced by its findings were the classicists Jane Harrison, F. M. Cornford and Gilbert Murray. For a summary of the controversy engendered by the search for 'pagan origins', see 43, pp. 7–16. My own views, expressed in *The Theatre of the Middle Ages* (41, pp. 1–14), have undergone drastic revision at the kindly hands of Tom Pettitt (375–377). See also the discussion of traditional or folk drama in chapter 12, pp. 340–2, below.

8 Joseph Fontenrose, *The Ritual Theory of Myth*, Folklore Studies 18 (Berkeley: University of California Press, 1971).

9 See Peter Dronke, *The Medieval Lyric* (London: Hutchinson, 1968), p. 190.

10 Roger Fowler (ed.), *Wulfstan's Canons of Edgar*, EETS, OS 266 (Oxford: Oxford University Press, 1972), pp. 6–7.

11 See 4, pp. 289, 171, 305. For the Robin Hood playlet, see 381, pp. 32–42, 71.

12 For *miracula*, see 4, pp. 82, 125, 173; for William of Wadington, see F. J. Furnivall (ed.), *Robert of Brunne's Handlying Synne*, EETS, OS 119 (London, 1901), pp. 154–6.

13 The Anglo-Norman text of the *Adam* is given with parallel English translation in 62, pp. 78–121; see also Axton and Stevens, *Medieval French Plays*, pp. 3–44, which includes transcriptions of the music. The critical and scholarly literature is extensive: see Lynette R. Muir, *Liturgy and Drama in the Anglo-Norman Adam* (Oxford: Medium Ævum Monographs 3, 1973), and her subsequent discussion in 33, pp. 57–8.

14 For varied views on this issue see Kolve (*130*, pp. 8–32) and Nelson (34, pp. 1–10); for a summary, see Tydeman (*41*, pp. 127–9).

15 For good general surveys of medieval drama both in Britain and on the continent see the contributions under 'Medieval Drama in Europe' in Martin Banham (ed.), *The Cambridge Guide to World Theatre* (Cambridge: Cambridge University Press, 1988). Recent attempts to bridge the gap between the British Isles and Europe include two important chapters in Briscoe and Coldewey (*12*): Robert Potter, 'The Unity of Medieval Drama: European Contexts for Early English Dramatic Traditions' (36) and Lynette R. Muir, 'Medieval English Drama: the French Connection' (33).

2

MEG TWYCROSS

The theatricality of medieval English plays

Medieval plays were not written for the theatre. They were put on in city streets, in churches, on playing fields, in college halls and in private houses, and they exploited each of these venues in its own distinctive way. The shape and acoustics of the venue, the skills of the actors, the nature of the audience and of the occasion, all presented certain constraints and certain opportunities. Add to this a variety of types of subject matter, and we have not one but a whole range of theatricalities.

Plays are for performing, and one recent branch of medieval theatre research has specialised in the informed 'recreation' of medieval performance conditions. This has been an eye-opening and salutary exercise. Because medieval theatre is so different from modern commercial theatre both in setting and intention, we modern investigators have had to break down our prejudices about the practical limits of staging and acting style. We have discovered, among other things, that actors can perform on a stage eight feet by ten feet; that twenty-foot-high pageant wagons are not necessarily doomed to overbalance; that long rhetorical speeches are not by definition 'boring'; that spectacle can speak more strongly than words; that it is possible to look the audience full in the face. Above all we have learnt to trust the plays themselves: that if we take them seriously as theatre, they will work. Medieval theatre has emerged not as childlike or primitive, but as different, and often highly sophisticated.

One of its strengths was clearly the way in which it acknowledged and engaged its audience, but this is one relationship we can never fully reconstruct in performance. There was no such thing as casual theatregoing: each of these plays was the centrepiece of a special occasion for a close-knit community. The mystery plays were at the same time a religious festival and a tourist attraction: their players could draw on a charge of heightened religious emotion and civic pride which we can never recreate. Similarly, a great hall play was initially written for a household group who knew each other's quirks and foibles, and who were sensitive to status and ceremony. Both were 'community theatre' in the true sense. Modern revivals have to face the fact not only that they cannot recapture this relationship, but that there is probably nothing they can substitute that will not do violence to or distort the plays' premises. Thus the National Theatre's *The Mysteries* (474, 486) (1985), which have arguably done more than any other production, the York Festival Mystery Plays included, to popularise mystery plays in Britain, tried to draw on a spurious sense of community created by appeals to a romantic nineteenth-century trade unionism that never was, as a substitute for the religious fervour and knowledge that the director probably rightly felt had gone for ever.

For the purposes of this chapter, our main line of demarcation lies between plays performed indoors and plays performed outdoors. Not only were there, broadly speaking, seasonal differences, the nature of indoor and outdoor playing was different. Under indoor venues come the great halls of noble or collegiate households, guildhalls and churches (whose drama reflects the liturgical seasons). Outdoor plays were performed on pageant wagons in the streets of cities like York, Chester, Coventry or Norwich, or in the type of staging called place-and-scaffold. This could be mounted in a sizeable arena or be merely a matter of two or three booth stages in a country churchyard. Of these, only place-and-scaffold possibly played to a paying audience: all the others were funded by levy or subsidised by the person or group for whose benefit they were mounted.

There is no room here to talk about mummings, royal entries, disguisings or tournaments, though they are all part of the theatrical picture of the fifteenth and early sixteenth centuries. Their intellectual content and production values were on the same level as those of the plays of which this book treats, but they have no easily discernible narrative (they cannot be treated as 'literature'), and thus are omitted. But it should not be forgotten that they, with the ephemeral 'Christmas games' and 'king games' of folk-drama, were a substantial part of the theatrical activity of their era, and that their style fed into what we recognise as plays.

OPEN-AIR STAGING: PAGEANT WAGONS

In Britain, large-scale open-air theatre must almost by definition belong to the summer. The civic cycles of mystery plays were traditionally performed on or around Corpus Christi Day, the Thursday after Trinity Sunday. This is a moveable feast, as it depends on the date of Easter, but it must fall within the period 21 May to 24 June, when, as far as possible in our uncertain climate, we may expect (moderately) good weather and long hours of daylight. The summer solstice, when the sun is above the horizon for seventeen hours in the northerly towns of York and Chester, falls on 21 June, but in the fifteenth and sixteenth centuries, before the reformation of the calendar, the longest day would in fact have been about ten days earlier.

The long hours of daylight were necessary in York, for there the cycle of over fifty plays was performed all in one day. In Chester the cycle moved back from Corpus Christi Day to Whit Week some time between 1475 and 1521: by the 1530s the twenty-five plays were spread over three days, the Monday, Tuesday and Wednesday of Whit Week. I am going to refer mainly to these two cycles, as for them we have not only almost full scripts, but also sufficient independent civic and guild records to be able to piece together something of the methods of performance. Besides this, enough remains of the original city centres to give the visitor a sense of how the pageant wagons may have fitted into their settings. In the last decade there have in fact been various small-scale practical 'recreations' of wagon plays over part of the original routes, most notably at Chester in 1983 and York in 1988 and 1992, and this chapter incorporates some of the discoveries made during these experiments.

As the following chapters will show in more detail, all the surviving pageant-wagon cycles have a basic structure in common. The great story that composed the Corpus Christi play (the whole cycle was called a *play*, while the individual portions were *pageants*: this is the terminology adopted in this chapter), a history of the universe from just before its Creation to its ending at the Day of Judgement, was parcelled up into episodes. Each episode was delegated to a separate group, a trade or religious guild, which was totally responsible for its production. Each group had or shared a mobile stage also called a *pageant*, which when their turn came they pulled through the city along a traditional route, stopping at prearranged *stations* (the word means 'stopping places') to perform their episode.

True processional staging, as this is called, is more complicated to de-scribe than it is to execute. Let us take York as an example. There were between twelve and sixteen stations along the processional route, which ran from Holy Trinity Priory just inside Micklegate Bar down the main streets of the city in a lefthanded sickle shape to end on the Pavement (*170, 174*; see below, illustration 1). On Corpus Christi Day, as the city ordinance declares, the actors of the first plays were to be ready at their pageants at 4.30 a.m. (*158*, p. 25). Then the first guild, the Barkers (Tanners), would move its wagon out to the first station by Holy Trinity Priory and act its play of the Creation and Fall of the Angels. When this was finished, the wagon would move on to the second station, a few hundred yards down Micklegate, where the same pageant would start all over again; meanwhile, the Plasterers would have moved their wagon up to the first station, and

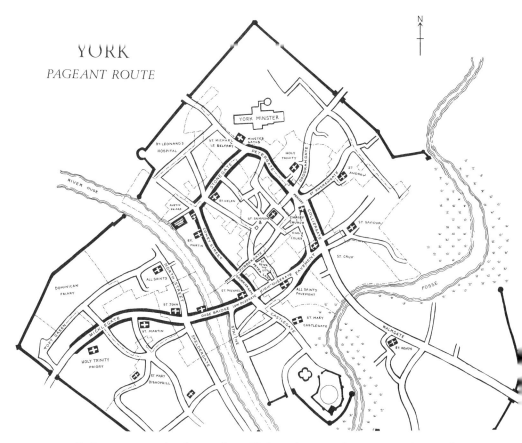

1   York pageant route, late fourteenth to mid-sixteenth century. See pp.39–41, 98–100, 298–9.

have started playing the *Creation*. If it was a twelve-station year, by the time they had finished, the Barkers would have moved on to the third station further down Mickelgate, so the Plasterers would move on to the second station, and start all over again, while the Cardmakers drew up at the first station to play the *Creation of Adam and Eve*. By the time the Barkers had finished at the last station of the route on the Pavement, the Spicers would be playing the *Annunciation* at the first station, and the whole of the route would be alive with plays on the Old Testament. To proceed forward in historical time, you would only have to walk briskly from the Pavement back along the route towards its beginning at Holy Trinity. Chester followed the same principle, save that the twenty five plays only played at five stations, and by the 1530s, as noted above, were spread over three days.

In practice, it was not quite as tidy as this. Apart from the problems caused by guilds not being ready and holding up the whole proceedings (which we know of because they were fined for it by the city council), this would work mechanically perfectly only if every play were the same length, whereas they vary from ten minutes (the *Creation of Adam and Eve*) to about forty (*Moses and Pharaoh*). If a long play were followed by a short one, the short one would have finished at Station 1 well before the long one had finished at Station 2, so the short play would have to wait by Station 2 until the long play had finished and vacated the space. The actors in the short play would thus have had a lot of breaks between performances. This 'back-up effect' would also happen if a short play were followed by a long one, only in this case the audience would have the break. (By a mathematical quirk, these intervals get longer in an arithmetical progression, which can prove very disconcerting to an untrained modern audience.) The actors in the long plays get the worst of all possible worlds, as they have to play continuously, like a tape loop. Because of this knock-on effect, the actual playing time of the cycle at the later stations is much longer than the mere sum of the lengths of the individual plays. In 1988, with four plays playing over only four stations, the overall playing time of two hours at Station 1 had stretched to three hours by Station 4. However, far from being a blot on the aesthetic effect of the performance, this was actually very useful, as we shall see later.

One might imagine that the plays would interfere with one another. In practice, this does not happen. In York, the streets curve sufficiently for almost every station to be just out of sight of the previous one: in Chester, they are round the next corner. In any case, the wagons block the street so that the audience cannot see what follows. Sounds drift across, but are not really intrusive, though one can imagine that a *Harrowing of Hell* accompanied by really loud explosions could wreak havoc with the more plangent mood of the *Death of Christ* and *Resurrection* on each side. It may be that some plays took the opportunity to play in tandem: the 1415 description of the York Tilethatchers' play –

> Mary, Joseph, a midwife, the new-born boy lying in a manger between the ox and the ass, and an angel speaking to the shepherds and the players in the following pageant [i.e. the Chandlers' *Nativity*] (*158*, p. 18) –

suggests that the two pageants were linked in some way: unfortunately in the manuscript the page where the angel speaks to the shepherds is missing from the Chandlers' play, and there is no speaking part for an angel in the Tilers' play. The situation with the *Herod/Magi*, shared by the Masons and Goldsmiths, is even more curious: they appear for at least some time to have used two wagons, one Jerusalem (Herod's court) and one Bethlehem (the stable).[1] Several other plays seem to call for two locations: *Moses and Pharaoh* and the *Resurrection* are conspicuous examples.

Though processional staging is complicated to explain, it is in fact a beautifully simple and economical solution to a severe logistic problem: how to bring a vast play to a large holiday audience without losing either detail or an intimacy of approach. The problem was solved by playing each episode over and over again to audiences which must have been relatively small – as many as can crowd into an ordinary shopping street around a pageant wagon, perhaps between one and two hundred. But cumulatively it adds up to an impressive number.

This parcelling out had implications for the actors, the audience, the set, the organisation, and what judges of ice-skating competitions call the 'artistic impression'. The organisation and funding made use of the existing social and commercial infrastructure of the trade guilds, who put on their individual pageants from a mixture of religious devotion, civic pride and showmanship. The production was funded by an annual mandatory levy on each guild member called (in York) 'pageant silver': as street theatre practitioners know, you cannot charge for entrance to a street event, and passing round the hat almost always attracts charity rather than real-cost contributions. This levy was collected by 'pageant masters' who were also in charge of 'producing' the play in our modern sense: making sure that it got on the streets. Their term for 'produce' was *bring forth*, a literal translation of the Latin *producere* and in the case of the pageant wagon practically appropriate as well:

> youe wrightys and slaters wilbe fayne   *glad to*
> bryng forth your cariage of marie myld quene

say the Chester Early Banns (*179*, p. 35). A huge job was thus shared out in manageable chunks, and the spirit of competition between the guilds would ensure that each attempted to outdo the others, as in the Siena Palio or Philadelphia Mummers Parade today.

For the actors, even though playing the same play twelve or sixteen times must have been a severe test of physical and vocal stamina, especially for the major roles (for example, the York *Last Judgement* is virtually a solo for God, and it must have taken seven to eight hours of pretty well continuous playing), at least it was repetition. (When one actually mounts a processional performance, one realises why such phenomenal sums were spent on beer. Besides the strain on the voice, the actor gets very dehydrated under mask and wig, and for the pushers it is of course hard physical work.) Also the great roles were shared out. In York, there were at least twenty-two actors playing Christ. This meant that there was less danger of identifying the role with any one star actor. In performance, it creates an extremely strong sense of the role itself, detached from any one particular performer.

This happens – not totally accidentally – to mesh very well with medieval views on the relationship between 'images' (pictures or statues) and the sacred persons and truths they represent. The actor, as image, does not become but represents the person he plays (428, pp. 33–4; 471).

The implications of this view on acting style have become the subject of dispute: was the acting highly stylised or moderately naturalistic? We shall never really know. The use of masks for supernatural characters, the gilding of God's face, haloes and the way in which some characters carry attributes, suggests a certain measure of stylisation, as does the rhetorical structure of the dialogue. But it is possible for both to coexist in the same performance: they are not opposites, but a matter of degree. The argument has raged most violently over the topic of women's roles. These, as in the Elizabethan theatre, were played by male actors (the words 'youths' or 'young men' both suggest the wrong connotations to us, as it seems likely that in those days the advent of puberty was later, and an experienced actor in his late teens might not yet have a broken voice). Japanese Kabuki actors show how convincing female impersonation by a mature male adult can be, but then they operate in a very stylised form of theatre (see 428 (masks); 471 (haloes and attributes); 403, 417, 418, 424 (men in women's roles)).

The Proclamation to the York Play recorded in 1415 calls for the guilds to provide 'good players well arayed & openly spekyng' (158, p. 25). In 1476 the city council attempted to set up a vetting process by which four of 'þe moste Connyng descrete and able playeris within þis Citie' should visit the actors of the projected productions,

> And all suche as þay shall fynde sufficiant in personne and Connyng [*physical presence and skill*] ... for to admitte and able and all oþer insufficiant personnes either in Connyng voice or personne to discharge ammove and avoide.
>
> (158, p. 109).

This concern with 'insufficiant' voice is endemic to open-air theatre, and probably one of the many reasons why women did not play. The pageant-wagon player in the street was luckier than his counterpart who played in place-and-scaffold on a village green, for he had walls off which to bounce his voice. Even so, acoustics remain a problem. Practice has shown that actors should project their voices outwards and upwards to a convenient wall, not down into the crowd. The verse helps: it tends to have a strong alliterative beat (even in Chester, where the main stanza form is octo-syllabic), which it combines with a regular if sometimes complex rhyme scheme. The actor thus has a rhythm which underlines the most important words and is encouraged to keep his voice up to the end of the line; dropping the voice or running out of breath are common faults of amateur actors. The alliterative and rhyme patterns also help the audience to recognise potentially evanescent words. Even the apparently otiose tags and repetitions of the minstrel style – 'When I am dead *and laid in clay*, Till God's Son come, *the sooth to say*,/And ransom his folk *in better array*/To bliss come never we' – gives the audience a chance to assimilate the information they are being given which a more condensed form of dialogue would not under the circumstances allow.

Each pageant is written for the resources of an amateur dramatic society. There is usually one strong acting part, sometimes two, requiring high amateur standards, though we have to remember that in the fifteenth century at least there were no professional actors as such, and the mystery play casts probably contained many a good amateur who might nowadays have become professional, with all of the talent but none of the training. Singing by members of cathedral choirs is the only real professional skill required. Popular recreational skills developed elsewhere were also pressed into service for the play, such as the staff- and sword-twirling of the Chester Herod, or the stilt-walking of the Chester Dobye brothers (see *442, 443* (singing); *186* (skills)).

The other parts are within the range of good to reasonable amateurs, who can be typecast. Overall, the characterisation is strong and can be subtle, but is generic, not individual, in the sense that the actor has to take on a completely different personality from his own, with markedly individual quirks of character. Provided the actor can carry the main lines of the character, his own personal appearance and traits will provide all the individuality that is necessary. Character is always subordinate to narrative and depends for its effectiveness largely on how well the playwright shows the recognisable patterns of human relationships – father and son, son and mother, husband and wife (sometimes with a dose of stereotyped caricature), brother with brother, lord with servant, teacher and disciples. In any case, there is not enough time within the limits of the individual pageant to develop anything at length or show subtle changes of character, but since many of the characters are traditional, the playwright does not have to spend much time establishing, for example, St Joseph's confused goodness of heart, or Herod's bloodthirstiness.

Processional production also gave rise to a perception of the play, on the audience's part, which is unfamiliar to us. Our modern concept of the captive audience is irrelevant. In York, for nearly twenty hours, some part of the play would be going on in some part of the town. It was more like a party one could drop into and out of at will. Even for those who watched the whole play through continuously at one station (the Lord Mayor and aldermen were officially obliged to view it every year from their chamber at the Common Hall Gates), the one-act arrangement provided welcome breaks between episodes: these breaks were further extended by the back-up effect discussed earlier. Audience who were not tied to one station by hospitality or because of having paid for seats on a scaffold, and who were particularly taken by one play, could follow it on to the next station and get an instant action replay. In any case, it seems unlikely that the ordinary member of the audience, however stage-struck or devout, would watch the whole sixteen-hour play through from start to finish. It is of course possible: medieval people had far greater staying power in the face of both entertainment and edification than we have, and recently even modern audiences have become accustomed to the experience of the nine-hour theatrical marathon. If one or two episodes were missed, one could always catch up on them the following year.

Structurally, each of these episodes is engineered as a self-contained unit. Though this can lead to some curious inconsistencies, especially where one guild has apparently adapted its pageant without reference to the others in the same run of plays, these are advantages. Each pageant wagon can establish its own scale and setting, from Eden to Ark, stable to temple, bedroom to the Heavens. It can also set a new tone and mode. This is particularly striking at the end of the Passion and beginning of the Resurrection sequences. In York, the *Crucifixion* concentrates on the soldiers' brisk indifference to Christ's suffering, whilst the *Death of Christ* is more formal and iconic, with the Seven Words from the Cross, and the lament of Mary. The *Harrowing of Hell* shows the implications of these human events on a cosmic scale, and the *Resurrection*, how the characters involved reacted to Christ's rising from the dead. *Christ's Appearance to Mary Magdalen* discloses how it affects the individual soul. By the end, the audience has seen the Redemption from many different angles.

One view sees the pageants as a picture sequence, the same in kind and intent as those of Books of Hours or stained-glass windows which feature the events of Incarnation or Passion frame by frame: a parallel emphasised by the framing effect of the pageant wagon. The overall effect is thus cumulative rather than integrated. There is much to be said for this view, but the effect was in fact more coherent. Apart from the Passion sequence, which is a continuous narrative divided into scenes according to their different locations, the whole play is held together not only by a traditional story-line, but by a general sense that it is history: 'this is what happened'. The characters act as they do because that was what they did: any motivation (as provided by Satan in the *Fall of Man*, or Judas in Towneley 32) is a bonus. The other dimension, the warp to history's weft, is the recurring strands of doctrine and imagery (often expressed in terms of prophecy and biblical typology) drawn from the reservoir of the medieval interpretation of the Christian faith. No production can afford to disregard this in favour of the narrative line alone.

What was the pageant wagon like, and what was it like to act on? Our clearest description of one is a laconic pair of items in an inventory of 'particulars appartaynyng to the Company of the Grocers' of Norwich in 1565:

> A Pageant, that is to saye, a howse of waynskott paynted and buylded on a carte with fowre whelys
> A square topp to sett over the sayde howse   (85, p. xxxv)

(*Wainscot* is the sheet wood used for panelling; our modern equivalent is plywood.) The word *cart* and our modern coinage *pageant wagon* suggest something rural and basic – a haywain, perhaps, decorated for a harvest home. Nothing could be further from the truth. The pageants of York or Chester or Coventry were custom-built theatrical machines. A seventeenth-century Warwickshire antiquary, William Dugdale, described the Coventry pageants as 'Theaters ... very large and high, placed upon wheels, and drawn to all the eminent parts of the City, for the better advantage of Spectators' (51, p. 558 n. 77). When they were not in use, they were stripped down of their more perishable scenery and stored in special large garages called pageant houses, to be rolled out the following year.

Though we have no contemporary pictures of English pageant wagons, paintings and drawings of sixteenth-century Flemish pageants (the most familiar is the 1615 painting by Denis van Alsloot now in the Theatre Museum in Covent Garden; see illustration 5)[2] suggest something of the elaboration and variety that might have appeared at York or Chester. It is clear that the sheer display of the wagons themselves was an important feature of the theatricality of the whole event. The citizens of York described their play in 1426 as 'quemdam ludum sumptuosum' (a certain lavish entertainment) (158, p. 42) and in 1399 spoke of the 'graundes espences & costages' that it caused them (158, p. 11). Both Early (1530s) and Late (recorded after the end of the Whitsun Plays in 1609) Banns in Chester refer over and over again to the 'full fayre syght' of the 'caryage' itself, and its 'grett costage' (costliness) (179, p. 36, line 35, and p. 38, line 15). It is specifically stated that the richer guilds are expected to demonstrate their prosperity by the amount they lay out on their carriage:

> Of the Drapers you the welthie companye
> The creation of the worlde. Adam & Eue
> Acordinge to your welthe sett oute wealthelye
> (179, p. 242, lines 17–19)

Banners, pennants, processional singing and music – all features taken up by modern productions – emphasise that one of the main features of the Corpus Christi play was this processional quality, a sense of marvel following upon marvel. We should remember that the whole event was a performance, not just the individual pageants enclosed in it.

This sense of procession has been at the centre of the recent dispute about how the wagons were aligned for performance.[3] The traditional view, based on the Coventry antiquarian Thomas Sharp's early nineteenth-century reconstruction, is to see them as booth stages on wheels. The stage picture produced is the horizontal oblong, familiar from our proscenium-arch stage (39, frontispiece). Recently, however, a fresh look at both the Flemish pictures and the Spanish Holy Week floats has suggested that in fact the most logical way to use the wagon is as a thrust stage surrounded on three sides by the audience. The front stage opening would be more nearly square than oblong. This cuts down on the time and effort spent manoeuvring the wagon to the side of the street, especially if, as seems likely, it had no turning circle, avoids the danger of collision with jettied overhangs in the upper storeys and leaves much more room for the audience, and for backstage activities. It also gives the audience the full frontal view of the wagon approaching down the street, something which most of those present would agree was one of the most successful features of the 1988 and 1992 York reconstructions.

We have no recorded dimensions for an English mystery-play pageant wagon, but comparative material suggests that the standard width (possibly regulated both by the practicable axle-tree length and by the width of the streets through which it had to pass) was eight feet (2.45 metres): length varies from ten feet (3.05 metres) to fourteen feet (4.27 metres – all metric lengths are approximate).[4] One clearly has to throw away all one's modern preconceptions of how much acting space actors need. One result is that there is no space for casual 'naturalistic' movement, as every flicker shows up. Movements have to be, not necessarily stylised, but deliberate and significant.

It is of course possible to use the street as an extra acting space, as suggested by the famous stage direction 'Here Erode ragis in the pagond and in the strete also' (Coventry Shearmen and Taylors' Play, stage direction at line 783), but in practice a scene played at street level tends to disappear among the audience and have audibility problems, and it is best saved for special effects such as devils rioting or apostles appearing from among the crowd, or the various scenes that demand journeys.

As for height, all surviving pictures suggest a stage floor at audience head height, four to five feet (1.22 to 1.53 metres) from street level, or even higher. Experience proves that this is necessary in crowded streets where the audience stand or move about in order to get a better viewpoint. Here the people who paid to have the plays stop before their houses had an advantage: they could watch from an upper window (first-floor windows in surviving buildings in York give a very good and only slightly raised angle on the lower stage), or because they hired out seats on temporary scaffolds. One thing that reconstructions have taught us is that our modern ideal of everyone in the audience getting an equally good view just cannot have obtained, any more than it does for modern processions. It is only later in purpose-built theatres that everyone has a reasonable expectation of hearing and seeing everything. An ergonomic approach suggests a roof eight feet (2.45 metres) above the stage floor, except in the case of an extremely sedate play in which none of the characters raises a sword or even an arm above his head. This gives one at least twelve to thirteen feet (3.66 to 3.96 metres) for a single-storey wagon. However, several wagons for episodes such as the *Ascension*, the *Assumption of the Virgin* and *Last Judgement*, which require lifts, were double-deckers.

The effect of placing these wagons in an ordinary city street is striking. To begin with, they act as frames which mark the play and its actors off from the audience. They localise the actors and give the audience a focus. This is very noticeable when actors who have been on the ground go up into the wagons. In return, the street gives the wagons and actors added emphasis. Plays like the *Creation* or the *Last Judgement* represent events on a cosmic scale. Modern theatre directors tend to interpret this in terms of a sweepingly wide set and scores of actors. But this is unnecessary: it is all a matter of context. When you stand in the street in front of a *Last Judgement* pageant wagon, and your head tilts back to follow the angels climbing up to take their places on the Heaven deck among the rooftops, you get a real sense of height, and of hierarchy: the three layers – the highest of Heaven, the area 'in the clouds above the earth' where God comes to judge and the ground from which the dead rise and out of which the mouth of Hell opens. Here, as elsewhere, height is used thematically.

Sheer spectacle plays a vital role in this drama. It acts as a metaphor for divine power and glory: the York Mercers' inventory of 1433 (printed in full in chapter 3, p. 94 below) colours in their wagon with blue and red, and gold sunbeams and stars – and it creates a sense of wonder. Stage machinery can be mounted on wheels as well as on a fixed base, provided it is stable, and medieval pageantry was full of 'devices'. Many of the cosmic plays call for lifts, others for trapdoors and other kinds of reveals. Some apparently static plays, like those of the Creation, which appear to consist purely of a monologue by God, may well have been a fantasy of 'devices'. We have to remember that these were guilds of craftsmen as well as salesmen,

The text within the image reads:

> Omne la paix entre dieu et les hommes.
> Par le moyen de la Vierge marie.
> Fut iadis faicte ainsy a present hommes.
> Bourgoys franços deschargez de nos hommes
> Car marie auecq nous se marie.

2   Pageant stage for the royal entry of Mary Tudor (sister of Henry VIII) into Paris, 1514, on the occasion of her marriage to Louis XII of France (British Library MS Cotton Vespasian B. ii, f. 15r). This shows a mixture of biblical and allegorical figures of the kind found in some mystery plays. In the centre are the actors representing Louis and Mary. Above, on the upper stage, in allusion to Mary's name and in the hope of her providing an heir for France, is the Annunciation. To the left and right, two of the Four Daughters of God, Justice (with a sword) and Truth (with the Bible); cf. the N-Town plays and *The Castle of Perseverance*. Below, the Shepherds, representing the common people of France.

3   Pageant stage for the royal entry of Mary Tudor into Paris, 1514; cf. illus. 2 (British
Library MS Cotton Vespasian B. ii, f. 13r). This shows a group of allegorical and mythological
figures, as in some of the morality plays. Justice and Truth enthroned preside over Phoebus
(carrying the sun, representing Louis) and Diana (carrying the moon, representing Mary); to
the left Bon Accord and to the right, linked by Minerva (dressed in armour, a symbol of
readiness for war), the *Stella maris* ('Star of the sea' a title of the Virgin, here applied to Mary
Tudor). The costumes and attributes are typical of stage costume of the early sixteenth
century.

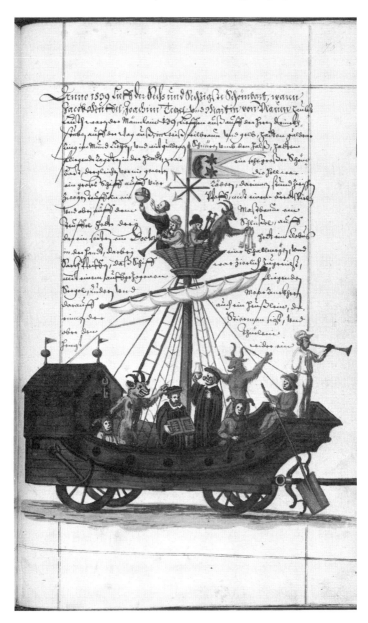

4 Ship on wheels, with devils; German, early sixteenth century (British Library MS Additional 15707, f. 70r). This gives some idea of how Noah's ark may have appeared in processional pageant productions, and incidentally shows what devils looked like on stage.

5   Annunciation pageant wagon, Brussels, 1615. Detail from Denis van Alsloot, *The Triumph of Isabella*, the Theatre Museum, London. See p. 46.

6   Nativity pageant wagon, Brussels, 1615. Detail from Denis van Alsloot, *The Triumph of Isabella*, the Theatre Museum, London. See p. 83, n. 1.

and professional expertise was one thing that was available, for money if not for love: account books are full of payments to painters, carpenters, wheelwrights and tailors.

The medieval love of pyrotechnics, not only to assist the devils, but also for more supernatural events, is much in evidence (399). The Chester *Pentecost* demands that God should send forth the Holy Spirit 'in spetie ignis' (in the form of fire), and while two angels sing the antiphon *Accipite Spiritum Sanctum* they 'projecient ignem super apostolos' (shall cast fire upon the apostles; 73, Play 21, line 238, s.d.). Modern productions have simulated this with ribbons and streamers, but it seems likely from other medieval accounts (409, pp. 107, 119) that the apostles were showered with real fire. In Coventry's Doomsday play, the world was set on fire at each station (51, p. 230). Though the Chester *Harrowing* was played in the open air, it seems to have recreated 'the people that walked in darkness have seen a great light': a stage-direction reads 'fiat lux in inferno materialis aliqua subtilitate machinata' (let there be material (i.e. genuine, not imaginary) light in Hell contrived by some ingenious device; Play 17, first s.d.). Despite the Coventry record of the visit by Queen Margaret of Anjou in 1457, at which *Doomsday* could not be played 'for lak of day' (51, p. 37), it seems very likely that the last plays of the York cycle, notably the *Last Judgement*, had some form of stage lighting. Again, continental records of mechanical heavens suggests that they were full of oil lamps with reflectors, something that, like the fireworks in an enclosed space, no modern fire officer would sanction.

Other more localised special effects include human animals: the Chester Magi are instructed, 'Then goe downe to the beastes and ryde abowt' (Play 8, line 112, s.d.). The beasts are wickerwork camels animated by two 'porters' apiece. Balaam's Ass was sufficiently a favourite to be featured in the advance publicity of the Banns: the Cappers and Linendrapers are to 'Make the Asse to speake and sett hit out lyuelye' (179, p. 243). Other stage effects include the dramatic moment in the Chester *Judgement* in which Christ produces fresh blood from his side (Play 24, line 428, s.d.).

Stage effects like these stand for real-life miracles, and the sense of wonder they produce is translatable into religious awe. In the Chester *Purification* (485), a piece of stage conjuring becomes the persuasive centre of the play. Simeon disbelieves the prophecy 'Behold a virgin shall conceive' on rationalist grounds, and attempts to emend the verse in Isaiah that says this. He scrapes the words away, and writes 'a good woman' instead. An angel thereupon alters the book back to 'a virgin', in red letters for emphasis: when Simeon tests 'whether this miracle be verray' by altering the wording back to 'a good woman' it reappears as 'virgin' in the shining certainty of 'golden letters'. Because the audience are trained to see the realities behind the stage action, the spectacle can become part of the message (471).

It is not only in the spectacle that these plays give a sense of being artefacts, presented for our delight and edification. The way in which the narrative is conducted is often far more like story-telling than what we would regard as drama. (This tendency is general in medieval biblical plays, not just those performed on pageant wagons.) We have to remember that at this time there was no hard and fast line between 'literature' and 'drama': both were performance arts. Plays were described as 'quick [living] books' (40). Every character can be his own story-teller. Modern theatre, under the influence of Brecht, is partly returning to this stance: it is not as unfamiliar to us as it was a few decades ago. Medieval theatre is merely less self-conscious about it. There was no need to create the 'illusion' of naturalistic theatre, the self-contained hermetically sealed world in which the characters are aware only of each other, and on which we eavesdrop. If the audience needs to know something, it is told directly. A character unselfconsciously tells the audience how he feels. He also tells you 'what he is doing at the same time as he is doing it' (228, p. 47). Presumably this running commentary draws the audience's attention to actions that some of them might not be able to see: it also adds an emphasis to significant action, as in the York *Crucifixion*; sometimes, as in the *Baptism* or the *Last Supper*, it has the effect of ritual. Besides this, for the characters to pass on this information is to emphasise the fact that they are communicating with the audience: these actions are not private, but are done for the benefit of the audience, that they may see.

The extreme manifestation of this is the creation of the Presenter figure, sometimes called Expositor or Doctor, whose sole function is to be an interface between the play and the audience. The plays are openly meant to teach. The actor in a mystery play must make himself first and foremost a communicator of his material, not a medium of his own personality and feelings. Actors trained in modern schools are often very uncertain at this, because they are not used to giving prominent expression to the content of what they are saying: they look for the motivation and emotion behind it. Working on these plays requires a lot of strenuous thinking over and above what is needed to tease the meaning out of the unfamiliar fifteenth- and sixteenth-century English. For all their apparent simplicity or even naivety of mode, these are extremely intellectual plays, written by people whose main training was theological and rhetorical.

Modern actors also, apparently, find it initially difficult to face the audience close up, without the comforting glare of the footlights to insulate them. But pageant-wagon playing is street theatre, where the actors must fight to grab and then hold their potential audience's attention. Most writing on the subject concentrates on the mechanisms developed to signal that the play has begun: cries of 'Peace!', threats, prayer (which has a soothing effect). Even the warm-up man is not a modern invention: see Towneley's Pikeharness in the *Mactatio Abel*, or Chester's Goobett-on-the-Greene. Once hooked, the audience have to be continually played, lest their attention should stray. This may be one reason for the story-telling mode: it insists on the presence of the listener as well as the story-teller. The Latin word *audiens* means 'listening', and the audience are constantly reminded that they are to listen actively: 'Lo, lo, sirs, what told I you?' 'What think you, sirs, thereby?'. They are used as sounding boards for the characters' opinions and reactions. The true amount of direct address in these plays becomes apparent only when they are performed. There is no such thing as a soliloquy: the character shares his fears and distresses with the audience's willing ears.

> Shuld an angell this dede haue wroght?
> Sich excusyng helpys noght,
> ffor no craft that thay can;
> A heuenly thyng, for sothe, is he,
> And she is erthly; this may not be,
> It is som othere man.
>
> (Joseph, in Towneley 10, lines 293–8).

In direct audience address, as with York's John the Baptist –

For if we be clene in levyng,	*living*
Oure bodis are Goddis tempyll þan,	
In the whilke he will make his dwellyng.	*which*
Therfore be clene, bothe wiffe and man,	
Þis my reed;	*advice*
God will make in yowe haly þan	*wholly*
His wonning steed	*dwelling place*
	(Play 21, lines 36–42)

– the use of *ye/you* and *thou/thee* (the singular and thus more direct and intimate form of the pronoun) is frequent; so is the way in which the characters will associate themselves with the audience by using *we/us*. This mode of direct address is again not exclusive to the drama: it is an essential feature of the movement of popular piety that sought to bring the individual into a personal relationship with Christ, suffering for his pain, and loving him for his love shown to us (40).

OPEN-AIR STAGING: PLACE-AND-SCAFFOLD

The other main pattern of open-air staging has been christened 'place-and-scaffold'. Here the acting area consists of an open space (the *place*) surrounded by individual stages (the *scaffolds*), each localised as a structure (house, palace, temple, Hellmouth) or natural feature (a mountain). Other scenic elements may be disposed in the *place*: trees, crosses, a pillar, rocks, fountains, even rivers and lakes. The French loan-word *place* is descended from the Latin *platea*, which basically means 'a flat open space'. Latin stage directions in these plays use *platea* where English ones use *place*, and this type of staging is sometimes called 'platea-and-mansion staging', *mansion* meaning 'stopping place': the reason will become apparent later.

To the British reader 'place-and-scaffold' usually conjures up the theatre-in-the-round stage plan of *The Castle of Perseverance* (illustration 8, p. 61), but in fact this layout can be adapted to fit whatever open space is available. (It could even be used for indoor theatre, provided the space was large enough – in a church, for example, which in those days would be free from fixed seating, though the natural orientation of the altar would have to be respected.) On the continent, the paved main squares (also called *places*), normally used for markets and martial displays, could accommodate multi-locational plays such as the Easter Play at Lucerne, for which detailed stage plans survive (409, endpapers). If the traditional recreation area was outside the town walls, as at Clerkenwell Fields in London, then the play would be performed there. This area was sometimes called a 'playing place' or 'game place' and was also used for ball games and shooting at the butts: theatrical 'games' or 'plays' were only another type of entertainment, though they required rather more in the way of construction work to set up.

Compared with the pageant-wagon plays, we have distinctly less information about actual performances of place-and-scaffold plays, and none about productions of the surviving scripts. The evidence that marks them as place-and-scaffold is internal: references to the *place* in stage directions, the obvious use of a multi-locational set, or, in three manuscripts, an actual stage plan.

Of the plays we can definitely tie to it, *The Castle of Perseverance*, the Digby *Mary Magdalen*, the N-Town Passion Plays and Mary Play, the Croxton *Play of the Sacrament*, *The Killing of the Children* and *The Conversion of St Paul* (which is a rather curious case, as it appears to be a genuine promenade performance in our sense of the word) come from East Anglia. The earliest Scottish example, the surviving version of Lindsay's *Ane Satyre of the Thrie Estaitis*, was adapted from the original indoor version for outdoor playing at Calton Hills Fields in Edinburgh. The others, the Cornish

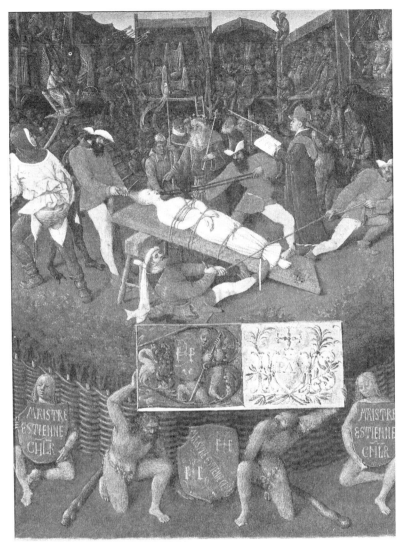

7   Jean Fouquet, 'The Martyrdom of St Apollonia', from *The Hours of Etienne Chevalier*.
See p. 58.

Ordinalia and *Beunans Meriasek*, are written in Cornish, and thus do not lie
within our main brief, but we need to introduce them here as comparative
evidence.

    We have a certain amount of independent evidence about 'playing places'
in East Anglia and in Cornwall. Both are largely rural areas of prosperous
villages and small towns, groups of which seem to have clubbed together to
put on performances in churchyards or purpose-built 'rounds', like the

Cornish *plen an gwary*. There are two existing Cornish rounds at Perran-porth and St Just-in-Penwith, though there is no direct evidence that these were used for plays rather than other games, and their diameters are three times the size of the forty to fifty feet (12.3 to 15.2 metres) described by the antiquarian Richard Carew in his *Survey of Cornwall* (1602). Besides this, the manuscripts of the Cornish *Ordinalia* and the saint's play *Beunans Meriasek* include schematic 'stage plans' which resemble the famous drawing in the manuscripts of *The Castle of Perseverance*. These all have some puzzling discrepancies but suggest a circular acting area enclosed in a raised bank which is punctuated with scaffolds.

The central *place* acts as a No Man's Land into which the characters descend to converse, fight or otherwise interact. Here there is a possible visual parallel in the famous Fouquet miniature of 'The Martyrdom of St Apollonia' from *The Hours of Etienne Chevalier* (illustration 7): it shows a semicircle (perhaps a circle cut in half to allow us to see in?) composed of tall roofed scaffolds like those put up for the spectators at a joust. Some indeed hold spectators, but some are clearly theatrical stages: on the left is Heaven, where God sits surrounded by angels, opposite him is Hellmouth attended by devils, and diametrically opposite the viewer is a throne room with an empty throne. Its occupant has descended into the arena to super-vise the martyrdom of the saint, which is proceeding somewhat theatrically in the centre. In *Meriasek*, and in the first N-Town Passion Play, there is a permanent structure in the middle of this arena, respectively a chapel and 'a lytil oratory' used as a council house (Play 26, line 288, s.d.). In the *Castle* plan this structure is the Castle of Perseverance itself, with its teasing caption 'þis is þe castel of perseueraunce þat stondyth In þe myddys of þe place, but lete no men sytte þer, for lettynge of syt, for þer schal be þe best of all' (83, p. 1; 115, pp. 152–3).

This immediately raises the question of where the audience was supposed to be. Did they sit or stand? The answer actually makes a considerable difference to the effect of the play. From our experience of sports arenas, from pictures of their medieval equivalent, the tournament ground, and from the ground plan of the Lucerne play (which is oblong rather than cir-cular), we would expect the audience to be seated on the circular bank. This was the solution adopted by the Toronto Poculi Ludique Societas pro-duction of *The Castle* in 1979 (483). It is reinforced by the fact that the Flesh tells the audience

> Perfor on hylle
> Syttyth all stylle
> And seth wyth good wylle
> Oure ryche aray.   (lines 271–4)

This is tidy, and has the merit of keeping the audience out of the way of the actors and of danger, especially during the great siege of the castle that is the central feature of the play. It also has its drawbacks: one is that acoustics can be very difficult for characters on the opposite side of the arena (though it may be that the original playing area was not as large as it appears to have been at Toronto). The other is that from the perimeter it is almost impossible to see every scaffold equally clearly, let alone with the Castle in the centre 'lettynge of syt.' Again, as in the wagon plays, perhaps it is being too modern to expect everyone to be able to see everything. But if this was the procedure, why does the diagram also warn 'and lete nowth ouer many stytelerys be with Inne þe plase', if stitlers are, as has been suggested, crowd-control marshals?

The alternative is to adopt the solution tried by the Poculi Ludique Societas' production of the N-Town Passion Play in 1981 (484), which is to allow the audience free access to the arena, and have crowd marshals to clear the way for the characters. This has the advantage of allowing the characters to use the audience as 'crowd' as the pageant-wagon plays do. But the spatial organisation of a place-and-scaffold play is far more complicated than that of a pageant-wagon play, where there are at most two focuses of interest. If this is solved by getting the stitlers to lead the audience from one scaffold to the next, then it turns into a sort of promenade performance, but this depends on the audience being not only biddable and trained (which modern audiences are not), but not overwhelmingly large in number. If they are not guided in this way (and it does slow down the action), it is very difficult for them to know where the next scene is coming from. The other problem of having an audience at ground level has already come up à propos of pageant wagons: ground level action, of which there is a lot in place-and-scaffold plays, can be properly seen only by a very restricted audience. Besides this, without a sufficient overview of the acting area, the audience cannot keep the allegorical or geographical scheme of the setting and the current positions of the different players in the game in their mind's eye.

A third possibility, though it can only be proposed for plays that do not stipulate a circular layout, is to use the Valenciennes pattern, as used at John McKinnell's production of the Digby *Mary Magdalen* at Durham in 1982. In 1547, a Passion play was performed in Valenciennes in the Hôtel de Croy. The director later recorded a detailed set drawing and 'comic strip' snapshots of each scene.[5] The set drawing shows an apparently straight line of scaffolds running from Heaven at the left hand to Hellmouth at the right, ranged along a raised stage. In Romans in 1509 a raised stage 30 by 15 paces (90 by 45 feet: 27.43 by 13.7 metres) was set with 'towers, turrets, castles, towns of wood and stakes, and canopies as necessary . . . ' (409, p. 73). This presupposes an audience set facing the stage in the modern way. However, it is frequently pointed out that the Valenciennes drawing is a schematic artist's impression rather than a design blueprint, and that the houses might be arranged in a curve (482, p. 127). The Durham production set its scaffolds in a semicircle backed by a quarry (as at Shrewsbury, and possibly at Edinburgh), with the audience on the ground in the centre of the semicircle facing the action. This layout would also work for the N-Town Mary Play (the same episodes are dramatised in Valenciennes), but we cannot prove that it was so.

There are a variety of technical terms for the scaffolds: *scaffold*, *stage*, *house* and *tent*, which implies a temporary construction of 'stretched' (*tentum*) cloth, either a booth stage or a pavilion as set up for the contenders in tournaments. Presumably they could be as simple or elaborate as funds and taste allowed. Their inhabitants call them *houses*, *castles*, *towers*, *halls* or *bowers*, which gives a sense of their function. They represent identifiable locations, such as Jerusalem, Marseilles, the castle of Magdala or the mount of Olivet, or the unnamed 'seats' of earthly potentates such as Herod, Pilate or Caesar Augustus, or of psychological and moral forces such as the World, the Flesh and the Devil, enemies of God who dwells in the Heaven scaffold. Like pageant wagons, scaffolds focus the audience's attention and frame the characters, giving them a scale. The difference is that there are far more scaffolds visible to the audience, and the action switches cinematically from one to another, or to the space between them.

The scaffolds seem to be set high: 'Cum vp to me above', says Mankind to Envy in *The Castle* (line 1139); 'I clymbe fro þis crofte/Wyth Mankynde to syttyn on lofte', responds Envy (lines 1144–5). This height allows the characters who preside over the scaffolds to dominate the arena, and of course the audience. It is noticeable how many of them are presented as enthroned kings, such as the World, the Flesh, and the Devil in *The Castle* (lines 456–7). They look down on the *platea*, their field of action, like generals. When they come down, it is deliberately significant. When in *The Castle* the Three Enemies, each with his entourage, descend to launch the assault on the Castle they are like medieval kings taking the field: it is a declaration of all-out war. Otherwise they communicate by messenger, a character who is far more visible in performance than he is on the page: he traces the skeins of relationship between the chief characters.

The circular stage diagrams of the manuscripts resemble the medieval *mappa mundi*, and it has been seen as significant that the stage plan of the Castle (see illustration 8) is carefully oriented on the points of the compass, with God to the East, 'an hiegh to þe sonne' (*Piers Plowman*, B-text

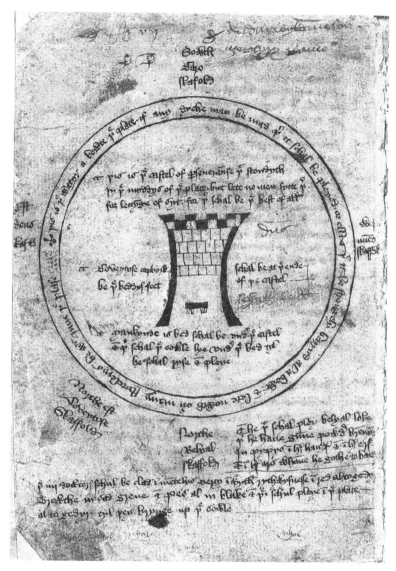

8   Staging plan for *The Castle of Perseverance* (Washington, D.C., The Folger Shakespeare Library, MS V. a. 354, f. 191v). See pp. 59–60, 245–7. For transcriptions of the text included in the diagram, see 83, p. 1, 115, p. 153.

Prologue, line 13), the materialistic World to the West, and Hell to the North, as was traditional (235, pp. 166–94). The effect is that of a microcosm, an interior world over which the battle for man's soul is to be fought. This battle is mapped out for us by the movements of the main character between the scaffolds. These scaffolds, even in the geographically-based plays, are often not so much locations as the 'home ground' of the characters who preside over them. These are their spheres of influence, where their power is greatest. If one character 'goes up' into the scaffold of another, he becomes his subject. *The Castle* and its like give physical expression to the common metaphors for psychological and moral processes. We see the Good and Evil Angels trying to pull Mankind towards Heaven or the World, both visible locations; when he says, 'I now forsake my synne iwys/And take me holy to Penaunce' (lines 1422–3), he literally leaves the Seven Deadly Sins and goes down to Penance.

The large-scale 'historical' plays such as *Mary Magdalen* (a hybrid which overlays the geographical map with a moral one in the opening scenes), or the N-Town Passion Plays and Mary Play, and the smaller plays like *The Conversion of St Paul* and the Croxton *Play of the Sacrament* are organised on a geographical basis. Here multi-locational staging is based on the perfectly logical premise that if you want to represent two locations, they should be in two separate places. This gives the playwright the opportunity, not taken up as often as one might think, of 'split-screen' action. The most famous example of this is in the N-Town Mary Play, where Joachim, lamenting in the desert, full of anxiety about his wife Anna, is echoed at another part of the stage by Anna herself, left at home, and worrying about Joachim. The idea that the characters' location could be changed while the play was in progress by altering the scenery, so that the location as it were moves while the characters remain still, did not occur to anyone: scene changes began to happen only later, in professional theatres with a confined stage space and a static audience. If the characters went from Nazareth to Jerusalem, they changed their physical location, however short a distance they went in real terms. In *The Conversion of St Paul*, the audience apparently travelled with them, from station to station, conducted by an author figure called Poeta:

> Fynally, of þis stacyon thus we mak a conclusyon,
> Besechyng thys audyens to folow and succede
> Wyth all your delygens þis generall processyon . . . (lines 155–7)

> *Finis istius stacionis et altera sequitur.*   (line 161, s.d.)

> (*End of this station and another follows*).

(A possible model with which everyone would be familiar is the Stations of the Cross.) The narratives of several place-and-scaffold plays seem to be linked with the theme of life as a journey, a romance as well as a religious motif. The protagonist has no home, or cannot stay in it (otherwise, at the most basic, there would be no story). Mary Magdalene leaves the Castle of

Magdala to travel to Jerusalem and sin; after a brief return at her conversion, she sets out on another journey, to convert Marseilles and die in the desert, where she is nearer (physically and spiritually) to heaven. Heaven is the ultimate home, and when it is achieved the play perforce comes to an end.

In the case of *Mary Magdalen*, the plot is organised on a series of encounters which involve the heroine moving from location to location. In the second 'Marseilles' part, the play is so episodic as to be almost picaresque. There is some interrelation between the other characters, but on the whole they are there to shape her destiny and show her powers (as in the *Pericles*-like episode of the marooned queen), not to live an independent life. Conversely, when secondary characters do communicate, as in the N-Town Passion Play, the web of comings and goings about the place works up the mounting atmosphere of conspiracy and the net closing on the protagonist.

The plays exploit to the full the potential for sheer spectacle in these movements about the place. The audience's eyes are drawn to the messenger as he runs from one scaffold to another, though the most dramatic use of the solitary moving figure comes at the beginning of Passion Play II, when 'Here xal a massanger com into þe place rennyng and criyng "Tydyngys! Tydyngys!" and so rownd abowth þe place, "Jesus of Nazareth is take Jesus of Nazareth is take". . . . ' (Play 29, line 89, s.d.). Passion Play II starts with a procession which delivers Herod, Annas and Caiaphas to their scaffolds. In the Digby *Killing of the Children*, the Purification is solemnised with a formal procession 'about the temple' by Simeon carrying the Child and Anna, escorted by 'virgynes, as many as a man wylle' holding 'tapers in ther handes' (line 464, s.d.) and singing Nunc Dimittis. The triumphant procession in Passion Play I of the Entry into Jerusalem, with Christ riding on an ass, is paralleled in II by the Via Dolorosa. Mounted journeys create even more theatrical excitement: Saul's horse is given a great build-up, 'a palfray, Ther can no man a better bestryde!' (*The Conversion of St Paul*, line 123). But the *pièce de résistance* is always the ship, whether it is the Ark, or the boat that takes Meriasek to Brittany and back, or Mary Magdalene's Mediterranean galley with its crew of singing sailors and cheeky ship's boy who is sent up to the crow's nest to act as look-out. It is of course necessary that these vessels should be caught in a storm, to allow the sailors to deploy their full range of mime skills.

The stage directions in these plays display their dramatists' awareness of the necessity of planning moves about the place: indeed, they are a distinctive feature of place-and-scaffold plays. Journeys from one scaffold to another take time: in *Mary Magdalen* a messenger from the Emperor Tiberius in Rome leaves at line 139 for Herod: he does not arrive until line 208, though it takes him only twenty lines to get from Herod to Pilate. Such stage directions can prolong time as convenient: 'Here the knyghtes and Watkyn walke abowght the place tylle Mary and Joseph be conveid into Egipt' (Digby *Killing of the Children*, line 232, s.d.). The N-Town Passion Plays have a penchant for simultaneous action, though only one group of characters actually talks. In Passion Play II, Christ is to be clothed in white and led to Pilate at the same time as Satan plots and puts the Dream of Pilate's Wife into action on her scaffold: Christ must arrive at Pilate's scaffold 'be þe tyme þat hese [Pilate's] wyf hath pleyd' (Play 31, first s.d.). A stage direction at the Crucifixion (Play 32, line 92, s.d.) envisages three separate actions going on at the same time, though all are in the same area: 'þe sympyl men' press-ganged by the executioners hang the thieves on their crosses, while the executioners themselves dice for Christ's garment 'and fytyn and stryvyn', while 'in þe menetyme' Our Lady, the Three Maries and John come and cast themselves down in front of the Cross – then Mary laments. There are quite a number of other 'in þe menetyme' stage directions, but most of them seem concerned with keeping up the pace of the action, ensuring that the next scaffold picks up its cue promptly: 'Here Cryst enteryth into þe hous with his disciplis and ete þe paschal lomb; and in þe menetyme þe cownsel hous befornseyd xal sodeynly onclose schewyng þe buschopys, prestys and jewgys syttyng in here astat lych as it were a convocacyon' (Play 27, line 76, s.d.).

It is possible that the scaffolds had curtains, like a modern stage, to conceal characters who are not involved in the current action, and to be drawn back as if by an invisible hand to reveal significant tableaux. In *Mary Magdalen* both Heaven and Hell are double-deckers, fitted with traps for mysterious and sudden appearances and disappearances and lifting machinery. Since the scaffolds in place-and-scaffold staging are fixed, pyrotechnic effects can be even more elaborate: a 'feruent' (representing lightning) is sent down a wire in *The Conversion of St Paul* (line 182, s.d.) and stage directions in *Mary Magdalen* call for two major conflagrations (line 743, s.d.; line 1561, s.d.).

It will have become apparent that in terms of organisation these plays are everything that pageant-wagon playing is not. Those who have been fortunate enough to be at the Toronto performances of *The Castle* and the N-Town Passion or the Durham *Mary Magdalen* will have been impressed and horrified at the size, cost and sheer complexity of the operation. *The Castle* calls for a cast of thirty-five speaking parts and the building of six scaffolds, and lasts four and a quarter hours. The N-Town Passion Play I has fifty-six speaking parts (and possibly sixty-two in Passion Play II, though it is difficult to tell where this text originally came to an end), and eight to ten scaffolds. *Mary Magdalen* has over forty speaking parts and nineteen separate locations. The *Thrie Estaitis* has forty-three speaking parts. Even given some doubling (and this is not as possible as one might at first think), the logistics are daunting. Fortunately it is not necessary to assume that the existence of Banns proclaiming a performance 'at N. Town', or 'At ... on þe grene in ryal aray' (*The Castle of Perseverance*, line 134) means that these plays toured. As Peter Meredith (*104*, pp. 19–20) has pointed out, N-Town is not so much a touring play as a touring manuscript: churchwardens were intended to hire the script and organise the performance out of local resources. We know that in Essex and Kent in the early sixteenth century they could already call on professional help from 'property players' (producers) from London who would organise the set and special effects, using their expertise and local labour (244, 427). But even they pale in comparison with the grand continental plays: Valenciennes has 169 speaking parts plus extras, which were shared among sixty-three actors (409, p. 17), and Renwart Cyzat, the director of the Lucerne Easter Play, calculated that without doubling he would have to find over 400 actors (409, p. 53).

Clearly one of the main theatrical features of the plays was their sheer impressiveness of scale. They were conceived on heroic lines, a marathon for the audience as well as the actors. The Cornish *Ordinalia* was divided to play over three days, and *Meriasek* over two. The N-Town Passion Play was divided into two parts, to be played alternate years. *The Killing of the Children* is the second part of a lost Nativity group in honour of St Anne. We are looking here at an appetite for theatre that can stand comparison with the days of ancient Athens.

INDOOR THEATRE: LITURGICAL DRAMA

The Bodley MS e Museo 160 *Burial* and *Resurrection of Christ* (84) is the one complete surviving example of vernacular liturgical drama.[6] A rubric to it reads

> This is a play to be played, on part on Gud Friday afternone, and þe other part opon Ester Day after the resurrection in the morowe.   (84, p. 142)

It could easily be integrated into an Easter Sepulchre ceremony. Each section takes about an hour to play. The *Resurrection* calls for professional plainchant singing. There is no need for costume other than ecclesiastical vestments as adapted for the *Quem Quaeritis* in the *Regularis Concordia*, save that the risen Christ is disguised as a gardener.

INDOOR THEATRE: THE GREAT HALL

Lydgate's various mummings, *Mankind* and *Wisdom* (1460s) probably, Medwall's *Fulgens and Lucres* and *Nature* (1490s) certainly, *Mundus et Infans* (*The World and the Child*, 1507/8) possibly, *Youth* (?1513), *Hick Scorner* (?1514), *The Four Elements* (1517–20), Skelton's *Magnyfycence* (?1519–20) and John Heywood's various interludes and farces, which lie outside the remit of this book, were all written for a great hall venue. The great hall was the chief room in any substantial household, whether the court of the king or of a lord temporal or spiritual, or a corporate body such as a guild, a school, an Oxford or Cambridge college, or the London law schools, the Inns of Court. It was the social and administrative heart of the household, used for public business, for dining and for what we would call 'functions': any occasion for which space was needed for a large number of people.

Many great halls still survive, and a visit is by far the best way to bring the plays to life. Sizes vary: apart from the hall of the Palace of Westminster, the largest great hall in Europe, which is a staggering 239′6″ by 67′6″ (73 by 20.6 metres), they range from the merely vast, like Lambeth Palace, the London home of the Archbishop of Canterbury, Medwall's patron (93 by 38 feet, 28.3 by 11.6 metres), through the grand, like Penshurst (62 by 49 feet, 18.9 by 14.9 metres) to the more intimate, like Rufford Old Hall in Lancashire (*c.* 1500: 47 feet by 23 feet, 14.33 by 7 metres).[7] The variations in size must have made a difference in acoustics – playing in one of the 100-foot halls must have been almost like playing outside – and intimacy, and it would be helpful to be certain that particular plays were performed in identifiable halls, but unfortunately, despite various educated guesses, we do not really *know* where any of them were acted, or indeed for whom: the fact that Medwall was chaplain to Archbishop Lord Chancellor Cardinal Morton does not necessarily mean that *Fulgens and Lucres* was performed at Lambeth Palace.

Though their dimensions vary, the late medieval/early Tudor great halls themselves follow a fairly standard shape and pattern, which was constrained partly by building materials and methods, and partly by the social role that they played in the life of the household. This pattern in its turn dictates much of the stagecraft of the plays. A diagram will help (see illustration 9).

As a visitor came through the main entrance into a busy hall, he would see at the far end a dais, on which the lord of the household (henceforward this term can also stand for King, Archbishop, Lord Mayor, Master of a College, etc.) was seated, usually under a *celure* (canopy or 'cloth of estate').

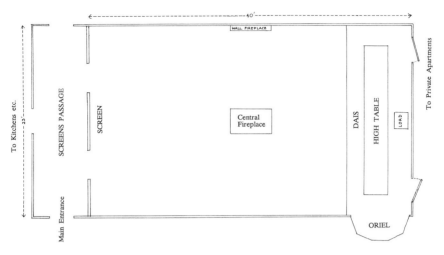

9   Floor plan of a great hall.

He was thus instantly recognisable and, like the head teacher on the platform at a school assembly, had a commanding view of all the events in the hall. Looking down from his seat, *he* would see at the far end of the hall an arrangement of three symmetrically-placed permanent wooden screens masking the wall containing the kitchen and exterior doors, with entrance gaps to either side of the centre screen (see illustration 10). These screens might be joined together at the tops to form a partition wall, and the entrances might or might not have doors. Through these doorways the household assembled, visitors entered and the servants brought meals from the kitchens.

At mealtimes the servants would set up a table (known, for obvious reasons, as a board) on trestles on the dais before the lord's seat: this was called the high table. Other tables were set up in the rush-strewn body of the hall, end on to the high table (as in their survivals in Oxbridge colleges). Diners sat on benches or stools. There might be a large open fireplace on one wall or a huge raised hearth in the centre of the room, with the smoke drawn out by a louvre in the roof.

Into this space came the play. (See illustration 11.) It will be immediately apparent that this makes the hall something rather different from a theatre. It was someone's living space temporarily converted, familiar working surroundings which accommodated, for an hour or two, an alternative world of make-believe. There must have been a sense of transformation, of being *en fête*, especially since indoor dramatic entertainment was reserved for festive occasions: the birth of an heir, the visit of foreign dignitaries, the

10   The great hall of Gray's Inn, London, built 1556 (?), view from the dais towards the screens.

11   The *Bal des Ardents* (Ball of those who caught fire), from Froissart's *Chronicle* (British Library MS Harley 4380, f. 1). This shows the famous French court disguising (1393, but as seen in the mid-fifteenth century) of wodewoses dressed in hemp stuck on with tar, which caught fire when a spectator leaned too close with a torch to see who they were. The great hall is cleared for the disguising, with only the queen and two of her ladies shown seated on the dais. The king was one of the masqueraders, but was saved by his aunt, the Duchesse de Berri, who rolled him in her voluminous skirts and put out the flames. Most of the others were burned to death.

foundation feast of a guild or college. Above all it was a traditional part of the festive seasons of winter. One of these was the pre-Lent Carnival extravaganza of Shrovetide, though this seems to have been celebrated to a much lesser extent in Britain than it was (and still is) on the continent: however, we know of English Shrovetide plays, and *Mankind* bears signs of being one of them (335). In England, the main festive season was the Twelve Days of Christmas, when the usual workaday world was pushed aside for a marathon of feasting, churchgoing, carols, dancing, mumming and card- and dice-playing. Instead of the summer world of the mystery plays and outdoor moralities such as *The Castle of Perseverance*, we are indoors, at the coldest and darkest time of the year, 'When the day waxeth short and the night long' (*Hick Scorner*, line 89), keeping the cold and dark at bay. At the Court, and in lesser courts and households throughout the country, Twelfth Night was the final and culminative party, ending the festive season with a programme that followed dinner with a 'play as an entirlude A comody or trigidy' (56, p. 34), followed by a 'disguising', an entertainment featuring lavish costume and dancing, which might incorporate a 'pageant', a spectacular set-piece of wheeled staging representing a castle, a ship, a mountain, an arbour, or what you will, bearing characters who performed a romantic scenario with formal speeches and balletic action, and out of which might emerge a *moresk* (another form of dancing team). This was followed by a *banquet* (what we would call dessert or a buffet, though it could be extremely lavish) and more dancing, and the evening was finally brought to an end with the *voidee*, a ceremoniously-served nightcap of wine and spiced cakes.

To appreciate the mode and stagecraft of these plays we have to realise what their context was: they were not isolated flourishes of dramatic art, but part of a continuum of festivity, an entertaining pause for digestion in the Christmas eating and drinking. Different households presumably had their own variations on the usual timetable (314). The disguising can turn up embedded in the play, as in *Fulgens and Lucres* Part 2. *Wisdom*, with its relatively static mode (at least on paper), is more like these lost pageant disguisings than the usual surviving interludes: its production values are lavish, it calls for very professional choral singing and it brings in *three* elaborate disguisings with attendant musicians. Similarly, the play could be adapted to the timetable of the household, or to less grand festive days. Rastell, the printer of *The Four Elements*, is quite happy to suggest that this interlude, which he estimates at an hour and a half's playing time, could be cut to 'not ... paste thre quarters of an hour of length' by missing out 'muche of the sade [serious] mater', such as the Prologue, and some of the speeches of Nature and Experience: 'Also', he suggests, 'yf ye lyst ye may brynge in a dysgysynge.' *Fulgens* is written to be played in two parts, the first 'at dyner' (Part 2, line 11), which would begin about noon, the second 'in the evynyng aboute suppere' (Part 1, line 1362), and *Nature*, written by the same author possibly for the same household, has the same kind of bipartite division.

Clearing the hall floor for the play was thus no different in kind than clearing the floor for dancing. In the earlier period with which we are concerned, there was no special provision for staging: the actors were down among their audience, on the same floor-level. We know of lavish and spectacular stage sets in the Court Revels, but they belonged to the quasi-balletic pageant disguisings, not the interludes which preceded them. An interlude usually made do with a chair for Wisdom or the World or Lucres as Judge, and that was virtually that.[8]

The actors came in through the screen doors like any other visitors or members of the household, and entered into the same space as the audience. Consequently, the 'stage' space is seldom imagined as a particular fictional *location*. In *Magnyfycence* it is often called 'the place', just as if it were in an outdoor place-and-scaffold production. Its fictional *function* is defined by the characters who assume temporary command over it: it is the place where Fulgens meets Cornelius, or Hick Scorner brawls with Imagination, or Mischief holds court: but it is noticeable that these are all activities that might, given other participants, take place in the hall itself in its normal life. It is not incongruous to be told that Lucres

> hathe appoynted hym [*Cornelius*] to be *here*
> Sone, in the evynyng aboute suppere
>
> (*Fulgens*, Part 1, lines 1362–3)

because though Fulgens and Lucres are ancient Romans, they occupy the same space and have the same preoccupations as the modern audience. 'Real' locations are elsewhere: for example, though the morality hero's fall often takes place in a tavern, the tavern is always offstage, described lubriciously by the tempters. Even when Mankind (in *Mankind*) starts to dig, and it would appear that the hall floor has become a field, it only becomes so by reason of his present activity. His mime sketches in an imaginary half acre, but when Titivillus afflicts him with a sudden anguished movement of the bowels, it is 'I wyll into þi ʒerde, souerens, and cum ageyn son' (line 561): the field vanishes with the actor.

Neither do the players attempt to disregard their surroundings: on the contrary, they draw attention to them. One reason why we know so much about the venue is because they comment on it all the time. In *Fulgens*, one of the characters is stuck outside the hall doors trying to get in. His fellow inside comments with interest:

> He knokythe as he were wood!   *mad*
> One of you [*i.e. the audience*] go loke who it is.
>
>   (Part 2, lines 74–5)

On a January evening, the fire becomes a focus of attention (if it was indeed in the middle of the hall, it must even have been a hazard). In *Nature*, when Man and Pryde go out, Worldly Affection stays behind to keep warm:

> Thys good fyre and I wyll not depart!
> For very cold myne handys do smart –
> It maketh me wo-bygon!
> [*To a victim in the audience*]
> Get me a stole! Here, may ye not se?   *stool*
> Or ellys a chayr! Wyll yt not be?
> Thou pyld knave, I speke to the!   *hairy*
> How long shall I stande?   (*Nature*, Part 2, lines 512–19)

The players do not only take over the floor, they attempt to commandeer the furniture, and order the audience about. If people are blocking the entrances:

> Geve rome there, syrs, for God avowe!   *by God*
> Thei wold cum in if thei myght for you.
>
>   (*Fulgens*, Part 1, lines 193–4)

A lot has been talked about the folk play 'ritual' of clearing the magic circle for the players: it is also a physical necessity, as anyone who has performed with an unstructured audience will tell you. The impression from the pre-1520 plays is that the audience encroached on the acting space rather more than we might expect from our traditional visualisation of the gentry seated, while the servants crowd round the doors. It is even possible that only the lord and lady on the dais actually had seats. It is clear that in the chiaroscuro of the torch- and firelight it was perfectly possible to lose a character in the audience. In *Hick Scorner* two of the characters accuse them of hiding the eponymous hero:

IMAGINATION: Some of these young men hath hid him in their bosoms,
     I warrant you.
FREE WILL: Let us make a cry that he may us hear.
IMAGINATION: How, how, Hick Scorner, appear!
     I trow thou be hid in some corner.   (lines 297–300)

Much of this capitalises on practical necessity. If an actor has to push his way through the audience, he can't just pretend they are not there, so one might as well write the pushing into the part:

> Aback, fellows, and give me room,
> Or I shall make you to avoid soon!   (*Youth*, lines 40–1)

Other cries of 'room!' are to stop the audience getting damaged in a stage fight: 'Make room, sirs, that I may break his pate!' (*Hick Scorner*, line 718) – naturalistically, 'Let me get at him!'. But what starts as a technical convenience is turned into a metatheatrical game: the players treat the audience as if they and the characters were in the same world, which physically of course they are. In *Nature*, when Bodily Lust tries to escape, Envy tells the audience to stop him:

> Hold hym in, syrs, I you requyre!
> [*which of course they fail to do*]
> Alas, wold ye not at my desyre
> Do so myche for me?
>
> (*Nature*, Part 2, lines 687–9)

This game depends on the audience keeping to their role as audience and not responding to these appeals. It then goes one further, and pretends that the audience has the same licence to answer back as the players have to speak. Enter a character:

> Who dwelleth here? Wyll no man speke?
> Is there no fole nor hody peke?   *simpleton*
> Now by the bell, yt were almys to breke   *a good deed*
> Some of these knaves brows!
> A gentylman comys in at the dorys
> That all hys dayes hath worn gylt sporys,   *gilded spurs*
> And none of thys knaves nor cuttyd horys   *shrewish whores*
> Byddys hym welcom to house!
>
> (*Nature*, Part 1, lines 723–30)

It takes far longer to analyse what is happening here than it does to recognise it. The character abuses the audience for behaving like an audience: for not answering him when he asks a question, for the very act of being silent, which is a prerequisite of being an audience; he then tells them that it is discourteous of them not to welcome him, as if he were a genuine visitor and they were in their everyday non-audience roles. The game becomes a power play. He pulls rank on them, the rank of his assumed character, *and* the temporary authority of the actor while the play is in progress. In this case, this attitude and the hectoring tone are built into his characterisation. When next he demands their approval of his wardrobe, thus drawing attention to it –

> How say ye, syrs, by myne aray?
> Doth yt please you? Ye or nay?
>
> (*Nature*, Part 1 lines 739–40)

the combination of arrogance and high fashion clinches his identity: he must be Pride.

In moralities, it is particularly the vicious characters who play this meta-theatrical game. As actors, it gives them the chance to dominate and control their audience; for the purposes of the plot, which requires that the Vices should capture the central ground until the climax of the play, it reinforces their particular kind of manipulative authority. Moralities are a struggle between the good and evil principles as much for the attention and loyalty of the audience as for the soul of the protagonist. Since he represents them, the audience have to feel as well as observe the attraction of vice. (There is no Brechtian alienation here.) The Virtues also address the audience:

> O souerence, I beseche yow yowr condycyons to rectyfye,
> Ande wyth humylite and reuerence to haue a remocyon   *inclination*
> To þis blyssyde prynce þat owr nature doth gloryfye
>
> (Mercy, in *Mankind*, lines 13–15)

but their appeal is direct, honest and emotive, as one would expect. The Vices seduce, hector and mock. While the Virtues exhort and appeal to the audience, the Vices play games with them.

The opening encounter of *Mankind* is an epitome of this process: Mercy, at the beginning fully in command of our attention and emotions, is subverted by Mischief, who mocks his authority, parodies his language (the language of authority) and perverts his logic, with the excuse, 'I am cumme hedyr to make yow game' (line 69). Like the actor playing him, he is there, he suggests, purely to entertain. His henchmen, Newgyse, Nowadays and Nought, having failed to get Mercy to respond to their jokes, dismiss him as a spoilsport:

> Men haue lytyll deynte of yowr pley   *little pleasure*
> Because ჳe make no sporte.   (*Mankind*, lines 267–8)

Virtue is no fun: vice is. They themselves are supremely theatrical. They play games with the conventions of acting, continually working up illusions and then dropping them: the 'beheading-game' where serious injuries are immediately cured by the threat of amputation; the mock court of Mischief which breaks up into a football match; getting the audience to pay to see the devil. They are magicians of a kind, making us see things that are not there, winning our admiration, and our cash, for their expertise. Their tour de force is getting the audience to consent to their own discomfiture in the community-singing of the 'Christmas song'. For the actors, getting them to carry on once they realise what is happening is the supreme test of their power over the audience: a paradigm of progress into sin, seduced by high spirits.

The devil Titivillus is an arch-magician who 'goeth invisible' (302), the extreme trial of the theatrical imagination. His scene with Mankind is a repertoire of theatrical tricks: slipping the board under the earth, which makes Mankind think that the ground is too hard to dig, stealing his seed-corn, making off with his spade. The success of his sleight of hand and his self-confidence that the audience are on his side will them into complicity:

> Ande euer 3e dyde, for me kepe now yowr sylence!
> Not a worde, I charge yow, peyn of forty pens.
> A praty game xall be scheude yow or 3e go hens.
> 3e may here hym snore; he ys sade aslepe.
> Qwyst! pesse! . . . . . I xall goo ronde in hys ere.   *whisper*
> (*Mankind*, lines 589–93)

All the Vices invite and expect our complicity, and we go along with it because they let us into their secrets. Another ruse is disguise or changed names, as in *Nature* or *Magnyfycence*, where the audience is made privy to the deception and almost forgets what this deception represents in terms of real life. We are so swept up in the excitement of the illusion that we disregard the fact that we are accomplices in crime. In one way it does not matter because we know it is all only a play. This might seem to suggest that the moral lesson is also a fake. But the play signifies a real-life process, and as the dramatic mood begins to shift back to seriousness (though this again is a matter of theatrical technique), so the signified surfaces from under the signifier. Once normal values come back into the play, the game turns ugly – 'A roppe, a rope, a rope! I am not worthy!' (line 800) – and dangerous.

The game does not always have to be a weapon of evil. In *Fulgens and Lucres* Medwall plays with its possibilities largely, one feels, for the fun of it. He allows the actors to build up the familiar theatrical illusion, and then deftly flips it over. A, for example, breaks into a promising *tête à tête* between B and the Maid, on whom he also has designs and, discovering they have been together for a whole hour, voices his disquiet. B replies comfortingly,

> Nay, nay, here be to many wytnes
> For to make ony syche besynes
> As thou wenyst, hardely!   *imagine, truly*

to which the Maid responds indignantly,

> Suppose ye that I wolde be nowght   *immoral*
> Yf no man were by?   (*Fulgens*, Part 1, lines 1017–21)

A consummate piece of theatrical impudence, as up to this point she and B have been acting as if they were alone in the world.

A and B are not malicious, and their subversion of the rules seems to be done out of pure high spirits and opportunism. Medwall's great tour de force with them is merely the logical extension of the audience game. He stands on its head the pretence that the audience are in the play, and pretends that the players are audience. It is difficult to say how long this deception could have been kept up in practice – not for very long, one suspects, as genuine members of the audience do not usually speak in rhymed verse. (A's entrance is in fact very like the opening speech of Pride, which we analysed earlier.) Medwall then compounds it by playing exactly the same trick with B. The joke is based on the motif of the naive member of the audience who doesn't realise the difference between theatre and real life. B reacts to a shameless piece of audience address by Cornelius, who invites them to volunteer for the job of go-between in his courtship with Lucres. As soon as he is safely out of the door, the audience strikes back: B declares that he is going to volunteer. A is horrified and tries to restore the theatrical boundaries:

> Pece, let be!
> By God, thou wyll distroy all the play!

B acknowledges the boundaries by expressing a joyous determination to rearrange them:

> Distroy the play, quod a? Nay, nay,
> The play began never till now!
>
> (*Fulgens*, Part 1, lines 362–5)

The suggestion here is that he is going radically to disrupt the plot, and one can see how in another kind of play (*The Knight of the Burning Pestle?*) this might happen, but in fact despite a few minor skirmishes – A tries to persuade Gaius to give up wooing Lucres, B delivers an obscenely malapropised love message from Cornelius – neither of them manages to mar the fortunes of their respective masters, and the plot finishes just as the prologue has promised. A and B's main energies are diverted into the subplot, where they cause mayhem harmlessly enough.

However, they are used for another purpose. The subplot, though virtually self-contained, mirrors the situation of the main plot: two men competing for the hand of a girl. The difference is in the type of competition thought suitable for the aristocracy and for the servant class. While Gaius and Cornelius behave scrupulously correctly, and dispute formally and with due etiquette, 'to eschew the occasion of strif and debate', A and B squabble, tell tales about each other, try to steal kisses, and compete for their lady's favours by singing, wrestling and 'jousting' in a game rudely called 'fart prick in cule'.[9] The play is enhanced on several levels. The audience is treated to a full range of popular entertainments and 'Christmas games': the servants are allowed to express the sexual drive and jealous physical aggression that their civilised social superiors must keep under control, and they give tongue to less than elevated sentiments about the matter at issue.

The subplot thus adds a necessary extra dimension to the theme of the play. *Fulgens* is a serious play about social status and power and who should have the right to it – old blood, or new intelligence. It was a live political issue in the 1490s, when Henry VII was displacing the old aristocracy of the Wars of the Roses with new-blood administrators 'of poor kin and birth'. Cardinal Morton himself, Medwall's employer, was one of them.[10] But though its content could to some of its audience have seemed radical in detail, it does not challenge the overall assumptions of its time about the necessity of social hierarchy. Gaius Flaminius, the plebeian, does not wish to overthrow the status quo, but to prove his right to be granted admission to it.

If we could take ourselves back to the original performance, we would see quite how unthinkable any other attitude would be. The very seating (or standing) plan of the audience for whom it was written was a declaration of social hierarchy, and so was the conduct of the occasion for which they were gathered. The kind of people who could afford to support plays in their houses lived ceremoniously and in public. Dinner in the great hall of a late medieval magnate was itself a kind of social theatre, regulated by a fixed etiquette from the processional entry of lord and lady to the *voidee* after which they retired. During the dinner lord, lady and honoured guests were displayed on the dais like figures on a stage. The household and lesser relations and dependants sat in the body of the hall, again according to a protocol which dictated that the lower down the social scale one was, the further from the high table one sat.

The fact that the actors entered through the service doors actually accorded with their status. They were servants of the household: until the very late fifteenth century, a group of talented amateurs got together purely for the occasion, in everyday life the almoner, tailor, glazier, usher. Even in the court of Henry VII the four-man team of 'Kings pleyers' had other jobs: John English was a joiner and Richard Gibson a tailor. Visiting acting troupes were either townspeople or technically the servants of another noble household: 'my Lorde of Essex pleyers', 'my lorde of burgeyveney pleyers'. (The later professional troupes known as the King's Men or the Lord Chamberlain's Men, were their linear descendants: 314, pp. 216–9; 58.) The other 'professional' theatre group at Court was the Gentlemen (and children) of the Chapel: any household of status maintained its own chapel and its singing men and choirboys, the latter useful for playing female roles. Joan in *Fulgens* is invited to join in the singing match with a third (treble) part, because she 'can gode skyll' (Part 1, line 1120). Their natural place is at the lower end of the hall.

Making their entrance through the hall doors, the actors would be literally confronted by their master. They present the play to him; its success, or even its continuance, depends on his approval:

> ... we shall do oure labour and trewe entent
> For to play the remenant
> At my lordis pleasure.   *(Fulgens*, Part 1, lines 1430–2)

The important speeches and action of the play were presumably directed primarily at him. In plays like *Fulgens*, which present authority figures, whether Lucres or the World or Magnificence, the actor who plays a king or a justice does it in the face of an audience who are always aware that he is a counterfeit authority, since they have the touchstone of the real authority sitting watching them.

Any play dealing with power and its abuses, either by the protagonist or his advisers, is potentially political. Usually the dangerous edge is taken off because the morality format deals with a generalised concept of authority (Magnificence, Manhood in *The World and the Child*). *Fulgens* deals with its delicate subject by another time-honoured device: it sets it up as a formal debate between two generic heroes, and in practice invites the audience to adjudicate. In the Prologue B tells us that in the end, because of the public dissension aroused over it,

> This matter was brought before the cenate,   *Senate*
> They to gyve therin an utter sentence
> Whiche of these two men sholde have the preeminence.
>   *(Fulgens*, Part 1, lines 116–18)

But when we reach that part of the plot, Gaius starts his oration with

> what so ever I shall speke *in this audience*,
> Eyther of myn owne meritis or of hys insolence,
> Yet fyrst unto you all, syrs, I make this request:
> That it wolde lyke you to construe it to the best.
>   *(Fulgens*, Part 2, lines 588–91)

The Senate of ancient Rome has been superseded by the jury of 'this honourable audience'. In the fiction, Lucres agrees to act as judge, but insists that the sentence will be 'After myne owne fantasie' (Part 2, line 429) and will not be binding on anyone: 'It may not be notyde for a generall prece-dent' (line 432). Gaius replies that since her decision will be purely private,

'None other man ought to have thereat disdayne' (Part 2, line 438). These polite disclaimers give one the sense that both author and actors are walking warily. At the very beginning of the play, B goes out of his way to point out that no one present is *personally* involved: 'here is no man of the kyn or sede / Of either partie' (Part 1, lines 178–9), as of course they were all ancient Romans. The reminder that this is only a fiction keeps topicality at a safe distance, just as the generalisations of allegory (usually) protect the author and actors from the charge of slander.

The fiction that A and B are members of the audience in theory allows them to speak as their surrogates, to comment on and challenge the decisions and attitudes presented in the main plot. In fact, the joke is that, like the Duck in Chaucer's *Parlement of Foules*, theirs is a below-stairs viewpoint far more simpleminded and materialistic than any of the audience would actually confess to holding:

A Let me se now, what is your oppynion
  Whether of them is most noble of condycion?
B That can I tell hardely:
  He that hathe moste nobles in store,   *gold coins*
  Hym call I the most noble ever more,
  For he is most sett by.   (*Fulgens*, Part 1, lines 1374–9)

They have no pretensions to gentility or finer feelings:

  I am nether of vertue excellent,
  Nor yet of gentyl blode. This I know well
        (*Fulgens*, Part 1, lines 141–2)

indeed, they deny all knowledge of any such things. Lucres decides that she will have Gaius 'for his vertue'; 'Vertue? What the devyll is that?' asks A (*Fulgens*, Part 2, lines 840, 842) and proceeds to ask the women in the audience if they usually choose their husbands this way. It sounds like subversion but in fact reinforces the attitudes of the main plot. A and B give the audience a chance to acknowledge and laugh at the pragmatic point of view while being too discriminating to buy it. They are not even consistently radicals: because their attachment to their masters is essentially self-serving, B actually speaks up for the most conservative viewpoint (he has almost by accident become Cornelius's servant), when he simplifies Lucres's decision for Gaius into

  by a chorles son she wolde set more
  Than she wolde do by a gentylman bore.
       (*Fulgens*, Part 2, lines 771–2)

The audience are before her in the reaction, 'Nay, syr, then ye report me amys!'

The game probably has a final twist. For us, A and B are the names of the characters. But they are also lawyer-speak for 'Fill in appropriate name here' (like the N for *nomen* in 'N Town'). It seems very likely that A and B are playing themselves. We shall never know (despite the wishful thinking that B was played by Thomas More as a page (88, p. 17)) what their personal mannerisms and histories were, or how many in-jokes are lurking in the dialogue and situations.

Like the costume trick ('I thought verely by your apparell / That ye had bene a player' (*Fulgens*, Part 1, line 51) the effect of this is almost impossible to replicate in a modern production. A random paying audience lacks the essential prerequisite: it isn't part of a family, in the medieval sense of 'household'. Most of these plays were written to be performed by members of a closely-knit in-group for their fellows. Even if the group was highly stratified, nonetheless they were all part of this 'family' and shared the same private jokes. Editors have laboured manfully to recover these (partly in order to establish dating). *Magnyfycence*, as one would expect from Skelton, is positively rattling with puns and allusions, including, according to Paula Neuss, a running joke about a Mistress Lark who was Wolsey's paramour (90, pp. 34–5). These topical allusions and in-jokes, though they hold a modern audience at arm's length, must have acted as a cohesive force on the original audience. They create a feeling of group loyalty. Even a play like *Mankind*, so full of purely theatrical tricks, depends for some of its effects on the audience understanding Latin well enough to play with it (which suggests a university or at least educated venue), and thus, by implication, a solidarity against those who don't.

The indoor plays feel much more 'professional' than their outdoor counterparts. This may be owing to a variety of circumstances. Indoor acoustics are much less defeating than outdoor ones, making it possible for dialogue and plotting to be more subtle. But the main factor must be that they were written for actors who were at least approaching professionalism.

The ability to sing, or at least field a trio (the standard part song at the time), is taken for granted: not difficult, if some of the actors are members of the Chapel. It also seems to be taken for granted that there will be minstrels available (they would already have played for the diners). Newgyse falls into the scene in *Mankind* with 'Ande how, mynstrellys, pley þe comyn trace!' (line 72), the basic bransle with which, according to Thoinot Arbeau's *Orchésographie* (1589), an evening of dancing was started. Dancing was a skill taught to all children in polite society almost as soon as they could walk. The disguising, an expected part of a grand Christmas entertainment, was usually provided by the young noblemen and sometimes women of the court, thus having a rather higher social status than the play that preceded or enclosed it. Fighting was another standard skill, in which the audience would be knowledgeable: in *The World and the Child*, Folly entraps Manhood by letting him win two rounds of sword-and-buckler play. Both of them appeal to the audience about a disputed hit (lines 560–5). A and B demonstrate the more plebeian skill of wrestling:

> That were a game accordynge   *suitable*
> For suche valyaunte men as we be!
>
>   (*Fulgens*, Part 1, lines 1144–5)

At Court the Christmas company was entertained by fighting at the barriers (sword play on foot across a waist-high partition), so display of skill at arms was one of the indoor 'disports' they were used to; in any case, stage fights are always good theatrical value.

Other skills are more actorly. Some of them perhaps belonged to the professional fool (see *Magnyfycence*, lines 1175ff.). The actor playing the Mankind figure in *The World and the Child* needs to be able to tumble. Conjuring is another skill: Titivillus seems to do a piece of sleight of hand at *Mankind*, lines 569–72, and Folly in *Magnyfycence* seems to suggest that he too is a conjurer: 'I can do mast'ries, so I can' (line 1192), though his challenge to Crafty Conveyance that he will 'magic' him out of his coat depends on a verbal trick – ironic, because 'Conveyance' was another word for 'sleight of hand'. We even find trained animals, or at least biddable livestock, in Fancy's hawk (is it a hawk? is it an owl? is it stuffed?) and Folly's dog. The 'fiddler's bitch' is a familiar character in popular theatre from the thirteenth-century proto-interlude *Dame Sirith* to Lance's dog in *The Two Gentlemen of Verona*.

All the comic actors need to be skilled in mime. The actor who plays the Mankind figure in *The World and the Child* needs to be able to play all the Five Ages of Man from birth to extreme age. The remarkable amount of reported speech and incident in the interludes also demands graphic physical acting: Sensuality in *Nature* telling his accomplices how Man fell for the whore Margery at his first visit to the tavern; Newgyse and Mischief explaining, with actions, how they escaped from jail (*Mankind*, lines 612–45). The Vices need to be good at mimicry, especially in *Magnyfycence*, where Skelton asks them to imitate the butts of their satire, from a coy housewife and her lover (lines 452–61) and an all-too-willing damsel being had in a corner (lines 1348–53) to a splenetic lord making himself throw up with rage (lines 1615–19). Typical Vice dialogue demands really advanced verbal skills, to be able both to sustain solo comic routines and flights of fancy and to toss dialogue to and fro, from the popular 'echo' routine in which one character wilfully mishears the other (Folly and Fancy in *Magnyfycence* (lines 1059–1159) behave like a couple of stand-up comics) to the slick ensemble playing of Newgyse, Nowadays and Nought. The actor has to be adept at spinning quick-change fantasies like plates.

Even if 'four men and a boy' was not the standard size of the Tudor acting troupe (*The World and the Child* seems to be a virtuoso piece for only two actors), the general practice of doubling would require not only considerable versatility but great reserves of stamina in the actors, and great resource in the playwright. It is noticeable that even though these are plays about the clash of vice and virtue the Vices rarely encounter the Virtues en masse, and there are a fair number of 'bridging' speeches, in which one character soliloquises or sings to cover the others' quick changes. *Magnyfycence* is almost dizzying in its manipulation of the actors between the roles. Skelton decides to capitalise on this thematically, so that not only do his actors change characters and costumes, but so do his characters: each of the Vices has a *nom de guerre* – Fancy calls himself Largesse (possibly also a joke about his size), Crafty Conveyance is Sure Surveyance, Counterfeit Countenance is Good Demeanance and Cloaked Collusion is Sober Sadness. The changes of name and costume, confusing on the page, become perfectly clear (if giddying) onstage.

Because the plays cannot call on complex scenery for effects, a great deal of play is made of costume and hand props. Some standard props come in over and over again, like the situations that necessitate them: purses, fetters and a hangman's noose are permanent inhabitants of the props box. Clothes are used not only to reflect status, but as a metaphor for it. The World invests the Mankind figure with clothes: in *The World and the Child*, the baby is sent into the world 'poor and naked' (line 45); he asks the World for 'Meat and cloth my life to save' and is given 'garments gay' (line 67); presumably the World adds a little more at each seven-year visit, until at twenty-one he vests him in 'robes royal right of good hue' (line 197) and dubs him knight. This image would be a familiar one to an audience who were used to getting their annual wages partly in clothes; theatrically it gives the figure more physical substance the more garments he puts on. It also underlines the dilemma in all anti-materialistic plays, that one needs a modicum of garments to keep one warm, and that one gets these from the World. Conversely, once Man has been seduced by the Vices who follow in the World's train, he often changes his garments for extravagant high fashion. In *Mankind* the transformation becomes part of a running gag in which his good 'side-gown' (side = 'wide') is cut down to 'a fresch jakett after þe new gyse' (line 676): it comes back twice, each time more ridiculously abbreviated.

How did the original audience see the comic element in the plays? Leaving aside the publisher's blurbs – 'A goodly interlude and a merry' –

there is still a general stress on the entertainment value of the play as a whole: *Magnyfyence* is variously described in the closing speeches as 'This treatise, devised to make you disport' (line 2534), 'This matter we have moved, you mirthes to make' (line 2548), and 'this disport and game' (line 2567). It is salutory, however, not to say bracing, to see some of what was considered to be entertaining. *The Four Elements* is more like a Royal Institution Christmas lecture than a Boxing Day pantomime: 'A new interlude and a mery, of the nature of the four elementis, declarynge many proper poyntys of phylosophy naturall, and of dyvers straunge landys, and of dyvers straunge effectis and causis'. The prologue insists on the author's mission to inform: this, and the debate in *Fulgens*, with the serious discussions of statecraft and of the condition of the human soul in other plays, acknowledges that there is pleasure in exercising the mind as well as the funny bone. But there is a general feeling that too much unadulterated 'sad matter' might lose the audience's attention. To this end,

> This phylosophycall work is myxyd
> With mery conseytis, to gyve men comfort.   *diversions*
> (*The Four Elements*, lines 136–7)

In *Fulgens* the whole subplot (which is not in the original source) could be seen as an inventive 'conceyt'. Certainly Medwall uses several comic routines – the 'lost letter' routine, the 'distorted message' routine, the 'forgotten name' routine, even the 'are the actors going to turn up for Part Two?' routine – which could be cut without serious damage to the main plot, though at considerable loss to the general hilarity. In more strictly moral interludes, as we have seen, the 'japes' are integrated by being given to the Vices, who use them to distract the hero from serious study, work or consideration of the state of his soul. In the end he is rescued and restored to sobriety by the Virtues. One could make comparisons with the general pattern of the holiday season, intended to relax but return one refreshed and perhaps a little sated to the sober comfort of everyday routine. But before we become too Bakhtinian, we should remember that Misrule in these plays is always brought back sharply to heel.

Being more in sympathy with Misrule, we tend to be interested mainly in the 'tryfyllis', but we should give proper consideration to the theatrical mode of the 'sad matter', which is after all the 'matter principal' of the plays. Because we no longer have a ceremonial mode in ordinary social life, it is difficult to find our way through to the serious characters and the issues they represent. The process of history has landed us in the camp of the Vices: they are the norm instead of being an entertaining but unstable divergence from it. Our laid-back, colloquial ethos gives us no way of relating to people who keep the forms of courtesy and talk in rhyme royal. We must resist the tendency to send them up. Mercy in *Mankind* is *not* silly, just because Mischief tries to make a fool of him: the play loses its force unless he is the anchorman. One of the first things one has to teach actors in these plays is how to behave with the proper flourish, to use the forms of politeness, to bow and curtsy with just the proper degree of reserve or humility to each person. There is a link between costume and dignity: you cannot slouch in the kind of bodice that the lady in the frontispiece to *Fulgens* is wearing, or do anything but stand up straight in that gentleman's gown and hat. With bodily poise comes the right internal poise. The best training for *Fulgens*, as the frontispiece hints, is to learn the basse dance. The way in which the characters covered the space in the centre of the hall floor must have been very like the way they covered it in a dance. The patterns of their encounters – Gaius' courtship of Lucres, the disputation itself – are formal and restrained. Again as in dancing, once the control has been established, the emotion can begin to show through. Actors also need to learn the skills of rhetorical delivery, which requires a scrupulous attention to the structure and meaning of what you are saying. You will never persuade others of the nature of true nobility, the operations of God's grace, or the shape of the cosmos, if you have not worked it out yourself. It is also necessary to see that proper solemnity (in their sense) does not preclude a sense of humour. In this respect alone, Lucres is a creation worthy to stand among Shakespeare's comic heroines.

These plays are perhaps more than any other a mirror of the society that bred them, and of the occasions on which they were performed. Though they can explore potentially tragic situations, the closure is optimistic. Magnificence is rescued by Good Hope before he commits suicide; Mankind is lifted out of his despair by Mercy. To have it otherwise would not suit either the Christian framework or the festive setting. They are socially self-confirming; hierarchy is restored; everything returns to its proper place, 'as shall stond with treuth and reason / In godely maner according to the season' (*Fulgens*, Part 1, lines 159–60).

NOTES

1 See the tentative discussion of the possibility of tandem playing at York by Beadle (70, pp. 425–34). In the van Alsloot painting (see illustration 6 on p. 52) an angel perched on the Nativity stable roof sings to the shepherds following the wagon on foot.

2 See also Meg Twycross, 'The Flemish Ommegang and its Pageant Cars', *METh* 2 (1980), 15–41, 80–98, Figs. 7 and 8.

3 The debate, which has been largely oral, has been mentioned by White (174) and

McKinnell (479), and began with the inaugural issue of *Medieval English Theatre* (Alan H. Nelson, 'Easter Week Pageants in Valladolid and Medina del Campo', *METh* 1 (1979), 62–70). In organising the four groups who performed at York in 1988, I suggested that we should all play end-on. The results were persuasive, though not all of Eileen White's objections have yet been met. For the Seville Holy Week *pasos* see Manuel J. Gomez Lara and Jorge Jimenez Barrientos, *Semana Santa: Fiesta Mayor en Sevilla* (Seville: Ediciones Alfar, 1990).

4 See L. J. Morrisey, 'English Pageant Waggons', *Eighteenth Century Studies* 9 (1975–6), 368; Albert Feuillerat (ed.), *Documents Relating to the Office of the Revels in the Time of Queen Elizabeth* (Louvain: Uystpruyst, 1908), pp. 157–8, 160, 162; Jacques Thiboust, *Relation de l'ordre de la triomphante et magnifique monstre du mystère des 'S.S. Actes des Apostres' par Arnoul et Simon Gréban* (Bourges: Au Grand Bourdaloue, Chez Vermeil, 1836), pp. 22, 70, 72. John Marshall, for practical reasons, estimates the dimensions of the Chester carriage at 'little more than twelve feet in length and seven feet six inches in breadth' (*185*, p. 34).

5 For a reproduction of these drawings see Elie Konigson, *La répresentation d'un mystère de la Passion à Valenciennes en 1547* (Paris: CNRS, 1969).

6 The 'Shrewsbury Fragments' (in *85*) appear to contain the part for one actor/ singer who took the roles of the Third Shepherd in a *Shepherds* play, the Third Mary in a *Resurrection* and one of the Disciples in a *Peregrini* (Travellers to Emmaus). They appear to be from a semi-vernacular liturgical play, but give very few clues about performance. A comparable vernacular/liturgical fragment of an *Ordo Prophetarum* (Procession of Prophets) has recently been discovered in Cambridge, Magdalene College MS Pepys 1236 (from Christ Church, Canterbury, *c.* 1460–75); see Rosamond McKitterick and Richard Beadle (eds.), *Catalogue of the Pepys Library at Magdalene College Cambridge: Medieval Manuscripts*, vol. v, Part 1 (Cambridge: D. S. Brewer, 1992), p. 13.

7 Dimensions from Margaret Wood, *The English Mediaeval House* (London: Dent, 1965), pp. 62–6. On practical arrangements for drama in early Tudor households see also Westfall (*314*, esp. pp. 18–28).

8 Arrangements for the staging of academic plays in Cambridge college halls during the sixteenth century, which could vary considerably from one another, as they do from the picture of great hall playing given here, are examined by Alan H. Nelson in *Early Cambridge Stages* (Cambridge: Cambridge University Press, forthcoming). He shows that in the universities, at least, other methods of hall staging had developed by the mid-century, and may have existed even during our period. We need to take into consideration the possibility of a much more 'modern' staging when looking at plays that do not, for example, show much audience interaction, as is the case with much of the early academic drama. But one should not react against the traditional view of great hall staging, which fits the evidence given here well.

9 See Peter Meredith, '"Fart Pryke in Cule" and Cock-Fighting', *METh* 6 (1984), 30–9; Alan J. Fletcher, '"Fart Pryke in Cule": a Late-Elizabethan Analogue from Ireland', *METh* 8 (1986), 132–9.

10 See Alexander Grant, *Henry VIII* (London: Methuen, 1985), pp. 16–21.

3

RICHARD BEADLE

The York cycle

INTRODUCTION

I EGIPTIUS	My lorde, grete pestelence
	Is like ful lange to last.
REX	Owe, come þat in oure presence?
	Than is oure pride all past. (Play 11, lines 345–8)

In chapter 12 of the book of Exodus, God's final vengeance upon the Egypt-
ians for the enslavement of the children of Israel is the death of the firstborn.
Called upon to mention the incident in the play of *Moses and Pharaoh*, a
writer in medieval York chose to substitute 'grete pestelence' for the biblical
episode, a striking alteration to the canonical source, for in later medieval
England 'the grete pestelence' had come to be the customary way of referring to the Black Death of 1348–9. Upon hearing the grim words, the tyran-
nous and verbose Rex Pharaoh is immediately deflated, capitulates and
orders the release of the Israelites – in performance, a moment of chill stasis
after the pell-mell black comedy with which the reports of the preceding
plagues of Egypt would probably have been presented. When the play was
new, this may also have been a moment of remembrance for survivors of the
Black Death and those born in the succeeding generation, for the York
Hosiers' play of *Moses and Pharaoh* was probably composed when the
memory of this, the most destructive of all the plague's visitations, was still a
living memory. The earliest possible documentary reference to the existence
of cycle drama in York dates to 1376, though our extant copy of *Moses and
Pharaoh* was not set down until much later. In its subsequent career in the
fifteenth and the first half of the sixteenth century the cycle changed in many
ways, but there is no evidence to suggest that the Hosiers did other than
bring forth the same pageant, more or less annually, through to the last
recorded performances in the late 1560s. Moreover, it appears that they
continued to use the same script, with its sombre echo of the great mortality

over two centuries before, from which (like the Israelites in the plagues of Egypt) only a chosen few had survived. Survival from plagues and other disasters has traditionally moved communities to great acts of collective expression, often artistic expression. Whether or not this was the case in York after 1350 can only be a matter for speculation, though it is worth observing that social and economic circumstances were, paradoxically, in some ways more favourable to an undertaking on the scale of the Corpus Christi play during the city's period of recovery from the Black Death, than beforehand.[1] Whoever conceived of the cycle set themselves the formidable problem of showing an immense, occasionally spectacular, but conceptually subtle play to a large and diverse audience within crowded urban confines. The solution proved to be at once a practical *coup de théâtre* and a complex expression of the community's character, which systematically embodied both its spiritual aspirations and its day-to-day material preoccupations in the form of poetic drama.

Later in the cycle, after the Resurrection, at the end of the Woolpackers' and Woolbrokers' play of the *Supper at Emmaus* (Play 40), there is another contemporary allusion in the York text, which introduces a quite different modulation in the dramatic illusion. The play is concluded with an apology to the audience spoken by one of the actors, as it were half in and half out of the character of one of the pilgrims who encounter the risen Christ on the road to Emmaus:

> I PERIGRINUS Here may we notte melle more at þis tyde,
> For prossesse of plaies þat precis in plight.
>
> (Play 40, lines 191–2)

(We cannot remain here talking any longer at the moment, because of the procession of pageants pressing urgently [behind us]).

As has been explained in detail in chapter 2 (pp. 39–41 above), the York plays were presented *seriatim* at a succession of stations along the streets of the city, and the presence of other pageants (the wheeled vehicles that furnished the sets) waiting to perform at the station occupied by the Woolpackers and Woolbrokers provides the cue for the end of their play. This is an unusually explicit instance of that sense of pregnant metadrama that underlies the text of the cycle as a whole. The text is essentially a performance script, never intended as reading matter, and it repeatedly insists on the presence of an audience, who are thereby drawn to participate almost physically in the illusion, finding themselves implicated in the events portrayed. At the beginning of the Passion sequence, in the Skinners' play of the *Entry into Jerusalem* (Play 25), biblical episodes such as the healing of the blind man and the lame man, and Zacheus in the sycamore tree, must have been transacted at street level amongst the audience, who were thus obliged to imagine themselves as the first Palm Sunday crowds, and their own city as the place where Christ was coming to suffer and to die. This effect is again brought home effectively by the conclusion of the play, which consists of a series of florid set speeches of welcome delivered (probably from the pageant wagon), by eight burgesses. The style of address is unmistakably that favoured for pageants celebrating the formal royal entry into the medieval city, and the play is rounded off with singing, almost certainly of a piece from the contemporary liturgy of Palm Sunday:

VIII BURGENSIS	Hayll domysman dredful, þat all schall deme,	
	Hayll þat all quyk and dede schall lowte,	*worship*
	Hayll whom worschippe moste will seme,	*befit*
	Hayll whom all thyng schall drede and dowte.	*fear*
	We welcome þe,	
	Hayll and welcome of all abowte	
	To owre ceté.	
	Tunc cantant.	*Then they sing*
		(Play 25, lines 538–44)

(538 ... stern judge who will pass sentence on all)

Though each play in the cycle was (as the documentary records repeatedly put it) 'brought forth' by a craft guild or a group of guilds in collaboration, much remains uncertain as to precisely what 'bringing forth' involved. The documents indicate that it meant at least the obligation to provide funding for a performance annually, to maintain a pageant wagon and the necessary properties and costumes, and to attend to the quality and conduct of the performance. These circumstances occasionally gave playwrights the opportunity to display the cycle's duality of perspective in yet another mode. In the Shipwrights' *Building of the Ark* (Play 8), the biblical shipbuilder Noah is presented as a divinely-directed contemporary shipwright in the act of constructing a clinker-built vessel, which in symbolic terms represents the Church, the sole hope of salvation for all mankind. Again, it is the closing words of the script which embellish what has been the playwright's intention throughout, to blend the daily labour of the York Shipwrights with the divine scheme of redemption, for they revolve around a felicitous play on the word 'craft', which signifies both the play-Ark, the vessel which has just taken shape before the audience's eyes, and at the same time the divinely-inspired craft or 'mystery' of shipbuilding which God has taught Noah:

[NOE]	He þat to me þis Crafte has kende,	*taught/given*
	He wysshe vs with his worthy wille.	*May he guide us*
		(Play 8, lines 150–1)[2]

The full repertoire of the York Corpus Christi cycle, some fifty separate pageants, ran to well over 14,000 lines of Middle English stanzaic verse, of which about 13,500 survive. It is important to bear in mind that the script as preserved reflects for the most part a version of the cycle current in the third quarter of the fifteenth century, already much revised from earlier forms, and itself subject to substantial alteration until the religious drama was finally suppressed in York about a century later. The script called for over 300 speaking parts, and there was an unknown but undoubtedly much larger number of supernumeraries – musicians, stagehands and other assist-ants – required to mount the performance, which normally took place annually on Corpus Christi Day, beginning at dawn and probably not ending until after midnight. A certain amount of documentary information also exists concerning the financial and practical requirements of the production – the movable stages known as pageant wagons, properties, costumes and stage effects; regulation, income and expenditure of the guilds that brought forth the individual pageants; the total control over the production exercised by the governing body of the city; the processional route through the streets, at intervals along which (as most scholars now believe) the pageants were repeatedly performed in series. These immense physical demands in relation to a single artistic enterprise by one community have no significant modern analogue, and the practical conception answers to an equally singular gran-deur and complexity of thought: the idea of a unified drama of the Fall and Redemption of mankind presented in such a way as to implicate the spirit-ual lives of the audience throughout. Within this fundamental binary struc-ture of Fall and Redemption the cycle rises impressively, in the text as we have it, to its theological and dramatic occasions, unfolding the story in individual plays of high quality portraying the Fall of the Angels (Play 1, the Barkers), the Fall of Man (Play 5, the Coopers), the Incarnation (Play 14, the Tilethatchers' *Nativity*), the Crucifixion (Play 35, the Pinners; Play 36, the Butchers), the Resurrection (Play 38, the Carpenters) and the Last Judgement (Play 47, the Mercers). Herein, however, lies a paradox. Though these are the episodes that do much to create the strong sense of an under-lying unity of artistic purpose behind the cycle, they could – judging by the varying attitudes displayed to theme, characterisation, style, metre and prac-tical stagecraft – all be attributable to so many different authors. Several of them were certainly composed at different dates in the cycle's career, and not all of them remained as part of the York repertoire throughout that time. What is true of these paradigmatic episodes is equally the case amongst the intervening plays which fill out the narrative and furnish the traditional network of figural correspondences that binds the cycle yet more firmly together in theological terms (*130*, pp. 57–100) – for example, the lesser cycle of Old Testament plays (7–11), or the plays on the life of Christ (10–25), or the Marian sequence (44–46) inserted between the Pentecost play and the Last Judgement. Here again an extraordinary variety of dramatic and poetic styles is displayed, and a number of the plays can be shown to date from different periods, or to have been replaced by new (but un-recorded) versions during the later life of the cycle, or to have been dropped from production altogether.

All the evidence of diverse authorship and rolling revision of the cycle through the years nevertheless fails to displace the powerful submerged consistency of intent that informs the writing at every point. The York cycle's success in achieving the essential 'Gothic' aesthetic virtue of diversity-within-unity perhaps confers upon it the status of norm against which the other cycles or cycle-type compilations may be judged. It contrasts variously with the eclectic approach to the cycle structure adopted by the compiler of the N-Town manuscript, or Chester's self-conscious attempt to recreate the genre in a form appropriate to the changing times of the sixteenth century, or the radical experimentations with the individual components of a cycle found in the plays of the Wakefield Master, all of which are discussed at length elsewhere in this volume. As we have seen above, the York cycle's specific self-referential or metadramatic allusions to 'medieval time and English place' (130, pp. 101–23) are studiedly discreet and quietly assimilated to its greater purposes. This is characteristic, and contrasts with the freer but less clearly motivated references to the contemporary scene that form an attractive feature of the Chester cycle and the Wakefield group. York impresses with a gathered sense of grandeur and monumentality, within which variegated detail and the changes wrought by time are effectively subsumed. We began by suggesting that the York Corpus Christi cycle may conceivably have been invented as the city's united response to specific circumstances in the later fourteenth century: in the almost complete absence of factual evidence, no 'evolutionary' theory offers any more plausible explanation of its origins. However that may be, its evident antiquity, and a documented career that suggests more or less annual performances in a basically stable form for up to two centuries, cannot but have attracted attention as a paradigm, though by no means one that was slavishly imitated elsewhere.[3]

THE TEXT: THE REGISTER OF 1463–77

Prior to studying the York cycle, either as a whole or in the form of one or several of its parts, it is important to be clear about both the range and the nature of the information that can be brought to bear. To invoke the idea of the 'text' of the cycle or indeed the texts of many of the individual pageants is not necessarily a straightforward matter, since both the whole and the parts were, throughout their history, often in a state of becoming rather than of being. This is a characteristic which the York cycle shares not only with its immediate congeners, but also with a number of other major medieval literary works. The fact, however, that it was a public work of art, a social product that renewed its form annually, renders it a text more radically 'unstable' or dynamic in its nature than other *œuvres mouvantes* of the time, such as the *Canterbury Tales* or *Piers Plowman*. Our surviving copy of the text was assembled at some time between 1463 and 1477, which happens to be exactly half way through the cycle's documented life-span. It is contained in a large manuscript book, now British Library MS Additional 35290, which seems to have been compiled from 'prompt copies' of the individual pageants (known as 'originals') held by the fifty or so separate guilds who had responsibility for them.[4] The manuscript now in the British Library had official status in the city, where it was known as the 'Register' of the Corpus Christi play, and the scribe who compiled it succeeded in obtaining copies of nearly all the guilds' originals, leaving a few gaps in the sequence where texts were not forthcoming, or plays defunct. A facsimile of the Register has been published (*109*), and the manuscript has twice formed the basis of critical editions of the cycle since the discovery of its identity during the nineteenth century (*72*; *70*, pp. 1–2).[5] Both the introduction to the facsimile and the textual commentary in the more recent critical edition show that the Register is an object of singular and formidable complexity, revealing not only the text of the cycle as it happened to be captured at an arbitrary moment in its career, but also something of its earlier history in fossilised form.

It is not known for certain why the civic authorities called for a consolidated copy of the whole cycle text in the third quarter of the fifteenth century. However, it was during this period (between 1465 and 1476) that the Corpus Christi play, an exclusively civic affair, began to displace the ecclesiastical procession of Corpus Christi from its own official liturgical occasion (the first Thursday after Trinity Sunday) to the day after (*152*). At the same time as the play got Corpus Christi Day to itself (in 1476), the governing body of the city instituted, apparently for the first time, an official vetting procedure for the cycle, involving 'iiij of þe moste connyng [*skilful*], descrete and able playeres within þis Citie to serche, here and examen all þe plaiers and plaies and pagentes throughoute all þe artificeres [*craft guilds*] belonging to Corpus Christi plaie' (*158*, p. 109). Scrutiny of the plays under these circumstances could well have prompted the compilation of a master copy, in which case the appearance of the York cycle text as we now have it was the result of practical rather than literary considerations.

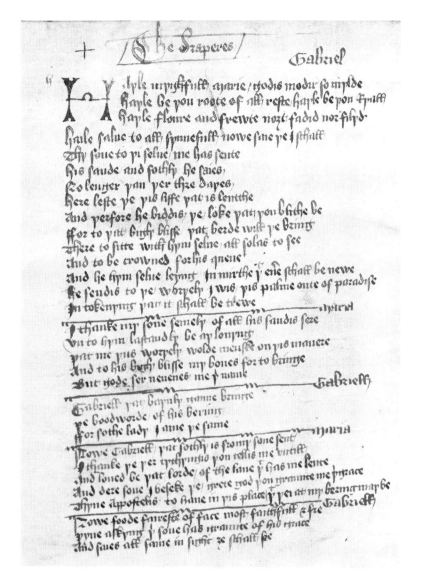

12 Register of the York plays, the Drapers' pageant of *The Death of the Virgin* (British Library MS Additional 35290, f. 230v). See p. 92.

The Register was certainly much used for practical purposes during the sixteenth century, in particular by a civic official who took it into the street at the first station to check the text against what the actors were actually saying and doing whilst the plays were in progress. This was John Clerke, servant of the Common Clerk of York from the 1540s to the 1560s, whose annotations in the British Library manuscript provide us with precious eyewitness information about the cycle in performance (*162*). Amongst other things he noted music cues, pieces of stage business and places where anything from a single speech to a whole play had been revised or rewritten. During his time the Marian plays became doctrinally suspect in the eyes of Protestant zealots and were dropped temporarily from the cycle between 1548 and 1553, before disappearing for good in 1561. There is no evidence, however, that Clerke was in any way concerned with censoring the text of the cycle on ideological grounds, and indeed none of the annotations by later hands in the Register can be convincingly traced to religious controversy (*162*, pp. 247–9). It was probably Clerke who added the small ' + ' against the heading of the Drapers' *Death of the Virgin* (Play 44, see illustration 12), and similar crosses are found against the heading of the Weavers' *Assumption* (Play 45) and the Hostelers' *Coronation* (Play 46), presumably to indicate their suspension, seemingly the only signs in the manuscript of the changing times in which he lived.

To speak, then, of the text of the York cycle is to involve oneself in some understanding of the complex means whereby it has been transmitted to us. For critical and interpretative purposes, the Register should be thought of as representing, for the most part, as complete a text of the cycle as the civic authorities were able to collect during the third quarter of the fifteenth century. External references in the documents and the annotations of Clerke and others in the manuscript itself indicate some of the ways in which the Register soon passed into obsolescence as a fully accurate record of either the content or the organisation of the cycle. By Clerke's time, performance practice showed that a number of the plays had changed hands amongst the guilds, that the texts of others had been partially or completely rewritten and that some had been suppressed. The Register as originally compiled gave copies of forty-six pageants that were then in the 'repertoire' of the cycle. Though it is usually assumed that all of them would have been brought forth on each and every occasion that the cycle was performed, we have no hard information that this was the case, and there may indeed be evidence to the contrary (*143*, pp. 118–19).

THE RECORDS: (i) CRAFT ORGANISATION

The Register of the Corpus Christi plays tells only part of the story. Much of the evidence for what we know of the development of the cycle, of its fluid nature and of the practical arrangements for performance from year to year comes not from the bibliographical or literary quarter, but from documentary sources held mostly in the archives of the city of York (*158*). The interpretation of the 'records' of the early drama in York (as they have come to be called) is also an area where caution must be exercised, since they are the scanty and random survivals of a once much larger body of material, often frustratingly ambiguous in their import, which should ideally be seen in the broader context of the city's structures of social, political and economic organisation as a whole, rather than in the form of the snippets and extracts that appear (however scrupulously presented) in modern editions (155, 52). They range from official memoranda and minutes of the city's governing body, through its financial accounts, rentals and legal records, documents pertaining to the craft and religious guilds (particularly the ordinances and accounts), wills of prominent citizens, to the ecclesiastical records generated by the archiepiscopal see and the religious houses of York (158, pp. xvii–xlii). All of these classes of document yield external information which may be brought to bear on the understanding of some aspect or other of the cycle: the endless changes in the guilds' arrangements for financing and 'bringing forth', as they put it (i.e. staging), their pageants; information about the pageant wagons themselves, and where they were stored when not in use; entries concerning properties and costumes; rents for stations on the processional route along which the plays were presented; identifications of named individuals concerned in some way or other with the production over the years; and a mass of other detail, which amongst other things provides a basis for reconstructing the annual routine for staging the cycle.

Early in Lent the governing body of the city would decide whether to authorise a performance of the Corpus Christi play for the coming season, occasionally preferring to substitute one or other of York's great civic plays, the Creed play or the Paternoster play, the texts of which have alas been lost (153). If, as normal, the Corpus Christi play went forward, specially appointed officers of the individual guilds, the pageant masters, put in hand arrangements for their plays. It was the pageant masters who in effect produced the plays, collecting financial contributions (pageant silver) from the members of the guild and raising money from other sources (169). Though the evidence is scanty, it suggests that the next step was for the pageant masters to engage a person whom we would nowadays call the director to attend to the pageant wagon, actors, props, costumes and rehearsals, and the day of performance itself. Insufficient information survives from York to generalise about who the directors and actors were (70, p. 38). At 4.30 a.m. on Corpus Christi Day the pageant wagons, stage crews and actors assembled on Pageant Green (now Toft Green) within the southwest corner of the city walls, and the performance was ready to commence. The stations along the processional route were marked by official civic banners set up the night before. The rising of the sun was greeted at the first station outside the gates of Holy Trinity Priory, Micklegate, by God's opening speech in the Barkers' pageant, creating his bright angels and the first heavenly light.

From amongst the mass of business records and accounts, one document in particular deserves to be quoted here, for, rather than representing what has been preserved, it reveals all too vividly the enormous wealth of fascinating information about the appearance of the plays in performance which has been lost. At the same time it illustrates some of the difficulties encountered in interpreting material of this kind. In 1433 the Mercers' guild drew up an inventory of the pageant wagon, properties and costumes used at that time in bringing forth their play of Doomsday (Play 47) which gives some idea of the visual components in a presentation of this type. Together with the version of the Mercers' text recorded later in the Register, which may not relate in every detail to the items listed, it has served as the basis for various discussions aimed at conjectural reconstruction (*156, 157, 160*), and as a blueprint for modern productions of the play:

> ... ffirst a Pagent With iiij Wheles; helle mouthe; iij garmentes for iij deuels; vj deuelles faces in iij Versernes [*two-faced masks*]; Array for ij euell saules, þat is to say ij Sirkes [*shirts*]; ij paire hoses [*stockings*], ij vesenes & ij Chauelers [*wigs*]; Array for ij gode saules, þat ys to say ij Sirkes, ij paire hoses, ij vesernes & ij Cheuelers; ij paire Aungell Wynges with Iren in þe endes; ij trumpes of White [*silver*] plate, & ij redes [?*red garments*] and iiij Aubes [*albs*] for iiij Appostels; iij diadems with iij vesernes for iij Appostels; iiij diademes with iiij Cheuelers of ȝalow for iiij Apostels; A cloud & ij peces of Rainbow of tymber; Array for god, þat ys to say a Sirke, Wounded, a diademe With a veserne gilted; A grete coster [*curtain*] of rede damaske payntid for the bakke syde of þe pagent; ij other lesse costers for ij sydes of þe Pagent; iij other costers of lewent brede [*eleventh breadth – ?a standard measurement*] for þe sides of þe Pagent; A litel coster iiij squared to hang at þe bakke of god; iiij Irens to bere vppe [*support*] heuen; iiij finale coterelles [?*special bolts of some kind*] & a Iren pynne; A brandreth [?*frame*] of Iren þat god sall sitte vppon when he sall sty [*ascend*] vppe to heuen, With iiij rapes at iiij corners; A heuen of Iren With a naffe of tre [*wooden pulley*]; ij peces of rede cloudes & sternes [*stars*] of gold langing to heuen; ij peces of blue cloudes payntid on bothe sydes; iij peces of rede cloudes With sunne bemes of golde & sternes for þe hiest of heuen, With a lang small border of þe same Wurke; vij grete Aungels halding þe passion of god, Ane of þame has a fane of laton [*brass banner*] & a crosse of Iren in his hede [*sic*] gilted; iiij smaller Aungells gilted holding þe passion; ix smaler Aungels payntid rede to renne aboute in þe heuene; A lang small [*thin*] corde to gerre [*cause*] þe Aungels renne aboute; ij shorte rolls of tre [?*wooden rollers*] to putte forthe þe pagent
>
> (*158*, pp. 55–6, punctuation and glosses added)

Though not itself typical of the York records in general, the Mercers' inventory nevertheless illustrates the characteristic way in which their richness of suggestion can be combined with seemingly irreducible obscurity or ambiguity, especially where customary expressions or terms of art are concerned. Precious pieces of hard information emerge: the actors, for example, seem all to have worn masks (probably a convention in the portrayal of supernatural figures), and God's costume is evocatively termed a 'Sirke, Wounded', evidently a close-fitting garment displaying the wounds suffered in the course of the Passion, literally the 'bludy serk' of Henryson's later allegorical poem of that name. On the other hand, as the studies cited above have shown, some of the technical terms used in describing the decoration and mechanical features of the pageant wagon remain too elusive to provide a basis for a definitive reconstruction.

THE RECORDS: (ii) CIVIC ORGANISATION AND THE *ORDO PAGINARUM*

Little can be said for certain about the scope and nature of the Corpus Christi play during the first few decades of its existence. The very scanty records of the late fourteenth century indicate that some sort of presentation was taking place as early as 1376, and that by 1399 proper regulations were being called for to control a performance that was over-running its allotted time span in its progress along the processional route. The first episode to be identified by name is *Moses and Pharaoh* (see above), which was assigned to the Hosiers in 1403 (*158*, pp. 3–12, 13–14). The picture suddenly becomes clearer in 1415, when the civic authorities caused the town clerk, Roger Burton, to draw up a document still known by its original name, the *Ordo Paginarum* – the 'Order of the Pageants' – which was enshrined in the city's principal register of its official instruments, the Memorandum Book. The *Ordo Paginarum* takes the form of a long list of the guilds that brought forth plays at Corpus Christi, the names of guilds or groups of associated guilds in a column on the left being accompanied by a brief description of the subject matter of their plays to the right. These summary descriptions of the plays seldom run to more than two or three abbreviated phrases, but sometimes include valuable details such as the *dramatis personae*. A second, even briefer list, probably of much the same date, accompanies the *Ordo* proper, and indicates that at this time the cycle was subdivided into some fifty-seven separate pageants. Between the two lists is a copy of the *Proclamacio ludi corporis christi*, 'Proclamation of the Corpus Christi play' to be made on the vigil (day before) Corpus Christi, stating the regulations for public order on the occasion of the performance and prescribing in general terms how the pageants should be played, and their procession expedited.

13   The York *Ordo Paginarum* of 1415 (York, City Archives, A/Y Memorandum Book, f. 253r). See pp. 95–7; visible at the top of the page are the entries for the Tile[thatcher]s', Chandlers' and Goldsmiths' guilds, together with brief descriptions of their respective pageants of the *Nativity*, the *Shepherds* and the *Three Kings*. For transcriptions see 158, pp. 18–19, 704.

The York *Ordo Paginarum* of 1415 is a document of outstanding importance, essential reading for any student of the cycle, but, partly owing to heavy alterations made during the years it was in use, and partly owing to disastrous flood damage in 1892, no fully satisfactory transcription has yet appeared. A photographic reproduction was included with the facsimile of the text of the cycle issued in 1983 (*109*; see also illustration 13).[6] Though the *Ordo* probably began life as the city's first attempt to establish an official record of the basic content and organisation of the cycle, revisions to the scripts being used in performance and alterations in the assignments of guilds to plays meant that it started to go out of date soon after 1415. It therefore provides a record of some, but by no means all, of the changes in the organisation of the cycle and the content of the individual plays that took place during the rest of the fifteenth century and earlier half of the sixteenth.

The *Ordo Paginarum*, examined with caution, provides an interesting point of comparison with the version of the cycle registered between 1463 and 1477. In some cases the description of a guild's play in the *Ordo*, unaltered from its original form of 1415, matches well with the general content and *dramatis personae* of the script registered in the name of that craft during the third quarter of the fifteenth century, and the extant text may indeed go back to the earlier date. However it should still be borne in mind that, since the *Ordo* descriptions are so brief and the plays are based on standard biblical and apocryphal subjects, scripts could be revised or entirely rewritten without calling for any alteration to the relevant *Ordo* entry. On the other hand it is possible to point to various instances where comparison between surviving plays and the *Ordo* descriptions reveals information of historical or critical interest about the cycle (see below).

The main general conclusion that may be drawn from the *Ordo Paginarum* is that by 1415 York possessed a long play, designed to be performed annually on the occasion of Corpus Christi, consisting of individual pageants on biblical and apocryphal subjects arranged in a 'Creation to Doomsday' cycle, for which the responsibilities and costs were divided amongst the craft guilds of the city. How the shape of the whole was conceived, and how the interrelationship of the parts was first achieved are interesting questions for which there are no easy answers. There are good reasons for thinking that at this time, and indeed for the greater part of the fifteenth century, the city retained no consolidated text of the cycle as a whole, and performance must have proceeded on the basis of the individual copies of their plays held by the guilds themselves, marshalled according to the 'Order of the Pageants' set down in the Memorandum Book. In practice this meant that the impressive, unified cycle, so instantly perceptible to the user of a modern edition of the text, with all its intricate network of figural correspondences and 'overarching patterns of imagery that echo from one episode to another' (155, p. 128), existed solely on the occasion of performance, and only achieved what we recognise as literary form with the compilation of the Register, apparently as a matter of practical convenience, half a century or so later.

RECONSTRUCTING PERFORMANCE, THEN AND NOW

Important new dimensions have recently been added to the study of the York cycle with investigations into the historical topography of the city itself, and the use of the ancient locations for modern productions of a number of the pageants in something like their original setting. Amongst the most interesting documentary records of the Corpus Christi play are the lists of 'stations', stopping places along the fixed processional route through the streets, at which the individual pageants were performed. The earliest of these lists of 'places to hear the play' dates from 1399, and the latest from 1569, and they reveal amongst many other things that the number of such stations could vary from year to year, though the number often favoured was twelve. York has been fortunate in retaining much of its medieval street layout, including virtually all the thoroughfares used for processional performances (see illustration 1, p. 40), and patient research has in some cases established the exact physical locations where the pageant wagons were drawn up and the plays acted. Even details such as the width of the streets at these points, and the identities of those who paid rent to the city for the privilege – and probably the commercial potential – of having a station in front of their houses, have been discovered (170, 174, with maps; maps also in 70, 71).

A major step forward in the understanding of how the York plays might have worked in performance came in 1988, when the invaluable opportunity arose to use conjecturally reconstructed wagons on part of the original processional route, playing to a street audience at the very locations that were probably first used for such a purpose over six hundred years earlier (478, 479, with photographs, 488, 490). The significance of this new dimension to the study of the cycle should not be underestimated, since it defines with remarkable precision many of the key questions about the kind of 'theatre' for which the plays were designed, and about the capacities of the audiences who saw them. When wagons were drawn up at a station, were they arranged like a small proscenium stage, pulled over to one side of the street, playing towards the house opposite? Or were they set up as 'thrust' stages occupying the centre of the roadway, facing down the street, with the audience in front and at both sides? Were, indeed, both of these dispositions, and possibly others, used? How much of the remaining street area could be used as acting space in the quite numerous plays whose action demands a second or third location apart from the deck of the wagon? Given the lifting tackle in the Mercers' inventory above, but bearing in mind the low over-hangs on the buildings, how high might a second storey on a pageant wagon have been? Could two pageant wagons really be deployed to play 'in tandem' at one station, as the bibliographical and documentary evidence strongly suggests was the case with the Tilethatchers' *Nativity* / Chandlers' *Shepherds* (Plays 14/15) and the Masons'/Goldsmiths' *Herod*/*Magi* (Play 16) (70, pp. 425–34)? How accurately can the size of the audience gathered at a single station be established?

The aesthetics of playwriting for and staging under these newly and sometimes precisely definable circumstances have as yet been little explored, and the dynamics of audience response to modern productions using these original locations have much to tell us. The topographical evidence indicates that the stations were sometimes within sight and usually within earshot of the one preceding and the one after, so that a sense of simultaneity in the presentation of adjacent episodes – an uncanny sense of being both within a specific narrative time and outside it – must have been perceptible to the audience throughout the performance as a whole. Alexandra Johnston has remarked how one of York's typical dramaturgic techniques, that of begin-ning a play with a greeting to the audience and ending it with a farewell, is a conceptual extension of the actual repeated comings and goings of the pageants of the stations, invoking 'the constant sense throughout each episode that the story of salvation history being unfolded ... consists of many journeys' (154, p. 367).

The performance space itself probably had rather less of the feeling nowadays associated with 'outdoor theatre' than is commonly assumed. The acting space on the wagon and in the street was closely bounded by buildings on either side, with the characteristic jettied upper storeys, still preserved here and there in York (illustrations in 174) cutting out a good deal of the sky. It is becoming clear that the York pageants individually were played to a relatively small audience at each station. In medieval street con-ditions, standing room was probably even more limited and unsatisfactory than it is at the same places now, and those who hired the temporary raised seating or looked out from upper windows undoubtedly had the best view. Unlike most of their modern counterparts, the medieval audience, under these conditions, seem to have been very susceptible to a collective vulner-ability to the contagious emotions of the dramatic moment, for which the closest parallel might be the experience of a crowd on an important sporting occasion these days (171, pp. 285–6). The traditional image of medieval drama as a theatre of large gesture and heavy bombast, conveyed through doggerel verse in continuously raised voices, is rapidly evaporating. As far as York is concerned we are now discovering that its audience was in the best position to respond to the subtle patterns of emotional and conceptual inter-play set up in the dramatic structures of the cycle. Descended from gener-ations who were more accustomed to hearing their literature than to reading it, they were connoisseurs of the remarkable metrical intricacy displayed in many of the plays, which, as we shall see in a moment, often demand a finely-tuned ear for allusion, wordplay and the verbal embodiments of psychological nuance. As the most detailed study so far of the topographical evidence concludes, 'Perhaps we need to consider the performance of the York Corpus Christi play not as an epic, but as a very intimate dramatic experience' (174, p. 57; cf. 478, p. 114).

STUDYING THE YORK PLAYS: TEXT, DOCUMENTS AND PERFORMANCE

Most of the York cycle still awaits detailed study along lines that move towards an integration of the textual, documentary and theatrical evidence, complex and resistant to consensual interpretation though some of it is. Recent illuminating accounts of the *Nativity* (Play 14; 134, pp. 60–80) and the *Resurrection* (Play 18; 171) show what can be done. An extended com-mentary on the cycle as a whole, along the lines of that provided by Lumiansky and Mills for Chester (73) or Spector for N-Town (78), is a major desideratum, and, where appropriate, attention must be paid to the presence of music in the plays (443), and the possibility of iconographic influences (148). The close attention devoted to the Passion sequence by J. W. Robinson (167, 134) has been well placed, though scrutiny of the textual, documentary and literary evidence for the existence of a dramatist whom he dubs the 'York Realist' is long overdue. In the space available here it is only possible to gesture towards the critical and interpretative impli-cations of the points drawn together in the preceding sections, and the Passion sequence – in particular the texture of its dramatic poetry – may be allowed to serve as an initial touchstone. Two plays from the York Passion sequence, seen in the context of the *Ordo Paginarum*, provide a point of entry into discussion of the styles of dramatic writing being practised in York in the 1420s. Play 35, the celebrated York Pinners' pageant of the *Crucifixion*, may be set alongside the Tilemakers' *Christ before Pilate 2: The Judgement* (33), a play regularly attributed to the 'York Realist'.

There is good reason to think that the *Crucifixion* as we now have it probably came into being in 1422. The situation prior to that date, from

1415 at least, is preserved unaltered in the brief pageant list that accompanies the *Ordo Paginarum* proper, which shows that the nailing of Christ on the cross and the rearing of the cross on Calvary were originally played as separate episodes by different guilds:

Payntours	Expansio & clauacio christi
latoners	leuacio christi super montem
(Painters	The stretching out and nailing of Christ
Latteners	The raising of Christ on the Mount) (*158*, pp. 26, 711)

Another document of 1422 in the Memorandum Book, however, makes clear that a decision had been made to amalgamate the two episodes into one pageant, under the control of the Pinners and Latteners. The intention was to simplify the organisation of the cycle, which because of the profusion of short pageants was proving cumbersome in performance (*158*, pp. 37–8). Careful examination of the relevant entry in the main *Ordo* list shows that erasures and substitutions (visible in the facsimile, but not recorded in the Johnston and Rogerson *REED* transcription) were made by Roger Burton, no doubt in or soon after 1422, in order to reflect the new circumstances. In the absence of evidence to the contrary it seems very likely that our extant text of the Pinners' pageant (copied 1463–77), which covers both the corresponding episodes, was originally composed in response to a practical need to shorten the cycle.

The York *Crucifixion* has never lacked high praise as a work of dramatic art, not least for the quality of the 'realism' that has gone into the portrayal of the executioners' work. The tools of their trade – hammers, nails, ropes, wedges, timber – are all studiedly displayed to the audience and constant reference made to them in the dialogue, largely to enhance the realistic impact of the presentation, but also because some of these objects later become the 'Instruments of the Passion' displayed by the angels at the Last Judgement (mentioned as properties in the Mercers' inventory above). The dialogue is expertly managed, and in such a way as to make the blocking of the play reasonably clear to any director, since it is possible at all important points to infer where each speaker is and what he is doing (*173*). The vivid realisation of the gruesome actions involved in stretching out and nailing Jesus to the cross owes much to the late medieval tradition of affective meditation on every minute physical detail of the Passion (*138*, pp. 262, 402, n. 54). This, when it becomes embodied in dramatic form, compels the audience's absorption in the work (a key word in the play) of the executioners, so that when the cross is reared and Christ utters his lyrical appeal to 'Al men þat walkis by waye or strete', an onlooker's silent complicity in what has gone before precipitates a guilty sense of implication in the Crucifixion.

Some idea of the dramatist's range of style and technique may be gained by considering this climactic moment in the play and the cycle as a whole. 'Where are oure hameres laide / þat we schulde wirke withall?' asks the third soldier:

IV MILES	We haue þem here euen atte oure hande.	
II MILES	Gyffe me þis wegge, I schall it in dryue.	
IV MILES	Here is anodir ȝitt ordande.	*prepared*
III MILES	Do take it me hidir belyue.	*quickly*
I MILES	Laye on þanne faste.	
III MILES	ȝis, I warrande.	
	I thryng þame same, so motte I thryve.	
	Nowe will þis crosse full stabely stande,	
	All-yf he raue þei will noght ryve.	
I MILES	Say sir, howe likis you nowe,	
	Þis werke þat we haue wrought?	
IV MILES	We praye youe sais vs howe	
	ȝe fele, or faynte ȝe ought.	*whether you faint*
JESUS	Al men þat walkis by waye or strete,	
	Takes tente ȝe schalle no trauayle tyne.	
	Byholdes myn heede, myn handis, and my feete,	
	And fully feele nowe, or ȝe fyne,	*pass*
	Yf any mournyng may be meete,	*equal*
	Or myscheue mesured vnto myne.	
	My fadir, þat alle bales may bete,	
	Forgiffis þes men þat dois me pyne.	*cause me pain*
	What þei wirke wotte þai noght;	
	Therfore, my fadir, I craue,	
	Latte neuere þer synnys be sought,	
	But see þer saules to saue.	(Play 35, lines 241–64)

(246 I'll thrust them in together, so may I prosper 248 Even if he writhes about they will not split 254 Be sure that you miss none of my suffering 258 Or suffering compared . . . 259 . . . who may relieve all torments 261 'They know not what they do' 263 . . . visited upon them)

In this dramatist's hands the twelve-line stanza, abababab$_4$cdcd$_3$, is assimilated equally well to the very different dramatic requirements of Jesus's serene address, and the demotic hammerblows of the executioners' stichomythia. 'All men þat walkis . . .' describes not only the actual posture of much of the audience, but also calls forth emotional associations of the medieval liturgy, quoting 'O vos omnes qui transitis per viam' (Lamentations 1.12) from the Good Friday *Improperia* or 'reproaches' (138, pp. 260–1). The strong deictic element in the language of the soldiers ('*oure*

hameres', '*þis* wegge', '*þis* crosse' and so on) emphasises the nascent symbolic nature of the objects they are handling, and at the same time 'covers'
the difficult and undoubtedly dangerous stage actions that the actors are
called upon to perform. Powerfully integrated and nuanced dramatic poetry
of this kind would be likely to find its best-attuned audience in the more
intimate circumstances of performance described above. The play's verbal
and thematic emphasis on *work*, for example, converges on a kind of pun
arising out of the third soldier's question in lines 249–50, followed by Jesus's
oblique, delayed answer in line 261, via 'trauayle' in line 254: the ignorant,
physical, painful work of man in the cause of sin and death is transfigured
into the sublime, spiritual work of redemption in the cause of life ever-
lasting.

Whether the work of the York *Crucifixion* playwright occurs elsewhere in
the cycle is largely a matter for speculation. A natural starting point is the
metrical evidence, though one would not want to suggest either that this
writer possessed a monopoly of the twelve-line stanza, or that he did not
compose in other metres. Nevertheless, the same stanza, with more or less
ornamental alliteration according to subject matter, occurs in a substantial
number of other plays. It was adopted, for example, in the Doctor's long
prefatory speech rehearsing the Old Testament prophecies of the birth of
Christ, which was grafted on to an earlier *Annunciation and Visitation* (Play
12; 70, p. 424). Roger Burton recorded this as an addition to the cycle in an
alteration to the *Ordo Paginarum*, and it evidently dates from much the
same period as the revision that produced the *Crucifixion* of 1422. Unlike
the latter play, however, the Doctor's speech is a significant enlargement of
the cycle (144 lines), aimed at articulating more clearly the previously abrupt
transition from the Old to the New Testament story. The twelve-line stanza
of the *Crucifixion* is also the metre of parts or all of ten other plays: the
Parchmentmakers' and Bookbinders' *Abraham and Isaac* (10), the Hosiers'
Moses and Pharaoh (10), parts of the Chandlers' *Shepherds* (15), most of the
Masons'/Goldsmiths' *Herod / Magi* (16), most of the Spurriers' and
Lorimers' *Christ and the Doctors* (20), the Curriers' *Transfiguration* (23),
the Cappers' *Woman Taken in Adultery / Raising of Lazarus* (24), the
Bakers' *Last Supper* (27), the Saddlers' *Harrowing of Hell* (37) and the
Potters' *Pentecost* (43). At least one of the plays in this group, the *Woman
Taken in Adultery / Raising of Lazarus*, seems in its present form to be, like
the *Crucifixion*, the result of an amalgamation of two episodes that feature
earlier as discrete plays in the *Ordo Paginarum* lists (70, pp. 441–2), and
could well be another part of the same campaign to reduce the number of
separate components in the cycle. Other plays in the group have interesting
compositional and stylistic links which have recently come to light. The

Abraham and Isaac and the *Moses and Pharaoh* both rely to differing extents on a specific source, a northern vernacular narrative poem of around 1400 (which also happens to be in the same twelve-line stanza), now known as the *Middle English Metrical Paraphrase of the Old Testament* (*139, 141*). The *Moses and Pharaoh* is in turn linked to its closest figural relative in the cycle, the *Harrowing of Hell*, by specific structural and verbal echoes, particularly in the respective treatments of Pharaoh and Satan (*138*, p. 154; *141*, pp. 20–1).

Turning to the other play in the Passion sequence under consideration here, the Tilemakers' *Christ before Pilate 2: The Judgement*, it is also possible, with the help of recent research in the documents (*161*), to date the period of the writer's work fairly specifically. It appears that from at least the time of the original *Ordo Paginarum* until 1422, the events portrayed in the extant play, together with others that have not survived,[7] were separate pageants brought forth by different guilds. Between 1422–3 and 1432 a series of documents in the Memorandum Book records the progressive acquisition of responsibility for the episode as a whole by the Tilemakers, during which time it appears that the new play came into being, perhaps developing through more than one phase. The end product, the extant text *Christ before Pilate 2* recorded in the Register a generation or so later, is thus very likely to date from the decade between 1422 and 1432. It could, therefore, be exactly contemporary with the revision of the *Crucifixion*, and, though the documents do not say so explicitly, it seems likewise to have been written as a result of a prevailing desire to simplify the organisation of the cycle.

The Tilemakers' pageant is devoted to the events between Jesus's return from Herod's court and Pilate's decision to hand him over to the Jewish authorities for execution. It includes an apocryphal episode, elaborately developed from a brief allusion in the contemporary narrative poem the *Northern Passion*, to the legend that the banners held by the soldiers at Pilate's court bowed down, and that Pilate and the High Priests involuntarily sprang to their feet when Jesus was brought in. The script was one of the longest in the cycle, running to over 500 lines when complete (a leaf now missing from the manuscript has carried away some fifty), and in the play as we have it only one short speech of eight lines is given to Jesus. Most of it is devoted to the ceremoniously wordy manoeuvrings of the High Priests and the evasions of Pilate, which break down suddenly into a prolonged scourging scene of ferocious violence:

> PILATUS   Why suld I deme to dede þan withoute deseruyng in dede?
> But I haue herde al haly why in hertes ȝe hym hate.
> He is fautles, in faith, and so God mote me spede
> I graunte hym my gud will to gang on his gate.

CAIPHAS	Nought so ser, for wele ʒe it wate,
	To be kyng he claymeth, with croune,
	And whoso stoutely will steppe to þat state
	ʒe suld deme ser, to be dong doune
	And dede.
PILATUS	Sir, trulye þat touched to treasoune,
	And or I remewe he rewe sall þat reasoune,
	And or I stalke or stirre fro þis stede.
	Sir knyghtis þat ar comly, take þis caystiff in keping,
	Skelpe hym with scourges and with skathes hym scorne.
	Wrayste and wrynge hym to, for wo to he be wepyng,
	And þan bryng hym before vs as he was beforne.
I MILES	He may banne þe tyme he was borne,
	Sone sall he be serued as ʒe saide vs.
ANNA	Do wappe of his wedis þat are worne.
II MILES	All redy ser, we haue arayde vs.
	Haue done,
	To þis broll late vs buske vs and brayde vs
	As ser Pilate has propirly prayde vs.
III MILES	We sall sette to hym sadly sone.

(Play 33, lines 324–47)

(*Pilate* Why should I condemn him to death, then, if he doesn't deserve it? But I have heard in full how you hate him in your hearts. So help me God, he is innocent, for certain. He has my ready permission to be on his way. *Caiaphas* By no means, sir, for as you know well, he claims to be a crowned king, and whosoever will boldly lay claim to that dignity, you should judge, sir, to be struck down and put to death. *Pilate* Sir, that indeed appertains to treason, and before I go he will repent that claim – before I move or stir from this place. You noble knights, take charge of this offender, lash him with whips and hurt him with blows. Twist him and wrench him, too, until he cries with pain, and then bring him again before us. *1st Soldier* he will curse the day he was born – soon he shall be treated as you command. *Annas* Rip off his tattered clothes. *2nd Soldier* Sir, we are already well prepared. Enough – let us hasten and apply ourselves to this wretch, as Sir Pilate has personally commanded us. *3rd Soldier* Soon we shall deal with him diligently.)

The metre is distinctive: the line consists, when fully extended, of a four-stress long alliterative line, all four stressed syllables being commonly reinforced by alliteration, a a ‖ a a, rather than the 'classical' a a ‖ a x pattern favoured by most fourteenth-century writers of alliterative poetry, such as Langland and the *Gawain* poet. Unstressed syllables tend to be numerous and irregularly distributed. It is not really appropriate to speak of the metre in terms of syllabic scansion, but the unstressed syllables are commonly paired before an alliterating stave ('hym my *gud* will to *gang* on his *gate*'), lending the dialogue an anapaestic drive, and probably making it easier for the actors to memorise. In its own time it was dubbed 'tumbling' verse in remarks attributed to the poet-king James I of Scotland, and a taste for the long alliterative line combined with complicated stanza forms seems to have been prevalent in Scotland and northern England during the fifteenth century. The analysis of the stanza form here is abab₄bcbc₃d₁ccd₃, and to provide over 500 lines of alliterative dialogue in this shape must have been no small challenge to the dramatist. But in spite of the artificiality of the mode, the natural, demotic tone of the exchanges is very marked. The use of spare lines or half-lines to pad out the verses or achieve the stanzas is avoided, the phatic expressions, on the contrary, being assimilated to every-day speech rhythms, and sometimes carrying a resonance beyond them-selves. Lines and phrases like 'He is fautles, *in faith*, and *so God mote me spede*' and 'Sir knyghtis þat ar comly ...' carry an ironic weight in this context.

More arresting, however, is the authentic sense of psychological move-ment captured in the texture of the verse. Pilate's genuine or affected exasperation with the continuous importunities of the High Priests is most effectively communicated in his turning of a real question into a rhetorical one, not waiting for an answer:

> Why suld I deme to dede þan withoute deseruyng in dede?
> But I haue herde al haly why in hertes ȝe hym hate.

Such evasions are called to a halt by Caiaphas, the senior and more calculat-ing of the two High Priests, and the observant actor will notice the carefully placed 'ser's (lines 328, 331), which are minor features in the extended apparatus of deadly *politesse* Caiaphas employs throughout the play, con-verging here upon the unanswerable point, that Jesus, in claiming to be king, has challenged the Roman governor's own authority. In contrast with Caiaphas, Annas's taste for physical violence is instantly unveiled, for as soon as the order for the scourging has been given, he calls (true mark of the sadist in office) to see the naked flesh (line 343). After the scourging comes the now-famous moment in the play when, returning to the biblical narra-tive, Pilate is presented with the bowl wherein to wash his hands, an act whose symbolic significance is unconsciously embellished with a quotidian proverbial gloss in the obsequiousness to the servant who brings it:

> Here is all, ser, þat ȝe for sende.
> Wille ȝe wasshe whill þe watir is hote?
>
> (Play 33, lines 442–3)

Like the *Crucifixion* play of 1422, the script provided for the Tilemakers at much the same time depends for its effect on an audience's fine attunement to the minutiae of a distinctive style of dramatic poetry. Other plays in the Passion sequence written in the long alliterative line (though the stanza forms vary widely) are the Cutlers' *Conspiracy* (26), the Cordwainers' *Agony in the Garden and the Betrayal* (28), the Bowers' and Fletchers' *Christ before Annas and Caiaphas* (29), the Tapiters' and Couchers' *Christ before Pilate 1: The Dream of Pilate's Wife* (30), the Litsters' *Christ before Herod* (31) and the Cooks' and Waterleaders' *Remorse of Judas* (32), any of which will repay the kind of close attention focused upon the episode from the Tilemakers' script above. Attractive though it is to attribute this group to one writer, it should be borne in mind that several other plays, whose subject matter did not perhaps lend itself to similar treatment, are nevertheless written in a comparable metrical form.

A variation on the alliterative mode within the Passion sequence is found in the Butchers' *Death of Christ* (Play 36), one of the most impressive plays in the cycle, where the number of alliterating staves to the line, in a characteristically complex stanza, is reduced from the usual four to three in the *frons*, ababbcbc$_3$d$_1$eeee$_2$d$_3$:

> On roode am I ragged and rente,   *cross; torn; gashed*
> þou synfull sawle, for thy sake;   (Play 36, lines 120–1)

Though commonly assumed to be by the same dramatist as the alliterative Passion plays listed above, the *Death of Christ* actually differs from them considerably in both dramatic technique and the handling of the verse. A series of devotional icons familiar to the audience from the visual arts of the period – the Man of Sorrows, the lamenting Virgin, the Deposition and so on – are caused to melt into one another through a metrical medium that is best described as lyrical, the sublimity of the subject finding its most eloquent expression, then as in later ages, in image and music (71, p. 222).

We may end with the beginning of the cycle. The superb Barkers' pageant of the *Creation and Fall of the Angels* (Play 1, and cf. Plays 40 and 44 for the same metre) is composed in yet another variety of the alliterative medium, a kind of rhetorical and expository 'high style', with no less attention to verbal nuance and structural detail than in the Passion plays. Here, the basic formal units are the stanzas taken as a whole, which are apportioned to the speakers on a numerological basis according to their roles, and in harmony with the symbolic development of the action. Since all the characters were supernatural, the actors would have worn masks, and the otherworldliness of the visual impact is reinforced by the stylisation of the language. God and the loyal angels in heaven speak throughout in complete stanzas, whilst the rebellious angels divide the stanza amongst them as they fall into hell. The effect is to absorb the audience's attention to dramatic language in a way quite different from the alliterative Passion plays, but no less imaginatively inventive (142).

God the Father opens this first pageant and the cycle as a whole, bringing together, as had been suggested above, the dawn of creation and time with the annual dawning of Corpus Christi Day in the city of York:

Ego sum Alpha et O: vita, via, veritas primus et novissimus.

The opening line, pregnant with allusion, stands as a kind of epigraph to the cycle as a whole: 'I am the way, and the truth, and the life: (no one cometh unto the Father, but by me', John 14.6), from Christ's parting words to the disciples after the Last Supper, is conflated with 'I am the Alpha and the Omega (the first and the last, the beginning and the end'), the closing words of the Apocalypse (22.13). The audience is invited to contemplate from this first, but effectively extra-temporal, moment the two events which at the same time form the structural cruxes of the cycle about to be played, and constitute the central facts of their spiritual lives – the episodes where Christ, having come from instituting the Eucharist (literally, Corpus Christi), embarks upon the work of redemption in the Passion – and then his general judgement of all mankind at the end of time on Doomsday.

NOTES

1 For references see 70, pp. 21–2. Heather Swanson, *Medieval Artisans: an Urban Class in Late Medieval England* (Oxford: Basil Blackwell, 1989) is largely devoted to the development of guild organisation in later medieval York.

2 See further 140. It is not known how the guilds came to be assigned to their particular episodes, some being more or less 'appropriate' to the craft, others seemingly unconnected; see 70, pp. 29–30, and 159.

3 A hint of York's wide influence resides in the fact that its version of *Christ and the Doctors* (Play 20) is echoed variously in the Chester, Towneley and Coventry plays on the same subject (references in 70, p. 438). The 'Shrewsbury Fragments' (see in 85), which are probably from the Lichfield area, include dialogue also found in the York *Shepherds* (Play 25). For the more pervasive influence of York on the Towneley/Wakefield plays see below, chapter 5.

4 A sixteenth-century copy of the Scriveners' 'original' of their *Incredulity of Thomas* (Play 41) survives at York (145).

5 A concordance to the text, based on the 1982 edition (70), has since been published (109, including corrections, pp. xxxi–ii), and a selection of the plays in modern spelling (71) has also been issued.

6 The best transcription of the *Ordo* so far published is in 158, pp. 16–26. The introduction to the *Ordo* section of the facsimile gives some improved or amended readings, and cf. Meredith, in 161; but a revised transcription of the whole with a detailed commentary remains a desideratum.

7 One of the casualties of this revision, an early York Millers' pageant of the soldiers dicing for Christ's garment, is recognisable in the Towneley/Wakefield repertoire as the *Processus Talentorum* (163). The Towneley *Judas* also seems likely to have been a York pageant of this era (see below, p. 147).

4

DAVID MILLS

The Chester cycle

INTRODUCTION

Critics of medieval drama locked into an evolutionary thesis of dramatic development that valued 'realism' and 'comedy' as marks of later and more highly developed dramatic 'organisms' found Chester's less exuberant style reflective of a primitive, undeveloped form of drama characteristic of an early date of composition. They were strengthened in this view by a persistent tradition in Chester that the plays were the oldest in England. Since the 1950s, however, the myth of early composition has been exposed and, after re-examining the internal and external documentary evidence relating to the plays, recent critics believe that Chester's cycle in its present form was the product of the sixteenth century and hence probably the latest of the English cycle texts. Moreover, there are indications in the prefatory Banns of the post-Reformation period that the cycle was even then considered different both from 'sophisticated' contemporary drama and from the cycle plays of other towns that were falling under disapproval because of their association with Roman Catholic doctrine.

Chester's distinctive interpretation of cyclic form and function should therefore be recognised as a conscious creation with its own goals and strengths. Freed from the condescension of earlier critics, Chester's achievement can now be appreciated as an attempt to articulate the mystery cycle as a coherent dramatic genre rather than as a conveniently loose chronological framework for the containment of dramatic and thematic diversity. In contrast to the sometimes urgent demands for empathetic response made by York and Towneley, Chester holds its material at a contemplative distance, inviting its audience to ponder its plays calmly and thoughtfully.

TEXT

From the later sixteenth century Chester's cycle was considered to be worth preserving as a book in its own right. Indeed, only two of our manuscripts may date from any earlier period. (73, vol. 1, pp. ix–xxvii). Two grimy fragments with lines from the beginning of Play 18 (*The Resurrection*), found in a book-binding in Manchester's Central Library (MS M), have been variously ascribed to the fifteenth and to the late sixteenth/early seventeenth centuries; and a complete version of Play 23 (*Antichrist*), preserved among the Peniarth manuscripts of the National Library of Wales, Aberystwyth (MS P), is probably from the later fifteenth century, though its value has been reduced by the inking-over and occasional alteration of its text by someone during the last century. With these two exceptions, all our other manuscripts of the plays – six in all, each signed and dated – postdate 1575, the year of Chester's final performance.

The earliest of these, Huntington MS 2, now in the Henry E. Huntington Library, California (MS HM), was written in 1591 by 'Edward Gregorie, scholler at Bunburye'. Bunbury is a village near Chester, and Gregorie served for a time as churchwarden under its strongly Puritanical minister, Richard Roe; he was perhaps the second son of a yeoman-farmer from Beeston, within Bunbury parish. The next three manuscripts in date were all written by the same man, George Bellin of Chester's Ironmongers' Company. Bellin was a man of some antiquarian interests, a scribe to a number of Chester's companies and the parish clerk of Holy Trinity Church, Chester (179, pp. xxxv–xxxvi). His two copies of the complete cycle, Additional MS 10305 (MS A) made in 1592 and Harley MS 2013 (MS R) of 1600, are both in the British Library. Bellin's third manuscript, written in 1599 (MS C), is of Play 16, *The Trial and Flagellation of Christ*, which was the responsibility of the Bowers, Coopers, Fletchers and Stringers; Bellin was clerk to the Coopers' Company and the play survives bound in an Apprentice Book which the Company still owns. The fifth manuscript, Bodley MS 175 (MS B) in the Bodleian Library, Oxford, was copied in 1604 by William Bedford, the clerk to Chester's Brewers' Company and parish clerk of St Peter's Church, Chester. Finally, in 1607 the scholarly rector of St Michael's Church, Chester, James Miller, who was also the precentor at Chester Cathedral, completed what must be termed an 'edition' of the cycle which had been begun – perhaps at Miller's instigation – by two other scribes whose identities are not known, that text is now Harley MS 2124 (MS H) in the British Library. Possibly this manuscript was intended as an addition to Miller's collection of books on music, theology and history mentioned in his will of 1618.

This spate of late copying may attest a number of impulses: the pride and affection with which the cycle continued to be regarded in the Chester area, particularly by clerics and devout laymen with scholarly aspirations; the strong antiquarian movement in Chester, which valued the plays as part of the city's history and traditions; and interest in the play text as a book for private reading as well as a piece of practical theatre. Mistaken beliefs about the cycle's authorship may also have contributed to the interest. It is remarkable that a text of the cycle was available for copying over a quarter of a century after performances ceased. No other English cycle attracted such scholarly interest, and consequently no other cycle text is attested in so many manuscripts.

The manuscripts present modern editors with the kind of decisions more usually encountered when editing literary than dramatic texts. The first EETS editors, Hermann Deimling and Dr Matthews, offered a critical text based on Miller's 1607 copy in the belief that its readings were generally both 'older' and 'better', although on occasion they 'emended' Miller's text in accordance with their understanding of those terms.[1] The most recent edition (73, vol. I, pp. xxvii–xxxiii) rejected these criteria and their under-lying assumptions, preferring Gregorie's 1591 text, unemended, as base because, as the most conservative, it simplifies the problem of presenting variant readings to the reader. The editors elsewhere argue (182, pp. 1–86) that all our extant manuscripts derive from a lost manuscript which had been used as a working document for a number of years. By the late sixteenth century that document was a record of repeated revision and selection, with words, phrases, long sections and even whole plays obscured, emended, or offered in alternative forms – in effect, 'a cycle of cycles'. When copying, the scribes made decisions at such points according to their differ-ent priorities and critical intelligence, and allowance must be made for these differences. Gregorie, the earliest, was also the most scrupulous and accurate in deciphering the text, preferring wherever possible a 'non-interventionist' approach. Miller, the latest, did not hesitate to emend intelligently according to clear priorities – meaning, rhyme, verse-movement, stanza form, structural coherence, etc. – and his version therefore contains a number of unique readings, some very extensive (73, vol. I, Appendix I). Bellin's and Bedford's versions are closer to that of Gregorie but treat the text less consistently. Their variants, however, can give important clues to 'original' readings.

AUTHORSHIP AND ORIGINS OF THE CYCLE

Writing in 1618–19, the Chester antiquarian David Rogers (on whom, see *179*, pp. xxiii–xxxvi) states:

> In the yere when this Sir Iohn Arneway was mayor of Chester, the whtson
> playes made by a monke of Chester Abbay named Rondoll, was by the said
> maior publıshed and caused to be sett forth and played at the Charges of
> euery Company within the said Cittie with theire Pagiantes ... And the said
> Rondoll the author in the prolouge before his booke of the whitson playes
> doth shew more fully.   (179, p. 326)

Rogers writes as if the 'book of the plays' was a literary work with an
'author' and a 'prologue' which could still be inspected in 1618–19. The
'prologue' was certainly the post-Reformation Banns, the verse-announce-
ment which was proclaimed in Chester's streets on St George's Day in the
year of a performance (text in 182, pp. 285–310). Both Bellin in 1600 and
Bedford preface their cycle texts with these Banns, and Rogers himself provides two other copies, one of 1609 now in Chester City Archive (MS CH)
and the other, Harley MS 1944 (MS L), in the British Library. While these
Banns do not correspond exactly to the text as we now have it (178),[2] they
contain and sanction a persistent version of the plays' origins which Rogers
describes above.

According to this version the responsibility for originating the plays was
shared between two men, Sir John Arneway and Randle Higden. During
the sixteenth century Arneway's name appeared on Chester's mayoral lists
as the city's first mayor, in 1328. But in 1594 – after performances had
ceased – William Aldersey established that the city's first mayor had actually
been Sir Walter Lynett, and that Arneway's mayoralties had occupied
successive years from c. 1278 to 1288. Higden was a monk who had entered
the Benedictine abbey of St Werburgh in Chester (later, the cathedral) in
1299 and died in 1363/4. The author of a number of Latin works, he became
famous for his universal Latin history of the world, the *Polychronicon*,
which was translated into English twice in the later fourteenth century. One
of those translations, by the Wycliffite John of Trevisa in 1387, was printed
by William Caxton in 1482 and remained influential in the sixteenth century.
Though the two men's dates were historically incompatible, as long as the
error in the mayoral lists went undetected, it was possible to claim that the
plays began in Arneway's mayoralty of 1327/8, making Chester the oldest
cycle in England. F. M. Salter conclusively disposed of that fabrication in
1955 (191, pp. 32–42). It had itself replaced an earlier official ascription, in a
proclamation by Chester's Town Clerk, William Newhall, in 1531/2, (179,
pp. 27–8), which retained Arneway as the initiator of productions but
affirmed that the text was 'devised and made' by another monk of St Werburgh's, Henry Francis. That name appears on three lists of monks, of 1377,
1379 and 1382, but nothing is known about the man or his possible connection with the plays, and his dates are also incompatible with Arneway's.

The Banns weave an interesting case around Higden. They defend the cycle as an early attempt to bring the Scriptures to the people in the vernacular at a time when the Bible was available only in its Latin form and to priests, and hence as an initiative compatible with Reformation ideals. Higden is reconstructed as a monk of Protestant inclination who knew his Bible (Banns, line 8), who was willing to face possible death for his evangelising zeal in bringing the Scriptures to the people (line 25), and who taught sound doctrine (line 27). Though these claims are spurious and propagandist, they suggest a determination to defend the cycle against possible attack from Reformers by referring its origins to the two most famous citizens of Chester; they attest the contemporary local belief that the plays were ancient and unusual; and they imply curiosity about their origins and purpose. They also suggest that the plays might be defensible in their antiquity as a civic tradition, and in their material as a now outmoded but once revolutionary attempt to disseminate the true Scriptures. The Banns attribute non-scriptural material either to other recognised authorities (lines 147–50) or to a desire to inject light relief (lines 94–5), and emphasise the alterity of the plays in language (lines 49–55) and performance (lines 192–208). Moreover, although phrases such as 'not altered in menye poyntes from the olde fashion' (line 156) suggest that the text had changed within living memory, the belief that beneath that adapted text lay the one vernacular work of a reputable Chester historian may have been another factor impelling the authorities to preserve the play-book and the local antiquarians to continue copying it for private reference and use. Even though the fiction of Higden's authorship cannot be sustained, it offers a further indication of the thematic and structural coherence of the cycle which seems to predicate the controlling hand of some author or overall reviser.

SOURCES

Both the traditions of authorship and the nature of the cycle itself may be linked to the question of source. Chester's primary source was, of course, the Bible, supplemented on occasion from the apocryphal New Testament gospels which supply features such as the midwives at the Nativity (Play 6, lines 469–563), and from familiar standard compilations such as Peter Comestor's *Historia Scholastica* or Jacob da Voragine's *Legenda Aurea* in which are found incidents such as the appearance of the Virgin and Child to the Emperor Octavian (Play 6, lines 185–372, 644–98). But to a greater extent than the other cycles, Chester signals the 'authenticity' of its material to the audience by numerous explicit allusions to scriptural passages and by direct quotations from the Vulgate text (*182*, pp. 99–110).

Most of this material was so widely available that it is now impossible to establish a single immediate source for the cycle, even if (as is unlikely) such a source ever existed. Early critics, noting the presence of corrupted French passages in the cycle and misled by the supposed early date of composition, suggested derivation from French drama, but such links are tenuous; the French serves primarily as a stylistic class-marker signalling that the speaker is a worldly ruler, in the same way that Latin is used as the mark of the spiritual authority by God, angels, clerics (*182*, pp. 89–90).[3]

But one English vernacular poem, *A Stanzaic Life of Christ*, provides material in at least seven of Chester's plays (Plays, 6, 8, 9, 11, 12, 17, and 20), and possibly other less distinctive material elsewhere.[4] Although the modern editorial title aligns that poem with the many other medieval works about Christ's life, this poetic account is liturgical rather than biographical in organisation. Its format is that of the liturgical year, beginning at the Nativity rather than Advent and ending abruptly (and possibly incompletely) at Whitsun. Most of its material derives from the *Legenda Aurea*, though significantly it also draws upon Higden's *Polychronicon*. Its three extant manuscripts, all of the later fifteenth century, evidence ownership by Cheshire families. It is usually therefore assumed that the *Life* was written at Chester and that a playwright/reviser incorporated material from this local text of limited circulation into a large-scale revision of the cycle. Neither its date of composition nor the date and circumstances of the incorporation of its material into the cycle can now be determined.

Although Chester's borrowings are distinctive, they constitute only a small and unrepresentative section of the 10,840 lines of the *Life* and the material has, moreover, been transformed in its adaptation from poetry to drama. The poem is not an obvious source-book for a playwright, for, as Elizabeth Salter puts it: 'There is little proof that the poet was interested in dramatic dialogue and event, or in compassionate treatment of the Humanity of Christ. His concern is with the moral teaching to be drawn from the events of Christ's life.'[5] Chester's selective use of the *Life* may therefore suggest the playwright's didactic priorities and desire for distinctiveness. The incorporation of material from a text far removed from those meditational works springing from Franciscan piety which seem to influence other cycles implies an intention to educate by information and explication rather than by empathy and catharsis.

Both cycle and poem generate thoughtful reflection. Both predicate a mixed audience of laity and clerics – made explicit by the Devil in Play 24 who self-consciously cites his biblical text in Latin 'which wordes to clearkes here present I wyll rehearse' (lines 579–80). Both defensively specify the authorities for their material:

> That Clerkus shal not after say   *later*
> these newe fables wrote a fonne   *fool*
>   (lines 31–2)

as the *Life* explains. So the cycle, in addition to its numerous biblical references, also cites 'Freere Bartholemewe' (Play 6, line 565), St Gregory (Play
12, line 170), St Augustine (Play 12, line 285) and St Jerome (Play 22, line
263) to authenticate explications. Both manifest an interest in the origins of
contemporary ceremonies, sacraments and rituals – in the cycle, marriage
(Play 2, lines 157–60), tithing (Play 4, lines 133–6), baptism (Play 4, lines
197–200), Candlemas (Play 11, lines 143–50), the Eucharist (Play 15, lines
73–104) and the Creed (Play 21); the cycle has the further advantage of being
able to make links with the liturgy by incorporating liturgical song, to a
greater extent than any other English cycle (*189*). The *Life* 'is intended to be
read privately as well as aloud';[6] one reason for the late copies of the cycle
text may be that it too was regarded as suitable for private devotional study.
Miller's manuscript includes supporting biblical references and quotations
alongside the text of the opening plays, and a Latin side-note in all
manuscripts authenticating the fifteen Signs of Judgement (Play 22, line
260 + Latin) would be available only to a reader. That impression is furthered
by the cycle's stanzaic uniformity: the majority of the text is written in the
'Chester stanza', $aaa_4b_3aaa_4b_3$ or $aaa_4b_3ccc_4b_3$ (*182*, pp. 311–18), giving a
metrical regularity more characteristic of a devotional poem than a play-
book.

Chester's awareness of civic drama in other parts of the country is suggested by its isolated borrowings from other plays (*182*, pp. 90–5). Lines
240–7 of Play 9 correspond to lines 750–3 and 764–7 of the Coventry
Shearmen's Pageant. The episode of 'Christ Before the Doctors' which concludes Play 11 is common also to Coventry, Towneley and York. 'The Sacrifice of Isaac' with which Play 4 concludes is an adaptation of the version
found in the Brome Hall commonplace book, although the original provenance of the Brome play is unknown. Such correspondences strengthen the
impression that in its final form Chester represents a conscious attempt to
reshape cyclic drama as a textually controlled genre in reaction to models
available elsewhere.

STRUCTURE AND PERFORMANCE

The starting-point for a cyclic dramatist was the reassuring framework of
universal history from the beginning of Creation to the end of historical
time. The disadvantage of that framework for artistic purposes was the
intractable simplicity of chronological/narrative sequence. The 'artistic

[*artificiale*] beginning' commended by Geoffrey of Vinsauf, whereby a poet could open with 'later material' and introduce 'earlier' material by subsequent allusion, was not an available option. But Chester experiments with that historical structure, breaking up its monolithic effect by a number of interconnected structural markers while strengthening its overall coherence.

The cycle's performance history is an important consideration in this restructuring process (*178*; *182*, pp. 165–202). From the earliest reference to the cycle in 1422 (when it was already established and being performed by the city companies) (*179*, pp. 6–7) and throughout the sporadic sightings of its production in Chester's sparse fifteenth-century records until a final reference of 1472 (*179*, pp. 13–15), the play was associated with the Corpus Christi Day procession from the church of St Mary-on-the-Hill to the church of St John. It was apparently performed in its entirety on that day, and, on the slim evidence of probable timing, the absence of records of processional performance, and its replacement in the sixteenth century by a play performed by the clergy at St John's, it has been suggested that Chester's Corpus Christi play was performed only when the procession reached St John's.

When the play is first mentioned in sixteenth-century records, in 1521 (*179*, pp. 24–5), it had become the 'whitsun playe', pluralised by 1531–2 as 'the plaies' (*179*, pp. 27–8). Subsequent records indicate performance in three parts – on the Monday, Tuesday and Wednesday of Whitsun week – processionally, along a different route from that of the Corpus Christi procession. The wagon route was conveniently downhill. The first station was at the gate of St Werburgh's Abbey, the ecclesiastical centre of the city, in front of the clergy. The second was at the High Cross in front of St Peter's Church where Chester's town hall, the Pentice, stood and where the mayor and aldermen could watch the performance. The route continued along Watergate Street and thence through the side lanes to Bridge Street, perhaps for the general citizenry.

We do not know why the plays were transferred to Whitsun or why they were divided into three parts. There is no evidence to date the change of occasion, but there is some indication that the move to a three-day performance was recent in 1531/2. A cause or by-product of the latter change was the possibility that companies performing on different days could share a single wagon, and our first recorded 'wagon-sharing agreement' dates from 1531/2 (*179*, pp. 26–7). The cycle was an occasional event, not annual, and subject to the approval of the city authorities, but the three-day division seems to have continued until the last performance, in 1575. Then the cycle was performed in censored form over four days at Midsummer, the time of Chester's secular Midsummer Shew. Subsequently, Sir John Savage, the mayor in 1575, had to answer to the Privy Council for the production (*182*, pp. 192–4).

Whatever the reason for these changes, Chester's authorities had decided to separate their cycle from its traditional association with Corpus Christi and to break the chronologically continuous play of universal history into three distinct but interconnected parts. The cycle was now enacted not under the sacramental pressure of the Eucharist but in the context of the Whitsun commemoration of the coming of the Holy Spirit and of the following Trinity Sunday in honour of the triune God. The change also has artistic implications, for the tripartite division changes the audience's perception of cyclic cohesion. Each day's production becomes a distinct unit moving towards its own affirmative conclusion. The first day's performance encompasses the action from Play 1, *The Creation and Fall of the Angels*, to Play 9, *The Magi's Gifts*, a formal and symbolic act of homage to the infant Christ. The second day's action continues from Play 10, *The Massacre of the Innocents*, to Play 17, *The Harrowing of Hell*, the triumphal accomplishment of Christ's redemptive mission. The third day takes up the historical action with Play 18, *The Resurrection*, to culminate in the impressive *Doomsday*, Play 24.

UNIVERSAL HISTORY

Perhaps because this tripartite division cuts across our perception of the framework of universal history, Chester insists strongly upon the integrity of that framework. Its first lines are a statement of its axioms, set apart formally from the remainder of God's opening speech as if delivered by a disembodied voice before God enters and identifies himself:

> Ego sum alpha et oo,
> primus et novissimus.
> It is my will it shoulde be soe;
> hit is, yt was, it shalbe thus.   (lines 1–4)

These lines describe the confined and providentially controlled world of the universal history. As 'alpha et oo' (alpha and omega), God locates himself beyond the start and end of time, and through this claim the player-God affirms his role of initiating and terminating the dramatic action. The simple monosyllables of the English lines assert that in all historical time – present, past and future – events move at God's will, and hence that the subsequent dramatic action lies in the control of the player-God. From the outset the dramatist establishes God as initiator and contriver whose authority is unchallengeable and whose Will will be supreme. History is an action shaped within the mind of God and the cycle offers a selection of his significant interventions.

The Latin is the first of many instances in which the cycle reaches out to the authenticating text of God's book which will underpin all statements of importance and which, as the devils indicate in Play 24, lines 557–80 + s.d., contains the ground-rules for God's activities. He cannot renege on his own Word. Hence the cycle concludes not with the end of time at the completion of Judgement but with an a-historical coda by the four evangelists, corresponding to these opening lines, which exhorts the audience to confirm from their gospels the truth of what they have witnessed in the play (Play 24, lines 677 + s.d.–708). As God's hidden purpose has been progressively revealed, increasing responsibility has been laid upon human free will. Post-Pentecostal man has been given the historical revelation on which to base faith, the Eucharist for its perpetuation, the model of Christ for charity, culminating, in the final play of time past (Play 21), with the gift of Holy Spirit for confirmation. That process, only partially revealed to former ages, is now available to all in God's book. As the final three plays show, man is free to choose his course knowingly. The risen dead already know their judgement and acknowledge its justice. As God concurs with the claims of the Devil at Judgement, a kind of accommodation between the opposing forces of Play 1 is finally reached.

Within this framework, the threefold division of time enables the cycle to focus in turn on each Person of the Trinity – the interventions of God the Father on Day 1, the Incarnation of God the Son on Day 2, and the coming of God the Holy Spirit on Day 3 – so that the tripartite division of the cycle's artistic structure becomes a kind of mimetic trinity. The cycle's trinitarian concern is stressed in the continuation of God's opening speech, which defines the Godhead in terms of its attributes and constituent Persons. Loaded with Latin terms and Latinate vocabulary, and embellished by resonant alliteration and an insistent rhyme scheme, lines 5–35 of Play 1 sound impressive, but their sense if fully recoverable only from the page because the vocabulary is abstruse and the theological concepts technical. God reveals himself as timeless, the origin of all being, the indivisible Trinity, the source of wisdom and grace, omnipotent, providential and established in truth. These attributes will through time seem questioned as sin enters creation and God's justice inevitably appears to conflict with his grace. The Trinity responds through time by manifesting itself sequentially in its three Persons, until finally the plan is complete, time and creation return cyclically to their Creator, and the opening unity of the Trinity and its attributes is reaffirmed.

The remainder of Play 1 addresses the theological issue of the origins of evil. God's style modulates towards a more colloquial level as he addresses his creation (cf. 'Nowe, Luciffer and Lightborne, loke lowely you bee', line

68) and sets roles for his players ('to walke aboute the Trenitie', line 67), forbidding them to know why ('cast never comprehension', line 70). In apparent foreknowledge, he extends creation – in dramatic terms, his set-building – to the world (line 73) and the dungeon of Hell (line 74), warns Lucifer and the others of the penalty for disobedience and then vacates the Director's chair and leaves the set, promising to return (lines 110–25). In theological terms God's warning emphasises that the angels can choose, and so explains how evil can enter a system created by a God of perfect goodness. The responsibility rests with the will of Lucifer, who can choose something outside God's comprehension by casting himself in the role of antagonist. God's lament,

> A, wicked pryde! A, woo worth thee, woo!
> My meirth thou has made amisse. *joy; spoilt*
> I may well suffer: my will is not soe
> that they shoulde parte this from my blisse. *thus*
> A, pryde! Why mighte thou not braste in two?
> Why did the that? why did they thus? *they*
>
> (lines 274–9)

is a statement of bewilderment. God knows that pride has caused the rebellion and that the fallen angels chose pride because he gave them choice; but he does not understand why they should make that choice. Though he grieves, he is bound inevitably to separate those who follow their will from those who follow his. The play is thus a prefatory statement of the origins of evil which prepares the way for God's education of man's will to make appropriate choices.

This progressive educational process falls into three stages. At the centre of the first day's performance is the chosen vehicle of God's grace, the Jews. In secular terms the cycle traces the origins of the Jewish nation from the covenant with Abraham, unquestioningly obedient to God's mysterious wishes (Play 4), to the emergence of a conquering nation under Moses, the custodians of God's Law and of his Messianic prophecies (Play 5). But a subsidiary theme to the rise of the Jews is the promise to the Gentiles, carried in the characters of Melchisadek (Play 4), Balaam (Play 5), Octavian (Play 6) and the Magi (Plays 8–9). Already, in the latter part of the day, the Jews are a subject-nation and the Roman Emperor Octavian is in command. Mary witnesses in a vision the withdrawal of favour from the Jews (Play 6, lines 437–52) which will be the subject of the next day's plays. On the second day, when the Originator of action is drawn into the dramatic narrative as the incarnate Christ, the plays extend the scepticism and hostility already evident in Plays 8 and 9 of the first day. Herod's unsuccessful attempt to kill the infant Jesus which begins the second day is the first manifestation of the threat to Jesus's life that is finally accomplished at the Crucifixion in Play 16A in which the hostility of the Jewish nation developing from Play 12 finds its climax. The irony of the death of Herod's own son and of the king himself (Play 10, lines 377–457) is paralleled by the irony inherent in Play 17, which shows how the apparent success of the Jews has effected the triumphal fulfilment of Christ's purpose. The third day completes the revelation of the Godhead in Play 21, *Pentecost*. The Resurrection itself is not enough. Christ enters and departs mysteriously as if testing the apostles, and finds doubt and vacillation even among his closest followers. But with the gift of the Holy Spirit their faith is fully confirmed, the tenets of future belief are formulated and the Church's task of preaching the Gospel to all nations begins.

The opening play is marked as a prologue to the cycle by the absence of the otherwise ubiquitous Chester stanza. The historical action starts with Play 2, where a new beginning is signalled by God's repetition of the opening Latin of Play 1 at its start. Time also begins again as God re-creates and separates light from darkness as a physical act to mark the first day (Play 1, lines 290–7; Play 2, lines 9–16). The cycle is already beginning to play tricks with our sense of chronology. From Play 4 a contemporary figure, the Expositor, is admitted into the historical action to interpret the coded meaning of events and prophecies and add supplementary material, in Plays 4, 5, 6, 12 and 22. In Play 5, in Miller's version (73, vol. 1, Appendix IB), after the Gentile soothsayer Balaam, possessed by God, has delivered a Messianic prophecy, the play abruptly moves forward in time along a line of Jewish prophets, each adding his prophetic utterance, and then reverts to the historical action with Balak's resigned acceptance of God's power (73, vol. 1, Appendix IB, lines 288 + Latin − 448). In a parallel time-shift in Play 22, following 'Pentecost', the action moves backwards in time to the Old Testament prophets of Antichrist.

Our sense of chronology is also disturbed by abrupt shifts of time within the apparently continuous action of individual plays which, in a manner characteristic of Chester, incorporate two or more self-contained episodes. Thus, at Play 2, line 425, the action suddenly jumps forward over thirty years, from the expulsion from Eden to the killing of Abel. In Play 4 three incidents from different periods of Abraham's life are juxtaposed (see further below). In Play 5 we move without warning from the giving of the Law to the account of Balaam and Balak. In Play 11, twelve years historically separate the actions of the 'Presentation' and 'Christ Before the Doctors'. Other conflations are less obvious. Herod's gruesome death in Play 10 occurred many years after the Slaughter of the Innocents but here seems causatively linked to it. The grouping of Christ's appearances in Play 19 conceals the fact that Christ's appearance to doubting Thomas (lines 216–75) occurred eight days after his appearances at Emmaus (lines 1–143) and Jerusalem (lines 144–215) on the day of Resurrection. Such discontinuities emphasise that Chester's material is selected and grouped on a thematic rather than a chronological basis.

Play 13 illustrates the method well (see *192*, pp. 156–62; *135*, pp. 281–8). Its literal 'actions' manifest Jesus's compassion and charity in response to human need. A blind beggar receives from Jesus the means of regaining his sight; a friend of Jesus dies and, grieving for his death, Jesus brings him back to life. In both episodes Jesus requires belief in his Godhead, and the miracles become means of demonstrating the power of faith. But both serve primarily as 'signs' – events that 'signify' something else – demonstrating God's power and glory. They illustrate Jesus's opening speech in the play in which he affirms the unity of the Godhead ('my Father and I are all on', line 8) and his role of leading his followers from darkness into the light of life. That speech is constructed of passages from different places in St John's gospel, framed at the start and end by quotations in Latin from that gospel. Its five stanzas, set apart formally from the rest of the play as seven-line stanzas, ababbcc$_4$, supply a prologue whose literary images then take dramatic form in restoration from blindness and from death. The two episodes dramatised also belong to different parts of John's gospel (9.1–38; 11.1–46), and the discontinuity between them is emphasised by Jesus's sudden non-scriptural disappearance after line 284 ('statim evanescit Jesus') and the equally sudden entry of the lamenting Maria at line 301 with no indication of a change of time or scene. Her claim that 'in feeble tyme Christ yoode me froo' (line 303) is meaningless within this dramatic context. The severing of chronological and causative connections emphasises that the play's coherence lies at the thematic level. Given that, the order of events here is potentially arbitrary, though dramatically climactic.

Chester's time-shifts and discontinuities of action emphasise that in this cycle history is not a sequence of immediately contingent events but a construct made in the light of the two advents of God, Incarnation and Judgement. Though dramatised as an unfolding process, the cycle's structure is determined and unified by a series of correspondences retrospectively recognised in the fulfilment of the prophecies and signs of those advents. Adam begins the series of prophecies when, as promised in Play 2, lines 138–40, he relates after his Fall the vision of God's redemptive plan he received in Eden (Play 2, lines 437–72). The prophets of Miller's Play 5 (lines 288 + Latin – 432) foretell the first advent and its consequences, and the fulfilment of the prophecies is confirmed by the Doctor in Play 8 (lines 268 + Latin – 349). Simeon in Play 11 disbelieves Isaiah's prophecy of virgin birth and has its truth confirmed by a miracle, to his comic bewilderment. Jesus claims to fulfil prophecies (cf. Play 13, line 5; Play 19, lines 80–95 + Latin) and prophesies his second advent (Play 16, lines 45–50; Play 20, lines 137–52). Peter cites Judas's death as prophetic fulfilment (Play 21, lines 17–32 + Latin); prophets in Play 22 affirm the coming of Antichrist as a sign of Doomsday; and Antichrist ironically announces himself as the fulfilment of prophecy (Play 23, lines 17–24 + Latin, 40 + Latin − 56 + Latin).

Prophetic fulfilment is supplemented by the typological links made between Old and New Testament events by the learned Expositor. Speaking with post-Redemptive knowledge, he links for us the three discrete episodes from Abraham's life in Play 4 as prefigurations of tithing and the Eucharist, baptism and the sacrifice of the Son of God by the Father, all well-established interpretations. In Play 12 he explains the three temptations of Jesus as paralleling those of Adam – in gluttony, vainglory and covetousness – citing St Gregory as his authority (lines 169–216). Herod ironically reverses typology in appealing to the scriptural example of Athalia in Play 8, lines 332–5, for she was a traditional prefiguration of Herod in her destruction of the royal children (2 Kings 11.1) and died a terrible death herself.

The recurring devices of prophecy and typology, however, serve also to reinforce the strangeness of the events dramatised. The past is a time of marvels which defy normal human understanding. In Play 6, the *Nativity*, for example, an angel visits Mary and later Joseph; the Sibyl prophesies to the Emperor Octavian and later shows him a vision of the Virgin and Child in a star; Mary sees a vision on the way to Bethlehem. A sceptical midwife doubts the miracle of Mary's painless virgin birth; her hand withers as she attempts a gynaecological examination but is healed at her prayer to the newborn Christ. The Expositor tells of Rome's marvellous Temple of Peace devised by the Devil which collapsed at Christ's birth, of three suns in the sky and the ox and ass kneeling at the manger. These marvels are signs of Jesus's divinity, a means of communicating his identity to the people of that time and strengthening their belief. Jesus's miracles – knowing the inner thoughts of his enemies ('For godhead full in thee I see that knowes worke that doe wee', Play 12, lines 277–8); healing the blind ('If he of God were not, iwis, hee could never worke such thinges as this', Play 13, lines 223–4); raising the dead ('By verey signe nowe men maye see that thou arte Godes Sonne', Play 13, lines 476–7) – are inexplicable other than as demonstrations of his Godhead. As the Janitor in Play 14 says:

> For his marvayles leeve aye upon   *believe*
> that he is verey Godes Sonne
> although hee in this [worlde] wonne.   (lines 173–5)

His healing of Malchus almost convinces that sceptic (Play 15, lines 345–6), and posthumously his pierced side miraculously and symbolically gives sight to the blind Longinus in defiance of Caiaphas's wish to prove Christ's mortality (Play 16A, lines 372–407). These wonders prepare for the greatest signs of all, the Resurrection (Play 18), Christ's mysterious manifestations to the disciples (Plays 18–20), the Ascension (Play 20), and the coming of the Holy Spirit (Play 21). The past as here presented is a time of marvels, made more marvellous by the absence of interest in logical causation.

Nevertheless, such signs belong in the historical past. During the first advent, prophecies are fulfilled and typology superseded, and in their place Christ establishes the intrinsically powerful sacrament of the Eucharist:

> for knowe you nowe, the tyme is come
> that sygnes and shadowes be all donne.
> Therfore, make haste, that we maye soone
> all figures cleane rejecte.　　　　(Play 15, lines 69–72)

Jesus introduces a New Law and a new sacrifice. The visible sacrament of the Eucharist re-enacts the continuing mystical sacrifice of Christ for sinful man going on in Heaven, for Christ's historical sufferings on the cross for man's sins are simply a local sign for a process that continues throughout time. Christ still bleeds in Play 24 ('Tunc emittet sanguinem de latere eius', line 428 + s.d. – 'Then he shall pour out blood from his side'), though by then his blood is not only a joyful sign of salvation for the penitent but also a terrifying sign of damnation for the obdurate (Play 24, lines 425–36). After Pentecost, God's grace and power are manifest in the Eucharist.

But to be efficacious, that sacrament must be taken in the redeemed present with the remembrance of its significance from the historical past. All prophecy, alluded to or recited, and the interpreted types, are now products of memory. The *Harrowing of Hell*, Play 17, begins with the recollections of the patriarchs and prophets. At the centre of contemporary faith, as the recurring stimulus to the Christian memory, lies the Eucharist:

> This give I you on me to mynd　　　　　*think of me*
> aye after evermore.　　　　(Play 15, lines 95–6)

The culminating play of Day 3, *Pentecost*, is a play of remembering, as the disciples strive collectively to remember the words of Christ and, under the influence of the Holy Spirit, formulate a Creed which is the summation of the events previously witnessed (cf. 192, pp. 205–22). Jesus in his great Judgement speech (Play 24, lines 357–420) reviews the purpose and events of the first advent and rebukes the unmindful:

> Howe durst you ever doe amys
> when you unthought you of this   *recalled*
> that I bleede to bringe you to blys
> and suffered such woo?   (lines 429–32)

The gospels to which the audience is directed finally by the four evangelists (lines 677–708) are similarly aids to memory. To retrieve the past with the understanding of faith is the spur to Christian salvation and the cycle's justification.

Pentecost, with its summary of the tenets of faith revealed in the cycle, marks the closure of the past age of marvels attending the first advent. Prophecy and marvel will return only in future time as the signs of the second advent. Antichrist confuses men by apparent miracles which replicate Christ's own miracles; but 'The[y] were no myracles but mervelles [marvellous] thinges' (Play 23, lines 410), wonders without significance which prove powerless against the consecrated Host. All miracles are superseded by the continuing miracle of the Real Presence in the Eucharist, validated by the historical knowledge of the Godhead summarised in the Apostles' Creed, resources available to every Christian in the age of the Church.

ASPECTS OF THE DRAMA OF SIGN

After our earlier discussion of theology in Play 1, we can now consider its impact as drama. God's initial warning to the angels not to touch his throne in his absence seems to provoke the very curiosity and disobedience that it forbids, to present a temptation or 'dare' which Lucifer takes up. His 'Goldilocks' occupation of God's chair is in literal terms foolishly impertinent rather than evil, deriving from his belief that his splendid appearance is a sign of his own intrinsic worth rather than a manifestation of the greater glory of God. Cast out of God's presence, he loses that light – he and Lightborne, now 'two feeyndes blake' (line 251), inhabit 'a dongion of darkenes' (line 74). At the end of the play God separates night from day as a physical sign of the separation of evil from good, introducing the 'light–dark' image which Jesus develops in Play 13, 1–35, and which is literalised in Play 17 (opening stage direction). 'Sitting in God's chair' is not a credible cause for expulsion but a literal and inadequate sign of Lucifer's wilful rebelliousness and a useful image by which we can apprehend, however inadequately, the process of temptation. Humanity finds Lucifer's literalised naughtiness amusing and even appealing, but recognises that the dramatic action is not mimetic but metaphoric, like eating the apple in Play 2.

The exploration of this kind of drama is seen in the way the Expositor's interventions in Play 4 emphasise the structural division between the play's three episodes: Abraham's meeting with Melchisadek, his consent to circumcision and his sacrifice of Isaac. Historically decontextualised, and separate from each other, the episodes assume the character of marvels, literally strange to the point of absurdity. Why should Abraham give tithes to Melchisadek ('as skyll is that I doe' (line 36), he says enigmatically)? Why should God demand the removal of male foreskins – surely not, in his omniscience, 'for therby knowe thou maye thy folke from other men' (lines 187–8)? Why should the renewal of his covenant be conditional upon Isaac's ordeal of terror? The participants never ask such questions but move mindlessly to the will of God. For the audience the episodes become riddles, solved and linked thematically by the Expositor's typological interpretations. But that Expositor is the representative not of God but of the playwright, and his dramatic function is to make explicit the underlying process of artistic selection by which these three episodes have subjectively been accorded significance within the play. In seeking to direct our reading and limit our range of interpretation, the Expositor persona alerts us to the way in which this drama has been shaped to reduce questioning.

The play's final episode, 'The Sacrifice of Isaac', is doubly revealing because there the playwright can be seen resisting the empathetic model of naturalistic drama offered by his source, the Brome play. Brome begins by showing Abraham's affection for his young son, which prompts God's decision to test Abraham's priorities by requiring Isaac's sacrifice. Much of the play consists of the dialogue between father and son as they move towards their seemingly inevitable goal. The sacrifice concludes with God's promised reward for Abraham's successful performance in the test but the play continues challengingly on to show a much disturbed Isaac rejoicing in his reprieve but traumatised by his experience.

In Chester's adaptation, God has already promised Abraham an only son as his heir (lines 157–60), but now seems perversely to countermand that promise. His command is without prelude or explanation:

> Take Isaac, thy sonne by name,
> that thou lovest the best of all,
> and in sacryfyce offer him to me
> upon that hyll there besydes thee.
> Abraham, I will that yt soe bee
> for ought that maye befall.   (lines 211–16)

Human affection ('lovest') is acknowledged in the defining phrases of the first two lines, only to be brutally trampled down in the chilling 'sacryfyce' of the third. The speech becomes thereafter angry and impatient; the directions are fired out, as if Abraham is looking around dazedly ('Upon *that* hyll!

There!! Besydes thee!!!'). Its last two lines are sternly peremptory: they brook no argument and offer no explanation – 'I will' is enough. Both content and tone invite our resistance, and consequently Abraham's facile agreement is naturalistically incomprehensible. Repeatedly thereafter he conceals the truth of the act from himself by euphemising it, most grotesquely as 'a little thinge' (line 230), and by concealing it under the pretence of routine observance until the pathetically trusting and obedient Isaac becomes suspicious of his father's strange conduct and the absence of a sacrificial beast. The child voices the enormity that the father, believing that God cannot mean it (cf. lines 269–72), will not confront:

> I hope for all myddylarde   *the world*
> you will not slaye your chylde.   (lines 267–8)

When the truth is known, Isaac tries to construct some sort of rationalisation – an 'over-the-top' punishment for some forgotten wrong, perhaps (lines 289–92) – and challenges Abraham: 'ys that your wyll?' (line 286). Abraham replies:

> O my deare sonne, I am sorye
> to do to thee this great anoye: *harm*
> Godes commandement doe must I.
> His workes are aye full mylde.   (lines 293–6)

The three statements stand separate, unconnected by logic or syntax. The grotesquely formal statement of anguish ('sorye') with its understated 'great anoye', the lack of logical support for 'doe must I', and the ironic pressure of the situation upon 'aye full mylde' raise questions that are never answered. It is Abraham's will to do God's will (lines 306–7), and surprisingly it becomes Isaac's will to do his father's will:

> ABRAHAM   But that I doe this dolefull deede,
>   my lorde will not quite mee my meede.   *reward me*
> ISAAC   Marye, father, God forbydde
>   but you doe your offeringe.   (lines 313–16)

Isaac's first line, with its suggestive conjunction of Mary, father and God and its forceful 'God forbydde', seems about to challenge Abraham's preposterous self-interest ('my meede'), which still evades the reality ('this dolefull deede'), but naturalistic resistance is deflected into unnatural acquiescence.

The action moves with slow formality, Isaac repeatedly invoking a domestic normality which allegedly exists somewhere outside the play but is never allowed to appear within it. Held in the audience's consciousness, it becomes the measure of the abnormality of this grim ritual – the blessing, blindfolding and binding of Isaac, his positioning on the altar by Abraham, and the sword being drawn. The magnificence of Isaac's final words –

> Almighty God in majestie,
> my soule I offer unto thee –   (lines 418–19)

yields finally to desperate, pleading pathos –

> Lord, to yt bee kynde! –   (line 420)

which challenges the cruelty of the action. God now reverses his earlier vow and arrests the action. Yet neither Abraham nor Isaac has stage-life beyond that moment of sacrifice. They are never shown reunited or given a chance to comment further upon what has happened. The action seemingly freezes into a picture-like tableau across which the Expositor offers his interpretation.

That typological interpretation accords with the suppression of naturalism. But when the Expositor then kneels to pray for 'such obedyence ... as this Abraham was beyne' (lines 476, 479), he seeks to introduce an inappropriate standard of naturalistic evaluation which invites resistance. The prayer serves as a measure of the alterity of the play-world which Abraham occupies; he cannot serve as a role model for contemporary man. Appropriately, therefore, the Expositor is interrupted in prayer by a Messenger (lines 484–91) returning us to the reality of Chester streets and the approaching wagon of Play 5.

The appearance of God, incarnate in human form, arouses suspicion of his marvels and confusion about his purpose. Chester, like the other cycles, shows the confusions that arise from the metaphoric extension of the word 'king' to spiritual kingship, but intensifies the issue by emphasising in Play 5 the authority of the Law – reasserted by the boy Jesus in Play 11 (lines 271–98) – and the connection between spiritual election and worldly power (Play 5, lines 104–7). The misunderstanding attending Jesus's separation of spiritual from worldly kingship and his claims to fulfil the Law present understandable difficulties for the sceptics in his dramatic audience.

Herod is drawn into the action in Play 8. The dramatist alludes to the traditional dramatic model for King Herod, the comically irate and ranting tyrant who, when he feels threatened,

> ... would goe wood, by my faye,
> and flye out of his skynne.   (Play 8, lines 134–5)

But this Herod is an actor comically at odds with his role. His court contains a library of true signs, the books of Jewish prophecy hitherto closed to the Gentile Magi who have only Balaam's star-sign to guide them. But

Herod is a false sign, a mock king whose public statements and kingly robes belie his true intentions.

His opening speech to the Magi assigns quasi-divine power to physical violence, with grotesque effect. It grandiosely appropriates to Herod the titles ('kinge of kinges', line 169) and powers of God. Herod claims to expel devils (lines 175–6), to control the planets and elements (lines 179, 183–5), to have the Christ-given authority to loose and bind (line 178), and a limitless supremacy that recalls God's opening claims:

> I am the greatest above degree
> that is, or was, or ever shalbe.   (lines 181–2)

Absurdly grandiloquent, these claims are undercut by the constant resort to physical violence ('beate', lines 174, 178; 'crack his crowne', line 188), by his own physical disorder ('my hart is not at ease', line 196) and by the stylistic descent into the colloquial ('What the devell should this bee!' line 201). Margin cues suggest that the speech is accompanied by violent gestures with staff and sword (at lines 196, 200, 206, 209–11). This contrast between his formal public image and his private fears carries into all Herod's speeches, which are a mixture of public bombast and private aside. Such an outlook cannot encompass the metaphoric application of 'king' to Jesus but literalises it as a political threat. Herod does not deny the interpretations of the Doctor, but his answer is to destroy the signs – the words ('Those bookes were rent and torne', line 351) – and what they signify – the Christ-child, in contrast to the rational Emperor Octavian of Play 6 who correctly reads the signs of his own mortality (lines 297–344) and accepts the star-sign of Christ's birth (lines 644–66).

As Herod seemingly takes control of the action in Play 10, the play moves into melodrama. Admitting that the slaughter is 'agaynst the right' (line 23), he dismisses his knights' objections ('a villanye yt weare iwys', line 155) with exultation in its scale. But ironically, the knights fail to recognise Herod's own son by his outer sign, his rich clothes (lines 409–12). In his despair Herod's physical decay as he rots before our eyes (lines 418–22) signifies his inner moral corruption. As he dies, he is hauled off to Hell by the gloating devils he earlier claimed to master. In resisting the signs of prophetic fulfilment, he becomes part of the cycle's system of signs himself, and typologically fulfils the Old Testament figure by whom he justified his actions.

Play 16 marks a significant suspension of the drama of sign. The Bible prompts a contrast between the wonders of the Nativity and the political priorities of the Trials and Crucifixion. But whereas the York Realist exploits the latter in an eight-play coverage of the Trials and Passion, Chester compresses those events into a single continuous action which records suggest was sometimes performed as a single play and sometimes as two (73, vol. I, Plays 16 and 16A). Though reminiscent of the multi-episode structure in other plays of the cycle, this rapid sequence of events, with its brief episodes and terse exchanges, reflects the pressure of time and circumstance upon the action (cf. Play 14, lines 354, 406, 425; Play 16, line 159; Play 16A, lines 9, 149–52). Significantly, in his interrogation by Herod (Play 16, lines 163–202), Jesus refuses the role of miracle-worker which he has occupied in the ministry plays and is seen willingly to accept the role of victim in his own drama. And, whereas Herod in Play 8 was drawn into the action 'fortuitously' by the arrival of the Magi, Caiaphas and Pilate are 'logically' impelled into it by the pressure from the mob which has built up throughout the preceding plays. They are caught up in events which they cannot control and, unlike Herod, their options are closed.

The Jews in Play 13, baffled by Jesus's sudden disappearance as they prepare to stone him, say 'to sir Cayphas I shall him wrye [denounce]' (line 295); in Play 14 the traders, beaten from the Temple and shocked at Jesus's Messianic claims, decide 'Cayphas I shall tell' (line 260); and Judas, later in the same play, thinks of the plans being laid by 'Sir Cayphas and his companye' (line 297). The orthodox, who have seen Jesus frustrate justice (Play 12), break the Sabbath and raise the dead (Play 13) and destroy commerce (Play 14), demand action from their leader, while the popular acclaim that greeted Jesus's entry into Jerusalem (Play 14), growing from the wonders that he has performed, signals a potential threat to public order (lines 358–9). Caiaphas is no Herodian tyrant but a politician trying to contain the situation, who is first discovered chairing a committee to determine a course of action that will not alienate public opinion (Play 14, lines 305–20).

Caiaphas defers to the mob in Play 16, turning (unbiblically) to the accusers ('What saye you men that nowe binne here?', line 58) when Jesus professes divinity. He accedes to their demand for violence against one 'that owr lawe so destroyes' (line 61), but in so doing despises their blind stupidity:

> Distroye shall hee not hit.
> Yee wretches, ye wanton wytt!   (lines 62–3)

The buffeting is the priests' cynical way of appeasing the people while they debate the next step, and at its end their deliberations are also concluding (lines 110–17). The mob's brutality is suggested not only by their violent actions but also in what Travis aptly characterises as 'the short, pulsating rhythms of a primitive chant' (192, p. 83) in the tormentors' speeches throughout the play, suggestive of the jeering sing-song of children releasing their own insecurities by reviling their victim.

Pilate too is compelled by popular opinion. Initially he is amusingly indifferent to the sixteen-line accusation presented (lines 118–33). He tosses a casual two-liner to Jesus, who deftly returns it, and then he denies the request! A passing reference to Galilee allows him to pass Jesus over to Herod, who returns him swiftly to Pilate. Pilate then indolently shrugs his shoulders – 'is best we lett him gonne' (line 217). The matter is trivial. But he is shocked by the 'noyce' (line 221) of the general outcry, 'nayle him, nayle him to the crosse' (line 220), and unsuccessfully tries to appease the mob by offering to release Barabbas. Almost pleadingly he turns to the priests ('yee prelates here everychonne, that will ye do?', lines 243–4), but they simply parrot the mob's cry ('nayle, nayle him to the crosse anonne', line 245). Like them he offers violence as appeasement (lines 305–6), exposing Jesus to public humiliation as a mock king, and repeats the offer of Barabbas, this time to the priests, but in vain. He reluctantly yields to popular demand and delivers Jesus to Caiaphas and the mob for execution, saying 'Save him I ne may' (line 369). Violence, which in this play has served as a kind of public rhetoric employed by politicians to satisfy the people, will now reach its popular climax in the Crucifixion. But, as Play 16A nears its end, Jesus signals his reversion to the role of miracle-worker by the healing of Longinus in preparation for the Harrowing of Hell and the wonders of Day 3.

The mob's response is replaced by a moment of calm and reasoned discussion. Exasperated by the priests, Pilate takes Jesus aside at line 252 for a private dialogue, emphasising his own detachment from the hostile mob ('Men of thyne owne nation shewen for thy dampnatyon', lines 259–60). This private conversation, with its sober exchange of views on Jesus's use of the term 'king' and on the nature of truth, goes to the centre of the theological issues and exposes the misunderstandings that fallen language can generate. Jesus admits his kingship (line 278) but denies its worldly sense ('my realme in this world, as say I, ys not', lines 264–5). Truth is the prerogative of God, and the present proceedings demonstrate its powerlessness on earth (lines 284–90). This exchange is in a different register from the bayings of the crowd; and though it satisfies a dispassionate Roman governor, it cannot satisfy the outraged Jews.

Chester's dramatisation of the interventions of God in past history is completed with *Pentecost* on day 3 and the cycle moves on to the second advent. But before that advent, it realises through Antichrist the dangers of trying to make the flesh into Word and, in an action of daring self-parody, demonstrates the limitations of drama itself. In moving from the summation of Christian faith in the clear and unambiguous language of the Creed (Play 21) to the prophets of Antichrist (Play 22), it reverts to the riddling obscurity of Old Testament prophecies. Once again words no longer seem fixed in meaning and the almost forgotten Expositor re-emerges, as on previous days, to call up the actors and determine the significance of what they say – with this important difference: the Expositor is setting out the programme for the plays to come instead of speaking with the benefit of hindsight. He is a herald of closure and, in this last appearance, out-prophesies the prophets themselves with his gratuitous account of the signs before Doomsday. 'Hee comes soone, you shall see' (line 340) feeds our expectations of the second advent by echoing Revelations 22.20: 'Surely I come quickly. Amen. Even so, come, Lord Jesus.' The figure who follows, speaking the Latin of authority (Play 23, lines 1–8), identifies himself as Christ. He turns out to be Antichrist. We, the audience, have been deceived.

Antichrist reveals the difficulties of reading signs by replicating the miracles that Jesus used to demonstrate his divinity – raising the dead (lines 97–112), dying and rising (lines 121–68), sending down his 'Holy Spirit' (lines 193–200). Moreover he offers tangible rewards – the titles to kingdoms – which win him more ready support than Christ's spiritual rewards. God's messengers, Enoch and Elijah, have no means of logically disproving his blasphemous parody. The comic frustration of both sides is manifest in their entertainingly abusive and unproductive slanging-match, for, though Antichrist's curse cannot harm the prophets, their arguments cannot undermine his credibility. Indeed, as they proclaim the theologically complex concept of the Trinity on which the cycle is structured. Antichrist ridicules its rational incomprehensibility:

> Owt on you, theeves! What sayen yee?
> Wyll you have on God and three?
> Howe darre you so saye?
> Madmen, madmen! Therfore leeve on mee
> that am on god – so ys not hee!   *one*
> (lines 498–502)

Debate yields to faith and sign to sacrament. By blessing bread in a way made familiar from Plays 19–21, Enoch and Elijah produce no visible change in it, but they effect a change visible to the 'spiritual' sight of the devils, who are put to flight. They and the kings are not spared physical death at Antichrist's hands, but they have the assurance of God's power while on earth, and of his ultimate justice. For their perseverance and martyrdom they will be restored to spiritual life and salvation – the prophets by Michael (lines 699–722) and the rest at Doomsday (Play 24) – while Antichrist completes his replication of Christ's signs with an ironic reversal of the Ascension (Play 20, a comic descent into Hell in the hands of the devils), becoming thereby a sign of the second advent.

The play warns us as audience against responding only to the artistic effect of this drama, as it warns us as Christians against sensory response guided only by normative experience and uninformed by faith (*192*, pp. 299–41; *135*, pp. 313–20). In detaching miracle from its spiritual signification, Antichrist illustrates how an author/actor can convincingly appropriate familiar signs to his own ends, and so emphasises our responsibility, as readers/audience, for constructing meaning from the text/play. A fine line divides miracle from stage trick and illusion. If turning the trees upside down (lines 81–8) is the appropriate paradigm for Antichrist's signs, why not also for Christ's? So read, Antichrist represents the cycle itself, which replicates God's signs ostensibly for the edification of its audience, but also exploits their 'marvellous' quality, their effectiveness as dramatic material, for its own artistic ends, diverting us from their transcendental truth. If religious drama is not to be blasphemy, a distinction must be maintained between the God who said 'Ego sum alpha et oo' (Play 1, line 1) and the actor who continues 'I ame greate God gracious' (line 5); the actor 'is not' God but merely 'represents' God in the play-world of the cycle. We must learn to read through and beyond the action played before us.

For Christians the play is disturbing in making explicit both the 'fantastic' aspect of the material wonders of the past and the logical impossibilities of contemporary Christian teaching. Chester confronts those impossibilities by affirming the reasonableness of historically founded faith. Its message of rational belief anticipates that of Sir Thomas Browne in 1642:

> [I] believe [Christ] was dead and buried and rose againe; and desire to see him in his glory, rather than to contemplate him in his Cenotaphe, or Sepulchre. Nor is this much to beleeve, as we have reason, we owe this faith unto History: they only had the advantage of a bold and noble faith, who lived before his comming, who upon obscure prophesies and mysticall Types could raise a beliefe, and expect apparent impossibilities.[7]

As Play 24 demonstrates, in post-Pentecostal history man finds grace through charitable deeds performed under the redeeming grace of the ever-crucified Christ.

NOTES

1 Hermann Deimling and Dr Matthews (eds.), *The Chester Plays*, EETS, ES 62 (1892) and ES 115 (1916) (London: Kegan Paul, Trench, Trübner and Co.).
2 See also F. M. Salter, 'The Banns of the Chester Plays', *RES* 15 (1939), 1–17, 137 8.
3 See also A. C. Baugh, 'The Chester Plays and French Influence', in *Schelling Anniversary Papers* (New York: Century, 1923), pp. 35–63.

4 See Frances A. Foster (ed.), *A Stanzaic Life of Christ*, EETS, OS 166 (London: Oxford University Press, 1926), pp. xxviii–xliii, and Robert H. Wilson, 'The *Stanzaic Life of Christ* and the Chester Plays', *SP* 28 (1931), 413–32.

5 Elizabeth Salter, *Nicholas Love's 'Myrrour of the Blessed Lyf of Jesu Christ'*, Analecta Cartusiana 10 (Salzburg: Institut für Englische Sprache und Literatur, Universität Salzburg, 1974), p. 96.

6 Salter, *Love's 'Myrrour'*, p. 96.

7 L. C. Martin (ed.), *Sir Thomas Browne: Religio Medici and Other Works* (Oxford: Clarendon Press, 1964), *Religio Medici*, p. 10.

5

PETER MEREDITH

The Towneley cycle

Almost certainly the most anthologised of all medieval English dramatic pieces is the so-called *Second Shepherds' Play*, containing the double story of Mak the sheep-stealer and the visit of the shepherds to Bethlehem. Through this public exposure, not only the play but the 'name' of the author also has become familiar – 'The Wakefield Master'. Not everyone who knows of the *Second Shepherds'*, however, will automatically connect it with the thirty-two short plays (better called 'pageants') that together make up the Towneley cycle, or realise that it is not so much the 'second' as an alternative Shepherds' pageant: *Alia eorundem* (another of the same). Even knowing the relationship between the pageant, the Wakefield Master and the Towneley cycle does not, however, take you very far; why, for example *Wakefield* Master, but *Towneley* cycle?

'Wakefield' refers to the smallish industrial town in what used to be the West Riding of Yorkshire, once the centre of the extensive medieval manor of Wakefield.[1] Since early in this century it has been claimed, with varying degrees of certainty, as the original home and place of performance of this cycle of pageants (76, p. xxxv; 75, p. xxviii). As the York play was to York, so, it was said, the Towneley cycle was to Wakefield. The name 'Wakefield Master' was hence created as a convenient reference name for the anonymous author of a strikingly original group of pageants within the cycle.[2] His pageants contain a number of references to places in and around Wakefield and it is not, therefore, an inappropriate name. He is not, however, certainly known to be a Wakefield man. The name 'Towneley' comes from the family of Towneley in whose possession the manuscript of the pageants was when it came to public notice in the early nineteenth century (113, p. vii; 217, p. 137). The name was established as that of the cycle by the publication of *The Towneley Mysteries* in 1836 by the Surtees Society – the first of the complete cycles to be published. The family were Catholics and their main seat was Towneley Hall near Burnley in Lancashire. The manuscript formed part of the library of Christopher Towneley, a seventeenth-century antiquary and collector, but how it came into his possession or where it came from is not known. As a Catholic, Towneley may have picked up and preserved the manuscript as a sample of a time when his faith was the acknowledged faith of the whole of the country.

The first problem with the cycle is, then, one of names and origins. A second, in some ways related, problem is the kind of performance that is appropriate to it, related because knowledge of the place of performance can provide knowledge of the type of staging. With no town records to serve as a context for the cycle we are thrown back on the manuscript and the text itself. Unfortunately, unlike those in N-Town, the stage directions do not give 'staging' information. That is, they do not talk in terms of scaffolds or 'place' or curtains unclosing but in the narrative terms of the story. The staging information in the stage directions tends to be details of movement, gesture and action, not broad indications of stages and sets. Furthermore, the association with Wakefield, even if it were certain, would provide no more information about the physical theatrical setting of the cycle, since the burgess court records refer only to text and responsibility.

A more basic problem even than those of provenance and staging is the nature of the cycle itself. Comparison with York again reveals how our certainty about the York cycle derives from a combination of text with civic information. The relationship of pageants to crafts, the responsibilities for performance, the type of performance, the date and to some extent the development of the cycle are all matters of certainty or relative certainty because of this combined evidence (see above, chapter 3). Because of the absence of related records for Towneley, the smallest details of the writing, layout and make-up of the manuscript, and its later treatment, become of crucial importance in trying to understand the cycle.[3] There are any number of questions for which answers might be sought in the manuscript but three related ones stand out: What kind of manuscript is it? What function did it serve? and What is its date?

Its most likely function was that of register, or official copy of a play cycle, but this is difficult to prove. Only one register exists, that for the York play, so the evidence for the nature of a register derives from one example only. The York Register is a complete text of all the pageants (except for a number never entered but for which spaces were left). By its very existence it demonstrates a civic concern with the play, and this is borne out by the marginal annotations, which show the city authorities attempting to keep an eye on the extent to which the text as performed was differing from the text as recorded in the Register. Further civic concern is with the responsibility of individual crafts for specific pageants. Craft names, not titles, are used as running headings in the manuscript (see illustration 12, p. 91).

Even a glance at the Towneley manuscript will reveal how little these features are present. There are no running headings. The pageants are titled and the only craft attributions are later additions at the beginnings of four pageants, with one craft ('Lysters pagon') repeated, vertically, in the margin of the last (unfinished) pageant, *Judas*. It would certainly not serve as a check on craft responsibility. The annotations are few. There are two deletions relating to what can only be Protestant censorship (fols. 66 and 104v), one being annotated: 'correctyd and not playd' (fol. 66). There is a small scattering of notes written vertically and horizontally in the margin (e.g. fol. 31, 'note this very . . .'; fol. 61, 'no materes ben as sade') and a few alterations to the text. These include the addition of a missing line (fol. 81v), the correction (again for Protestant purposes) of a line relating to the Mass (fol. 67), and minor alterations of words ('lady' to 'lord', fol. 44; 'a pope' erased, fol. 57v). In no way are these comparable to the York annotations.[4] The Towneley manuscript looks like a register primarily because it has what looks like a complete cycle of pageants. There are gaps (no *Trial before Herod*, for example) and there are pageants out of order (*Pharaoh*, *Lazarus* and *Judas*) but it remains a cycle.

What the annotations do, it seems to me, is to suggest that this was a manuscript related (however distantly) to performance. This makes sense of noting that a passage was 'not playd'. That there are few annotations does not matter. We do not know whether the York Register was typical, or even whether there is such a thing as a typical register. Furthermore, if Towneley was from Wakefield the social set-up was of quite a different kind: a small town, the centre of a large manor and under the control of the lord of the manor and his bailiff, not, like York, a largely autonomous city. There is also no real reason why the craft names should appear in the same way in both play manuscripts. The craft guilds in York were directly responsible to the city authorities. We do not know what the relationship of the crafts to the Towneley cycle was. If we again use the Wakefield records, then it is clear that crafts were involved there and that they were subject to fines by the burgess court; but the records are of 1556. Could it be that the later additions of craft names in Towneley relate to a later development in Wakefield? There is at the moment no way of telling.

This raises the question of date. The manuscript used to be thought of as of the mid-fifteenth century, but the most recent study, the facsimile edition (*113*), puts it either very late in the fifteenth century or, perhaps more likely, into the sixteenth. The date of the manuscript is not, of course, the date of the cycle, but a late date for the one does allow a late date for the other, if there is no other reason for restricting it. It is also important to remember that the date of the cycle means the date of the compilation, the putting together of this group of pageants, and not the date of individual pageants. The nature of the compilation is somewhat complex but to take it at its simplest level there are three elements: pageants known to be from York, Wakefield Master pageants and pageants from another source or sources. Setting aside dubious cases, the Wakefield Master has added to or revised two of the York pageants, and also added (though only once substantially) to four pageants from other sources. No one has obviously revised or tampered with any of the complete Wakefield Master pageants and it would therefore seem a not unreasonable conclusion that his was the last revision of the cycle. 'Revision' sounds like a formal review of the whole work, but it would be wrong to think of it in those terms. These are plays, not acts of parliament, and no doubt the reviser added, altered and deleted only where he was specifically directed or where he saw an opportunity to improve. Certainly the Wakefield Master seems to have indulged his natural skill in extending the range of humour and grandeur of the ranting tyrants. The period of the whole compilation may well, therefore, be the period when the Wakefield Master was making his alterations. Unfortunately that does not provide a firm date. The most helpful internal evidence comes from the satirical costume references in the additions to the *Judgement*, but even that is open to question. Long hair and padded shoulders for men and low collars for women do suggest the late fifteenth century, but other references could as easily be earlier or not suggest any particular date. Hoods, which are referred to, apparently went out of fashion in the mid century; horned headdresses are usually taken to refer to the extravagances of the early part of the century, but could also refer to later fashions. The costume references cannot provide a firm date, but they certainly do not exclude the latter part of the century.[5]

The Towneley cycle has been fully edited twice: once by Joseph Hunter and James Gordon for the Surtees Society (the edition already referred to) in 1836, then, just over sixty years later, in what has been the standard text for nearly a hundred years, by George England and A. W. Pollard for the Early English Text Society edition of 1897 (75). The latter is a very considerable improvement on the former in accuracy and in its presentation of the text, but there are still confusions in stanza forms and still some errors, one or two lines missing, a very inadequate glossary and, for so complex a text, a sad absence of annotation. In view of these shortcomings, a new text is in preparation for the EETS by A. C. Cawley and Martin Stevens. Cawley has already produced an excellently accurate text of the six accepted Wakefield Master pageants, with full introduction, notes and glossary (76). This is the only part of the cycle that has so far been fully annotated and accurately edited, though fifteen of the pageants, nearly half of the cycle, are included in David Bevington's useful and reliable anthology, *Medieval Drama* (62). A complete modern-spelling edition is being produced by John Marshall and myself.

Cawley and Stevens in 1976 brought out a facsimile of the manuscript in the Leeds Medieval Drama facsimile series (*113*), which, besides providing an excellent description of the manuscript which supersedes Louis Wann's article (*217*), re-examined the date of the manuscript and provided the currently accepted dating of the end of the fifteenth century or the beginning of the sixteenth. There is also a useful concordance to the six pageants of the Wakefield Master based on the Cawley edition (*121*; cf. also *122*).

Martial Rose's pioneering translation (*77*) was valuable in making the cycle available to a wider audience and in putting the cycle back on the stage, but it is not always an accurate guide to the detailed meaning of the text. Since the performances at Bretton Hall, near Wakefield, in 1958 (part of the cycle) and 1967 (the complete cycle), and at the Mermaid Theatre in London in 1961 (part), there have been a number of productions, using a variety of staging layouts, of parts or of the full cycle: at Wakefield in 1975 (on pageant wagons, part) and 1980 (processionally at three fixed stages, complete), and in Toronto in 1985 (place-and-scaffold, complete).[6]

Though there have been dissenting voices (noted in *199*, p. 271; cf. *138*, pp. 142–4), the Wakefield Master's work has usually been highly praised. His skills are readily appreciated in the study, and criticism, often at a loss as to how to deal with the plays, has tended to concentrate on his work to the exclusion of the rest of the cycle. Two concurrent lines of investigation, apparently very diverse, have brought renewed attention to the whole cycle. One is the study of manuscripts. There the concern with understanding the nature of the manuscript, and in particular of explicating the relationship between play and performance, has brought attention back to the inter-relationship of all pageants and, surprisingly, encouraged an interest in cycles in performance. The other is the renewed interest in the plays as theatrical experiences: day-long, popular, open-air (often street), celebratory performances, not extracts made to fit into twentieth-century proscenium-arch theatres or single pageants forced into the one-act play format. This welcome revival of interest in the cycles – as opposed to individual pageants – as theatrical pieces is a necessary step before criticism looks, as it has still not done properly, at the Towneley cycle as a whole.

THE MANUSCRIPT

The Towneley cycle is contained in a single manuscript, now in the Huntington Library in California (MS HM 1), dating from the end of the fifteenth century or the beginning of the sixteenth (*113*, pp. ix–x). It is a large folio volume of parchment leaves made elaborate partly by the use of a fine series of decorative initials and partly, though to a more limited extent, by the use of rubrication. It is written throughout in the hand of a single scribe, with the exception of the final pageant, no. 32, *Suspencio Iude* (the Hanging of Judas), the hand of which is, however, of very much the same date (*113*, p. ix). The thirty-two pageants in the manuscript tell the history of mankind from the Creation to the Last Judgement. Four of these are out of sequence. The order of *Pharao* and *Processus Prophetarum* (the Prophets) has been reversed, and *Lazarus* and *Suspencio Iude* occur at the end of the manuscript instead of in their correct positions, between *Johannes Baptista* and *Conspiracio* (the Conspiracy) and between *Coliphizacio* (the Buffeting) and *Flagellacio* (the Scourging) respectively. There are a number of gaps in the manuscript where leaves have been lost or removed: (i) between pageants 1 and 2, the *Creation* and *Mactatio Abel* (the Killing of Abel); (ii) between pageants 4 and 5, *Abraham* and *Isaac*; (iii) between pageants 17 and 18, *Purificacio Marie* (the Purification of Mary) and *Pagina Doctorum* (the pageant of the Doctors); and (iv) between pageants 29 and 30, *Ascensio Domini* (the Ascension of the Lord) and *Judicium* (the Judgement). As a consequence seven pageants are incomplete (all those mentioned here except the *Killing of Abel*), some more seriously than others. The *Creation* lacks the temptation and fall of man; *Abraham* lacks only the conclusion after the reprieve of Isaac; *Isaac* lacks a beginning – a serious loss since the pageant is unique; half of the *Purification* is missing (the unusual beginning has fortunately survived) and the *Doctors* lacks an opening – perhaps containing further searching by the doctors for prophecies of Christ's birth, or perhaps the discovery by Mary and Joseph of Jesus's absence, as in the corresponding York pageant.

Most serious is the loss of twelve leaves towards the end of the manuscript. It apparently affects only the very end of the *Ascension*, but it is impossible to tell how much is missing at the beginning of the *Judgement* (*213*). The loss could represent more than a thousand lines of text; in other words, besides a missing beginning of the *Judgement*, possibly two lengthy, or three substantial, or even four ordinary length pageants. In this position all the extant cycles have a Pentecost pageant (missing in the Beverley list); York has as well a death of Mary sequence   Death, Burial (no longer extant), Assumption and Coronation; Chester has two Antichrist pageants and once had an Assumption. The extant York pageants, from Pentecost to Coronation, number 890 lines, so the missing leaves in Towneley could have contained a complete sequence of later life of Mary pageants up to her coronation, or something more unusual on the lines of Chester (a little over 1,000 lines). These calculations cannot be precise because the layout of the lines on the page crucially affects the number that can be contained, and the layout cannot be known. It is, however, important to realise how drastically the missing leaves could affect our view of the cycle.

The losses, except for the twelve-leaf one, are all of central leaves in a quire – the commonest position for accidental loss to take place, or for leaves to be removed when the removal has nothing to do with the text. The loss of the twelve leaves, however, looks like deliberate tearing-out, since it affects the middle and end of one quire and the beginning and middle of the next. If the lost leaves did contain Marian material it may well be that they were removed as part of the Reformation reaction against veneration of the Virgin Mary, which also accounts for the loss of the Chester *Assumption* and for the non-playing of the York pageants. There are a very few other signs in the manuscript of Reformation activity. In common with church service books the word 'pope' has been erased in the *Herod* (fol. 57v), though the reference is hardly flattering, and 'lady' has been altered to 'lord' once in the second of the *Shepherds* pageants, though not with much confidence (fol. 44). Further changes are the alteration of a line in *John the Baptist*, which clearly once contained a reference to the Mass (the rhymes are on -*es* and no doubt the last word of the altered line was *mes*) (fol. 67), and the deletion of a passage in the same pageant relating to the sacraments and marked 'correctyd and not playd' in the margin (fol. 66). A further deletion occurs at the end of Jesus's speech in the *Resurrection* – a stanza on transubstantiation (fol. 104v).

One other possible loss should perhaps be mentioned. It is normal for a planned manuscript to begin either with a quire marked *a* or with one marked with a cross (as in alphabets of the time). The Towneley manuscript appears to begin with a *b* quire. Since the manuscript consists of quires of eight leaves it is possible that eight or even sixteen further leaves are missing before the *Creation* pageant. There is no way of knowing what was contained in these leaves if they existed. If they contained material directly related to the play, then Martin Stevens's suggestion (213) that it was a set of banns or a proclamation for the cycle (as with N-Town and Chester) is the most likely, though they would hardly have required that much space. It is also possible that a blank quire was left at the beginning (not necessarily consisting of eight leaves) for possible additional introductory material, and that it was never used and later detached. It is important to note this absence because of its possible connection with staging, but it is clearly impossible to estimate its significance.

STAGE DIRECTIONS

Original stage directions can be of great value in providing evidence for recreating the staging of the pageants. As has already been said, there is none here that provides evidence for the overall staging, but many do provide evocative detail. The manuscript contains sixty-eight stage directions in all, some integrated into the layout of the text, some in the margin. They are spread unevenly through the pageants. Twelve have no directions at all, and those that do exist vary considerably in the kind and amount of evidence that they give. Most potentially striking is the single direction in *John the Baptist*: *Hic tradat ei agnum dei* (Here let him give to him the Lamb of God). The pageant combines Christ's baptism with Christian baptism, and the handing over of the Lamb of God to John adds another layer to the meaning. John is the historical prophet and the presenter of baptism as a sacrament; with the handing over of his traditional emblem he becomes also the familiar saint of the contemporary Church. He is not, like the shepherds, a biblical character becoming a contemporary human, but a biblical character becoming a contemporary icon. Unfortunately the pageant is so lacking in dramatic power that the further possibilities that the stage direction suggests remain merely potential and are never realised. The flat and repetitive verse which accompanies the action, with its inappropriate promise 'It may were the [protect thee] from aduersyte', kills the imaginative possibilities. Particularly valuable are the stage directions dealing with music not otherwise referred to in the text, even though there are only five of these. The singing of the angels in the *Purification* (after line 132): *Angeli cantant*: 'Simeon iustus et timoratus', adds an element of liturgical splendour to the marvel of the self-ringing bells (after line 102). The singing of the first verse of the *Salvator Mundi* by the souls in hell ironically explains the nature of the 'din' which irritates the devils in the *Deliverance* (after line 44), and the singing of the angels at Christ's resurrection enhances the wonder of the moment of his appearance (after line 225). Most unusual of the musical occurrences are the two suggested by the stage directions in *Thomas of India* (after lines 83 and 91). Each time Christ appears he sings *Pax vobis* etc. and passes amongst the assembled disciples, like the spirit which they at first take him to be.

Stage directions also establish the use of horses by the three kings in the *Oblacio Magorum* (after line 504), and Centurio in the *Resurrection* (after line 44). Only one special effect is mentioned, the common one of the disappearing of Christ at the meal in Emmaus (after line 290). The oddest stage direction is that in *Jacob* (after line 58). Between lines 58 and 59 several years have passed covering Jacob's sojourn with his mother's kinsman Laban, when he has married Rachel, had several children and amassed considerable possessions. All this is covered by the direction: *Hic egrediatur Iacob de Aran in terram natiuitatis sue* (Here Jacob leaves Haran for the land of his birth). He arrives a single man and leaves with wives, servants, children, flocks and possessions (and pursued by his uncle Laban), yet nothing is said of this. The immediately following stage direction is puzzling in a different way: *Hic scrutetur superlectile* (Here he examines his belongings). It seems to be no more than a response to Leah's 'Go and see [whether our things have passed the Jordan]'. Why does it deserve a stage direction? Merely to set him apart to struggle with the angel? Oddly the words are reminiscent of an earlier part of the biblical story when Jacob angrily asks Laban why *scrutatus es omnem suppellectilem meam?* (have you searched all my household stuff?). The word *suppellectilem/superlectile* is not so uncommon as to make a connection certain,[7] but it is possible that the biblical account has become woven into the stage direction. The 'stage direction' in *Lazarus: Et lacrimatus est Jesus* is, of course, an exact quotation from John 11.35. A further long direction describes the meeting of Jacob and Esau, here more satisfactorily translating into dramatic terms what in Genesis is a long and complicated series of devices that Jacob employs to turn away his brother's anger. There is much of interest here for performance, but, as has been said already, there is nothing in the stage directions that gives a hint as to the type of staging involved.

WAKEFIELD AND TOWNELEY

Because of the amount of speculation that there has been about the provenance of the Towneley cycle it is important at the outset to set out the documentary evidence as clearly and fully as possible. It takes three forms: the Wakefield burgess court rolls, a letter from the ecclesiastical commission in York and the manuscript itself. The burgess court material has recently been re-presented by A. C. Cawley, Jean Forrester and John Goodchild (*197*) because the rediscovery of the originals of the lost rolls has shown without doubt that part of the evidence presented by J. W. Walker in 1929 does not exist. There are two relevant rolls, for 1556 and 1559, which contain between them the following items:

> 1556. Item a payne is sett that everye crafte and occupacion doo bringe furthe theire pagyauntes of Corpus Christi daye as hathe bene heretofore veed, and to gyve furthe the speches of the same in Easter holydayes in payne of everye one not so doynge to forfett xls.

> 1559. Item a payn ys layd þat Gyles Dolleffe shall brenge in or cavsse to be

broght þe regenall of Corpvs Christy play before þis and Wytsonday in pane
...

Item a payn is layde þat þe mesteres of þe Corpvs Christi playe shall come
and mayke thayre acovntes before þe gentyllmen and burgessvs of þe town
before thys and May day next in payn of euere on not so doynge xxs.

(For 'before' in each of the latter entries read, presumably, 'between'.)

The 1556 roll is headed: Paynes layde by the burges enqueste at the
Courte kepte at Wakefelde / nexte after the Feaste of Saynte Michaell thar-
chaungell in / thirde and fourte yeares of the Reignes of oure Soueraigne
Lorde / and Ladye kinge Philyppe and quene Marye 1556'. Since this shows
that the court was held after Michaelmas (29 September) the threatened
penalty must relate to a performance in 1557. The entry establishes a
number of things: the involvement of the crafts, the existence of pageants
(without specifying the meaning of the word), the relationship with Corpus
Christi Day (leaving it slightly uncertain whether it is the pageants performed on that day or, less likely, a generic title), the existence of performances before 1557, the presence of speeches and the need to distribute them
during the Easter holiday. If the distribution of speeches is the handing out
of parts, as seems likely, then an ample two months was allowed for learning and rehearsal.[8] The first 1559 entry establishes the existence of a text.
We cannot be certain that it is a complete copy of the play rather than a
craft original of a single pageant, but the words used seem to imply the
former. The second entry apparently shows that the money for the play was
collected by the masters of the Corpus Christi play – whether collected from
crafts, wards of the town or parishes is not specified. Whoever they were
they were responsible to the burgess court, not to any individual group.[9] If
the period of the 1559 roll is the same as that of the 1556 one, then the
entries refer to 1560 – accounts to be made before 1 May, 'regenall' to be
brought back before 2 June (Whitsunday). This makes sense if the 'regenall'
was the town copy of the complete play and performance was in Whitsun
week. The first (1556) reference is to a performance in the reign of Philip
and Mary, therefore perhaps a revival or at least an affirmation of an old
custom, the second (1559) to performance in the second year of the reign of
Elizabeth – a survival.

The instructions from the ecclesiastical commission in York sent on or
around 27 May 1576 to the bailiff (the lord of the manor's official), the
burgesses and other inhabitants, presumably refers to a projected performance two weeks or so later (in that year Whitsunday was 10 June, Corpus
Christi, 21 June) (76, p. 125; 210, pp. 330–1). The commissioners understood that it was intended that 'in the towne of Wakefeld shalbe plaied this

yere in Whitsonweke next or theraboutes a plaie commonlie called Corpus Christi plaie which hath bene heretofore vsed there'. The letter specifies the abuses that it seeks to prevent, but these specifications seem rather more like blanket prohibitions: no representation of any of the Persons of the Trinity, or the administration of either sacrament (in the Reformed Church there were only two, baptism and Lord's Supper or Communion), nothing encouraging superstition or idolatry, or contrary to divine or civil law. It is impossible to know how much the authorities in York knew about the play and hence to what extent these prohibitions were specific. There does not seem to be any direct connection between these instructions and the Towne-ley manuscript. Certainly there is now no institution of the Eucharist ('administration' of the sacrament of the 'Lord's Supper') in the Last Supper section of the Towneley *Conspiracy*, but it seems there never was. The removal of one of the references to the seven sacraments in *John the Baptist*, marked 'correctyd and not playd', clearly refers to an occasion when these lines were not performed but presumably the pageant (and the play) was. It is more likely that the letter was an attempt deliberately couched in very broad terms to get rid of the play altogether. The instructions from the commissioners are therefore important witness to continuing attempts to perform the play at Wakefield in Whitsun week or thereabouts as late as 1576, but they give little other information.

The manuscript provides three kinds of evidence (76, pp. xiv–xvii). The link with Wakefield is established by the appearance of the name at the head of the *Creation* (fol. 1) and after the title of *Noah* (fol. 7v). Though there is therefore no doubt about the existence of a connection, the appearance of the name twice, instead of strengthening the connection, weakens it, since the name at the beginning of the whole manuscript might seem to establish a relationship between the town and the whole play, while the name at the beginning of the *Noah* makes it seem as though it relates only to individual pageants (217, pp. 151–2; 135, pp. 101–8). There are next the local refer-ences within the text. The most specific of these is to 'Gudeboure at the quarell hede' (*Killing of Abel*, line 367) referring to a lane, Goodybower, to the north of the parish church in Wakefield (where Brook Street now is). There are three references to the Wakefield locality in the *Shepherds* pageants. The most certain is to 'Horbery shrogys' (II, line 455) to the southwest of Wakefield. There are also 'ayll of Hely' (I, line 244), perhaps referring to Healey, a hamlet beyond Horbury, and 'the crokyd thorne' (II, line 403), reputed to be a reference to the Shepherds' thorn that appar-ently once stood in Mapplewell, though possibly a rather vaguer reference to one of the many 'thorn' placenames in the district. There is finally the reference to 'Watlyn strete' in the *Judgement* (line 126). This is a name given to a number of stretches of old Roman road, one not too far distant from Wakefield. It is also, however, a name for the constellation of the Milky Way, to which it could easily refer in the pageant. All five of these local, or possibly local, references occur in the work of the Wakefield Master, so that once again what appears to be a link between Wakefield and the whole play becomes a rather more specific connection with a portion of it.

There are finally in the manuscript the craft names added in the sixteenth century to six of the pageants: *Creation*, 'Barker' (fol. 1); *Killing of Abel*, 'Glover pag ...' (fol. 3); *Pharaoh*, 'Litsters pagonn' and 'lyster play' (fol. 21); *Pilgrims* 'fysher pagent' (fol. 107v); *Hanging of Judas*, 'Lysters pagon' (fol. 131v); and, possibly, 'Tyler' added below the title of the *Scourging* (fol. 78v). These are not in themselves references to Wakefield but they do establish a similarity in that some (and by implication all) of the pageants were performed by crafts, at least during the sixteenth century. They also establish, as do the corrections and cancellations, that this is a manuscript connected with the organisation of performance, not a reading copy for someone's library.

It is not really possible to take it very much further. Arguments have been levelled against Wakefield as the home of Towneley on the grounds that it was too small to have produced so complex a play. Many of these objections were made, however, when the play was thought of as of the early fifteenth century (*135*, pp. 97, 116–17; *210*, pp. 322–3). If it is later in the century then the chances are somewhat greater that it could have been performed in Wakefield. There is not really enough evidence either way as yet, especially in view of the uncertainty about the mode and organisation of the performance. Wakefield was the organisational centre of a very large manor – from the later fifteenth century, a royal manor. Towns, villages and hamlets in nearby areas were to an extent dependent upon it and it is possible that they could have been drawn as individual entities or as parts of larger groups into a centrally organised performance.[10] So far no evidence for such an organisation has been produced in the West Riding of Yorkshire. Nor is there any evidence for the site of the performance in or outside Wakefield.

LITERARY RELATIONSHIPS

THE YORK PLAY

As has been well known since Lucy Toulmin Smith's edition of the *York Plays* in 1885 (*72*), five of the Towneley pageants are closely related to the parallel pageants in York, or as Miss Toulmin Smith put it:

The Towneley plays are not only written in the same dialect, but five of them are the same as five of the York plays, with certain passages cut out or modified. (p. xlvi)

Since that straightforward (but incidentally misleading) statement was made, the battle lines have been drawn up between the various theories intended to account for the situation. Broadly speaking they are these: Towneley borrowed from York, or vice versa, or both derived from a common original cycle.[11] Much valuable work came out of the battle and now, some fifty years after the final salvoes were fired, it seems to be worth looking again at the relationship, drawing on what has been said already and adding some further suggestions.

The starting-point is inevitably the variation between the two versions of the five pageants: *Pharaoh*, the *Doctors in the Temple*, the *Deliverance*, the *Resurrection* and the *Judgement*. It is clear from a quick glance at the underprinted texts in the Toulmin Smith edition of *York* that the word 'same' has been used rather loosely. *Pharaoh* moves almost step by step with the York pageant and could indeed (allowing for minor variations) be said to be the same. The Towneley *Doctors* is also in a way 'the same', but here there are two major alterations: a totally different opening for the doctors themselves and an expansion of Christ's explanation of the ten commandments. The Towneley *Judgement* is far from being the same as York. The two have twenty-three stanzas in common (give or take a few lines) out of a total in Towneley of seventy-seven and in York of forty-eight stanzas. In other words just under half of the York pageant is incorporated into Towneley, and, despite the fact that the core of the episode is represented by the York sections, these are overwhelmed and transformed by the new Towneley material. There is a difficulty in making this comparison because the opening of Towneley is missing, but even if all the eighteen York stanzas that precede the opening of the Towneley pageant were added (and this would make for a very overweight pageant) it would still only make up a little over half of the present pageant. The 'sameness' of the *Judgement* pageants is clearly very different from the 'sameness' of *Pharaoh* or the *Doctors*.

The other two pageants are different again, but they are in some ways similar to each other. Each has a new introductory section, a speech for Jesus in the *Deliverance* and one for Pilate in the *Resurrection*, and then both continue alongside York but very freely altering, adding, omitting and reordering.

I have concerned myself first with the five major borrowings from York because, quite rightly, they have tended to dominate the discussion of the relationship between the two cycles. There is a danger, however, that concentrating on the five tends to conceal the extent of York influence elsewhere in Towneley, and also to a limit the discussion of possible influence. There are two other pageants that may well be from York: the so-called *Processus Talentorum* (probably a mistake for *Talorum* 'of the Dice' and hereafter called the *Dicing*) and the fragmentary *Suspencio Iude* (the Hanging of Judas). The evidence for the first being in origin a York pageant (or, to be precise, lines 190–351 of it) is reasonably strong, and no satisfactory argument has been brought against this attribution (*196*, *198*). Unlike the five others, however, its York counterpart dropped out of production in around 1422–3 and it is not therefore recorded in the York manuscript (*163*). For *Judas* there are two pieces of evidence. The first is the name, which is the same as that given to the York pageant in the so-called second list of pageants in the York A/Y Memorandum Book (*158*, pp. 25–6; *109*, pp. lii-lix). Like the *Dicing* it was no longer in performance after 1422–3 (*161*), and there is perhaps a greater likelihood therefore of the old name being retained. Secondly, it is written in one of the common York stanza forms (six-line, rhyming aaabab), used also in the Towneley/York *Resurrection*. The *Dicing* is to my mind almost certainly a York pageant in origin; *Judas* seems likely to be, but there is no final proof.

Besides these two possible York pageants there are a number of intrusions of York material into other Towneley pageants. The *Flagellacio* (Scourging) contains ninety-eight lines certainly from York, and a further fifty that are almost certainly so, out of the pageant's 416 lines. The Towneley *Offering of the Magi* contains only one York stanza, but the rest of the pageant is consistently in the six-line stanza of many York pageants, including the *Resurrection*. This is not in itself sufficient evidence to show that the *Offering* is an earlier version of the York pageant of the *Magi*, but the appearance of a single (insignificant) stanza from the current York pageant argues a proximity of some sort between the two pageants. Besides these borrowings there are a number of reminiscences of the York *Joseph's Trouble about Mary* in the Towneley *Annunciation*, and perhaps also worth mentioning is the obvious joining together of two or more pageants to make the present Towneley *Conspiracio* (Conspiracy). The pageant is oddly called *Conspiracio* at the beginning and *Capcio* (Taking) at the end. These hints of multiple breaks is a reminder that in the second list from York this section of the play was originally four separate pageants, the final one *Capcio Christi orantis in monte* (The Taking of Christ Praying on the Mountain).[12]

The York Register, to which reference has been made more than once in what has already been said, is a neat official copy made from craft originals of texts of the pageants of the Corpus Christi play in, as far as we know, the period 1463–77 (*70*, pp. 10–19; *109*). It clearly attempts to present a clean and accurate text. I have up to now used this text as a basis for investigating what 'Towneley' did to 'York', since there is no other text to use. It is, however, almost certain that the Register was not the exemplar for the Towneley versions of the York pageants and there is therefore a certain speciousness in talking about changes made to it as though they were the result of one person or several people in a single place (represented by Towneley) working on a known text (the Register). We do not know whether the versions of the York pageants borrowed by Towneley had already been revised to a considerable extent in York. There are one or two hints, however, that that was not so. If the borrowings were made before the Register was compiled in 1463–77, then the texts used are likely to have been craft copies of the text. But since the Register itself was compiled from craft copies, both texts, Towneley and York, are making use of similar originals, and so using the Register text to give an indication of Towneley's exemplar is not totally wrong-headed. On the other hand, if the Towneley borrowings were made after the compilation of the Register, but still from craft copies, we might expect to find some indication of any extensive changes in those copies in the annotations of some decades of Common Clerks or their deputies noting in the margins of the Register alterations in what they saw and heard at the first station of the play. For the five pageants under consideration there are no such annotations.

It is still important to remember, however, that we know very little about the circumstances of the borrowings. We do not know under whose auspices the changes in the texts were made, or who made them, or for what purpose. We do not know whether they were made in isolation or in connection with each other. We do not know whether the borrowings were made to fill in gaps or to replace unsatisfactory pageants in an already existing cycle, or whether they were the nucleus around which a new cycle was to be created. If all the suppositions about the origins of the pageants were facts, then York would have provided this new cycle, in part or in whole, with ten pageants, six still being performed in York – *Pharaoh*, the *Doctors*, the *Scourging*, the *Deliverance*, the *Resurrection* and the *Judgement* – and four disused pageants – *Offering of the Magi*, *Conspiracy and Taking of Christ*, the *Dicing* and the *Hanging of Judas*.[13]

NON-DRAMATIC LITERATURE

Examination of the way in which Towneley treats York is important for the light it can throw on the possible development of the cycle, but it is also important as an indication of the ways in which writers alter, adapt and develop their sources. The major vernacular source of the Towneley cycle is undoubtedly York, but there are also some minor vernacular pieces absorbed into the pageants. The most extensive of these is the lyric contained in the speech of the risen Christ in the *Resurrection* (lines 244–321) (*136*, pp. 26–7). The interpolation (measured by material added to the York pageant) consists of two additional stanzas for the soldiers set to guard the tomb, three stanzas for Jesus introducing the lyric and two stanzas rounding off the lyric. All seven of the stanzas outside the lyric are in the York six-line stanza, in one of them the rhyme scheme momentarily failing (Towneley line 224). The main interpolation here is, however, the thirteen stanzas apparently extracted from the lyric lament of Christ on the cross, 'Herkyne wordis wonder gud'.[14] The lyric exists in three manuscripts, none of which is the direct source of Towneley, and in a printed carol of 1550. The lyric and carol versions are all addresses of Christ on the cross to man and one might expect, therefore, some adjustment to fit the meaning to the risen Christ of the pageant. The playwright, however, though he has left out a number of stanzas, has not made that adjustment and the effect of the lyric is, at the joyous moment of the resurrection, to remind the audience of Christ's sufferings, and the bleeding figure before them acts, as the bleeding figure of Piers does in Passus XIX of *Piers Plowman*, as a visual transition from the crucified body of Christ to the sacrament:

> I grauntt theym here a measse   *meal*
> In brede, myn awne body. (*Resurrection*, lines 326–7)

The expansion of the child Christ's exposition of the ten commandments in the *Doctors* makes similar use of a series of verses. These, however, are found elsewhere, not as a single lyric, but scattered in the *Speculum Christiani*, a pastoral handbook of the fourteenth century (*193*).

As identifiable lyrics with a separate existence outside the play these two additions exemplify the use made of lyric poetry by the Towneley writer, especially, as here, in the revision and expansion of earlier work. Such use raises the question of whether lyrics underlie other apparently separable sections of the Towneley text. The most obvious example is the extended speech of Lazarus at the end of that pageant (lines 111–216). The speech is marked by a change to a more complex stanza form and to a heightened language, and, like the unexpected appearance of the crucified Christ in the *Resurrection* pageant, it is accompanied by an unorthodox presentation of a traditional scene. The figure of Lazarus is transformed into a *memento mori* or an image from a *transi* tomb, the lines he speaks demanding that the audience see a decaying body, a typical medieval figure of the dead, rather than the restored and purified body of the risen Lazarus.[15] The speech falls into two parts, one having much in common with many medieval lyrics on

Death (lines 111–73 and 198–211), the other with repentance lyrics and carols (lines 174–97).

The use of lyrics in the drama testifies to the common awareness amongst medieval writers of all kinds of the availability of literary and didactic texts for their own use. Re-use and adaptation of this kind are a commonplace of medieval literary work. The *Middle English Metrical Paraphrase of the Old Testament* that lies behind the York/Towneley *Pharaoh* is one kind – a formative, structural use of another poem (141); the assimilation of a lyric like 'Herkyne wordis wonder gud', for a specific limited purpose in the *Resurrection*, is another. Between these two and beyond them are all kinds of further exploitations of other literary work. The *Northern Passion* has frequently been cited as an important formative influence on the plays. Though the breadth of influence has sometimes been overplayed, there are undoubted connections between the *Northern Passion* and the drama.[16] One pageant in Towneley, the Last Supper section of the *Conspiracy*, certainly is affected by the *Passion* but in a very limited way. The influence appears most clearly at lines 320–9, where occasionally whole lines and frequently phrases and words are identical with one or other of the *Northern Passion* texts. This does not seem to be a sign of an overall influence, or even of a deliberate use of a specific section for a definite purpose, but rather of a familiarity with the poem spilling over verbally into the pageant. Or possibly a more immediate borrowing from the *Northern Passion* in an earlier version of the pageant is still showing through in the present Towneley text.

THE 'WAKEFIELD MASTER'

A. C. Cawley in his edition of *The Wakefield Pageants in the Towneley Cycle* puts forward three main pieces of evidence for the existence of the writer usually referred to as the 'Wakefield Master' (76, pp. xviii–xxi): the regular use of a particular nine-line stanza in five pageants (*Noah*, the two *Shepherds*, *Herod the Great* and the *Buffeting*), that the pageants written in this stanza are distinguished by a highly original use of colloquial idiom and that verbal parallels, as well as a number of other similarities of style and content, exist between the pageants. This may seem somewhat flimsy evidence upon which to base the existence of a writer, and yet anyone reading the five pageants will almost certainly be struck by their similarities of tone and style. To these pageants Cawley adds the *Killing of Abel*, which, though it has only one pure Wakefield Master stanza (and one with one line missing) (in 76, lines 450–62 and 463–70), seems to him and to most scholars to bear all the signs of Wakefield Master work. Cawley also draws attention to the existence of other uses of this characteristic stanza, equally in the same style, and concludes that the Wakefield Master had a hand in re-shaping or adding to the *Conspiracy* (stanzas 2–5), the *Scourging* (stanzas 5–27), the *Crucifixion* (stanza 57), the *Dicing* (stanzas 1–5 and 56–9), the *Pilgrims* (stanza 4), the *Ascension* (stanzas 57–8) and the *Judgement* (stanzas 16–48 and 68–76) (76, p. xviii). Apart from one or two minor uncertainties, this seems to be a convincing minimum view of the extent of his work.

I want to look at the Wakefield Master's work first through his revision of the York *Judgement*, where some of his talents and propensities are displayed in an extreme form.[17] Most noticeable of all is his verbal extravagance. His characteristic stanza form may in part have commended itself to him because it demanded a high degree of verbal ingenuity, and then allowed a display of the results of that ingenuity in its series of rhymes. There is no doubt at all of his love of words. He reaches out for them in all directions: the language of fashion, of the streets, the law courts, the cloister. Where he cannot find a word he invents it (*tristur*, 'post, job', line 208; *pransawte*, 'prancing', line 561), or perhaps trawls through the lower levels of the language to turn it up (*fryggys* ? 'fidget, jerk about', line 316; *skawte*, 'blow', line 559). There are constant reminders of his virtuosity:

> With hawvell and Iawvell   *babbling; jabbering*
> syngyng of lawvell   *?drinking songs*
> (lines 337–8)

> his luddokkys thai lowke like walk-mylne cloggys,
> *buttocks; look; fulling-mill blocks*
> his hede is like a stowke, hurlyd as hoggys,   *stook; bristly*
> A woll blawen bowke – thise fryggys as froggys,
> *puffed-out belly; jerk about*
> This Ielian Iowke, dryfys he no doggys
> To felter.   *?hunt*
> (lines 314–18)

The *Judgement* also reveals his enjoyment of lists of words. One stanza indeed is to all intents and purposes simply a list:

> Ye lurdans and lyars, mychers and thefes,   *rogues; pilferers*
> Flytars and flyars, that all men reprefes,   *scolds; fugitives; reprove*
> Spolars, extorcyonars, welcom, my lefes . . .   *spoilers; comrades*
> (lines 359–61)

He clearly delights in problems; series of rhymes on a Latin word, for example: 'thus/*eius*, tax/wax/*mendax*/' (lines 282–6); 'is/mys/*fecistis*' (lines 301–3); 'com/*eternum*, day/may/*mala*' (lines 381–5).

Sometimes he creates comically contrived rhymes: 'roll of ragman [a list of accusations] / breffes in my bag, man, / vnethes [scarcely] may I wag, man, / whils I set my stag [young horse], man.' (lines 224–7) or 'fill vs / till vs / Tutiuillus' (lines 246–8). He is only drawn once into identical rhymes in this pageant: 'hoket/hoket' (lines 233–4) or twice into nearly alike in: 'wedlake/ lake' (lines 586–7) and 'hande/nere-hande' (lines 189/191), but these are small failures amongst the eighty-six four-rhyme and forty-three three-rhyme series that are required.

Two things in particular, I think, undermine this bravura display. The first is that the words are not borne up by a sufficiently varied syntax. Though there are variations, the syntactical and rhythmic pattern is predominantly one of mid-line break and end-stopping. There is a considerable element of subjectivity here, but on my count the ratio of clear breaks (mid-line and end-line) to run-on lines is a little under two to one. Secondly, the thought and action of the additions are largely uncontrolled. The devils ramble and the lost souls (if we may consider their speeches also part of the Wakefield Master's revision) extend the laments by more than double. It is not that what they say is uninteresting, but that the impact of the Judgement is lost. The contrast is excellent between the ordered, rather old-fashioned, patterned statements of Jesus and the disordered verbal extravagances of the devils, but the delay in the action is too great between 'The tyme is commen I will make ende' (line 81) and the making of that end over three hundred lines later. What might have sustained the action would have been a continuous sense of the frightened compulsion to go to the Judgement occasionally apparent in the devils, but this is impossible to create out of the odd reference amidst an indulgent parading of sins. In addition the satirical descriptions do not grow into an absorbing of the audience into the dread of Doomsday. They become instead an entertaining display, as they are for the devils.

I have spent this long on the Wakefield Master's section of the *Judgement* because it demonstrates clearly some of the major strengths and weaknesses that reveal themselves, usually in a smaller way, in the rest of his work. His major strength, his command of a wide and varied vocabulary, provides the external appeal of many of his pageants and additions to pageants: an obvious example is the bravura Latin opening of the *Dicing*. It comes out clearly in the mock feast of the first of the *Shepherds* pageants, where the most exotic words of aristocratic cookery are laid side by side with mock French and comic English: 'oure mangyng' (eating, from French *manger*) where we 'foder/Oure mompyns' (feed our faces) with 'sawsed' and 'powderd' meat, 'chekyns endorde' (gilded), 'calf lyuer skorde with the veryose' (sliced and served with verjuice, lines 232, 209–10, 215, 216, 234, 236). It flourishes in the hypochondriac rages of Herod (though less exotically than in the vaunts of Pilate): 'losels, lyars, lurdans, tratoures, knafys' (lines 163–4), 'ditizance doutance' (Fr. 'say without doubt', line 171), 'Fy, dotty-pols' ('crackpots', line 231), and in his list of literary sources: 'Vyrgyll, Homere, legende, poece tayllys, pystyls, grales, mes, matyns' (lines 202–7). It is apparent too in the minor uses of Latin, not only the prophecies recorded by Herod's doctors and the shepherds, where it might be expected (though adding Virgil to the shepherds' catalogue, even if it is drawn from the well-known Pseudo-Augustinian sermon, gives it something of a virtuoso per-formance), but in night spells (*Shepherds* I, lines 290–4; *Shepherds* II lines 266–7) and to accompany the stretching and yawning awakening of one of the shepherds: *Resurrex a mortuus! . . . Judas carnas dominus!* (*Shepherds* II, lines 350–1). It exists too in his use of proverbs and proverb-like utter-ances and of traditional stories and incidents. Not only does he use them as a typical part of human language, but he uses them naturally; they are character-creating, not merely decorative, as with the proverb-capping meeting of the two shepherds:

2 SHEP.:	Poore men ar in the dyke and oft tyme mars,	*come to grief*
	The warld is slyke, also helpars	*like that*
	Is none here.	
1 SHEP.:	It is sayde full ryfe,	*commonly*
	'A man may not wyfe	*marry*
	And also thryfe,	*prosper*
	And all in a yere'.	
2 SHEP.:	Fyrst must vs crepe and sythen go.	

We must crawl before we can walk
(*Shepherds* I, lines 93–100)

This verbal abundance creates characters at all levels, not just that of the shepherds. The vaunts of Pilate and the rages of Herod are more enter-taining because of the words they use, but the words also individualise the characters. Words also create situation. The idea of the mock feast is good fun, the audience sees bread and ale (or maybe water) while it hears the words of medieval *haute cuisine*, but it is only the choice of those words that can give a reality to the artistocratic meal or create the kind of image that will make it parallel to the poverty of the stable embodying the royalty of the King of Kings.

The abundance of words and the images they carry with them might be expected to produce a sense of God's plenty, but instead they seem to me to convey man's plenty. This seems to be true in almost all the Wakefield Masters' pageants and adaptations. His major skill is an ability to create the variety of the world. Noah and his wife are a squabbling married couple. He is also a patriarch and the chosen of God, but first he is a hen-pecked husband. He is not a figure or type of Christ in this pageant because the play-wright makes no attempt to present him as such. The ark is not the Church, his wife is not the saved Christian, the Flood is not the Last Judgement. This is another well-told story. Maybe the fights go on a bit too long, maybe two is too many, but the comedy and the humanity are what make the story effective. It is the fun of 'ramskyt' (ram-shit); of the fearful husband knowing what's coming – 'And I am agast that we get som fray/Betwixt vs both' (lines 184–5); of the knockabout fights; of the presentation of the typical human situation, not the type–antitype situation, that govern the pageant.

The Wakefield Master's work is not open throughout to typological explanation, because he tends to draw attention to it when its use is appropriate. One of his skills lies in his ability to touch a stable reference point in the spiritual world beyond this one when he wants to. Little touches like 'This is boyte of oure bayll' (*Shepherds* I, line 147) in relation to a bottle of ale (or water imagined as ale) rather than Christ, are intellectual/spiritual fun because they hint at this other world, but like the anachronistic curses and asseverations they do not draw that world to the fore. It is at most the sudden shock of the strangeness, not a complex presentation of time, that is involved. Hints of the fall of man do not turn the widow's farmyard of the Nun's Priest's Tale into the Garden of Eden, they intellectually enliven the story Chaucer is telling by hinting at and suggesting unexpected associations. The oaths and refences are there primarily because they are what people say. They are part of a localised contemporary humanity. Only secondarily do they give a glimpse of a world beyond.

Individualised humanity lies at the root of almost all the Wakefield Master's techniques. He deliberately eschews the 'shepherds are pastors', *Pilatus id est diabolus* kind of equation. His shepherds and Pilates are individuals, made so by what they say and how they say it. This is why suggestions that all the tyrants are merely clones of Satan or Antichrist is so unsatisfactory. It is not their likeness that makes them interesting but their individuality. Pilate lives through the details he reveals of himself – each time different from or an extension of the last.

The second of the *Shepherds* pageants is remarkable because it is in this pageant alone that the individualised humanity and the presence of the spiritual world are integrated in a broader way. The shepherds are created separate: one moans of the inequalities of the social order, the second of the conflicts of marriage, the third of those of employer and employed. The structure of their speeches, however, links them together. Each complains first of the elemental disorder of the world (the weather – they are after all English shepherds) before going on to the specific complaint. Each complaint is contained within six stanzas. The first and second shepherds have six stanzas each of soliloquy, the third, for variation, has three stanzas, then one of dialogue, and then another two to himself. They also have a less obvious similarity in the movement from complaint to resolution. The first having made his complaint, shrugs it off, 'It dos me good ... Of this warld for to talk in maner of mone' (lines 46–7); the second rounds his off with a comic caricature of his own wife which allows any seriousness that the complaint might have had to dissolve in laughter. For the third shepherd the audience witnesses the complaint acted out, since he is the servant and the other two the masters. As the complaint is enacted, so is its resolution, in the singing of the three-part song. The naming of the parts – 'tenory', 'tryble' and 'meyne' – is not mere verbal gusto on the part of the Wakefield Master, but a deliberate indication that the song is in three parts and that they harmonise. The less obvious similarity in the *Shepherds'* opening, then, is one of movement in the case of each shepherd from discontent with one's state and with one's fellow human beings to content and harmony. Society may be grossly unjust, especially to the poor, marriage may be hell, especially if you're married (and a man), it may be no fun being a servant, especially with masters like these two, but it does not stop good fellowship and good humour from re-establishing contentment. The first part of the pageant is, then, a cleverly varied pre-echo of what most people now see as the main theme of the whole pageant, the movement from conflict to reconciliation, from a world at odds with God to one reconciled to him through the birth of Christ.[18]

In the major part of the pageant this conflict must be felt, hence the value of the Wakefield Master's skill in establishing a sense of a real situation: natural suspicion of the known thief, natural animosity between masters and men, natural (if typical) conflict between husband and wife. But as with all else he does, the sense of 'natural' is primarily a product of his verbal vitality, especially apparent in Mak: his southern tooth, his night spell, his 'magic', his (and Gill's) ingenious excuses for the state of their 'baby'. The reconciliation of this conflict is equally natural. It is turned into a very ordinary game; but this is also the way in which lyric, carol and sermon writers described the birth of Christ and the end of man's separation from God. The two halves of the pageant thus stand as unequal but matching sides of a figural diptych: birth and birth, reconciliation and reconciliation.[19] There is no need to read this into the pageant; it is there. Not so obvious as to be unexciting, but with sufficient indications as to be inevitable.

But what of the shepherds? The pre-echo of reconciliation that acted as a kind of prologue to the pageant is not merely another part of the matching diptych; it is also the first step in a demonstration that the shepherds are indeed the men to whom the angel's message should be addressed. Their coming to terms with their complaints in one way or another is a first sign of this. The second is the entirely natural (and heart-warming) reaction of the third shepherd and the others to their failure of common humanity in not giving Mak and Gill's newborn child a gift. The third is their common agreement to turn the punishment of Mak into a game. Thus the Wakefield Master's elaborate creation of three believable human beings is part and parcel of the spiritual meaning of the pageant. The audience does not just understand that the angelic message was to men of goodwill, it feels what goodwill is by being moved by the common humanity, common humaneness, of the three shepherds.

The *Shepherds* pageant is also a demonstration that the Wakefield Master's knowledge is not just of words. It is apparent that the description of the song of the three shepherds is not merely a demonstration of the writer's technical competence but is to draw attention to the abstract idea of harmony. The Wakefield Master repeats this use of music in the course of the pageant thereby creating a kind of choric comment on the action. The discordant singing of Mak (accompanied perhaps by Gill's groans) is the other side of humanity's music. The angel's song (and it is important to remember that there is only one angel) is the perfect music of heaven. Again the Wakefield Master uses technical terms for a spiritual purpose: 'Thre brefes to a long' ('Three short notes to one long') is, according to the theorists, perfect time.[20] It is also perfect audibly; the 'harmonies' are so true as to be indistinguishable from a single line. The shepherds then try to imitate it and fail comically. But the comic failure is a further sign of humanity. Laughter becomes in this pageant a sign of man's goodwill, a parallel to the game that is Mak's punishment.

The Wakefield Master is, then, as capable of controlled. structured writing as he is of boisterous exuberance. He is quite able to handle a complex parallel presentation of the spiritual and human world, but even here humanity dominates. His achievement in this pageant is to make his proven skill in the depiction of humanity subserve a spiritual aim (and to interweave with it) without losing any of its natural life.

Martin Stevens has recently suggested that the Wakefield Master was the 'guiding intelligence' for the whole cycle (*135*). This is impossible to prove or disprove but it does usefully raise the question of the extent to which his hand can be traced. The normal way of recognising his work is through the use of the characteristic nine-line stanza. Yet it is unlikely that such a skilful and ebullient writer would allow himself to be confined in such a way, and the fairly general agreement amongst scholars about his authorship or at least his participation in the writing of the *Killing of Abel* shows a willingness to accept this. But looking for his work outside the nine-line stanza can only be based on his work done in it, and judging only from that we may be getting a false impression of his complete range. In particular we know very little about what might be called his 'solemn' style. Almost everything that survives is for shepherds, devils, hen-pecked patriarchs, tyrants and the like. We have very little for God (ten stanzas, many of them directions for building the ark), for Mary (two stanzas), Jesus (four lines), for angels (two stanzas). Outside the five pageants there is a tiny sample for the apostles: Luke, one stanza in the *Pilgrims*; Matthew, one in the *Ascension*. Neither of these, though competent, is anything out of the ordinary, and anyway they are too brief to give a fair sample. It may, therefore, be that in our assessment of his work we are missing an important side of his output. The *Thomas of India* pageant should perhaps be looked at closely. It has what looks like a series of Wakefield Master rhymes in one of Peter's speeches:

> Bot euer alas! what was I wode! myght no man be abarstir;
> I saide if he nede be-stode to hym shuld none be trastir;
> And for a woman that there stode, that spake to me of frastir,
> I saide I knew not that good creature my master.
> (lines 73–5, with the missing line, 74a, supplied from the manuscript)

The invention and adaptation that has gone into producing the rhymes 'abarstir/trastir/of frastir' (more ashamed/more trusty/?questioningly) are typical of those found elsewhere. Besides this, the argument between Thomas and the other apostles is handled with considerable ingenuity and naturalness. The fact that it goes on too long may also seem characteristic of some of his work. It is difficult to speculate about what the 'solemn' side of his writing would be like but at least this might be a starting-point for investigation.

THE CYCLE

It has been suggested that the pageants of the Towneley cycle do not combine well together. Rosemary Woolf expresses it most clearly:

> The only cycle in which the different styles and stages of revision have not grown together into an organic whole is the Towneley cycle ...
> (138, p. 310)

This apparent lack of unity is up to a point a scholarly and literary problem rather than a theatrical one.[21] The fact that we know that the York pageants in Towneley are from York gives them a separateness that they would not have if their different origin was unknown. Besides which the briefness of pageants like the *Salutation* or the *Flight into Egypt* that we can see in reading them is not nearly so noticeable in performance, where they have their own individuality and physical space. Equally the rather simple language of pageants like the *Creation*, *Isaac* or *Jacob* is less obvious when the pageant is seen as well as heard. Only the Wakefield Master's work, perhaps, because his pageants are so much more developed, literary and structured, stands out. There is a danger that they hold up the flow of the narrative. In performance again this seems not to be so. Pageant performance involves the isolation of incidents and episodes while at the same time allowing them to be part of the same story. Their temporal and spatial relation to the whole is therefore not the same as scenes in a continuous action. Pageant performance can absorb very different styles of writing as well as of playing – as it must if the responsibility for the playing is divided amongst a number of individual craft guilds, with, as far as we know, no overall control.

There are some odd gaps in the cycle, apart from those caused by the losses in the manuscript. There is no temptation of Christ, no institution of the sacrament at the Last Supper, no trial before Herod (though it is referred to). There are also unexpected additions: the *Isaac* and *Jacob* pageants, *Caesar Augustus*, the *Dicing*. But these do not prevent the cycle from being a whole. David Mills has suggested that the pageants exist within a known story and that there is therefore no need to perform every part of the story (*209*, p. 96). This is surely right. How many people in seeing the cycle are aware that there is no Nativity or are worried by the fact that there has been no trial before Herod, even though the first torturer says that that is where they are coming from? As for the additions, *Isaac* and *Jacob* form part of an integrated family group with *Abraham*, and the *Dicing* provides yet another interesting sidelight on Pilate (and, for those who know the story, a lead into his later life) as well as providing an entertaining break between the horrors of the crucifixion and the joys of the harrowing and resurrection. *Caesar Augustus* is more difficult to justify. Trivial in language and oversimple as verse, it lacks any interest of plot and seems merely a tame preparation for Herod.

There is also a more positive unifying element, a sense of a concentration on human nature which gives the cycle a certain homogeneity. All the cycles translate biblical into human. It is good teaching practice – a way of making the Bible live; it is an obvious way of expanding what are often the bare hints of a story; and it is, in the fourteenth and fifteenth centuries, the normal approach to Christ's life.[22] To say, therefore, that a cycle is characterised by its humanity would seem to be stating the inevitable. In Towneley, however, there seems to be far more particularising of human language, character and action than elsewhere. It is especially noticeable, of course, in the Wakefield Master and it may well be that the dominance of his presence in the cycle draws the reader's attention to this element in the other pageants. Even before the scatological humanity of Cain, however, there is a Lucifer who even before he falls doesn't care a 'leke' (*Creation*, line 129) and a Cherub who leads Adam into Paradise by the hand, giving him and Eve distinctly elder-brother/sisterly advice (lines 210–25). What gives a strong sense of humanity to the cycle is the number of particularising words or phrases, or individualising emotions, actions or idea. The image of Cain's debased humanity is largely created by his individualised language. We may be used to God's 'back parts' (*posteriora mea*, Exodus 33.23) but 'his ars' (*Abel*, line 238) still seems the most incredible blasphemy. Cain's language not only particularises his humanity but attempts to re-create others, including God, in his image. In the main action of *Abraham* the human element almost of necessity predominates, but from the beginning that element is there. In his first speech Abraham recalls the past. Partly this links him into the story; but he does not do it impersonally, instead he sees it through a veil of pity for the sadness of it all. Remembering brings no comfort, only a longing for death (lines 33–6). Later, as Abraham pictures the return home without Isaac, he very sharply particularises Sarah's reactions and words.

> What shal I to his moder say?
> For 'Where is he?' tyte will she spyr;   *at once ask*
> If I tell hir 'Ron away',
> Hir answere bese belife – 'Nay, sir!'   *will immediately be*
> (lines 225–8)

Even some of the small additions to *Pharaoh* are in the direction of additional individuality of speech (e.g. lines 219, 225, 230, 232). The biblical account is altered at the end of *Jacob* in order to give greater weight to the reconciliation of Jacob and Esau and to the reuniting of the family in Esau's last words. In Genesis the reconciliation is rather a cold one and there is no invitation from Esau that they should together go to see their parents. Apparent anachronism can also be an individualising device, as it is most frequently in the oaths and asseverations of shepherds, torturers and others, but also in the tithes of Cain (lines 104–5 in particular) and Jacob (lines 55–8).

David Mills has seen a unifying element in memory in the cycle (209). I am sure he is right but I would prefer the term 'recollection'. In York, also, it is not uncommon for a character to run through earlier history at the opening of a pageant, but in Towneley this recalling occurs elsewhere as well and is far more personal to the character. It has already been suggested that Abraham's first speech is an individualising one, but its subject is the recalling of the past. *Noah* opens not with God recalling the past but with Noah, and what starts as an address to God in his majesty and might turns into a contemplation of sin and a fear of God's vengeance. Again the recalling has a personal and emotional basis. The same is true of other acts of recalling. The precise recollections of Christ's miracles are by the torturers, angrily condemning his failure to conform to the law (*Scourging*, lines 152–87), or, less individualised and more conventional, by Annas and Caiaphas trying to convince Pilate of the need for action (*Conspiracy*, lines 92–133). The lyric added to the *Resurrection* acts as a recalling of the crucifixion in the middle of the triumph of the resurrection. The disciples in the *Pilgrims* and in *Thomas of India* recall the same events in grief, and in disbelief of the fulfilment of remembered promises. The other element of recalling is prophecy, which, except for the *Prophets*, almost always appears as recollection. Like the moments of recalling, the prophecies are usually part of some human reaction to events: the kings' excited realisation that the star they are following is the fulfilment of Balaam's prophecy (*Magi*, lines 205–28), Simeon's pondering on the fate of his predecessors and gratitude for the prophecies that have been sent (*Purification*, lines 9–24), the doctors' faith that the prophecies will be fulfilled but their doubt about when (*Doctors* lines 1–48), the souls in hell recalling at the moment of fulfilment the prophecies of Christ's coming (*Deliverance*, lines 25–88). There are also the formal researchings into the past by Herod's doctors/councillors. Not all of these recall events present in the cycle. Some function instead within the Christian consciousness of history, but whether they are inside or outside the cycle they create an interweaving pattern of past and present.

Though recollection is important in the cycle, typology is not. There is one striking moment of poise between past and future when God at the beginning of the *Annunciation* balances past and future acts:

> For reson wyll that ther be thre,
> A man, a madyn, and a tre:
> Man for man, tre for tre,
> Madyn for madyn; thus shal it be. (lines 31–4)

It is the nearest that the cycle comes to explicit typological interpretation. Typology has for some time now been a way of approaching the structure and meaning of cycle plays. Not all critics have found it a satisfying approach, but the charismatic force of such works as Kolve's *Play called Corpus Christi* (130) coupled with the scholarship of such writers as Rosemary Woolf (138) has carried it into an almost automatic acceptance. I have said it is an approach to structure and meaning; I mean that it has been used to give order and coherence to what may have seemed haphazard and ill-

constructed, and to give depth to what may have seemed shallow and superficial. Much good has come of it in the right hands, but there has also come
a danger of feeling the typology and forgetting about the context. Typology
needs exposition, or verbal reference or visual reference to make it effective,
or it needs the structure of cycle or pageant to create an appropriate framework; in Towneley as a whole none of these seems to me to be present.
Humanity and recollection, and the humanity of recollection, create a web
of interrelation in the cycle which holds it together. It is a cycle of human
beings, humble and natural, gross and inflated, but all human, not types and
figures.

NOTES

1 The medieval manor and town of Wakefield are discussed in M. L. Faull and
  S. A. Moorehouse (eds.), *West Yorkshire: an Archaeological Survey to A. D.
  1500*, 3 vols. (Wakefield: West Yorkshire Metropolitan County Council, 1981).

2 Alfred W. Pollard refers to him as 'the Wakefield or Woodkirk editor' in the
  introduction to the EETS edition (*75*, p. xxii), but Charles Mills Gayley, *Plays of
  Our Forefathers* (London: Chatto and Windus, 1907) seems to have been the first
  to use the name 'Wakefield Master'.

3 The best brief description and discussion of the manuscript is the introduction to
  the facsimile (*113*), but the earlier ones by Wann (*217*) and Stevens (*214*) are still
  of value. There is no substitute, however, for looking at the manuscript itself,
  now made possible (if through a glass, darkly) by the existence of the complete
  facsimile.

4 Some doubt has been cast on the authenticity of the annotations, but there seems
  no real reason for this, except extreme scepticism (see Palmer, *210*, pp. 321 and
  342 n. 14). Mendel G. Frampton (*203*) very strongly defends the idea of the
  Towneley manuscript as a register.

5 The most convenient check on costume dates is C. Willett and Phillis Cunn-
  ington, *Handbook of English Medieval Costume* (London: Faber, 1952); see
  pp. 98–168 for the fifteenth century. Frampton (*203*, 631–43) has investigated the
  evidence provided by the costume references most fully, but his discussion makes
  clear what shifting sand this is upon which to base a firm date for the work of
  the Wakefield Master.

6 John R. Elliott, Jr gives a useful but selective list of productions of medieval
  plays in England between 1901 and 1980 (*472*; see pp. 111–13 for productions of
  the Towneley plays). Reviews of complete productions of the cycle will be found
  in *METh* 2 (1980), 49–52, and *RORD* 23 (1980), 81–4 (Wakefield, 1980); *METh* 7
  (1985), 51–4, and *RORD* 28 (1985), 189–99 (Toronto, 1985).

7 It occurs, scattered through the Old Testament, twenty-five times, relating to
  temple and household furnishings, material and general commodities.

8 Barbara D. Palmer understands this rather differently, but is worried by the
  inappropriateness of parts of the cycle to performance at Easter (*210*, 329, 345
  n. 51).

9 The plural 'mesteres' could mean a single group of people responsible for

financing the whole play, or a number of individual groups responsible for several pageants, such as the pageant masters of the York craft guilds.

10 Palmer moves towards this kind of arrangement (210, pp. 340 1), whilst admitting that there is so far no evidence for it from this part of the country.

11 Hardin Craig gave a very partisan view, and listed many of the contributions to the debate (25, pp. 214–15).

12 Of the many earlier discussions of these matters, those by Frampton (204, 205) are still of value, though his conclusions are often undermined by too great a reliance on the then accepted dating of the *Ordo* and the second list.

13 Besides the York association there is the brief reflection of Chester (*Resurrection*, lines 325–332, and, sporadically, Chester *Resurrection* lines 162–76), and the complicated interrelation of the Doctors pageants, investigated by W. W. Greg (*181*, pp. 101–20).

14 The lyric is no. 1119 in the Brown-Robbins *Index of Middle English Verse* (though the description there of its appearance in British Library MS Additional 37049 is rather inaccurate).

15 Some idea of the usual fifteenth-century presentation of Lazarus can be gained from 469, figs. 580–1.

16 Frances A. Foster (ed.), *The Northern Passion*, EETS, OS 147 (London: Kegan Paul, Trench, Trübner and Co., 1916), pp. 81–101. Foster certainly overstresses the relationship between the poem and the plays, as a close inspection of her examples will show.

17 Martin Stevens has also used the *Judgement* to characterise the work of the Wakefield Master, though his prime concern is to reveal the theme, as he sees it, of the 'abuse of language' in his work, the devils ironically condemning themselves by their extravagant language (*135*, pp. 164–8).

18 V. A. Kolve's very perceptive and subtle discussion of the Shepherds' pageants (*130*, pp. 151–74) seems to me to overstress the depiction of the 'world at its worst' (p. 167), and to underestimate the skill of the Wakefield Master by seeing such a subtle approach as common to all the English Shepherds' plays.

19 The two parts are not only linked thematically, but are also joined by numerous reflected details. Many scholars from Homer A. Watt (*218*) onwards have dealt with this, notably Arnold Williams (46, pp. 128–9) and Rosemary Woolf (*138*, pp. 190–1).

20 See Carpenter (*195*, p. 698), and also Manfred F. Bukofzer, 'Speculative Thinking in Medieval Music', *Speculum* 17 (1942), 165–80, at 177–8, for theorists relating ternary rhythm to perfection and the Trinity.

21 David Mills (*209*) emphasies the incoherence of the manuscript: 'The manuscript could almost be an idiosyncratic assemblage of material from a variety of sources into a sort of presentation volume, using a Creation–Doomsday framework of organisation' (p. 95). He stresses, however, the ability of the framework to contain the diversity. In my opinion he overstresses the diversity.

22 The tendency to expand and fill the gaps in the story of Christ's life exists from an early date, as the apocryphal gospels show. The later tendency, that of affective piety, is to elaborate on the feelings and experiences of the characters, as in the *Meditationes vitae Christi* and its successors.

6

ALAN J. FLETCHER

The N-Town plays

INTRODUCTION

'Corpus Christi plays', 'cycle plays': these are just two of the more familiar boxes in which modern critics have tried to contain the resisting diversity of much late medieval English drama. Indeed, such pigeon-holing has a long pedigree. Whoever wrote 'The plaie called Corpus Christi' on the first page of the play manuscript that concerns this chapter, British Library MS Cotton Vespasian D. viii, is the earliest known member of this critical family tree. He would hardly have foreseen that his sixteenth-century attempt to sum up the plays in front of him would have provided the title for one of the most successful studies of medieval drama in recent years, a study whose equally unforeseen consequence has been the encouragement of some homogenised ways of thinking about what a 'Corpus Christi cycle' might be (*130*). The fact is, however, that the plays of Cotton Vespasian D. viii are not tidily compliant, and resist the totalising project that the idea of a 'Corpus Christi cycle' has sometimes risked becoming. There is no evidence that these plays ever had anything to do with Corpus Christi, at least not in the most basic sense of their having been performed then; on the contrary, some were originally intended for performance on a Sunday. Nor has the Creation-to-Doom scope of the manuscript's content, which superficially invites comparison with the other three major mystery play collections of Chester, Wakefield and York, come about for comparable reasons. The former independence of some of its principal component parts has been suppressed: originally, these parts were never arranged according to any grand Creation-to-Doom design whatsoever. So in sum, it is juster to recognise the fascinating *difference* of this manuscript, and this sense of difference will, I hope, be an undertow to my introduction of it and of the plays of which it is no neutral transmitter.

A MANUSCRIPT IN SEARCH OF A CONTEXT

If the scribe-compiler of Cotton Vespasian D. viii (for so I shall refer to him) ever made a note of where and when he was working, the place in which he might well have recorded it, in some *explicit* at the end of his manuscript, no longer exists, for what was likely the final play in his collection, *Judgment Day*, lacks its concluding folios, finishing imperfectly with the promise of a speech from God that we never get to hear. When and where, then, was Cotton Vespasian D. viii compiled? Answers to these questions, far from being merely incidental, would help to contextualise the manuscript and so illuminate it as a material product of a specific cultural and historical matrix. The first question seems the less problematic: the scribe-compiler probably worked sometime after 1468, the date written on fol. 100v at the end of the Purification play, perhaps *c.* 1500, the period to which his handwriting seems best to correspond (114, p. xiii; 78, vol. I, p. xxii). But the question of where he worked is more difficult and has set scholars hunting widely afield, even though their excursions have mainly taken them through the same general part of England. The earliest critics, misled by a description written on the flyleaf of the manuscript by Sir Robert Cotton's librarian, Richard James, believed the plays were from Coventry.[1] Indeed, James's note that *vulgo dicitur hic liber Ludus Coventriae* ('this book is commonly called the Play of Coventry') gave rise to one of the most popular names for the plays, the *Ludus Coventriae*, a name which stuck even when critics had come to doubt their Coventry connection. It was the late-nineteenth-century investigation of the dialectal affinities of the manuscript's Middle English that started to shift attention away from Coventry to the east of England. As late as the 1960s, Lincoln was often championed as the home of the plays, even though any Lincoln affiliation of their written dialect had already by then been seriously undermined,[2] and East Anglia looked increasingly like the area in which the main scribe had been trained to write. Of course, a scribe raised on the spellings of his region might move to a part of England where others prevailed yet continue to spell as before, but, this granted, the extant records of dramatic activity in medieval Lincoln were hard pressed to correspond to the sort of drama Cotton Vespasian D. viii actually contains (34, pp. 100–18; 227). Although Lincoln rightly fell from favour as the city in which the plays were written, the tendency to foster them on a centre of cultural importance persists, and there are persuasive reasons why it should: the scribe-compiler was working somewhere where he had access to at least four different exemplars of dramatic texts (one of these, the Assumption play, he incorporated bodily into his compilation), and possibly to even more;[3] and secondly, he seems also to have been somewhere where he could consult theological material, about which more later.[4] So although in theory he could have been working anywhere, what little is known of his circumstances suggests at least that it was not in some utterly out-of-the-way place, nor, probably, very far from East Harling in south-central Norfolk, where the latest study on Middle English scribal dialects would seek to place him.[5]

Assuming he did not stray too far from home, the question then arises, where in East Anglia would have provided the right kind of cultural context for the manufacture of a play manuscript such as his? Norwich once seemed attractive until it was observed that whatever its provenance, the manuscript probably had no relation to the Norwich civic play cycle, for the content of this, as far as it can be determined, differed from that of the manuscript in several important respects (250). Moreover, the famous lines at the end of the banns of the plays: 'At vj of þe belle we gynne oure play/In .N. town' (Proclamation, lines 526–7), from which the plays derive their most appropriate modern name, the N-Town plays, are now generally thought to mean that the name of whatever town the plays were to be performed in should be substituted for the 'N' just as, for example, the letter N. (for *nomen*) in many a medieval liturgical manuscript was a cue to its reader to insert whatever name he required.[6] In short, the N-Town plays (or more precisely, the plays that the banns referred to, for they apply only to a portion of the manuscript's contents) were probably intended for touring, not for performing in one specific city. It is worth bearing in mind, though, that since there is no evidence that the plays in Cotton Vespasian D. viii ever came from any civic cycle, lack of correspondence between them and the civic cycle of Norwich is not the best reason for rejecting Norwich as the manuscript's home. Even so, Norwich has lost ground and has been eclipsed in some of the most recent criticism by a case argued powerfully in favour of a home in Bury St Edmunds (227). This argument requires scrutiny.

Bury St Edmunds was undeniably an important dramatic centre throughout the fifteenth century, and even before then there are signs of an interest in drama there (227, pp. 61–2). It was in its prosperous abbey of St Edmund that the Benedictine monk and poet John Lydgate spent much of his life, and his concern with drama is well attested in the mummings and pageants that formed part of his copious output.[7] Possibly the style of some N-Town plays betrays Lydgatean influence. Possibly, too, certain of the morality plays in the Macro and Digby manuscripts were at one time in the abbey's possession, and there is a little evidence that players or minstrels were hosted there (84, p. xiv; 252, p. 148).

But does all this therefore mean that Bury was the town in which the N-Town plays were compiled? There are difficulties in believing so that should not be minimised.[8] One is theoretical. Once an important dramatic centre is established, and undoubtedly Bury was, there may be a temptation to foster on it any play text that can be shown to come from the same general area of England in which the centre is located but whose exact provenance is otherwise unknown, as in N-Town's case. Records prove, however, that late medieval East Anglian drama might sometimes get written down in places that were not conspicuous cultural or dramatic centres. For example, Robert Reynes, a late-fifteenth-century churchwarden of the village of Acle in Norfolk, copied play extracts into his commonplace book.[9] Had all evidence of his whereabouts been removed from his manuscript, a comparatively out-of-the-way Norfolk village would surely not have struck critics as its likely provenance. Notwithstanding the undisputed existence of dramatic centres, cases like this should encourage respect for the diffusion of dramatic activity throughout East Anglia in the fifteenth century (see below, chapter 7). Yet as noted earlier, the scribe-compiler's access to several source texts suggests that the compilation of N-Town probably did somehow depend upon a centre of relative cultural significance. Are we back, therefore, to Bury St Edmunds? A glance at a map of East Anglia in the fifteenth century suggests another possibility with as good a claim, and this is the town of Thetford in south-central Norfolk, about twelve miles north of Bury.

Apart from the fact that it is the nearest big cultural centre to the area indicated by the spelling of the scribe-compiler, Thetford too is linked with drama. Its Cluniac Priory of St Mary, one of East Anglia's greatest monastic houses, is known to have made payments towards plays in Thetford and its surrounding villages (237). These payments might also fit a context of touring, inter-village drama such as is known to have existed in the region (266), and some kind of touring drama, as we saw, seems implied by the N-Town banns. Another contemporary East Anglian play with banns, the Croxton *Play of the Sacrament*, has also been thought to have a Thetford connection (85, pp. lxxxiv–v). N-Town's unique series of plays on the early life of the Virgin Mary were conceivably organised by some lay religious guild, as were also its plays on the Passion (79, pp. 9–12; 80, pp. 15–19). (These groups of plays will be discussed later.) If they were, Thetford too had social infrastructures suited to producing them. A well-endowed guild of St Mary was active there, and as early as 1422 Thetford had a guild of Corpus Christi.[10] One small hint at provenance may be contained in one of the marginal glosses that the scribe-compiler appears to have added to his manuscript. On fol. 74v is a note of the date of the feast of the translation of St Mary Magdalene. This feast, though rare in English liturgical use, was commoner in continental, especially French, uses of the sort that might be expected in a place like a Cluniac priory.[11] All this does not establish Thetford as a home of N-Town, of course, but it makes Thetford as persuasive a cultural epicentre as Bury St Edmunds.[12]

Wherever exactly the scribe-compiler worked, some of the plays he collected, those to which the banns refer, were evidently once intended for touring, and in the present state of our knowledge, it seems safest to say that this was to villages around the Norfolk and Suffolk border in the late fifteenth and early sixteenth centuries.

THE ARCHAEOLOGY OF THE MANUSCRIPT

Precisely because the plays of N-Town cannot be convincingly linked to any known external records of performance, as can plays from places like Chester or York, their manuscript assumes a singular importance. As the sole source of information on everything to do with them it needs careful searching for clues to the nature of the East Anglian dramatic milieu of which it is in some sense a reflex and which in turn it once helped to sustain; various revisions made in it by someone who had acquired it shortly after completion by the scribe-compiler show that it was eventually being used in actual play production (*114*, p. xxiv). Whether that was the scribe-compiler's original intention for it is, however, much less clear. Basically, it looks as if he wanted to compile a play repertoire, organised within a Creation-to-Doom framework, which would be more comprehensive than anything available in any one of his sundry individual exemplars, even if doing so meant replacing some plays in whole or in part with others. This repertoire he gradually pieced together, sometimes taking the trouble to co-ordinate coherently its originally disparate materials, sometimes not bothering, or sometimes beginning and then simply abandoning the attempt part way through. Probably a cleric, he was also someone with access to certain non-dramatic, theological writings which it seemed worth his while to draw upon for providing his manuscript with a set of marginal glosses. These argue for a rather learned or readerly interest in the material he worked with.[13] Perhaps his manuscript was destined for actors – without question it soon fell into their hands – yet its glosses betray a desire to give it a certain literary 'finish' indifferent to practical dramatic use. Whoever the scribe-compiler was, he seems to have been acquainted with the ethos of glossed and annotated texts, for in its own small way his manuscript reveals, too, the sort of concern for respectable textual presentation, for *ordinatio*, that might be expected in someone clerically trained.[14]

So distinctive an artefact is his manuscript that it stands apart from those of all other early English plays. However difficult now to pinpoint the purposes for which it was intended, they were evidently quite different from those served, for example, by the antiquarian compilers of the Chester manuscripts, by the medieval York scribes employed to copy their city's official play register, or by the scribe of the plush Wakefield manuscript (see above, chapters 4, 3 and 5). It is much humbler than any of these. But another important aspect of its distinctiveness, its manufacture from texts many of which once had utterly independent dramatic existence before being compiled, highlights a radical critical question: how is a critic to speak about a composite entity like N-Town?

There is no doubt that it is composite. From about the beginning of this century an appreciation has slowly grown of its textual complexity (233, p. 79 n.2). The scribe-compiler had access to a major play collection which seems to have formed the basis for his work, and for which the banns at the beginning of the manuscript were written. These banns were composed to describe a sequence of forty different episodes (each is called a 'pagent') from the Creation, through events of the Old and New Testaments, to the Judgement Day. The banns refer to plays that had already been subject to revision and editing before the scribe-compiler started copying them.[15] I will refer to the banns and their pageants as the Proclamation Play, reserving the word 'pageant' for episodes that derive from it (though critics have sometimes referred to it as the 'banns' or the 'pageant' play). The Proclamation Play was the one intended for touring and whose performance someone had imagined as happening on Sunday at N-Town 'at vj of þe belle'.[16] Possibly the scribe-compiler, in being content to copy this, envisaged similar production circumstances for his own collection. But as we have seen and will see again later, he reveals himself less as being interested in the practical dramatic aspects of what he copies than as being a literary editor who, while not zealous to remove every narrative discrepancy to which his magpie collection is prone, is still concerned enough to make a few gestures in the direction of logical narrative continuity. In view of his apparent disposition in this respect, it is not at all clear that the staging envisaged by the banns should be regarded as applicable to the contents of the entire manuscript in any really meaningful way. If he had intended this, he would have removed the mention at the beginning of Passion Play II that Passion Play I had been performed 'last 3ere' (Play 29, line 7). In fact, when the manuscript eventually does fall into the hands of a practical dramatist, Reviser B as he has been called, he quarries and adapts some of its contents for a two-day performance, and does not struggle to do what the banns seem to prescribe.

The scribe-compiler worked very roughly as follows. First he copied the Proclamation Play until the end of the seventh pageant, a procession of prophets foretelling the Virgin and her son. After this occurs the first major

14 The N-Town plays: *The Marriage of Mary and Joseph*, in the Mary Play (British Library MS Cotton Vespasian D. viii, f. 55v). See p. 170.

break in his copying process. Here he laid aside his Proclamation Play exemplar and took up another having in it a self-contained play on the early life of the Virgin. This Mary Play, in five episodes, presented her conception, presentation in the temple, marriage to Joseph, Annunciation (preceded by a

Parliament of Heaven, a deliberation among the three Persons in Trinity as to which of them should set in motion the machinery of man's salvation) and finally her Visitation to Elizabeth (79). Like the Proclamation Play, the Mary Play too had already undergone some revision in its exemplar before the scribe-compiler acquired it (223). Its first two plays, those of her conception and presentation, he copied more or less as they stood, but when he came to her marriage to Joseph, he decided to amalgamate it with another two pageants of similar topic that were also to be found in the exemplar of his Proclamation Play. The result was a blended text. Yet curiously, rather than hide the seams between Mary and Proclamation Play material, he chose rather to reveal most of them, and this he did by dotting in red the lobes of the paragraph marks before speeches lifted from the Mary Play, but leaving blank those before speeches from the Proclamation Play (see illustration 14) (*114*, p. xvii; *233*, p. 71).

After finishing this composite marriage episode, he put aside his Proclamation Play exemplar and resumed exclusively that of the Mary Play for the Parliament of Heaven and Annunciation, ignoring another Annunciation in the Proclamation Play. Then, taking up the Proclamation Play exemplar once again, and leaving that of the Mary Play (apart perhaps from lifting just a few lines from it (*104*, pp. 26–9), he copied the play of Joseph's doubts about Mary. Finally he returned to the Mary Play exemplar for the last time and copied its Visitation to Elizabeth.

From here on he worked steadily from the Proclamation Play exemplar until reaching the Purification Play, for this episode, not mentioned in the banns, had presumably therefore no pageant dealing with it.[17] After the Purification, the Proclamation Play exemplar was followed for a long stint. He copied its Slaughter of the Innocents, its Christ and the doctors in the temple, its pageants on Christ's ministry and Passion, through at least as far as the setting of the guard on Christ's sepulchre, and perhaps even farther, before radically changing his mind. At some point late in his copying from the Proclamation Play exemplar, he now decided to incorporate what was once an independent Passion Play. This was in two parts. The first, Passion Play I, which he had already copied into a separate booklet on some previous occasion, was originally free of any Proclamation Play material. He physically incorporated this booklet, suppressing in the process much of the Proclamation Play's Passion pageants that he had copied earlier, but retaining and interpolating a little of their material. I will explain this in more detail shortly. He produced Passion Play II, on the other hand, quite differently, for this time he copied it from the outset with a view to its amalgamation with the Proclamation Play material which he had already copied earlier.[18] This second part of the Passion Play is more substantially a blend of material than the first. It has no distinct ending, probably because the original ending of the play contained in the Passion Play exemplar was suppressed in the process of dovetailing it with pageant material. The Proclamation Play exemplar was now resumed and followed exclusively until the Assumption, a play that some completely different scribe had copied into a once independent booklet. The scribe-compiler incorporated it wholesale and rubricated it to conform it to the layer of the rest of his compilation. Finally he returned to the Proclamation Play exemplar to copy its Judgement Day pageant.

So a modern critic, viewing all this complicated textual architecture, has options like those available to someone viewing the interior of some great medieval cathedral: one may be content simply to take in an overall impression that the place makes, or looking more narrowly one may prefer to discriminate and trace the shifts of style between, say, Decorated and Perpendicular, from which overall impressions are finally constituted. Since either way of observing tends to shade into the other, the most natural thing might be to do a bit of both. Similarly, N-Town has had its general surveyors, mainly in the form of those who have perceived in it overarching thematic unity (224, 219, 135), just as it has had its textual archaeologists – those who have preferred to focus narrowly on its bricks and mortar (233, p. 79 n.2; 228, 231). Less effort, however, has been made to see how both views relate to each other, or to come to terms with the fundamental reason for their existence. In fact, the problem raised earlier of knowing how to speak about a manifestly composite text has created apparent critical alternatives. Alone, each has its limitations: finding N-Town to be inhabited by a presiding and coherent spirit, a sort of *genius loci* to whom thematic unity can be credited, even if in some sense true, is nevertheless a recipe for stifling its diversity and marginalising its undisputed textual disparateness;[19] conversely, seeking to excavate earlier textual structures, though informative, is finally an unachievable task and one indifferent to the possibility that the compilation they have been built into might have a structure of its own, whether planned or fortuitous. To put it briefly, is it useful to dwell on textual continuities at the expense of discontinuities, or vice versa? N-Town, the result of an unforeseen collaboration between texts (unforeseen in the sense that several of them were once discrete and formally unrelated to each other) tends therefore perhaps more than any other early play collection to polarise the critical approach.

Where both approaches originate, however, is in the activity of the scribe-compiler, and here may be the place to look for guidance about how to understand his collection. We may expose and thereby perceive the modernity of these approaches if we once apprehend something of his medieval textual practice. What are the attitudes to his text and its function that are implicit in his ways of working? We need to look at some text closely, holding critical and bibliographical issues simultaneously in focus.

BUILDING A PASSION PLAY

Passion Play I is written on five quires of paper: the first (quire N) is of twelve folios, with a singleton (fol. 143), bringing it up to thirteen folios, added after leaf seven; the second (quire O), is of three folios, wanting one leaf after the third; the third (quire P) is a bifolium; the fourth (quire Q) is similar; and finally the fifth (quire R) is a regular quire of eight leaves. The paper watermarks of quires N, P, Q and R are of the bull's head type, but quire O is the odd man out, employing a bunch of grapes type.[20] In itself a change of paper might not mean much, but other evidence confirms the suspicion that quire O (containing pageant material from the Proclamation Play) is, in fact, an addition made by the scribe-compiler to a set of quires he had already completed. If we therefore leave quire O aside for the moment and also the singleton added in quire N that probably belongs to this same phase of the scribe-compiler's revision, we can discern an earlier completed scribal stint in four quires (N, P, Q and R), and one of the interesting things to notice about it is the varied number of leaves that make this unit up: one quire is of twelve, two are of two and the fourth is of eight. We are evidently dealing with a scribe-compiler who is used to producing booklets, and he is happy to re-cycle one of them in the course of preparing his longer work.[21]

Let us return to quire O and the singleton fol. 143 in quire N to see how and why the scribe-compiler has introduced them. To take the singleton first. Originally fol. 142v (see illustration 15) ended with a stage direction: 'Here enteryth þe apostyl Petyr, and Johan þe Euangelyst with hym, Petyr seyng', and then the first six lines of the opening eight-line stanza of Peter's speech, which begins 'O ȝe pepyl dyspeyryng, be glad'. The last two lines of this speech's opening stanza would then have followed at the top of the next folio. However, the stage direction and the six lines of speech on fol. 142v were subsequently crossed out, and bracketed against the word *vacat* ('leave it out') in the left-hand margin. This was done to allow the new material introduced on the singleton fol. 143 to flow on sequentially. The new material starts at the top of this folio with a speech of Jesus which begins: 'Frendys, beholde þe tyme of mercy,/The whiche is come now, withowt dowth./Mannys sowle in blys now xal edyfy,/And þe Prynce of þe Werd is cast owth'. However, exactly the same four lines appear again a little later (on the top of fol. 145v), where they are addressed by Jesus to the citizens and children of the crowd at his triumphal entry into Jerusalem. Consider-

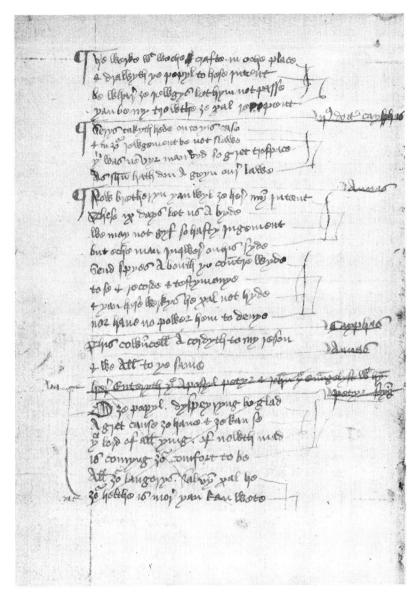

15 The N-Town plays: *The Entry into Jerusalem*, from Passion Play I (British Library MS Cotton Vespasian D. viii, f. 142v). See p. 172.

ing that nowhere else are plays given to such verbatim repetition, the lines at the top of the singleton fol. 143 begin to look suspicious. Moreover, the next thirteen lines, the rest of Jesus's speech in which his apostles are told to fetch the ass, plus the response of an apostle who says they are going off to get it, are written in the metre characteristic of the Proclamation Play (as indeed are the next two thirteen-line stanzas, which run over onto fol. 143v). It seems that what happened was this: the scribe-compiler, finding he had Proclamation Play material for the dispatch of the apostles for the ass, an episode probably not treated in the Passion Play, decided to incorporate it into his original Passion Play booklet when he was marrying the booklet into his larger compilation. In this respect his motives seem rather like those of some medieval gospel harmoniser who wants to produce the fullest possible account of the story; perhaps harmonies suggested to him a model. However, since the speech as it stood in the Proclamation Play exemplar would otherwise start much too bluntly ('Go to ȝon castel þat standyth ȝow ageyn ...'), he needed a lead into it. It is worth noting that here he had an opportunity to solve his problem by writing a line or two of connecting dialogue, an opportunity he did *not* take. Instead, he lifted the four lines that were roughly suitable for his purposes, even though they would be heard again later on.

If there is an important clue in this that our scribe-compiler may be a reluctant verse writer, nevertheless when necessary he does not jib at re-writing stage directions. It will be recalled that the deleted stage direction towards the bottom of fol. 142v, 'Here enteryth þe apostyl Petyr, and Johan þe Euangelyst with hym, Petyr seyng', originally prefaced the speech of Peter, 'O ȝe pepyl dyspeyryng, be glad', which, like the stage direction, was also later marked for omission. After the scribe-compiler had incorporated the Proclamation Play's episode of fetching the ass, he was free to bring back the suppressed six lines of Peter's 'O ȝe pepyl' speech, and did so at the bottom of fol. 143v. But this time the stage direction prefacing the speech has changed, and it is almost certainly the scribe-compiler who changed it: 'Here Cryst rydyth out of þe place and he wyl, and Petyr and Johan abydyn stylle; and at þe last, whan þei haue don þer prechyng, þei mete with Jesu.'[22] Realising that his interpolation had brought Jesus and the ass on early and that there was a lot of intervening text (the sermon-like speeches of Peter and John and the preparation of the citizens for the triumphal entry) before Jesus spoke again, he allowed him the option of riding off in readiness for his entry later. In his adjustment the scribe-compiler appears aware of the dramatic inappropriateness resulting from his compiling activity, although his desire to be inclusive can overwhelm his sensitivity in this respect – for example, the Virgin Mary exits twice from the cross (cf. 233, p. 73). His drafting in of a singleton to accommodate a Proclamation Play episode, while managed fairly efficiently, nevertheless damages the integrity of his earlier Passion Play text, for with great dramatic tact this had originally delayed the appearance of Jesus until the very moment of his triumphal entry.

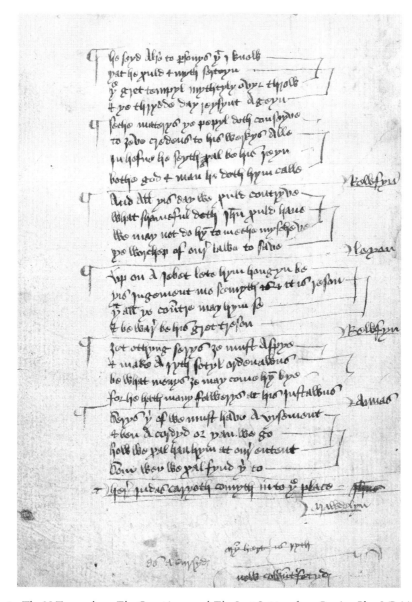

16   The N-Town plays: *The Conspiracy* and *The Last Supper*, from Passion Play I (British
Library MS Cotton Vespasian D. viii, f. 148v). See p. 176.

Quire O seems to have been intruded for similar reasons, and with
similar consequences. It contains Jesus's expulsion of the seven devils from
Mary Magdalene (a popular scene in medieval East Anglian drama, occur-
ring also in *Wisdom* and *Mary Magdalen*) and her pouring of the precious

ointment onto his feet (fol. 149r–v). After this, Jesus announces that he is to be betrayed by one of his disciples, and each, appalled, utters a four-line disclaimer, until finally Judas asks whether he is to be 'þat traytour' (this material occupies fols. 150–1). Judas then goes out with the stage direction: 'Here Judas rysyth prevely and goth in þe place and seyt "Now cownter..."'

The material contained in quire O again derives from the Proclamation Play exemplar, this time either from two different pageants or from an amalgamated one,[23] and, judging by tell-tale alterations at the bottom of fol. 148v (see illustration 16), it seems clear that the scribe-compiler added one lot of material, then changed his mind and added some more. Fol. 148v, the last before the insertion of quire O, originally ended with the stage direction 'Here Judas Caryoth comyth into þe place' and, in ink of similar dark colour at the very bottom of the folio, 'now cownterfetyd'. Both the stage direction and 'now cownterfetyd', the catchword referring to a speech of Judas that begins at the top of fol. 152 (the start of quire P), were subsequently deleted to make way for the first batch of new material. It appears that the scribe-compiler next copied the section where Jesus announces that he is to be betrayed (it begins at the top of fol. 150 with his speech 'Myn herte is ryght sory, and no wondyr is') up to the exit of Judas on fol. 151. He then noted the name of who was to have been the next speaker, Jesus, in the right-hand margin of fol. 148v, and wrote a new catchword, 'Myn hert is ryth', just above the old one, 'now cownterfetyd', that he had earlier deleted. However, now noticing even more material, a scene too good to miss about Mary Magdalene and her seven devils in another part of the Proclamation Play exemplar, he decided that he might also incorporate the scene here. So he copied this second batch of pageant material, probably on a second bifolium of similar paper (the bunch of grapes variety), which he then folded around what now became the inner bifolium of the quire, the one that began with the speech 'Myn herte is ryght sory, and no wondyr is'.[24] The consequence of this was that the catchword he had earlier revised to 'Myn hert is ryth', and the name of its speaker, Jesus, were now thrown out again. He crossed them through, and wrote 'Mawdelyn' as the name of the next speaker and the new catchword 'as a cursyd', the opening words of her speech on fol. 149.

Unravelling all this, complicated though it may have seemed, is important not for its own sake, but precisely because it exposes the scribe-compiler's working method, and implicit in this is an interesting attitude towards text. His procedure amounts to another critical approach, this time a medieval one offering an alternative that modern critics, often caught in the binary preoccupation with unity and its absence, can also usefully contemplate. There is no evidence in Passion Play I (or anywhere else in the manuscript for that matter) that the scribe-compiler ever wrote verse, even when he had ideal opportunities for doing so. On the other hand, he rewrites a stage direction ('Here Cryst rydyth out of þe place and he wyll ...') in a perfunctory attempt to salvage the narrative coherence lost as a result of compiling disparate material. Such activity is similar to his half-hearted renumbering of the pageants of the banns to try to correlate them with his finished compilation,[25] as well as to his fussing over small details of manuscript layout that bring the compilation into line with his concept of *ordinatio* (229, pp. 42–7). He changes his mind about what he wants to copy, and sometimes rapidly, which suggests limited forward planning. In sum, his involvement with his manuscript corresponds fairly well to medieval notions of the *compilator*, the scribe who adds little or nothing of his own to what he copies, but substantially rearranges and combines his materials in the way he thinks best suits the general terms of his *compilatio*.[26]

What those general terms seem to have been in his case – a Creation-to-Doom narrative – constitute a flexible framework, one with any amount of room for expansion or contraction between two nodal points. His inclination, as we saw, was towards expansion and inclusiveness, sometimes at the local cost of narrative coherence. Yet this inclusiveness implies no concomitant obligation for users of the *compilatio* to engage with all its compiled material; on the contrary, it facilitates their scope for *choice*. And this is once more exactly in the spirit of *compilatio*. A *compilator* often provided his work with an *accessus*, a means to open its contents for selective use as required. So too the *compilatio* of the scribe-compiler is not a closed text; it incorporates alternatives (as you wish, use of this or that ending, e.g. 'si placet' (if you wish) at the end of the Mary Play (79, pp. 134–7), options ('Here Cryst rydyth out of þe place and he wyll', and see also Play 27, s.d., lines 465 +), even perhaps in the Mary Play a guide to disentangling what is compiled with what (114, p. xvii), which opens its text to determination by its users. The banns too could even be regarded as a sort of index or *tabula* by which a user can find his way around the collection as he wishes. In short, responsibility for the final form that the *compilatio* takes is turned over to those who use it. Such selective use of it by Reviser B is an early instance of exactly this. The scribe-compiler foresees and provides for the fact that the form of his *compilatio* will finally be determined out in the community where it is used. In a sense its ultimate authorship is communal, and as such, repeatedly negotiable.

The implications of this for the two modern approaches noted earlier are weighty. A search for general unifying themes in the *compilatio*, though in some measure valid, risks closing its structure, and can claim no priority over the 'archaeological' approach, since it is liable to refuse the implicit invitation of the *compilatio* that the user undo it. But equally the scrutiny of individual plays and their textual layers, though it might appear happily aligned with this self-undoing aspect of *compilatio*, is only partially so, because it in fact proceeds from quite a different motive, the modern desire to discern, as one modern authority put it, 'the original purity of the most authoritative preserved forms of [an] author's words'.[27] Searching for the 'original purity . . . of [an] author's words' would have been largely alien to the scribe-compiler. Text for him, of this sort at least, was common property; it had not quite the private status of the kind accorded to texts in such modern textual criticism. Even if he added no dialogue of his own, he did not fully privilege the text in his exemplars. Like many another medieval *compilator*, he felt free to dismantle their structure where necessary. His attitude recognises the fact that since most of an author's words exist before he is born, they are to that extent a public domain over which he has no absolute control.[28]

To view N-Town as a *compilatio* is to expose the modernity of the ideologies underpinning both these modern approaches; it is also to remind us that the past is a country where people do things differently.

'SOMETHING RICH AND STRANGE'

A third modern approach to N-Town, one which sidesteps the literary double bind described earlier, is the question of how its plays were staged. Interest in this was shown even as early as the seventeenth century, when William Dugdale confidently described them as being presented in 'Theaters' which were 'very large and high, placed upon wheels and drawn to all the eminent parts of the City'.[29] But the 'City' he was thinking of as their home was Coventry. Subsequent critics have been less sure about N-Town's scope for a processional, pageant wagon staging. The Passion Play was early recognised as being a stationary, place-and-scaffold production, although as late as the 1960s it was still thought that other plays in the manuscript were produced processionally (220, 221; 25, p. 244). Since the 1970s, opinion has generally turned against theories of processional staging for any parts of N-Town (226, 232). A good case can be made that the Proclamation Play intended stationary, place-and-scaffold staging, and the Mary Play, a play even conceivably performed indoors, was probably similar. This would mean that the principal play exemplars of N-Town, though themselves originally unrelated, all shared a similar production mode.

The debate over N-Town's staging has been fuelled by its stage directions, which, after Chester, are the next richest in English mystery drama. Understanding them is a difficult business. It is clear that to some extent they correspond to the particular source texts that the scribe-compiler worked from: stage directions in Proclamation Play material are normally in Latin and are relatively few; the Mary Play has proportionally more, in Latin and in English, and the Passion Play has a wealth of them, predominantly in English. Less clear is which stage directions are original and which added later, whether as a result of armchair revision or actual play production. Yet in spite of their difficulties, they still give invaluable insight into what the drama of N-Town was like.

It has often been said that medieval drama presents the biblical past in terms of the medieval present (*130*, pp. 102–3), but the stage directions of N-Town lead one to wonder how useful this generalisation is. Take the first stage direction of Passion Play I:

> Here xal Annas shewyn hymself in his stage beseyn aftyr a   *shall; arrayed*
> busshop of þe hoold lawe in a skarlet gowne, and ouyr þat a   *old*
> blew tabbard furryd with whyte, and a mytere on his hed after
> þe hoold lawe; ij doctorys stondyng by hym in furryd hodys,
> and on befron hem with his staff of astat, and eche of hem on   *one*
> here hedys a furryd cappe with a gret knop in þe crowne; and
> on stondyng befron as a Sarazyn, þe wich xal be his masangere
>
> (Play 26, s.d., line 164 +)

The Jewish High Priest Annas is not dressed like a contemporary medieval bishop, but 'after þe hoold lawe' (*133*, p. 124). (The next stage direction will require the doctors attending Caiaphas to be clad 'aftyr þe old gyse': Play 26, s.d., line 208 +). Also, the messenger of Annas is a 'Sarazyn'. The thrust of the stage direction is clearly towards producing a sense of difference, of the exotic. Familiar things may be present, but are often combined in unfamiliar ways, or yet with things themselves unfamiliar, and noticeably when the divine or infernal are in view. In the same play, Christ is arrested by ten people 'with swerdys, gleyvys [halberds], and *other straunge wepoun*' – no average medieval militia this – and when in Passion Play II the Jews have crucified Christ, they dance around him:

> Here xule þei leve of, and dawncyn abowte þe cros shortly.
>
> (Play 32, s.d., line 76 +)

For a while they are like carollers dancing in a ring. Dances in the centre of which some action took place were familiar pastimes, but when, as here, that central action is a crucifixion, the familiar is suddenly estranged.[30] Collocations of this sort are like Ariel's sea-change: all turns rich and strange. N-Town repeatedly defamiliarises the medieval here-and-now in a polysemous play of signs. It self-consciously advertises its semiotic means in the process.

What its stage directions imply in this respect matches what is going on in its text. For example, N-Town's farting devil is not just scatalogically apt; he is presented for a moment doing something that medieval jesters often did.[31] Eve, costumed, presumably in such a way as to suggest nakedness, was nevertheless made by God 'a gret lady in paradys for to pley', and thus verbally glossed paradise too is presented not only as the traditional *locus amoenus*, but as a *hortus conclusus*, an aristocratic walled garden of delights opened with a private key.[32] Backbiter and Raise Slander, two common bedfellows in medieval theological literature, acquire a human habitation and name in the 'real' world of the bishop's court in the pageant of the trial of Joseph and Mary; and in the Parliament of Heaven in the Mary Play, familiar institutions are translated into unusual circumstances: petitioners (who represent mankind) make a plea (which angels transmit) to a deliberative council (of the Trinity) which determines in familiar judicial fashion a 'loveday' (the reconciliation of God's daughters Mercy, Truth, Justice and Peace).[33] Instances could be multiplied (e.g. Play 20, lines 151–4, Herod's feast; Play 26, lines 442–9 + s.d., Jesus's 'royal' entry). The Mary Play in particular is remarkable for such transformations of the familiar. But as a final illustration let us turn to the pageant of the doctors disputing with Jesus in the temple. This is a fine example of how defamiliarisation releases possibilities of meaning not otherwise readily broached. The doctors are taught to recognise superior wisdom where ordinarily it ought not to be, in a child, and their recognition is embodied in significant action:

> Hic adducunt Jesum inter ipsos et in scanno altiori ipsum sedere faciunt, ipsis
> in inferioribus scannis sedentibus . . .   (Play 21, s.d., line 144 +)

> (Here they lead Jesus into their midst and make him sit on a higher seat, while
> they themselves sit on lower ones)

In semiotic terms, the diminutive Jesus (an icon of childhood) nevertheless utters divine wisdom (an icon of Godhead, of the second Person in Trinity), and both are foregrounded by elevation on the highest *scannum* (literally, a seat or bench). An interesting contemporary stained-glass depiction of this scene in East Harling church, a church geographically close to the play's cultural origins, makes the seat of a throne, and thus takes the further step of putting the child Jesus on a traditional symbol of kingly authority (see illustration 17).[34]

While we can talk in this way about what stage directions and text suggest concerning the nature of N-Town's dramatic illusion, and even partially test our notions through practical production, there is a way of conceiving what is happening in more medieval terms: N-Town often engages a special sort of textual awareness, one prevalent in the culture of the time.

17   East Harling, Norfolk, parish church of SS Peter and Paul, fifteenth-century stained glass,
Christ among the Doctors. See p. 180.

Jesus in the temple alleges a Latin authority of scripture – *Omnis sciencia a domino deo est* – before he ever speaks in English, as would a medieval preacher who announces his scriptural theme before discoursing on its substance.[35] Indeed, N-Town is full of preachers and preaching method. Some are obvious, as when Moses turns preacher in his exposition of the Decalogue.[36] Some are less so, as when Death intervenes in Herod's feast after the Slaughter of the Innocents. Herod invites his knights to banquet, imagining all is well after eliminating Christ:

[Herod]

. . .

Þerfore, menstrell, rownd abowte,
Blowe up a mery fytt!   *tune*

Hic, dum buccinant, Mors interficiat Herodem et duos milites subito, et Diabolus
recipiat eos.

[Devil]

All oure! All oure! þis catel is myn!   *property*
I xall hem brynge onto my celle.   *shall*
I xall hem teche pleys fyn,   *fine*
And shewe such myrthe as is in helle!
. . .

[Death]

Off kynge Herowde all men beware,
Þat hath rejoycyd in pompe and pryde.
For all his boste of blysse ful bare,
He lyth now ded here on his syde.
For whan I come I can not spare;
Fro me no whyht may hym hyde.   *creature*
. . .

Thow I be nakyd and pore of array
And wurmys knawe me al abowte,   *gnaw*
ȝit loke ȝe drede me nyth and day;   *night*
For whan Deth comyth ȝe stande in dowte!   *are uncertain*
Evyn lyke to me, as I ȝow say,
Shull all ȝe be here in þis rowte,   *gathering*
Whan I ȝow chalange at my day,
I xal ȝow make ryght lowe to lowth   *bow*
And nakyd for to be.
Amongys wormys, as I ȝow telle,
Vndyr þe erth xul ȝe dwelle,
And thei xul etyn both flesch and felle,
As þei haue don me.   (Play 20, lines 231–6, 246–51, 272–84)

(s.d., line 232 + : Here while they are trumpetting let Death kill Herod and his
two soldiers suddenly, and let the Devil take them)

The way that Death explains the significance of his action is comparable to
the method of a medieval preacher who, having delivered a dramatic

exemplum, draws out for his congregation its moral significance. At the end of the play, Death takes his exemplifying procedure a step further. In making an exemplum of himself – the audience is invited to contemplate through him their own mortality – he introduces a new level of exemplary meaning. Such integumental layering of exempla is unusual in preaching, if exempla are common in themselves, and so, as here, reminiscence of preaching can be complex. But more importantly, N-Town's preoccupation with preaching and preaching method seems a function of something deeper.

At the heart of Passion Play I, at the institution of the Eucharist itself, Jesus explains 'by gostly interpretacyon' the meaning of the paschal lamb (Exodus 12) eaten with unleavened bread and bitter herbs, and initiates another transformation, as the rites of the old law cede to the new: 'þis fygure xal sesse; anothyr xal folwe þerby' (Play 27, line 361). The playwright may have derived the substance of Jesus's commentary, either directly or through an intermediary, from the *Glossa ordinaria*, the standard medieval Bible commentary that began in the great twelfth-century school of Laon.[37] Medieval exegesis raised a many-layered edifice of interpretation over the literal sense (the *sensus litteralis*) of the text.[38] At this point in Passion Play I, Jesus turns exegete. He glosses the *sensus litteralis* of Exodus 12 not only verbally (some of his terms are technical hermeneutic ones),[39] but also gesturally, by the elevation of a Eucharistic wafer, the new paschal lamb:

> And as þe paschal lomb etyn haue we
> In þe eld lawe was vsyd for a sacryfyce,
> So þe newe lomb þat xal be sacryd be me   *consecrated*
> Xal be vsyd for a sacryfyce most of price.   *of supreme value*

Here xal Jesus take an oblé in his hand lokying vpward   *Mass wafer*
into hefne, to þe Fadyr ...   (Play 27, lines 369–72 + s.d.)

Moments like this when exegesis is thoroughly enmeshed in the very narrative of the drama, when it surfaces, as it were, to be dramatised in its own right, may be a clue to what the playwrights of N-Town, consciously or unconsciously, were doing: they were making exegesis into a game, and this not only where exegesis is explicitly enacted in the drama's narrative, as happens in Passion Play I. In a more general sense too, the polysemous play of signs mentioned earlier could be regarded as drama's counterpart to exegesis, as an extension into dramatic terms of exegetical awareness: the *sensus litteralis* of the narrative is glossed and re-glossed into multivalence by a drama which, like exegesis itself, liberates audiences from the necessity of limiting apprehension of meaning to single possibilities. The excitement of N-Town's drama is partly founded in surprise, as dramatic signs, ever likely to display themselves in the unconventionality of their referrents, take spectators 'in aventure þer mervaylez meven', whether they intuited connections between their experience of what they saw and habits of thought characterising contemporary clerical culture or not; quite likely they just enjoyed all the heady exuberance in a spirit of play and game.[40] Moreover, it is a surprise liable to spring from the smallest details of the drama: wherever gaps are to be perceived between the words uttered and the actions enacted (and medieval drama in general is likely to have accentuated any discrepancy because often its words and actions occur simultaneously) there exists pretence, an awareness that, even if disbelief be suspended, everything performed is illusion, whatever the high seriousness, or otherwise, of the illusion in its effect. In such a context, where words may, but as equally may not, be referential, language itself can be defamiliarised; when their traditional referrents are prone to replacement by newer ones invented in the playful dramatic world, a curtain rises on the slipperiness of words themselves. Words too are actors, but this is a cause of delight rather than of any unsettling apprehension of how arbitrary words are, for the destabilisation of language in the dramatic context is only analogous, after all, to the established medieval pursuit of the higher levels of exegesis above the *sensus litteralis*. These levels, while holy games of invention, may nevertheless give access to salvation.

N-Town's spectators, whatever selection from the *compilatio* they were served with, could not have seen their world reflected as in a plane mirror, but playfully refracted into something rich and strange. For all that the possibilities of meaning may have been sumptuous, meaning's teleological end, the intimation of God's purposes for mankind, was nevertheless thought to be single. No doubt N-Town's playwrights hoped that by means of a drama that glossed the audience's perception of the world in this way, the audience might come to know the place for the first time.

NOTES

1 William Dugdale, *The Antiquities of Warwickshire Illustrated* (London, 1656), p. 116.
2 For studies promoting Lincoln, see 78, vol. I, p. xv n.5. Early authoritative cases for Norfolk language in the manuscript are Eric J. Dobson, 'The Etymology and Meaning of Boy', *MÆ* 9 (1940), 121–54; see 152–3, and 247; see p. 133. More recently, see Mark Eccles, '*Ludus Coventriae*: Lincoln or Norfolk?', *MÆ* 40 (1971), 135–41, and Jacob Bennett, 'The Language and Home of the *Ludus Coventriae*', *Orbis* 22 (1973), 43–63.
3 In order these four are the Proclamation Play, the Mary Play, the Assumption Play (physically incorporated into his manuscript) and the Passion Play. (These

groupings will be explained later.) The Purification Play, if not already in the Proclamation Play exemplar, would make a fifth.

4 Edmund K. Chambers (*English Literature at the Close of the Middle Ages* (Oxford: Clarendon Press, 1945), p. 49) thought he was a member of a religious house which had a library. Whatever his status, his access to a library seems likely; see further below.

5 See Angus McIntosh, Michael L. Samuels and Michael Benskin, *A Linguistic Atlas of Late Mediæval English* (Aberdeen: Aberdeen University Press, 1986), vol. III, p. 339. Since all four of the different scribal stints in the manuscript locate not far from each other, it is highly unlikely that the scribe-compiler was working far from home. I owe my understanding of their location to the generous assistance of Professor Michael Benskin, who has analysed N-Town orthography on my behalf.

6 Eccles, 'Lincoln or Norfolk', p. 135, strongly favours the N. = *nomen* interpretation. Spector (78, vol. II, p. 428, note to line 527) leaves open the possibility that N. designated some specific place. W. W. Greg ('Bibliographical and Textual Problems of the English Mystery Cycles', *The Library*, Third Series 5 (1914), 365–99) first proposed N-Town as the name of the plays (see p. 367). They have also been known as the Hegge plays after their former early-seventeenth-century owner, Robert Hegge.

7 Walter F. Schirmer, *John Lydgate: A Study in the Culture of the XVth Century*, trans. Ann E. Keep (London: Methuen, 1961), pp. 100–8 and 130–43.

8 The claim that the orthography of the N-Town Assumption Play booklet locates in Bury St Edmunds and that its scribe may have been a Bury man (78, vol. I, p. xxxviii; 227, p. 68) does not hold. More recent analysis by Professor Michael Benskin shows that its orthography belongs either to far northwest Suffolk, southeast Ely or northeast Cambridgeshire, and that an Ely location is more likely than a Suffolk one; also, that the Assumption Play archetype may have originated in west Norfolk.

9 Cameron Louis (ed.), *The Commonplace Book of Robert Reynes of Acle, an Edition of Tanner MS 407* (New York and London: Garland, 1980); also 85, pp. cxx–xxiv.

10 See F. Blomefield, *An Essay Towards a Topographical History of the County of Norfolk*, 11 vols. (London: William Miller, 1805–10) vol. II, pp. 80–3.

11 Thetford is also close enough to Bury to receive Lydgate's influence at an early date. The Benedictine connection between Bury's abbey and Thetford's Cluniac priory may explain it.

12 Professor Michael Benskin informs me that the spelling of Reviser B (114, p. xxiv) locates in the region of New Buckenham, about six miles northeast of East Harling. I interpret this to weigh against the Bury St Edmunds argument, otherwise one would have to imagine two independent scribes from the same part of Norfolk working down in Bury. Though not impossible, this entails inelegant multiplication of assumptions.

13 Greg, 'Problems', p. 399; on whether or not the scribe-compiler himself added the marginal glosses, see Alan J. Fletcher, 'Marginal Glosses in the N-Town Manuscript', *Manuscripta* 25 (1981), 113–17.

14 Malcolm B. Parkes, 'The Influence of the Concepts of *Ordinatio* and *Compilatio* on the Development of the Book', in J. J. G. Alexander and M. T. Gibson (eds.),

Medieval Learning and Literature: Essays presented to R. W. Hunt (Oxford: Clarendon Press, 1976), pp. 115–41.

15 The revisions in the Proclamation Play text are so extensive and complex that, given the scribe-compiler's working method to be described later, it is extremely unlikely that he alone was responsible for them.

16 This 'someone' was, presumably, the last reviser of the Proclamation Play banns who, if he did not compose it himself, decided to let the final banns speech stand.

17 It is not mentioned in the banns and its versification is unlike that associated with Proclamation Play pageants (or indeed with anything else in N-Town). It is undoubtedly interpolated, but conceivably it was already in the Proclamation Play exemplar *before* the exemplar came to the scribe-compiler.

18 Not *all* of the pageant material he had earlier copied was retained; much was displaced by Passion Play material during amalgamation. (On his treatment of Passion Play II, see *233*, pp. 72–6 and *80*, pp. 8–9 and Appendix 4.) It looks as if he decided to include the entire Passion Play only after already having copied extensively from his Proclamation Play exemplar, at least as far as its episode of the setting of the guard on Christ's sepulchre.

19 Thus Rosemary Woolf (*138*, pp. 309–10) can find 'a single controlling mind and individual sensibility' in the collection, and Martin Stevens (*135*), concurs.

20 *114*, pp. xv–vi. It is also important to notice that though the singleton fol. 143 has no watermarks, its chain lines appear to correspond with those of quire O (bunch of grapes watermark). This strengthens the suggestion I make below that the intrusion of this singleton and quire O occurred in the same phase of interpolation.

21 Pamela R. Robinson, 'The "Booklet": a Self-contained Unit in Composite Manuscripts', *Codicologica* 3 (1980), 46–69. As textually, so codicologically, N-Town is discontinuous. The scribe-compiler's inclusion of a booklet he had previously completed suggests some extended acquaintance with manufacturing play texts.

22 Peter Meredith (*105*, pp. 85–6) also comments on this. It is characteristic of the Passion Play that several of its English stage directions conclude with the expression 'þus seyng' (sometimes 'seyng þus' or just 'seyng') as an introduction to the words of the next speaker. Interestingly, the scribe-compiler's revisional stage direction is not of the 'þus seyng' type.

23 One lot of material, covering Mary Magdalene's exorcism and her anointing of Jesus's feet, is written in a stanza of thirteen lines characteristic of Proclamation Play pageants, plus one stanza with an aaabcccb rhyme scheme. This accounts roughly for the material on fol. 149r–v. Another lot, a Last Supper scene in which the disciples respond to Jesus's statement that he is to be betrayed, is written in another characteristic stanza, short-line octaves rhyming ababbcbc. This accounts roughly for the material on fols. 150–1. However, though both are characteristic of the Proclamation Play, the thirteener and short-line octave stanzas do not appear together in a pageant unless revision has taken place (as in the short-line octave Lamech episode that has been tailored onto the thirteener pageant of Noah; see *78*, vol. I, Play 4, lines 118–253 + s.d.). Who brought the two lots of material together is not clear. It may have been the scribe-compiler. Equally, the amalgamation may already have occurred in his Proclamation Play exemplar. Whatever the case, the stage direction at the juncture of the two lots of material on fol. 149v is probably revisional.

24 The fourth leaf of quire O is now wanting. The writing on fol. 149 starts comparatively cramped and becomes gradually more spacious on fol. 149v. This suggests that the scribe-compiler, anticipating difficulty in fitting all his intended material onto fol. 149r–v, cramped his writing to begin with, but relaxed as he realised that he had enough space.

25 The forty pageants of the Proclamation Play were numbered and briefly described in the banns. After N-Town was complete, the scribe-compiler realised that its interpolations created more episodes than the banns accounted for. He therefore tried to adjust the numbering of the banns to correspond to what N-town now contained. Finding this task too much, he abandoned it part way through.

26 Parkes, 'Ordinatio and compilatio', pp. 127–8.

27 Fredson T. Bowers, Textual and Literary Criticism (Cambridge: Cambridge University Press, 1959), p. 123.

28 Compare Chaucer's professed textual attitudes. He displays this democratising approach (even if as a literary pose) in his invitation to readers to 'encresse or maken dymynucioun of my langage' in Troilus and Criseyde; conversely, the curse of a scabby scalp will fall on Adam scriveyn if he does not copy Troilus and Criseyde exactly as Chaucer composed it (see Larry D. Benson (ed.), The Riverside Chaucer, 3rd edn (Boston: Houghton Mifflin Company, 1987), p. 531, lines 1335–6, and p. 650 respectively).

29 Dugdale, Antiquities, p. 116.

30 448, p. 166. Woolf (138, p. 258) says their action is like a dance round a maypole, but at this point the cross is not yet raised up. Comparison to a carole seems more apt. The episode may have been suggested by a passage attributed to St Bernard, commonly transmitted in Middle English and in popular Latin sources, where Christ reproaches man by comparing aspects of his Passion to man's merrymaking: 'tu tripudias cum pedibus et ego laboravi cum meis pedibus, tu in choreis brachia extendis in modum crucis in gaudium et ego ea in cruce extensa habui in opprobrium' (T. Graesse (ed.), Legenda aurea, 2nd edn (Leipzig, 1850), p. 227; compare Frances A. Foster (ed.), A Stanzic Life of Christ, EETS, OS 166 (London: Oxford University Press, 1926), p. 201, lines 5933–40)

31 As early as the twelfth century in the neighbouring county of Suffolk, Roland the Farter held lands of the king by performing at court a saltum, siffetum et bumbulum (a 'leap, whistle and fart') every Christmas (Constance Bullock-Davies, Register of Royal and Baronial Domestic Minstrels 1272–1327 (Bury St Edmunds: Boydell Press, 1986), p. 174). See also D. J. Gifford, 'Iconographical Notes Towards a Definition of the Medieval Fool', Journal of the Warburg and Courtauld Institutes 37 (1974), 336–42, esp. p. 338.

32 Play 2, lines 217–18 and 300–02; on medieval walled gardens, see D. Pearsall and E. Salter, Landscapes of the Medieval World, (London: Paul Elek, 1973), pp. 76–118.

33 Plays 14 and 11 respectively; on 'lovedays', see Josephine W. Bennett, 'The Mediaeval Loveday', Speculum 33 (1958), 351–70.

34 Compare the importance accorded the throne in the Secretum Secretorum (ed. M. A. Manzalaoui, EETS, OS 276 (Oxford: Oxford University Press, 1977), p. 411, lines 414–20); also, etiquette required that children cede place to their elders and betters (Frederick J. Furnivall, ed. Early English Meals and Manners,

EETS, OS 32 (London: N. Trübner and Co., 1868), p. 253, lines 85–7), hence the seating arrangement in N-Town, in worldly terms, would have seemed strange.

35 G. R. Owst, *Preaching in Medieval England* (Cambridge: Cambridge University Press, 1926), p. 316

36 Play 6, lines 47ff. The importance of the Decalogue in the preaching of catechesis was notably urged in 1281 in the decree *Ignorancia sacerdotum* of the Council of Lambeth. In the fifteenth century, the most important re-affirmation of *Ignorancia sacerdotum* was probably that of the Oxford Constitutions of 1407.

37 Compare *Biblia Sacra cum Glossa Ordinaria et Postilla Nicolai Lyrani* (Lyons, 1589)I, cols. 587–90, with Play 27, lines 396–436. Spector (78, vol. II, pp. 498–500) notes the close similarity of some of the play's lines (not as many as he might have) with Rabanus Maurus's exegesis on Exodus 12, the *Glossa*'s ultimate source at this point. However, the playwright's use of this or another such intermediary, rather than of Rabanus's *originalia*, seems more likely. For example, the unpublished Latin sermon 'Qui manducat hunc panem vivet in eternum' (Hereford Cathedral Library MS O.III.5, fols. 21v–24), for use either on Easter Day or Corpus Christi, contains most of the exegesis found in the Passion Play. Furthermore the written dialect of the Hereford scribe, who wrote in the first half of the fifteenth century, locates approximately in southeast Lincolnshire or northwest Norfolk, and is thus not far removed from where the author of the Passion Play probably lived. If nothing else, the Hereford sermon testifies to the currency in the playwright's region of the exegetical material that he has drafted.

38 A. J. Minnis and A. B. Scott (eds.), with the assistance of D. Wallace, *Medieval Literary Theory and Criticism c.1100–c.1375. The Commentary Tradition* (Oxford: Clarendon Press, 1988), pp. 197–276. For most medieval exegetes, the levels above the literal were the allegorical, tropological and anagogical.

39 Note 'fygure' and 'gostly interpretacyon' (Play 27, lines 361 and 278, and line 395 respectively). Other plays use technical terms, too (e.g. 'sygnyfure', Play 22, line 29 and Play 38, line 92). It might also be noted that typology, widely acknowledged in N-Town and interpreted as a source of its thematic unity, is essentially a technique of exegesis.

40 In which the polysemous play of signs was itself the chief object of delight; as Roland Barthes put it, 'Le plaisir du texte, c'est ça: la valeur passée au rang somptueux de significant' (*Le plaisir du texte* (Paris: Éditions du Seuil, 1973), p. 103).

7

JOHN C. COLDEWEY

The non-cycle plays and the East Anglian tradition

The predominance of East Anglia over all other regional theatrical traditions in late medieval England, as evidenced by the sheer number of recorded performances and by the variety of associated play texts, has been apparent since the time of Chambers. This fact, however, has ordinarily been obscured by the critical and historical attention (not undeserved) lavished upon the great civic cycle plays that flourished elsewhere in the country. Chambers, drawing together 'Representations of Mediaeval Plays' in Appendix W to his monumental *The Mediaeval Stage*, (23, vol. II, pp. 329–406), listed all known towns and villages sponsoring or partaking in some kind of dramatic performance. Forty-eight of his total of 127 locations, spread over thirty-four counties of England, Ireland and Scotland – that is, nearly forty per cent – were located in the four counties, or parts of counties, that comprised East Anglia. More recent scholarship has of course identified many other such theatrically inclined towns and villages since Chambers compiled his data at the beginning of this century, and the total for East Anglia, now easily double or triple the number he turned up, simply reaffirms its primary position (252). Chambers himself puzzled over his figures, noting that although 'a vigorous and widespread dramatic activity throughout the length and breadth of the land ... naturally finds its fullest scope in the annually repeated performances of several amongst the greater cities, yet it is curious to observe in what insignificant villages it was from time to time found possible to organize plays'. (23, vol. II, p. 109).

Despite the wealth of documentary evidence he amassed, Chambers was never able to shake his own bias to see cycle plays everywhere, nor could he recognise that most of the towns he had represented as performing 'Corpus Christi plays' instead represented places where plays were written and acted in an alternative, non-cycle tradition. Because of this, he was hardly in a position to see how the numbers might point towards East Anglia, and in this regard (as in so many others) Chambers's influence continues to the present day. Much modern scholarship and criticism has often simply followed suit, giving pride of place to the cycle plays as the characteristic form of drama played in the Middle Ages, and turning a blind eye to the communities all over the country – but especially in East Anglia – where non-cycle productions were the rule.[1] But current research is unearthing even more evidence of non-cycle theatrical practices in these places: the various Malone Society *Collections* and the *REED* county publications in particular are bringing forward detailed evidence of theatrical performances in hundreds of towns and villages far from urban centres that sponsored the cycle plays. And this research has begun to occasion some critical attention as well (235, 253, 265, 305). The more extensive documentation of non-cycle plays does not merely add to the numbers that puzzled Chambers and the several generations of scholars who followed him; it provides a frame of reference that can help historians of the drama understand and appreciate more fully the nature of the medieval theatrical experience itself. An important part of that experience was East Anglian.

But it is more than documentary evidence that points so strongly towards this region of the country. With few exceptions, the vast majority of surviving manuscript texts of medieval plays or play fragments that are unconnected with one or another of the civic cycles can be linked to East Anglia by language, manuscript provenance or place-name reference. The survival of these plays past the Reformation seems to have been an even chancier business than the survival of the great cycle texts, so we are left with precious few examples from which to make our observations, compared with what originally existed.[2] Even so, a preliminary list of the plays includes two-thirds of the texts now found in the EETS editions of the Macro plays, the Digby plays, and the non-cycle plays and fragments. The N-Town plays, too, are implicated, but since they form the subject of a separate essay in this collection they will not be treated here. When considered as a body of dramatic texts arising within a regional theatrical tradition, the East Anglian plays emerge as quite astonishing theatrical experiments. Taken together with the records of play performances, they suggest a richness and diversity of theatrical practices unmatched in any other region of the country. The purpose of the present essay is to explore and assess these texts and practices.

The region of England known as East Anglia has always been imprecisely defined geographically, and for good reason: the political boundaries of the ancient kingdom were often shifted by battle, treaty or convenience. The most conservative placement of its boundaries would limit the region to the two counties of Norfolk and Suffolk, homes of the original North Folk and South Folk of the Anglo-Saxons.[3] The most liberal definition of the region would extend its area considerably into a 'Greater East Anglia', the boundaries of which were spelled out in the treaty between Guthrum and Alfred during the late ninth century. According to this agreement the border of East Anglia ran from the mouth of the Thames, along the rivers Lea and Ouse to Watling Street, and so included not only Norfolk and Suffolk but also the adjacent counties of Essex, Cambridgeshire and Huntingdonshire, with parts of Bedfordshire and Hertfordshire (241, p. 158). Clearly the first definition is too narrow, for the Anglo-Saxons settled westward as far as the fens without regard to modern county boundaries, and eastern Cambridgeshire was considered part of East Anglia from the earliest times. Likewise, the second definition is too broad, its boundaries more an indication of Guthrum's greed and Alfred's hopes for appeasement than of any recognisable culturally viable region. For the purposes of this study East Anglia is taken to include the two main counties of Norfolk and Suffolk, and parts of the two main adjoining counties as well: Cambridgeshire east of the Ouse river, and Essex north of the Blackwater.[4] The northern and eastern boundaries of the whole region are of course formed by the North Sea.

Historically, East Anglia owed a great deal to its geographical position and topography, and these in turn influenced its theatrical fortunes. Its proximity to northern Europe and the Netherlands brought not just the recurrent threat of invasion, but the possibility of trade and the collateral development of roads, ports and inland centres of commerce. Its accessible shoreline, gently rolling landscape, meandering rivers and fertile, sometimes marshy soil invited early pioneering, the clearing of forests and the carving out of arable and pasture from woodland. The region supported a burgeoning population well before the Norman invasion, and from the eleventh century forward it ranked as the most densely peopled area in Britain.[5] According to the Domesday Book, Norfolk and Suffolk alone had 1,365 settlements by this time, but only three boroughs: Norwich, Thetford and Yarmouth.[6] During the next 300 years these communities continued to grow in size, number and prosperity, particularly during the fourteenth and fifteenth centuries as the cloth trade developed. By the late fifteenth century, Suffolk was the major cloth-producing area in England,[7] and Lay Subsidy and Poll Tax returns show clearly that the wool trade brought wealth to many East Anglian merchants.[8] Thus settlements became market towns, cathedrals and monasteries became ecclesiastical centres and holy sites became shrines for pilgrimage; uniquely in this region, however, only a few local fiefdoms became manors, and the prosperous village, peopled by a large proportion of free peasantry, remained the main social unit.[9] By the late medieval period, the time from which the earliest records of dramatic activity date, there was in place in East Anglia a densely packed network of towns and villages, evenly distributed over the region, with few distinguishable

urban centres. Except for Norwich, and to a lesser degree Ipswich, Bury St
Edmunds and Thetford, the dense population spread out in this tight matrix
of small communities, offering quite different kinds of theatrical opportunities from those afforded by the great population centres dominating the
midlands or the north – places like Coventry, Chester or York, that became
hosts to the civic cycle play tradition (235, p. 128 n. 11).

If East Anglia was a region marked by prosperity during the late Middle
Ages, it was also known to be pious, literate and politically active, though
in a more limited way, perhaps because of its geographical isolation. Its
commercial vitality from the fourteenth century onwards, with traders
moving across the countryside and along the rivers, farmers bringing their
goods to local markets or further afield to the market squares of Norwich
or Thetford or Bury, merchants setting up shop in the small towns, all
acted as the busy economic backdrop against which spiritual success could
be cultivated. Monasteries had grown up like mushrooms from well before
Domesday: by the year 1200 more than eighty of them were established in
Norfolk and Suffolk alone (241, p. 176). And now, in the fourteenth and
fifteenth centuries, the lay piety movement arose hand-in-hand with
middle-class fortunes. The East Anglians were by every account pious folk,
active parishioners who formed and supported spiritual guilds in impressive numbers, ordinary people whose personal good fortunes were reflected
not only in the donations and bequests made to their parish churches but
in the multiplication of the churches themselves. These 'wool churches' –
those magnificent perpendicular structures in Long Melford or Lavenham,
for example – were often wildly out of scale for the parishes they served.
The feverish building of parish churches reached its peak between 1475
and 1526. In Norwich, for example, by the end of the fifteenth century one
could walk to a different church every Sunday for an entire year and still
have a month of churches left before attending Mass at the Cathedral (251,
p. xv). And at this same time – indeed, for many of the same reasons – the
multiplication of endowments brought East Anglian monasteries, abbeys
and other religious houses into positions of unparalleled power and
influence.

As might be expected from such an economically and religiously potent
area, East Anglia shared in some larger political developments as well,
though its separation from much of the country by the fens tended to keep
politics recognisably local, and, in keeping with its rural character, a populist theme was often sounded. Bury St Edmunds, for example, famous from
the thirteenth century as the place where the barons had sworn to force the
terms of the Magna Carta upon King John, was prominent again in 1447 as
the site where Parliament assembled to issue a warrant for the arrest of

Humphrey, Duke of Gloucester (*305*, p. 132). The Peasants' Revolt of 1381 brought remarkable violence to East Anglia; and perhaps the best-known East Anglian event was Kett's rebellion in the mid-sixteenth century, another significant uprising. Still, while there was admittedly enormous power wielded by the Dukes of Norfolk from the Wars of the Roses until Elizabethan times, by other noblemen, and other powerful families in the region, or by Cardinal Wolsey during the early course of the English Reformation, there was never a 'King Maker' in East Anglia.

Taken together, the prosperity at almost every level of the social order, the development of lay piety and the consolidation of ecclesiastical and political power seem to have conspired to produce in East Anglia a uniquely rich and dense rural society – and one with very definite literary pretensions. It is not really surprising that a literary culture should flourish under such conditions, and when we come to consider the many play texts associated with this small region, we must recall that East Anglia was the home of quite an amazing array of writers in the late Middle Ages. They include the two most celebrated women authors in medieval England: Julian of Norwich (1343–1413) and Margery Kempe (1373–1439), both of whose works attest to the depth of mystical spirituality behind the lay piety movement in the region and to the radical edge that religious zeal could assume. But there were plenty of other writers who were not mystics: the dauntingly prolific John Lydgate (*c.* 1370–1449), from Lidgate, Suffolk, who spent most of his working life as a monk at the Benedictine Abbey of Bury St Edmunds; the Pastons, from Paston in Norfolk, whose letters testify to a generally high level of literacy, sophistication and business acumen among fifteenth-century East Anglian laity; John Skelton (*c.* 1460–1529), who retired to write poetry as rector of the parish church at Diss, Norfolk; John Bale (1495–1563), who had spent his early days as a Carmelite at the Whitefriars' House in Maldon, Essex, converted to Protestantism in the 1530s, resigned as Prior of the Ipswich Whitefriars, married and acted as a secular priest at Thorndon, Suffolk (*257*, pp. 159–60); and Nicholas Udall (1505–56), who served in the 1530s as vicar at Braintree, Essex, before assuming his ill-fated position as Headmaster at Eton. Later in the sixteenth century, Gabriel Harvey (1545?–1630) would be associated with Saffron Walden, Essex, his home town and the place to which he was wittily consigned again by Nashe; and, in the seventeenth century, Thomas Browne (1605–82) would retire in Norwich to practise medicine and write about urn burial. There were minor figures as well: the fifteenth-century John of Norwich, for example, author of the *Tractatus de modo inuendiendi ornata verba*; the poet John Metham, author of the romance *Amoryus and Cleopes* (1448); the chronicler John Capgrave, Austin Friar of Lynn (Norfolk); and Osbern Bokenham, Austin

Friar at Stoke Clare (Suffolk) and author of (among other things) an elaborate version of the legend of Mary Magdalene.[10]

No doubt there are other fifteenth- and sixteenth-century writers associated with the region who might be mentioned here, but the list above is surely long enough to make the point concerning East Anglian literary culture at the time. No other area in England during the 175 years between 1375 and 1550, except perhaps London, could boast of so many prominent, identifiable, bookish figures and literary accomplishments.[11] And we would do well to recall here that two of these authors, Lydgate and Skelton, are among the very few fifteenth- and early sixteenth-century names associated with playwriting and civic pageantry, mummings and devices;[12] that John Bale cast an enormous shadow over the second quarter of the sixteenth century as a playwright and polemicist (94); or that Nicholas Udall has long been considered a seminal figure in English drama (11, pp. 103–9).

These foregoing observations are meant to sketch out, briefly, the social, religious and intellectual contours of late medieval East Anglia, and to indicate something of its literary traditions. This background provides some larger cultural contexts for the remarkable proliferation of dramatic texts in the region from the late fourteenth century until the time of Elizabeth. The texts themselves are evidence that a startling number of anonymous playwrights flourished here as well: their works, too, display a connection with East Anglia, and they are firmly grounded in its language and habits.

EAST ANGLIAN DRAMATIC TEXTS

One group of dramatic texts with very strong East Anglian associations are the Digby plays – that is, the plays found in Bodleian MS Digby 133 – including *Mary Magdalen* (2143 lines), the most elaborate and theatrically demanding play outside of the cycles; the *Killing of the Children* (568 lines), that strange, humorous and vicious spectacle; *The Conversion of St Paul* (633 lines), with its morally illuminating and literal traverse from an early pagan stage to the local Christian church; and a large fragment (755 lines) of the arcane morality *Wisdom* (also called *Mind, Will and Understanding*) (84, p. 116). The plays have long been associated with East Anglia, not only on the basis of manuscript evidence, but also on the evidence of language and dialect. Originally the Digby plays were physically distinct manuscripts, as discolouration, wear and insect damage attest; they were bound together with a number of interesting alchemical and astrological works at some time during the seventeenth century (84, pp. x, liv, lxiii). But two of them, *The Killing of the Children* and the *Wisdom* fragment, were written by the same scribe. The *Killing of the Children* manuscript is dated 1512 and inscribed

'Ihon Parfre ded wryte this booke.' Whether John Parfrey was playwright or scribe, the family name of 'Parfrey' is found in Norfolk and Suffolk at this time, mainly in the area around Thetford. (*84*, pp. lv–vi). On three of the Digby plays (*The Conversion of St Paul*, *Mary Magdalen* and *Wisdom*) appear the name or initials of an early owner, Myles Blomefylde, about whom quite a lot has been discovered. Blomefylde was a native of Bury St Edmunds, born there in 1525; he attended Cambridge and was licensed to practise medicine in 1552. He was an avid collector of books, and at least eighteen early titles can be traced to his library. He also had a taste for dramatic literature, for besides the Digby plays he owned the sole surviving copy of *Fulgens and Lucres*. From the mid-1560s until his death in 1603 he lived in Chelmsford, Essex, where he practised alchemy and white magic as well as medicine, and where he was churchwarden for many years. It seems likely that he came into possession of the Digby plays while he was there, perhaps after their apparent final performance in 1562 (*242*). It has also been proposed that they may have come into Myles's possession through William Blomfield, an alchemical poet and monk of Bury St Edmunds, older than Myles but almost certainly related to him (*84*, pp. xii–xiii). In any case, Myles Blomefylde's ownership of the Digby plays marks a relatively late moment in their history, for the manuscripts all date from around the beginning of the century, and in the case of *Wisdom* it is clear that the play itself, of which the Digby fragment is only a copy, was nearly a hundred years old when he came into possession of the manuscript (*84*, p. lxv; *83*, p. xxxviii). The physical condition of all the plays in the Digby manuscript, and the evidence of copying and reworking of the texts, clearly point towards lengthy performance careers in this part of the country (*234*).

An additional chain of evidence linking the Digby play texts to East Anglia long before Myles Blomefylde's ownership involves another manuscript collection of plays – the Macro plays, named after their earliest known owner, the Reverend Cox Macro (1683–1767), also a native of Bury St Edmunds (*83*, *115*). The Macro group also includes the longest and most spectacular of the morality plays, *The Castle of Perseverance* (3,649 lines), copied by a south Norfolk scribe towards the middle of the fifteenth century (*83*, p. xi; *238*, p. 101, map). Slightly later are the Macro copy of the full text of *Wisdom* (1,126 lines), and the unique copy of a third morality, *Mankind* (914 lines; for all three, see further below, chapter 9). A comparison of the Digby fragment of *Wisdom* with the full text in the Macro manuscript has indicated that both are likely to have derived from a common exemplar, rather than one from the other (*84*, pp. lxv–lxvii), showing that at least one more copy must once have been circulating in the area. The scribe who copied the Digby *Wisdom* was also responsible for most of *The Killing of the*

Children in the same manuscript (*84*, p. lxiv), and was presumably someone concerned with compiling a small repertoire of plays circulating in East Anglia around the turn of the fifteenth century.

The Macro copies of *Wisdom* and *Mankind* are a slightly earlier example of the same activity. Important new light has recently been shed on their transmission by the discovery that their earliest owner, who in the Macro manuscript simply identifies himself as a monk named Hyngham (*83*, p. xxvii), elsewhere signs his name in full as Thomas Hyngham, monk of Bury St Edmunds. Moreover, this appearance of his full signature (in a copy of Walton's Boethius, now MS 601 in the Schøyen Collection, Oslo) lends further palaeographical support to the suggestion that he not only owned, but also copied out the whole of *Wisdom* and most of *Mankind* (*239*). The fact that a monk of Bury certainly owned and was probably himself responsible for the making of these copies of the two plays adds weight to recent arguments for Bury St Edmunds as a major East Anglian centre of dramatic activity (*253*, *305*). On the other hand, the presence in *Mankind* of the names of identifiable persons and places in neighbouring Cambridgeshire and Norfolk (*83*, p. 222) serve as a reminder that wherever, and for whatever purpose, Hyngham acquired an exemplar of it, *Mankind* is most likely to have been a travelling play. Likewise, if *Wisdom* was indeed, through Hyngham's agency, seen at Bury, the fact that he evidently had obtained a copy of the script from elsewhere suggests that it too may have been seen at other places, perhaps one or more of the neighbouring Benedictine or Cluniac foundations, such as Ely, Norwich, Wymondham or Thetford. Bury St Edmunds has also been strongly canvassed as the place where the N-Town plays originated or were performed (*227*), though as Alan J. Fletcher shows in the preceding chapter, the case for other possible locations still remains very much open.

The remaining Middle English non-cycle plays consist of six or seven apparently complete free-floating play texts, some dramatic fragments, and a few single actors' parts or speeches. More than half of these have links to East Anglia. Thirteen of them have been gathered together in Norman Davis's EETS edition of *Non-Cycle Plays and Fragments* (*85*, *117*). Of these, the ones that were composed, copied or performed in East Anglia include the following:

1)   The Norwich Grocers' Play, 'The Story of the Creation of Eve, with the Expelling of Adam and Eve out of Paradise'. Two versions of the play survive, modern transcripts of originals that had been part of the Norwich *Grocers' Book*, itself now lost or destroyed. The transcripts are preserved among the Kirkpatrick Papers in the Norwich Record

Office. One of the originals dated from around 1533, the other from 1565, and they seem to have been part of a larger sequence of pageants, if not a full civic cycle in Norwich (85, pp. xxii–xl). The later version shows clear signs of revision according to reformed doctrinal sensibilities.

2) The Brome *Abraham and Isaac*, which survives in a late fifteenth-century commonplace book now at Yale University Library. The book was discovered in the manor of Brome, in northern Suffolk, where it may well have been originally compiled and the play copied. About 200 lines of the play – nearly half of its 465 lines – bear a remarkable resemblance to the corresponding lines of the Abraham and Isaac play in the Chester cycle. The relationship of the play texts to each other has often been argued but never satisfactorily explained (85, pp. lviii–lxx, esp. lxiii–lxvi).

3) The Croxton *Play of the Sacrament*, surviving in a collection of miscellaneous texts in Trinity College, Dublin. Although the date 1461 is put forward in the play as when the dramatised events actually occurred, the surviving copy dates from at least fifty years later. The place-names of Croxton and Babwell Mill, mentioned in the banns and in the play, refer to places near Thetford and Bury St Edmunds respectively. The name of the quack doctor in the play, Brundyche, may also derive from the town of Brundish in Suffolk. Some understanding of the lines depends on recognising these names, so they would seem to have some bearing on where the play originated. The dialect, similar to that of *The Castle of Perseverance*, bears this out (85, pp. lxx–lxxxv).

4) *Dux Moraud*, in a manuscript at the Bodleian Library, Oxford, is an actor's part in a play of incest and murder, the plot of which can be reconstructed from a number of early poems that tell a similar story. Davis dates the handwriting of the play to the second quarter of the fifteenth century, though it is written on a much older vellum assize roll that contains matter relating to cases of William de Ormesby, an eminent judge active in Norfolk and Suffolk in the early fourteenth century. Davis identifies the language as having a 'strongly East Anglian character', and its versification as similar to that of *The Castle of Perseverance* (85, pp. c–cxi).

5) The Rickinghall (Bury St Edmunds) Fragment in the British Library contains an introductory pomping speech in Anglo-Norman, followed by a Middle English rendering of it. The speeches are written on the back of a fourteenth-century account roll relating to the manor of Rickinghall in Suffolk (which belonged to the Abbey of Bury St

Edmunds at the time). Davis notes that as far as can be ascertained, the dialect of the English is consistent with the origin suggested by the provenance of the manuscript (85, pp. cxiv–cxv).

6) The Reynes Extracts are found in another Bodleian manuscript, and consist of a speech belonging to the character Delight in a morality play, and an epilogue to a morality play. They appear in a commonplace book compiled by Robert Reynes of Acle in Norfolk in the late fifteenth century. Forms of some words like *therke* for 'dark' seem, according to Davis, 'typically East Anglian,' in keeping with the apparent provenance of the manuscript (85, p. cxxiii).

7) The Winchester Dialogues, found in Winchester College MS 33A, containing the semi-dramatic dialogue *Lucidus and Dubius* and the play *Occupation, Idleness and Doctrine*. The texts are written in a mid-fifteenth-century hand. The East Midland dialect they share contains forms unique to the southern Suffolk/northern Essex region, though the rhymes suggest that the texts may have originated further north (117, pp. 135–208).[13]

Thus, the full census of medieval play texts known to be of East Anglian provenance is as follows: all three complete Digby plays and the fragment of *Wisdom*, all the Macro plays, the N-Town plays, six out of the thirteen non-cycle plays and fragments, and probably the Winchester Dialogues.

By contrast, the remainder of the British Isles is rather sparsely represented in terms of the surviving non-cycle plays and fragments. Complete biblical plays are represented by a late antiquarian copy of the Shipwrights' pageant of Noah from an otherwise lost cycle of plays from Newcastle, together with an *Abraham and Isaac*, resembling the cycle play versions, in a fifteenth-century manuscript compiled at Northampton (both in 85). The *Pride of Life* (85) is a substantial fragment of a morality from Dublin, pre-dating the English examples of the genre by up to a century (see below, chapter 9). The early fifteenth-century Shrewsbury Fragments (85), from somewhere in the diocese of Lichfield, are a curious mixture, consisting of Latin liturgical presentations intercalated with vernacular dialogue of the kind found in the cycle plays, and the shepherds' speeches therein strongly resemble parts of York play XV. *Christ's Burial and Resurrection*, edited alongside but unconnected with the Digby plays (84), is an esoteric vernacular offshoot of the Latin liturgical tradition and seems to hail from one of the northern Carthusian houses in the early sixteenth century. A once flourishing tradition of secular farce is represented by a sole fragment of c. 1300, the *Interludium de Clerico et Puella* (117, no. 2), the complete action of which can be gathered from what seems to be a version for solo *jongleur* and dog, *Dame Sirith*.[14] For the rest, there are three short fourteenth- and fifteenth-century fragments of unknown provenance, apparently single actors' speeches jotted down as *aides-memoire*, named for the manuscripts where they are found: the Cambridge Prologue, the Durham Prologue and the Ashmole fragment (all in *85*).

Though the bibliographical and linguistic evidence for the provenances of all the texts in both of these groups has been very carefully sifted in the new editions and facsimiles published in recent years, we should not of course lose sight of the common-sense notion that plays originating elsewhere were copied by East Anglian scribes, just as East Anglian plays could find their way to other areas. The connection between the Chester cycle and the Brome *Abraham and Isaac*, or the hint of an earlier Lincoln connection for *The Castle of Perseverance* (*83*, p. xi), suggests as much. But the bulk and coincidence of the evidence point clearly towards East Anglia as the area to which more physical data links more surviving plays than any other region in the whole of the British Isles, and this phenomenon in itself deserves further investigation.

THE LANGUAGE OF THE PLAYS

The two most searching studies of the language of East Anglian drama remain unpublished PhD theses: Richard Beadle's 'The Medieval Drama of East Anglia' (1977; *235*) and Jean D. Pfleiderer's 'The Community of Language in the East Anglian Drama' (1981; *265*). These works offer analyses based not only on dialect but on orthographic conventions and poetic formulas shared by East Anglian plays. A full description of the language of each play appears in the introductions to the EETS editions by Spector (*78*) Davis, (*85*), Eccles (*83*) and Baker, Murphy and Hall (*84*). Characteristics of the East Anglian dialect receive the fullest articulation in Norman Davis's 'The Language of the Pastons' (*247*).

Beadle notes that phonologically based dialectology is an inadequate tool to distinguish those texts written in East Anglia from texts written in the larger east midlands region generally, and he offers a 'graphemic' or orthographic approach, one that incorporates scribal characteristics, notably spelling habits, as well as phonological indicators. His painstaking study reveals common orthographic variations in a wide range of texts and documents known to be of East Anglian origin in the late Middle Ages. Many of these are listed in a recent study (*238*), which includes a map showing the likely areas of dialectal origin for several of the East Anglian play manuscripts under discussion here.

Pfleiderer's approach to the language of East Anglian drama is stylistic.

She builds upon Beadle's observations regarding dialect and orthography, and uses computer-assisted concordances of the play texts to investigate a perceived 'community of language.' Pfleiderer first sets out to discover features of the language shared by these plays: characteristic suffixes, word repetitions, phrases, commonplaces, clusters and other rhetorical units. These features help establish a large East Anglian paradigm of dramatic expression. Circling back, she then traces the degree of affinity to that paradigm exhibited by individual play texts. Throughout, Pfleiderer relies on 'collocations', J. R. Firth's term, which helps determine 'artistic prosody':

> Alliteration, assonance, and the chiming of what are usually called consonants are common prosodic features of speech, and from the phonological point of view can be considered as markers or signals of word-structure or of the word-process in the sentence. Such features can be so distributed by a writer as to form part of artistic prosodies in both prose and verse. (265, p. 22n).

A good example of such a collocation is the expression 'to kill without a knife', found twice in *The Castle of Perseverance* (1617, 1124), once in *The Conversion of St Paul* (564) and once in the N-Town plays (Play 2, line 319), but not elsewhere in medieval drama (265, p. 43). Similar cases can be made for many other such stylistic tics, for words and phrases that echo again and again in these plays. The importance of Pfleiderer's work lies in its putting forward regional stylistics, locating a broad range of poetic expression used only, or in a special way, by the community of East Anglian dramatic texts.

Dialectical, orthographic and stylistic evidence thus corroborates other manuscript data to confirm the corpus of East Anglian play texts. It also suggests ways that these texts play off against each other to sound themes and expressions particularly familiar in the region. The language of East Anglian medieval plays, rooted as it is in vernacular speech, offers a means not only to identify the plays, but to bundle them together as a body of dramatic texts with common features and concerns.

EVIDENCE FOR PERFORMANCE AND STAGING

Evidence for the performance of plays in East Anglia comes from entries appearing in civic and parish records, in ecclesiastical and civil court documents and in occasional anecdotal references. Most of the documentary evidence is by its very nature localised, useful mainly as a kind of mapping exercise and a gauge, more or less reliable, of the frequency and distribution of dramatic activity in the region. But sometimes it can tell quite a lot about the kind of play that was performed and about theatrical necessities, props, costumes, the use of place-and-scaffold staging, or about performance conditions. Sometimes a text or manuscript can itself bear mute witness to its own performance history, with deletions, revisions, marginal notations or conditions such as worn and dirty cover leaves testifying to actual stage practices, as Baker has pointed out (234). Sometimes, as in *The Castle of Perseverance*, the text includes more specific information, like the map of the stage. In contrast to the documentary evidence, then, the texts, which are all unlocalised except for the Norwich Grocers' Play, can indicate more general characteristics of the East Anglian theatrical tradition.

In addition to Chambers's gathering of data in the appendices to his *Mediaeval Stage*, alluded to at the beginning of this study, a good deal of scholarly effort has been expended in the sifting and gathering of references to plays in local records, though the process is nowhere near complete. A primary source of information is David Galloway and John Wasson's Malone Society *Records of Plays and Players in Norfolk and Suffolk* (252); Galloway's *REED: Norwich, 1540–1642* (251) is also available now, though it leaves the early dramatic activities in the town unexplored. Alan Nelson's *REED: Cambridge* (59) offers some information about rural Cambridgeshire theatrical traditions, and sections of his *Medieval English Stage* (34) examine local evidence that indicates staging practices. For Essex drama the work of Andrew Clark (240) and John Coldewey (242–245), and some lesser-known articles by Robert Wright (266, 267) and W. A. Mepham (259–263) provide good starting points.

The picture of dramatic activity this evidence sketches out is unmatched in its variety of sheer 'busyness' in any other part of the country. The cycle play, that familiar expression of civic pride and power, appears here, although only in a truncated form at Norwich and in processions or *tableaux vivants* at Ipswich, and perhaps Bungay and Lynn. At Norwich, processions of pageants were mixed with performances, forming a kind of midget cycle that at its apparent peak in the 1530s consisted of twelve pageants. This number should be compared with the nearly fifty at York or twenty four at Chester (the shortest of the four great cycles). The cycle-like performances, beginning with the Mercers', Drapers' and Haberdashers' Creation play, continued past a Resurrection play to the Worstedweavers' 'Holy Ghost' play – an appropriate finale for a play sequence mounted on Monday and Tuesday of Whitsun week (85, pp. xxvi–xxvii; 249; 34, pp. 119–37). The Norwich Grocers' Play of Adam and Eve's expulsion from Paradise is the only surviving text from this group, and it exists in two versions, one pre- and one post-Reformation. This fact might be taken to argue for the longevity or tenacity of civic investment in dramatic enterprise, but this would be misleading. For although processions were common in Norwich as part of the civic fair or to promote Corpus Christi Day and

Whitsun week, records indicate that sponsorship of local *plays* there was a fairly rare event (251, pp. xxx–xxxii; 34, pp. 129–36). It is much the same elsewhere in the region. At Bungay in the early sixteenth century a series of pageants existed too, but here, at Ipswich, perhaps at Lynn and Bury St Edmunds, theatrical performances seem to have been only occasional additions to annual Corpus Christi Day or Whitsuntide processions (252, pp. 55–64, 140–8, 169–84; 34, pp. 189–91, 197–200).

Again, while consideration of the N-Town plays falls outside the scope of this essay, it is obvious from the banns alone that these plays do not conform to familiar patterns of sponsorship, organisation or performance shared by cycle plays elsewhere. But the patterns of organisation that emerge from non-cycle play productions in East Anglia are interesting in the extreme. Beside the very modest showing of cycle-like events must be placed the documentary evidence testifying to a startling amount of other local dramatic activities in the region. The number of places involved in one way or another with theatrical productions during the fifteenth and sixteenth centuries runs to well over a hundred, and these seem to have included almost every small corner of population, every village and town. Whatever the traditions in other parts of the country, putting on plays or taking part in them was not limited to a few large urban centres in East Anglia. Indeed, outside of Norwich there were no large urban centres with civic structures capable of supporting sizable theatrical enterprises, certainly nothing to compare with the well-established civic and social frameworks in place elsewhere in the country. The East Anglian plays were, like the cycle plays, expressions of a community, but with this difference: in other regions the community was urban, and guilds were the main facilitating agents making productions possible in the first place. In East Anglia the community was rural, a parish-based, densely populated network of villages and small towns. The agencies that made East Anglian productions possible were the parishes themselves, or, if the governance of the small community was handled by a municipal bureaucracy, the town hall or guildhall. Fiscal responsibility, and often even the oversight of local plays, then, fell into the hands of churchwardens and chamberlains, and it is from their accounts that much of our documentary evidence derives.

But another important distinction sets these non-cycle plays in East Anglia apart from the cycle plays put on elsewhere. By all accounts the non-cycle plays were performed for *profit* rather than as a display of power and wealth or as a means of pious education for the unlettered. These plays, in fact, sometimes acted as important parts of parochial capital building campaigns; they helped build whole church towers, replace roofs and add aisles to parish churches. They brought economic stability, financial well-being and a nearly surefire source of income to ailing or ambitious parishes everywhere in the region for three or four generations during the late fifteenth and sixteenth centuries. I have dealt with the matter of parish organisation and finance in some detail elsewhere (24, esp. pp. 93–8); what should be remarked upon briefly here are the two most familiar patterns of production that necessity seems to have invented, for they help explain the amazing proliferation of dramatic performances throughout this area. As might be expected from successful ventures, the patterns occur in other parts of the country as well, but never with such frequency as in East Anglia.

The first and most impressive pattern of production to emerge from surviving documentary evidence can be found in the elaborate collaborative celebrations that towns and parishes put on all over the region. These festive enterprises – at Snettisham the event was called, cryptically, a 'Rockfeste' (252, pp. 85–95) – were organised by one town with the cooperation and support of many others, and very often they included dramatic entertainment. Backed by subscription monies gathered in advance from neighbouring communities or by local men of substance, a town or a parish would set forth a day or more of eating, drinking, games and plays, in a kind of high-powered hybrid between a church ale and a parish play. The popularity of these events can only be guessed at from the astounding quantities of food and drink consumed by the crowds. In Bungay in 1568, to take but one example, whole beasts – nearly a dozen lambs, five calves and four stone of beef – were roasted; gallons of butter and cream and hundreds of eggs, and more, were used in cooking; barrel upon barrel of beer was brewed, amounting to more than a thousand gallons (235, p. 140). These were not church basement picnics. Frequently the ventures involved the cooperation of more than twenty towns and villages. In such places as Heybridge and Dunmow in Essex, Bassingbourn in Cambridgeshire, or Boxford in Suffolk (each of which had the support of between twenty and thirty other towns or parishes), records of the events have survived; many more places with communal plays and games, like Wymondham or Hadleigh, Stoke by Nayland or Kenninghall – places where full records have not survived – may be identified on the basis of payments to them appearing in the accounts of other communities.[15]

Importantly, the towns that sponsored cooperative ventures in effect also spread knowledge of theatrical practices far and wide, giving every supporting community a stake in the enterprises and financially successful models to follow. Not surprisingly, many did. But not all were able (or, perhaps, willing) to undertake productions on such a large scale, and there developed at this same time in East Anglia a second pattern of single performances, locally sponsored and more locally attended. Unlike single performances elsewhere, however, the towns that mounted these events often shared resources and skills in ways apparently unknown to the rest of the country. Indeed, the East Anglian performance tradition, whether it involved one town or many, can best be described in a single word: portable. As is clear from the above examples, audiences regularly moved from town to town to see plays. But play texts themselves could also move. Manuscript evidence makes it clear that texts led long stage lives in a variety of locations and conditions (234); and documentary evidence indicates not only that plays were composed locally,[16] but that play books were copied by towns and parishes, and sometimes rented out.[17] Moreover, a player in one town might perform a part in another town's play,[18] or an entire local troupe might take part of their performance on tour to a neighbouring town (243). If a town needed costumes or stage properties, these, too, were available for rent through a number of parishes; they became more available as the Reformation gathered force and ecclesiastical vestments were desanctified and transformed into players' garments (243).

In the records of many of these East Anglian plays, whether sponsored by one or several towns, a remarkable figure called a 'property player' shows up. He was a kind of early English music man, a semi-professional director, stage manager and producer all rolled into one. These property players were well paid and apparently worth the expense. They came in from out of town, bringing their expertise and their stage properties, and they seem to have taken some of the risk out of local theatrical enterprise (244). More light has recently been shed on one of them, Felsted of London, who certainly worked in East Anglia (427). Just how advantageous a position such figures put the parish in can be gathered from a note at the end of the Boxford (Suffolk) accounts from a large production in 1535:

> And it is to be remembryd that all the persons of the towne beforeseid (which brought in money to the profight of the pley) dyd ffynde all the townshippes mete & drynk of ther proper Cost & charge withowt any manner of Alowans to them made for any maner of Charge / by which meanys there is no maner of alowauns owt of this pley but oonley xxx^s to the propyrte pleyer and xv^s to dyuerse pleyers which cam owt of strange placys So that ther was made of the same pley clerely to the profyght of the Chirche – xviij^li xix^s v^d ob.
>
> (252, pp. 137–8).

It should be noted that the sum 'clerely to the profyght of the Chirche' is enormous, nearly nineteen pounds – at a time when the wages for a day's work was sixpence. Also of interest is the sum paid to the property player, thirty shillings, twice as much as that received by the 'pleyers which cam owt of strange placys'.

Thus audiences, play texts, players and stage managers moved about East

Anglia as a part of the region's locally sponsored plays. Yet the records also make it clear that some permanent performance sites were available, like the mid-sixteenth-century amphitheatre at Walsham-le-Willows (Suffolk) that Kenneth Dodd has written about (248), or the late fifteenth-century 'game place' mentioned in the Great Yarmouth records, with its 'game place hous' leased in 1538 (252, pp. 11–16). It may well be, as Beadle suggests (235, chapters 6 and 7) that the playing fields, camping closes and pightles or churchyards common to many medieval communities formed natural and convenient sites for theatrical entertainments. Evidence is too tentative, however, to support his further suggestion that the East Anglian tradition of theatre was related to Cornish tradition of theatre in the round, though John Capgrave of Lynn, on seeing amphitheatres in Rome in the 1450s, was moved to remark that there were such things in his part of the world as well (236). An alternative direction in which to turn might be across the channel to France, where some production practices are remarkably parallel, or the Dutch *Rederijker* tradition to which *Everyman* has been linked (33, 36). Meanwhile, internal evidence from the plays indicates that place-and scaffold staging was standard, and certainly a round playing place for *The Castle of Perseverance* is specified. Sometimes, as in the Digby *Conversion of St Paul*, the church itself was included as part of the playing area. The main point to note here is that, whatever theatrical practices may be echoed in the East Anglian tradition, playing spaces were available locally in a variety of forms all over the region, and they could be developed to accommodate large or small productions. Whether maintained specifically as theatrical spaces or simply as recreational areas for the communities, these were places where scaffold stages could be built to meet the stage requirements of surviving texts.

In addition to locally sponsored plays, East Anglian towns also hosted the obviously portable performances by a long list of travelling companies that no doubt used the same playing places. The history of these companies begins in the provinces during the fifteenth century. Their early success led to larger and larger numbers of them under the patronage of wealthy and status-conscious noblemen during Henrician and Elizabethan times, and their performances became increasingly popular during the sixteenth century. Indeed, some of the noblemen's companies were to achieve greatness as thriving London companies in Shakespeare's age, enjoying the largesse of royal patronage. Earlier, however, in East Anglia, the visits of these itinerant troupes at first supplemented and at last superseded town and parish ventures. Their growth and success are not phenomena specific to this part of the country, and details of their itineraries all over England have never been fully worked out.[19] Moreover, it has never been apparent whether the increased number and frequency of their visits reflects displacement of local performances or simply a filling of the void left when local plays ceased for other reasons. This is so in part because the records of their performances rarely indicate the kinds of plays they put on. Thus, little can be said about these troupes, who show up so often in local records, other than to note that their popularity grew rapidly and to observe that the performances by professional players lasted longer than any other form of entertainment in the region. Their days of success, however, like those of locally sponsored plays, were numbered, and their visits declined significantly during late Elizabethan and Jacobean times. Local resistance to their appearances, beginning late in the sixteenth century, seems to have been motivated by a combination of reformed religious sensibilities that frowned upon stage plays as immoral, and a genuine social concern about the fractious behaviour and privilege of playing companies. The fullest and most interesting evidence concerning such misbehaviour in East Anglia dates from 1583 in Norwich, where the Queen's Men were performing in the yard of the Red Lion Inn. A Norwich man named Wynsdon, accompanied by his servant George, attempted to gain entry without paying; one of the actors beat Wynsdon on the head with his sword, and, with two other actors and a servant of Sir William Paston's, pursued the servant and killed him (251, pp. 70–6). East Anglian towns had enough trouble keeping the peace and maintaining a reverent outlook without this kind of complication.

EAST ANGLIAN THEATRE AS SPECTACLE

Despite the wide variation among East Anglian play texts, despite the disparate venues for their performance and the differing patterns of production, the plays from this region all share a single distinguishing theatrical characteristic. Very simply put, they rely upon spectacle to a much greater degree than do the civic cycle plays. The spectacular form of East Anglian plays flows naturally from their function as profit-making enterprises. They *had* to be crowd pleasers and, as modern entertainment has demonstrated beyond doubt, nothing pleases so well as spectacle.

This is not to say that the cycle plays were *un*theatrical, only that the intentions, purposes and effects of civic cycle plays and the non-cycle plays seem quite different at the outset. The directions taken by scholarship and criticism regarding the two kinds of plays would surely bear out this contention. The cycle plays have attracted more attention for their historical circumstances and doctrinal implications than anything else, and more recently this has taken the form of tallying performance records with stage directions. The controversy over whether, or how, civic cycles might have been staged processionally in one town or another (34), how they met their death in a reformed age (129), or what benefits they brought to guilds have been questions eagerly attended to. Their literary features have not been neglected but the best-known critical works have puzzled over such matters as their formal framework (130) or doctrinal integrity (133, 192). How they worked their theatrical effects – or what those effects might have been – has never received the same kind of searching study, although Martin Stevens's recent *Four Middle English Mystery Cycles* (135) has begun to ask these kinds of questions.

By contrast, the best-known work on the non-cycle plays is Richard Southern's *Medieval Theatre in the Round*, a hypothetical account of the staging of *The Castle of Perseverance* (421), but with clear implications for the staging of other moralities. These plays, associated with East Anglia, are, as Robert Potter (311) and Robert Kelley (309) have shown, quintessential theatre. Who has written about *Mankind* without referring to its staginess, its ribald action and dialogue? It is nearly impossible to deal with any of the non-cycle plays without taking into account their unique and spectacular elements. None of the surviving *Abraham and Isaac* pageants in the cycles exhibits such shameless manipulation of audience sympathy for the fearful child as does the Brome version of the story. No pageant in the civic cycles, not even those where the notorious Herod appears, can boast of such a remarkable black-humoured and macabre scene-stealer as Watkyn in the Digby *Killing of the Children*, nor does any have a scene to rival his being beaten by distaffs. No known pageant from a civic cycle throws together an appearance of a quack doctor from folk drama, a removable hand nailed to a pillar and an exploding oven out of which Jesus might step, as does the Croxton *Play of the Sacrament*. Taboo subjects such as incest can act as the apparent mainspring of the plot in the non-cycle *Dux Moraud*, but not in any pageant of any surviving cycle, and not again until the taste for psychopathology is catered to on the Jacobean stage. And even *Wisdom*, generally noted for its learned tone, has a dance of whores to leaven the scholarly mood. In its largest sense, spectacle refers to special effects, apparent in the Digby *Mary Magdalen*, for example, with its emphasis on action, its rantings and ravings, its ship moving to and fro around the playing place, its burning temple and quaking statue of Mament (346). Play after play in East Anglia exhibits theatrical spectacle of the most challenging kind to directors and producers, then or now. That these essentially theatrical challenges *were* met in the plays' own times may go a long way to explain their success, power and proliferation. There is no question that on a play-for-play basis the East Anglian non-cycle plays easily out-Herod the Herods of the larger cycle plays.

CONCLUSIONS

This essay began by invoking E. K. Chambers's work. When Chambers wrote about the medieval stage, he projected upon his scattered evidence a chronological frame that was itself a dim reflection and distant echo of Darwin's *Origin of Species* and Frazer's *Golden Bough* (see below, chapter 12). Our own scholarship is informed by larger currents of thought and historical pattern as well, of course, though we no longer subscribe to the older evolutionary theory because it so often distorts rather than explains the evidence at hand. I am suggesting in this essay that instead of using time as our chief means of discovering the relationship of so many medieval plays to each other, we substitute, or augment, our investigations by using that other main coordinate of human experience, place. If we can narrow down the limits of time and place within which a performance or sequence of performances occurs, the plays themselves achieve new modes of meaning. It is more than a coincidence that so many early English play texts were written or performed in East Anglia. Both documentary evidence and internal evidence from the texts attest to a profitable, portable tradition, a theatrical inventiveness, an adaptability to local conditions and an exuberant sense of spectacle. Other reasons might be adduced to explain these phenomena, and further theatrical or historical significance might be attached to them, but the brute fact of East Anglian dominance looms large in the late medieval English dramatic heritage; it invites our recognition and requires our most careful attention.

NOTES

1 See, for example, the volume concerned with medieval drama published in the *Revels History of Drama in English* series in 1983 (19).

2 The survival of saint plays in the post-medieval period has recently been discussed by Clifford Davidson (344) and John Wasson (351).

3 D. C. Douglas adopts this narrower set of boundaries in *The Social Structure of Medieval East Anglia*, Oxford Studies in Social and Legal History 9, ed. P. Vinogradoff, (1927), p. 2.

4 Essex clearly figures in the concept of East Anglia from early times. For example, in the 'Little Domesday Book', a more detailed investigation which followed upon the main Domesday survey, the three counties of Norfolk, Suffolk and Essex were taken together as one region (235, p. 127, and further references there).

5 See David Hill, *An Atlas of Anglo-Saxon England* (Oxford. Basil Blackwell, 1981), pp. 18–19; H. C. Darby, *A New Historical Geography of England* (Cambridge: Cambridge University Press, 1973), p. 46, fig. 11; 241, p. 178.

6 Darby, *New Historical Geography*, p. 68, fig. 11; 241, pp. 162–3; Darby, *The Domesday Geography of Eastern England*, 3rd edn (Cambridge: Cambridge University Press, 1971), pp. 353–6.

7 P. J. Bowden, *The Wool Trade in Tudor and Stuart England* (London: Macmillan, 1962).

8 R. S. Schofield, 'The Geographical Distribution of Wealth in England, 1334–1649', *Economic History Review*, 2nd ser., 18 (1965), 353–6.

9 For further discussion of the relevant social and demographic factors see Beadle (235, pp. 128–30).

10 For John of Norwich see R. Weiss, *Humanism in England during the Fifteenth Century*, 3rd edn (Oxford: Basil Blackwell, 1967), p. 11, and 305, p. 135; for Metham, see Hardin Craig (ed.), *The Works of John Metham*, EETS, OS 132 (London: Kegan Paul, Trench, Trübner and Co., 1916); for Capgrave, see P. J. Lucas, 'John Capgrave, O.S.A. (1393–1464), Scribe and "Publisher"', *Transactions of the Cambridge Bibliographical Society*, 5 (1969–71), 1–35; for Bokenham, see Mary S. Serjeantson (ed.), *Osbern Bokenham, Legendys of Hooly Wummen*, EETS, OS 206 (Oxford: Oxford University Press, 1938).

11 An early and still useful survey of the literate community and its patrons in late medieval East Anglia is Samuel Moore, 'Patrons of Letters in Norfolk and Suffolk, c. 1450', *PMLA* 27 (1912), 188–207, and 28 (1913), 79–105. See also now Richard Beadle, 'Prolegomena to a Literary Geography of Later Medieval Norfolk', (238).

12 Derek Pearsall, *John Lydgate* (London: Routledge and Kegan Paul, 1970); Arthur Kinney, *John Skelton: Priest as Poet* (Chapel Hill: University of North Carolina Press, 1987), esp. chapter 3.

13 Norman Davis, 'Two Unprinted Dialogues in Late Middle English, and their Language', *Revue des Langues Vivantes* 35 (1969), 461–72; 235, p. 8.

14 Texts in J. A. W. Bennett and G. V. Smithers (eds.), *Early Middle English Verse and Prose*, 2nd edn (Oxford: Clarendon Press, 1968), pp. 80–95, 196–200; for discussion, see Axton (22, pp. 19–22). Late manuscript fragments and early printed plays of Robin Hood have recently been collected by David Wiles (381).

15 For the Heybridge and Dunmow accounts see Mepham (260, 262) and Wright (266, 267); for the Bassingbourn accounts, see J. C. Cox, *Churchwardens' Accounts from the Fourteenth Century to the Close of the Seventeenth Century* (London: Methuen, 1913), pp. 270–4; for the Boxford accounts, see Galloway and Wasson (252, pp. 135–8). For other places associated with dramatic activities in late-medieval East Anglia, see Lancashire (4, *passim*), lists in Galloway and Wasson (252, Appendix 3), Beadle (235, pp. 134–65) and Wright (266, p. 37).

16 In addition to such evidence of local composition as dialect, see the letter written by Thomas Wylley, vicar of Yoxford, Suffolk, to Thomas Cromwell, in 1537, complaining that he was at odds with his congregation over plays he had written (4, no. 1589, and further references there).

17 Stephen Prewett, for example, a priest of St Peter Mancroft, Norwich, in the 1530s, was paid to copy the 'game book' at St Mary's church, Bungay (Suffolk) in 1526 (85, p. xxxii n. 1); for the rentals, see the Maldon and Chelmsford (Essex) accounts (261, 263).

18 One of the *Hundred Merry Tales* attributed to John Skelton, 'Of Him that played the Devil and came through the Warren and made them that stole the Conies to run away', relates a story of a player of this type in an unnamed Suffolk town; see P. M. Zall (ed.), *A Hundred Merry Tales and Other English Jests of the Fifteenth and Sixteenth Centuries* (Lincoln, Nebr.: University of Nebraska Press, 1963), pp. 66–9.

19 The standard work listing companies, patrons and towns during these later years is still J. T. Murray's *English Dramatic Companies 1558–1642* (58). For the earlier period see Lancashire (4, *passim*), and Westfall (314, pp. 216–9).

8

BRIAN O. MURDOCH

The Cornish medieval drama

The earliest surviving dramatic use of Cornish is part of what may or may not be a play written on the back of a charter dated 1340, and the last is a single line in Richard Brome's *The Northern Lasse*, printed in 1632. The latter need not delay us; the somewhat garbled Cornish is used simply as something foreign. The former, however, has been seen as evidence for early secular drama in Cornwall and in England.[1] In forty-one lines of rhymed strophic verse similar to that of later plays, a speaker offers a young lady to someone as a wife, and then the girl herself is given some advice on handling a husband: agree to his wishes without any intention of carrying them out. It has been suggested that the *Charter Fragment* represents the bawd's part in a comedy, but there is too little of it for any certainty, and even the inclusion of a Cornish place-name is not particularly helpful. There *is* evidence for the performance of genuinely secular plays (most notably of Robin Hood) in Cornwall, but texts have not survived and what language they were performed in is unclear.

Between the *Charter Fragment* and Brome, however, most surviving literature in middle and early modern Cornish is dramatic. The exception is the late fourteenth-century poem *Pascon agan Arluth* (Passion of Our Lord), which served as a part-source for the earliest of the dramatic works, the trilogy known as the *Ordinalia*. Composed probably in the last quarter of the fourteenth century, the three plays are entitled in the fifteenth-century manuscript Bodley 791 *Ordinale de Origine Mundi*, *Passio Domini Nostri Jhesu Christi* and *Ordinale de Resurrexione Domini*. Related in content, though last chronologically, is the *Creacion of the World*, the first and sole surviving play of a sequence. It was copied by William Jordan in 1611, but composed probably around the middle of the previous century. The manuscript title is English (none of the plays has a Cornish title), but the Cornish equivalent *Gwreans an Bys*, taken by modern editors from the beginning of the work, is entirely justified. It covers the period from the Creation to Noah, and contains some passages from the earlier *Origo Mundi*, but the two plays are very different. Between the biblical plays comes a two-day *Ordinale de Vita Beati Mereadoci Episcopi et Confessoris*, known as *Beunans Meriasek*, the 'Life of Meriasek.' Meriasek (the Cornish version of Mereadoc) was a Breton saint with a cult in Camborne, and the broad themes of salvation, conversion and right belief in his dramatised *vita* are developed by the inclusion of stories involving the Virgin and St Sylvester. A colophon notes that it was finished in 1504 by Dominus Rad[ulphus] Ton. The Cornish plays each exist in a single manuscript, although later copies of the biblical dramas were made.

The language of these plays is not English, nor are they adaptations of English plays. In content, structure and staging there are considerable differences between the Cornish works and the English religious plays with which they most readily invite comparison, and it is sometimes more relevant to look at the French or Breton (though not in fact the Welsh) biblical drama.[2] The plays span two stages in the development of Cornish. The language of the *Ordinalia* is middle Cornish, while the other two exhibit the sound-changes that distinguish early modern Cornish, less so in *Beunans Meriasek* than in *Gwreans an Bys*, in which there is also a larger admixture of English.[3] Cornish ceased to be spoken in the eighteenth century, and its revival is relatively recent, so that the sound of the texts is not always clear. Unassimilated English words, or even whole phrases or couplets, are found already in the *Ordinalia*, but in spite of attempts to establish a dramatic pattern (275; 277, pp. 16ff.) none seems to exist (268, pp. 4–9). The first English phrase in the *Ordinalia* is indeed spoken by the Devil, but the most striking is a couplet sung in English in the *Resurrexio* by the three Maries. Lines of French and of Latin also appear. The linguistic skill of all three dramatists lies in the use of register and of formal variation, ranging from elevated, even quasi-liturgical verse to downright coarseness. Extended or complex imagery is rare in all of the plays, but there is great variety in tone and texture. Speeches by biblical figures (or the Marian prayers in *Meriasek*) contrast strongly with the scatological passages spoken by devils, jailers and torturers.

The dramas are composed in strophes which vary in form and rhyme scheme. The great majority of lines have seven syllables, with eight-syllable lines (though elision may have reduced them in speech) coming next. Four-syllable lines (treated distinctively in the manuscripts) also occur, and are alternated with longer lines for effect. T. D. Crawford (269) identifies nearly eighty strophic forms in the *Ordinalia* and there are further variations in the later plays, with some unrhymed lines in *Gwreans an Bys*. The maximum appears to be twelve lines, with six- and eight-line strophes very common. Rhyme patterns vary, too, though two or three

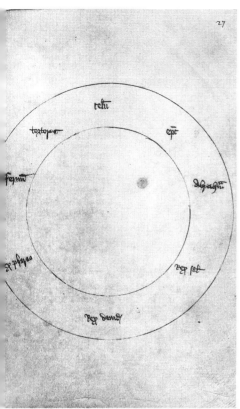

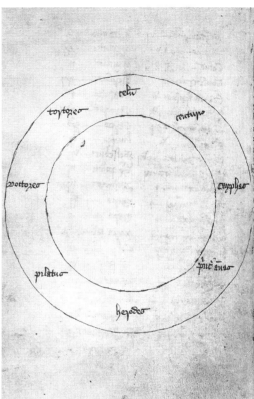

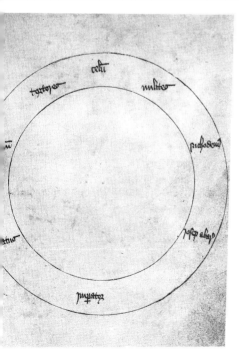

18–20 Staging plans for the three days of the Cornish *Ordinalia*: *Origo Mundi, Passio Christi, Resurrexio Domini* (Oxford, Bodleian Library MS Bodley 791, ff. 27r, 56v, 83r). The inscriptions indicate the positions of scaffolds around the periphery of the *platea*, by means of the name of the principal occupant: Heaven stands in the east, Hell in the north. Clockwise from the east (top): (18) *Origo*: Celum (Heaven), Episcopus (Bishop), Abraham, Rex Salamon, Rex David, Rex Pharaoh, Infernum (Hell), Tortores (Torturers); (19) *Passio*: Celum, Centurio, Cayphas, Princeps Annas, Herodes, Pilatus, Doctores, Tortores; (20) *Resurrexio*: Celum, Milites (Soldiers), Nichodemus, Josep abares (Joseph of Arimathea), Imperator (Emperor), Pilatus, Infernum, Tortores.

21   Noah's Ark, from the *Origo Mundi* of the Cornish *Ordinalia*, staged at Perran Round, Cornwall, 1969, by the Drama Department of Bristol University, under the direction of Neville Denny.

rhymes per strophe in forms like abababab, aaabcccb and so on are typical (269, 270).

The Cornish plays seem to have been performed not from pageant wagons, but in open-air amphitheatres known as rounds (in Cornish, *plen an gwary*). Two such rounds, between 120 and 140 feet in diameter, survive, one at St Just-in-Penwith and the other, Perran (St Piran's) Round, near Perranporth; place-names such as Plain-an-Gwarry in Redruth and possibly archaeological evidence indicate others. *Beunans Meriasek* is strongly associated with Camborne and was probably performed there, although it no longer has a round. It is unclear whether the *plenys an gwary* were custom-made or adapted from earlier earthworks (7, pp. 8–10; 268, pp. 26–30).[4] A much-reproduced engraving of Perran Round in William Borlase's *Natural History of Cornwall* of 1758 shows not only raised earth banks for spectators, entrances and a central *platea*, but also a trench and pit, used presumably to enable characters to enter under cover, as in the birth of Eve, for example. Critics of the rounds note that St Just has no such trench, but the suggested usage remains perfectly plausible.

Support for this method of production comes in the manuscripts. All three plays in the *Ordinalia* and both days of *Beunans Meriasek* include illustrations of staging in the form of a simple circle with names around the periphery (see illustrations 18–20). There appear to have been fixed plat-forms or scaffolding (the stage directions speak of *sedes*, *pulpiti*, *tenti* or even *domus*) at various points around the circle, each associated with a specific character, and stage directions call for characters to come down, and to enter the *platea*. The *Ordinalia* plays have eight names; *Beunans Meriasek* has more, but the characters do not all appear at the same time, and there were clearly shared platforms. *Gwreans an Bys* has no plan, but the text suggests only one platform, for heaven. In the *platea* itself few scenic features are indicated, apart from a chapel in the centre for the first day of *Beunans Meriasek*. The action will have taken place at different points, providing a varying focus of attention for an audience with a very good all-round view. It is not known at which time of the year the plays were performed, though Corpus Christi is possible, as is Meriasek/ Mereadoc's feast day in June. All of the plays have been revived in modern times and an attempt has even been made within the language movement to continue the tradition in writing (274, p. 188).

All manuscripts have detailed stage directions. Those of the *Ordinalia* are in Latin, those in *Gwreans an Bys* in English, the source apparently having been a stage-manager's copy indicating what props are to be ready at any point. *Beunans Meriasek* is particularly interesting in having primary stage directions in Latin, with later secondary comments sometimes in Latin, more often in English. Amongst the additions are references in English to costume, props and effects, which augment primary directions, as when the instruction *Hic pompabunt tortores* is followed by the note *w*[ith] *swerdys* (*BM*, s.d. at line 1172). The directions seem to refer to a specific per-formance:

> And John ergudyn aredy a horse bakke that was the Justis with constantyn
> ffor to play the marchont   (*BM*, s.d. at line 3460)

The indication of doubling-up is interesting in itself, although the cast is likely still to have been large, perhaps on the lines of the present Ober-ammergau play.

The length and scope of the plays, which clearly included music, and the general invitation at the end of *Beunans Meriasek* to dance and drink, indi-cate that they must have been social occasions of some importance. Con-sideration of the actual performances has been coloured, however, by an early description by Richard Carew in his 1602 *Survey of Cornwall* of a chaotic version of an unidentified Cornish drama (though he talks in general of the *guary-miracle*, 'miracle play'). He hangs onto this supposed pro-duction an early version of the stage joke in which an incompetent actor repeats literally everything the prompter says to him. Although cited in most secondary studies, Carew's comments must be treated with caution and their specific relevance is questionable (*301; 268*, pp. 12f.).

THE *ORDINALIA*

The plays of the *Ordinalia*, each around three thousand lines (2846, 3242, 2646), contain a number of individual stories, but are given a structural unity by the running theme of the defeat of the Devil and the Redemption promised at the Fall, although the typology is rarely explicit. The first play takes us from the Creation to Solomon, the next presents the Passion, and the last the Resurrection and Ascension, juxtaposed with the death of Pilate. Bodley 791 has separate headings for different sections of individual plays, but the manuscript is not the original, and these headings do not imply separate plays within the trilogy. Several Cornish place-names occur (in spite of the biblical setting), usually in the context of land given as rewards, and most of these names, which help in dating the work, are associated with Penryn (*275; 268*, pp. 12–49; *293*). The plays may be linked more specifically with Glasney College, the community of secular canons at St Thomas in Penryn, now destroyed. There are connections between Glasney and Camborne, the home of *Beunans Meriasek*, and passages from the *Ordinalia* appear in *Gwreans an Bys*. Since the writer of the *Passio Christi* also knew the Passion poem, there is a considerable concentration of the surviving Cornish literature in this western district. Glasney also had links with St Just-in-Penwith, the site of one of the surviving rounds, but it is not clear where in the Penryn area the plays were performed.

The basic source is the Bible, selected, and with embellishments that are exegetical (as with the links between the temptation in the desert and Adam's Fall), liturgical (the introit for a Mass of the Virgin is used in *RD*, line 455, for example), or devotional (as in the notion, repeated in the *Passio* and the *Resurrexio*, that the crown of thorns pierced Christ's brain). Specific incidents are emphasised, as with the story of David and Bathsheba in the first play and the emphasis on Thomas and the Magdalene in the last. Other additions are from apocryphal and legend sources, the most important being the widespread medieval story of the Holy Rood, which links the first two plays, and which is found in none of the English cycles. It traces the history of the cross from its beginnings as three seeds from the Tree of Life placed in the mouth of the dead Adam after a journey to Paradise by Seth in search of the Oil of Mercy. A slightly different version of Seth's quest is found in the older *Vita Adae et Evae*, but the *Ordinalia* has no traces of that apocryphon, although it is found in Breton and other continental dramas, and perhaps also in *Gwreans an Bys*. There is a further version of Seth's quest (probably the earliest of the Christianised forms) in the so-called *Gospel of Nicodemus*, other motifs from which appear in the *Ordinalia*. The Adamic *Vita*, the Holy Rood and the Nicodemus-Gospel, all flexible texts, are juxtaposed or indeed combined throughout the Middle Ages. A thirteenth-century French *Pénitence d'Adam*, for example, has elements of all three, and a Welsh text of the Holy Rood story is variously headed *Ystorya Adaf* (The Story of Adam) or *Euangel Nicodemus*.[5] Legend motifs from the *Gospel of Nicodemus* in the second and third plays include the dream of Pilate's wife, the Harrowing of Hell, the release of Joseph of Arimathea from prison and the idea of Enoch and Elijah in conflict with the Antichrist. The Harrowing is found in all the English cycles, but the dream and, particularly, the escape of Joseph are less common. Independent additional legends include that of the smith who refused to make the nails for the crucifixion, the healing of blind Longinus and the fate of Judas's soul. Not present in the English cycles at all is the death of Pilate, again found as a separate and flexible *Mors Pilati* and sometimes attached to the *Gospel of Nicodemus*.

Precise sources for the *Ordinalia* are difficult to establish, however, and the fact that many of these elements appear in such standard medieval source-books as the *Golden Legend* or the *Historia Scholastica*, or in English works such as the *Cursor Mundi*, merely confirms that a given tale was widely known. Positive identification requires closer correspondence of specific details than is usually found. Indeed, the only demonstrable vernacular influence is that of the Passion-poem, *Pascon agan Arluth*. Although Fowler (275, pp. 104–11) saw the borrowing in the opposite direction, the relevant strophes in the play are padded by repetitions and gratuitous assertions, and, more significantly, one passage of objective exegetical explanation from the poem is placed by the dramatist awkwardly into the mouth of Christ (291, pp. 823–5). Although actual verbal correspondences are not numerous, the *Passio Christi* contains a good number of exegetical and additional apocryphal motifs found in the poem, including several that are not common elsewhere, so that if the influence is not direct, then a shared source is likely.

The *Origo Mundi* opens with the Creation and Fall, Cain and Abel, Seth's quest, Noah, and Abraham and Isaac. The narrative of the Cross is continued when Moses finds and plants the miracle-working three rods or saplings that will combine to form the Rood and they are rediscovered by David, who determines to place them in a temple. After his love-affair with Bathsheba the remorseful David composes the Psalms, and the temple is built by Solomon, although the wood of the Rood fits nowhere. The play ends with Maximilla, whose clothing catches fire 'from the wood' (*OM*, line and the lame links with the similar miracles of Moses using the three rods in the *Origo Mundi*, and the events leading up to the Crucifixion are now juxtaposed with scenes between Annas, Caiapahas and Judas. The high priests swear by *mahomm* in striking the bargain, and Christ is taken at Gethsemane.

The trial of Christ before the high priests and Herod is juxtaposed with Peter's threefold denial, which is developed beyond Matthew 26.75 as Christ turns his eyes in a dramatic gesture upon Peter, who expresses his regret in a speech of five strophes. The brutality is realistic, as in the English and French dramas, the torturers delighting in the punishment.[6] Judas hangs himself in despair, and the motif found in the Passion-poem that his soul cannot leave through the mouth that had kissed Christ is introduced here by the Devil. The silver is used to buy the Potter's Field explicitly as a burial ground for Christians, rather than for strangers (as Matthew 27.7), so that their smell may not pollute the Jews (*PD*, lines 1545–8).

Christ before Herod brings in a debate between the *doctores* over whether or not Christ is a sorcerer. Jesus, of course, is silent, but here and before Pilate the image is invoked of the mermaid, which combines human and fish as Christ is God and man. The source is unclear, although mermaids do figure in Cornish church iconography, most notably at Zennor (278, pp. 260f.; 283, pp. 458f.). The dream of Pilate's wife, however, who is referred to only briefly in the Bible (Matthew 26.19), is not unique to Cornish, but is in the York and N-Town plays, and her role in all three plays (268, pp. 68–92) is fuller even than in the *Gospel of Nicodemus*. The diabolical council, realising that Christ is the son of God, and that the prophecy of the Harrowing is likely to be fulfilled, sends a dream to Pilate's wife in an attempt to have Christ released. The realisation by the devils of the divinity of Christ grows in strength as events unfold.

Much emphasis is laid upon the instruments of the Passion. Thus the crown of thorns pierces Christ's brain (a motif found also in *Pascon agan Arluth* and *Beunans Meriasek*), and the nails are emphasised by the legend of the smith, an episode again found in the Cornish Passion-poem, in English verse and the French drama. In this version the smith, who lives in *marghes yow*, Market Jew (Cornish *yow*, 'Thursday'), claims that his hands are too sore to make the nails, and they appear diseased when he is ordered to show them. However, his wife agrees to make the nails, aided by a torturer, who works the bellows. The unique use of a Cornish location that is not a land grant or a formula may, incidentally, be no more than a handy rhyme for *kentrow* (nails), although a vernacular source for this episode is possible (293; 269, pp. 150–2). The crucifixion scene itself includes, as does *Pascon agan Arluth*, the stretching of Christ, the cords and sponge, and later on the pincers used by Joseph of Arimathea to remove the nails. The stage directions call for the cosmic effects of the crucifixion too, (*hic sol obscuratur, hic fit terre motus*), again providing production problems.

The typological link between Adam and Christ is completed with the finding of the Holy Rood, now being used as a bridge across the Cedron, and it is carried, willingly, by Simon the Leper. The Virgin, who meets her son again on the way to Calvary, has a strikingly lyrical speech at the foot of the cross which mirrors her earlier encounter metrically and in tone (*Passio Christi*, lines 2591–2614 and 2931–48),[7] and the centurion also makes clear his feelings about Christ (lines 2965–72), asserting then that Christ is the son of God (lines 3079–98). The story of the Vernicle is missing (although it is adumbrated in the Passion-poem) but it may originally have been present; just after Mary's first meeting with her son, Bodley 791 has the blind stage direction *hic venit vernona et dicit* (*Passio Christi*, s.d. at line 2614). Veronica and the *sudarium* play a role in the *Resurrexio*.

Two non-biblical elements are added; first, the familiar curing of the blind soldier Longinus (here *Longeus*), whose spear, thrust into the side of Christ, releases the blood that restores his sight. The story is clearly eucharistic and Longinus expresses his newly-found faith and regret at what he has done in a lyrical passage which is a dramatic high point, based on the four-syllable unit:

> arluth thy'm gaf . del y'th pysaf
> war pen dewlyn
> an pyth a wren . my ny wothyen
> rag ny wylyn . . .   (*PC*, lines 3019–22)

> Lord forgive me I beseech thee
> on bended knee
> I did this thing all unknowing
> I could not see . . .

The body is taken to the tomb by Joseph of Arimathea, and the Virgin receives the dead Christ in a dramatised *pietà* which gives her a third lyrical *planctus*, with an anaphoric *ellas* (alas) and a recapitulation of the physical events of the Passion. Prior to the deposition, a brief but noteworthy scene is interpolated in hell, where the devils, whose confidence was never strong, now summon in desperation *kynyuer dyaul vs yn beys* (every devil in the world) (*PC*, line 3062) to defend hell against the Harrowing.

The first and the last plays of the *Ordinalia* close with a summons from a secular ruler to the minstrels. At the end of the *Passio Christi* Nicodemus calls simply for the audience to reflect on the events they have just someone who possesses concrete evidence, but does *not* believe. The emperor Tiberius is cured of leprosy when he is shown the image of Christ by Veronica, and he tries Pilate, who saves himself for a time precisely by wearing the seamless robe of Christ, but is eventually stripped of it and condemned, as happened to Christ. Like Judas, he commits suicide, and when the earth and the Tiber refuse to accept the body, devils take him to hell. Pilate's fate serves as a bridge between the Resurrection and the Ascension; his inglorious but supernatural death (with the expulsion of his body from the grave and its removal to hell by the devils) is a counter to the miraculous events of Christ's rising from the grave and the equally supernatural culmination, the Ascension into heaven with the angels.

The conclusion of the Pilate-section makes clear the skill of the integration. Devils carry off his soul *and* his body to the accompaniment of a grotesque and obscene song; Christ is greeted by the angels in an extended hymnic section. Just as the devils were baffled by the Harrowing, the angels want to know who comes to them in red rather than angelic white robes (the allusions are to Isaiah 63.1–3 and the liturgy for Holy Week), and Christ recounts the sufferings of the Passion after the angels have sung the *Gloria*. Man is redeemed, and *Deus Pater* welcomes Christ into heaven. The play concludes with a brief speech by Tiberius, the emperor physically and spiritually healed in the play, who summarises what has happened and pronounces a benediction: the plays are done and the minstrels are invited to strike up the music once more.

Man, with whose Creation and Fall we began, has been redeemed in a series of events for which the world was prepared both typologically (in the story of Isaac, for example) and in reality (in the continued physical presence of the Holy Rood). Those who witnessed (as the audience has just witnessed) the miraculous events are saved, and the literal opening of Longinus' eyes underscores this; those who (again like the audience) witness only an image, like Tiberius, or are told of the events, like Thomas, can also be saved. Only continued and obdurate rejection or complete despair leads to damnation, and that damnation is as real as Paradise.

GWREANS AN BYS

Just after the English title *Creacion of the World*, Jordan's manuscript adds 'the first daie of playe', and at its conclusion Noah's words to the audience imply that only one more day remained:

> Dewh a vorowe a dermyn:
> Why a weall matters pur vras,
> Ha redempcion granntys
> Der vercy a Thew an Tase,
>   Tha sawya neb es kellys.   (CW, lines 2542–6)

> Come tomorrow, in good time,
> to see great matters take place,
> redemption granted to men
> all through God the Father's grace,
>   to save the lost souls again.

Gwreans an Bys has always been overshadowed by the *Ordinalia*, partly for language reasons (the anglicisms in the passage just cited are clear), and partly because it has been misinterpreted (277, p. 21) as an adaptation of the earlier work. It does contain modernised passages from the first half of the *Origo Mundi*, but actual quotations (in three sections of the play) constitute only around two hundred of its 2,945 lines. Neuss (98, pp. 241–5) notes that most of the borrowings are speeches by God or cues for them, and others might simply be formulaic. She argues that the later dramatist was reconstructing from memory a part that he had played, and this is possible, although there might also have been a written source: single-role cue parts do exist, and the heading *Deus Pater* is once found, rather than the English equivalent used elsewhere. Biblical material has an inevitable uniformity, but some motifs shared by the plays are rare within dramatic adaptations of Genesis; nevertheless, although the plays may reflect a local tradition in the interpretation of Genesis, they remain very different.

The colophon states that *Gwreans an Bys* was 'wryten / by William Jordan the 12th of August / 1611'. In spite of a long-held notion that William Jordan of Helston was the author, Neuss has shown that he was transcribing a producer's or pageant master's working text or prompt-copy, and that the composition predates 1611. It has been assigned linguistically to the mid-sixteenth century, and comparison with the development of the late medieval Paradise play bears this out. The somewhat jerky series of biblical incidents in the *Ordinalia* is replaced by a smoother progression with few abrupt story changes. Additional pointers to the final stages of the medieval Paradise drama include the personification of Death, the serpent with a woman's face, and a strongly homiletic tone. The retention of the Holy Rood legend (which disappears from the continental Paradise play soon after the Reformation) seems, especially with the addition of a vision of the Virgin, to indicate a Catholic work, as does the consigning of Adam to Limbo. It is tempting to date it to the reign of Mary I (when John Tregear sources. Enoch, too, is absent from the *Origo Mundi*, and the story of Noah is fuller in the later work.

Calmana is a traditional name, but the mark of Cain is very unusual. The stage direction calls for it to be the letter *omega*, and Neuss (98, pp. 225f.) links this with the horns that often constitute the mark: Cain (echoed by Calmana and Lamech) refers to its position *in corne ow thale* (on the horn of my forehead) (*CW*, line 1643). A more likely source, however, is a tradition based upon Ezekiel 9, in which a letter is placed upon the foreheads of those who are to be spared, something which is the case, after all, with Cain.

Lamech does not appear in the *Origo Mundi*. The Bible has two Lamechs (Genesis 4 and 5), descended from Cain and Seth respectively, and the Cainite Lamech is seventh in line from Adam, (not from Cain, as in *CW*, line 1435). His wickedness is contrasted in commentaries and in texts like the *Legenda Aurea* with the goodness of Enoch, seventh in the Sethite line. In *Gwreans an Bys* he glories in his own wickedness, claiming to be worse than Cain and an oppressor of the weak. It is an exegetical commonplace to see him as the first bigamist, but this Lamech not only boasts of having two wives (the case, after all, with more respectable patriarchs), but of his womanising inability to keep away from pretty girls. This motif is not found elsewhere.

The story of the death of Cain is widespread. Old and nearly blind, Lamech wishes to go hunting, and that the dramatist is following a source such as the *Golden Legend* or Peter Comestor's *Historia Scholastica* is clear from details such as the assertion that he is hunting for skins rather than flesh. Mistaking Cain for an animal and misled by an unnamed servant, Lamech kills his ancestor. The story depends ultimately upon Lamech's sword-song in Genesis 4 in which he claims (unless the text is a Hebrew parallelism) to have killed a man and a boy. The Cornish Lamech blames the boy who was leading him and kills him in a rage. Even if the triumph of the sword-song itself is missing, Lamech appears not to repent, and Cain and the boy are taken to hell. Dramatisations of this tale (which is present in the stained glass at St Neot in Cornwall) are found in the N-Town plays and far more widely in the continental drama of the later Middle Ages (292).

Since the play ends with Noah, we do not know whether the story of the Holy Rood was developed. As in the *Ordinalia*, Seth is sent for the Oil of Mercy, but here sees two trees in Eden, the dry and the living, in a version rather different from that of the earlier play. He is again told that the child represents the Oil of Mercy, receives the three apple pips and returns to Adam. There are two major differences: the first is his vision not just of the child, but also of the Virgin at the top of the tree, recalling the Jesse tree iconography more than the Holy Rood legends; the second is Seth's decision to record the story of Adam and Eve and place them in pillars of brick and marble. This motif (recorded in Josephus) is found at the end of the apocryphal *Vita Adae* rather than in the Holy Rood legends, but the quest of Seth does link the two cycles, and other details in both plays clearly point to a Holy Rood text.

The death of Adam is unusual partly in that he is taken not to hell but to *Lymbo*, but more so because this is explained by Lucifer in what can only be thought of as an homiletic passage. The devils fail to understand why Adam cannot be tormented, and Lucifer explains that Adam, though a great sinner, repented, whereas Cain rejoiced in his sin. Lucifer is, of course, unhappy about Adam's fate:

> Hag Adam (vengens thotha!) –
> Lymbo ew ornys ractha,
> Ea, ragtha ef hay gowetha.
>   Ny dastyans an payne bras.   (CW, lines 2061–4)

> Adam (curses out of mind!)
> to limbo shall be consigned
> with all others of his kind
>   They shall not taste the great pains.

but an angel takes Adam away to await the Redemption.

Just as Lamech presented himself as the seventh Cainite, Enoch declares that he is the seventh Sethite. As in the familiar interpretation of Genesis 5.24, Enoch is taken by God to Paradise, but the passage serves again as a homily on the Fall when Enoch urges the audience to keep God's commandments if Paradise is to be regained. This has its closest resonance in the Protestant plays,[11] and it certainly belongs to the later stages of the Genesis drama. The idea of the expulsion from and the hope of a return to Paradise provides a structure, however, for *Gwreans an Bys*. Cain and Lamech as negative examples forfeit the hope by failing to repent, but Seth and Enoch are allowed to *see* Paradise, thus giving immediacy to their urging that men should keep God's commandments.

Noah's wife, compliant with her husband's wishes in the *Origo Mundi*, here dallies to gather up useful belongings before entering the ark. She is not quite the Noah's wife of the York play, although she is not unlike her Chester counterpart. More important, however, is the mocking of Noah by two of the Cainites, Lamech's sons Tubalcain and Jabal, chosen doubtless because Noah is the son of the Sethite Lamech. Noah warns them of the necessity of repentance, only to be asked:

Pew athe wrug ge progowther
Tha thesky omma theny?   (CW, lines 2347f.)

Who made you into a preacher
or sent you to teach us here?

Although Noah is mocked in the *Mistére du Viel Testament*, the use of
Enoch and of Noah to express points in this manner is closer to late works
like the *Adam und Heva*, of the Swiss Protestant Jacob Ruf[f] in 1550, and if
the sacrifice performed by Noah might have invited criticism by solifidian
Reformers, God stresses that the works are done *a leyn golan* (from a loyal
heart) (CW, line 2497). Hymns were sung at this point, perhaps by the spectators too: the stage direction calls for 'Some good church songys to be
songe at the alter' (CW, s.d. at line 2492). Beyond the brief appearance of
the Virgin in the Holy Rood episode and the reference to Limbo (rejected in
the Henrician Ten Articles in 1536) there is little here that the Reformation
could fault. *Gwreans an Bys* is well constructed and far more sophisticated
than the *Origo Mundi*. But there is a religious, linguistic and literary irony
in its partial preservation in the year of the Authorised Version and of *The
Tempest*.

BEUNANS MERIASEK

The play of St Meriasek is unique in British medieval drama. A non-biblical
saint's play of 4,568 lines, performed over two days, it presents the twin
soteriological themes of conversion and healing in a series of miracles
involving Saints Meriasek and Sylvester and the Virgin Mary. It is concerned, too, with intercession: where the biblical plays have full parts for
God and Christ, in *Beunans Meriasek* Christ's few interventions are made
always through the agency of an angel or saint. At first glance, the work
seems rambling. Attempt to identify historical characters have led to the
view that the action covers several centuries (281, p. 30), but this approach
is invalid: the play itself is consistent, and even apparently recognisable
figures are deceptive. Constantine is not the fourth-century emperor, but the
central figure of the eighth-century apocryphal *Donation of Constantine*.
The breadth of the play lies rather in distance, moving between Brittany,
Cornwall and Rome in the remote past of the age of conversion.

The work falls into sections, and although they have been performed
recently as separate plays, the linguistic and thematic coherence of the
whole, to which critics have now begun to draw attention (279; 270, p. 486),
must be stressed. The play opens with the childhood of Meriasek in Brittany, with a comic school scene designed to gain the attention, followed by

the hagiographical motif of his taking of the cloth rather than marriage to the king's daughter. Many of Meriasek's subsequent deeds, too, are commonplaces. In imitation of Christ he heals the blind and the lame and he calms storms when he sails to Cornwall. Meriasek establishes an oratory at St Mary's in Camborne, finds a holy well and heals the sick, but he comes into conflict with a pagan tyrant king, the first of many in a play in which paganism is a composite of non-Christian elements, with worship at different points of Mahound, Apollo (or Apollyon), Jove, Sol and various demons, including Belsebuc and Monfras (Cornish, 'good dung'). This particular tyrant, King Teudar, might possibly be an attack on Henry VII Tudor (which would date the work after 1485), but he appears in other Cornish saints' lives. Of greater interest is his debate with Meriasek, in which he rejects the idea of Virgin birth:

> Sevys oys a woys worthy
>   meryasek beth avysyys
> rag dovt cafus velyny
>   na govs tra na fue guelys
>   me a leuer
> erbyn reson yv a beys
> heb hays gorryth creys
> bones flegh vyth concevijs
>   in breys benen heb awer   (*BM*, lines 839–47)

> You were born of noble race,
> Meriasek, now be advised –
> do not bring yourself disgrace,
> telling impossible lies.
> I say to you:
> reason must be believed
> without seed no child's conceived
> in a woman's womb – it's true!

Meriasek counters with the image of the sun passing through glass,[12] but Teudar is unconvinced. Having tried to tempt Meriasek with riches (in analogy with the temptation of Christ, perhaps), he resorts to force, and Meriasek has first to hide in a rock which is then named *carrek veryasek* (Meriasek's rock), doubtless a genuine feature providing local 'evidence' for the truth of the tale. The saint flees to Brittany, where he tames a wolf, another hagiographic commonplace which, though apparently a blind motif, points on to later parts of the play.

A second strand is signalled in the manuscript as the 'Life of St Sylvester', but the central figure is first of all Constantine, and the theme again the conflict of Christianity and paganism, underscored symbolically with physical healing. The story is found in the *Donation of Constantine*, in the thirteenth century in the *Legenda Aurea*, and later in the French *Miracles de Nostre Dame*. Constantine is punished with leprosy for his persecution of Christians, and his cure (rather than a vision at the Milvian bridge) brings about his and Rome's conversion. After some failed attempts at healing, the blood of three thousand children is prescribed. Moved by the appeal of the mothers (which anticipates yet another strand in the play) and horrified by his bloodthirsty soldiers, Constantine reprieves the children, and because he has shown mercy, Christ sends Peter and Paul to tell him to send for Sylvester, who is in hiding from the persecutions on Mount Soracte (the form *Seraptim* in the text is not unusual in medieval versions). Sylvester baptises and heals the emperor, who decrees that the empire shall become Christian. The final part of the *Donation* story is not included, and the emphasis remains on Constantine's compassion.

The final part of the first day returns to Meriasek, now a hermit preaching holy poverty on a mountain in Brittany. Just as Constantine sent for Sylvester on Mount Soracte, Meriasek's aid is sought by the secular authorities, and he causes by prayer a forest fire (real or imaginary) that frightens into conversion a group of bandits. A grateful Earl of Rohan grants three festivals in the parish of Noyale-Pontivy (the Cornish text in fact misreads this reference to the saint's cult-centre in Brittany), and somewhat abruptly the action returns to Cornwall, so that the Duke of Cornwall can defeat Teudar, thus ending the day on a satisfactory note and with a good deal of action. The blessing of Christ and Mary is invoked, and we are told that this has only been a part of Meriasek's life-story (*BM*, lines 2500f.).

The second day opens with a single-strophe recapitulation by Constantine, after which Meriasek heals the blind Earl Globus and a demoniac. On the death of the Bishop of Vannes it is decided that Meriasek should succeed, and patents are sought from Pope Sylvester in Rome. In spite of the efforts of the Earl of Vannes and the Bishop of Cornouailles (*Kernou* is used both for Cornwall and the Breton district), Meriasek resists, preaching vigorously and doubtless with contemporary relevance against the desire for riches:

> Vn conduconn sur owhy
> kepar ha lues defry
>   hythyv an dus sans eglos
> pan lafuryens rag benefys
> ware y feth govynnys
>   py lues puns a yl bos
>   anethy grueys
> ny remembrons y an charych
> a reys dethe ry har lych
>   therag crist pan deer then vrueys. (*BM*, lines 2824–33)

> You are like the rest, I see.
> There are many, certainly,
> – today's men of Holy Church –
> working for a parish post,
> but what they want to know most
> is how many pounds it's worth,
> what it will bring,
> never thinking while they live
> of the account they must give
> to Christ, at the Reckoning.

Meriasek eventually capitulates, and continues to pray to the Virgin and to heal the sick. A new plot follows which has been dismissed quite wrongly as gratuitous padding. Sometimes called 'the woman and her son', the Latin heading *de filio mulieris* gives due prominence to the boy. The framework is again that of Christian king against pagan tyrant, and while the latter is unnamed, the former is King Massen, originally perhaps the Roman leader Magnus Maximus, who appears in the *Mabinogion* as Macsen Wledig (282, p. 61). A boy who has been sent to him with the repeated blessing of the Virgin by his mother is captured by the tyrant and is to be hanged because he refuses to renounce Christ. When the mother's pleas for Mary's help go unanswered, she takes hostage the image of the infant Jesus from a statue in the church. Mary herself intercedes with Christ, who gives her the power to release the boy, the statue is restored and the tyrant defeated. The story is found in various forms in Caesarius of Heisterbach, in the *Legenda Aurea*, Mirk's *Festial* and elsewhere, although dramatisations are very rare (290). Here it reinforces the idea of intercession, and links the mother not only with the Virgin but also with the mothers who appeal to Constantine. Meriasek prays frequently to the Virgin in the play as a whole (*BM*, lines 154–63, 704–9, 2970–5, 3134–41, 3865–8), and he is echoed by the woman's simply expressed prayers, which are, like his, marked by anaphora on the name of the Virgin. The woman also reiterates the mother–son relationship:

> Maria mam ha guerhes
>   me a vyn the luebesy
> maria ov map gueres
>   ha restoria thymo vy
> maria me reth cervyes
>   thum gallus bythqueth defry
> maria wyn rag ov les
>   y colmennov grua terry
> maria mar a mynnes
>   delyfrys bya surly   (BM, lines 3590–99)

Legend, too, the Cornish play lays greater stress on Constantine's mercy than on the conversion of the empire, and the integration with the Meriasek and hostage stories is well done, at whatever stage it was accomplished.

The source of the hostage tale is even less clear, and the reference in the manuscript to a collection of miracles of the Virgin is no help, since it appears in many such collections. The *Legenda Aurea* has been claimed as the source, but it differs from the Cornish in two important respects. In the *Legenda* and most other versions the son is a passive figure; here, threatened because of his firm beliefs, he is a potential martyr. Secondly, the fact that Mary does not work the miracle herself, but intercedes with Christ for help, is significant in a tale that might easily look like celestial blackmail. The dramatist, aware of the potential problems, makes it clear that only Christ can, at the last, effect the miracle. Although the version in the *Legenda Aurea* is followed by a tale of a thief rescued by the Virgin from hanging (the fate in store for the son), the change from a simple Marian miracle to an illustration of intercession through the Virgin is striking. Breviary readings for 7 June (St Mereadoc), 31 December (St Sylvester) and for the Nativity of the Virgin on 8 September are possible sources for the individual elements (290).

There is a careful thematic coherence between the three plots. Sylvester heals the emperor (who invests him with his papal authority) and rids his land of the dragon; Meriasek heals rich and poor alike, and rids the land of robbers; Sylvester and the secular authorities invest Meriasek with authority. No miracle converts Teudar, but he, like the later tyrant, is defeated, and the scenes in the hostage story in which demons appear make clear to the audience what will happen to unbelievers after death. Christ intervenes in all three plots, to provide for the salvation of a whole empire or to save a single believer, and a poor leper can be healed as well as an emperor: the range of characters is impressive. Christ, the Virgin and the angels, Pope Sylvester and Bishop Meriasek are part of a hierarchy extending down to simple believers like the woman and her son, the lepers and demoniacs. These are set against the hierarchy of unbelievers, from tyrants, soldiers, jailers and torturers, down to actual demons. Between these groups come the secular rulers – Constantine, the Breton dukes, King Massen and the Duke of Cornwall – and salvation in the physical and spiritual sense is available to all. If Meriasek himself, the central figure, is a character of 'shadowless innocence' (279, p. 2), he is no cardboard cut-out, but is given depth by the comedy in his childhood, by the adventure of his flight from Teudar, and by his resolute resistance to preferment, an ascetic forced to take high office against his will, but whose goodness makes him a fitting patron in his adopted country. The Marianism of *Beunans Meriasek* makes its disappearance after the Reformation less than surprising, but dramatic-ally it represents a considerable achievement, albeit in a doomed genre.

A NOTE ON TEXTS AND TRANSLATIONS

Recommending texts of the early Cornish drama for an English-speaking audience is difficult. Of the many translations, not all are accessible, and there is little uniformity. For the *Ordinalia*, Edwin Norris's nineteenth-century edition and literal translation (*97*) remains the only readily available full text, though there is also a modern prose rendering of the trilogy (*278*). R. Morton Nance and A. S. D. Smith edited the plays in Unified Cornish (*296*), a standardised language devised for revival purposes, and Nance translated all three. *Beunans Meriasek* is available in Whitley Stokes's nine-teenth-century text and translation (*100*), and also in a modern prose version (*279*). There is a modern scholarly edition and translation of *Gwreans an Bys* (*98*). Older and less easily accessible editions and trans-lations are listed in Evelyn S. Newlyn's bibliography of the Cornish drama (*7*). Recent interpretations of the texts are uniform enough for comparative work, though few convey any idea of the verse.

For the quotations in Cornish given above, and the accepted abbre-viations of the titles, see the list of editions cited, pp. xviii–xix. The *ad hoc* imitative verse translations are my own.

NOTES

1 By Richard Axton (*22*, p. 61). Texts differing slightly from that first given by Stokes (*99*) will be found in Henry Jenner, 'The Fourteenth-Century Charter Endorsement', *Journal of the Royal Institution of Cornwall* 20 (1915–21), 41–8; Enrico Campanile, 'Un Frammento Scenico Medio-Cornico', *Studi e Saggi Linguistici* 3 (1963), 60–80; and Lauran Toorians (ed.), *The Middle Cornish Charter Endorsement* (Innsbruck: IBS-Vertrieb, 1991). Ellis (*274*, p. 76) prints the Brome extract.

2 James de Rothschild (ed.), *Le Mistére du Viel Testament*, 7 vols. (Paris: SATF/ Didot, 1878–91); Omer Jodogne (ed.), *Le 'Mystère de la Passion' de Jean Michel* (Gembloux: J. Duculot, 1959) and *Le 'Mystère de la Passion' d'Arnoul Greban*, 2 vols. (Brussels: Palais des Académies, 1965–83). In Breton, see H. de la Villemarqué (ed.), *Le Grand Mystère de Jésus* (Paris: Didier, 1865), and for a Creation play, Murdoch (*289*). Watson Kirconnell, *The Celestial Cycle* (Toronto: Garland, 1952) lists further Paradise plays. In Welsh, see Gwenan Jones, *A Study of Three Welsh Religious Plays* (Aberystwyth: Bala Press, 1939).

3 See Jenner (*281*), Fudge (*277*), and Martyn Wakelin, *Language and History in Cornwall* (Leicester: Leicester University Press, 1975). Middle Cornish covers the period from about 1100 to 1500, with *Gwreans an Bys* at the beginning of the

modern period. Henry Lewis, *Llawlyfr Cernyweg Canol* (Cardiff: University of Wales Press, 2nd edn 1946, repr. 1980) is a primer of Middle Cornish.

4 On the archaeological evidence, see Longsworth (*284*, pp. 5f.) and Bakere (*268*, pp. 26–7). Borlase's illustration is reproduced in Nance (*294*), Bakere (*268*) and Fudge (*277*). Richard Southern (*421*) uses the Cornish round to argue for a wider use of this kind of staging but concentrates on St Just, dismissing Perran Round on the (slight) authority of Holman (*280*).

5 Longsworth (*284*, pp. 103–21) and Meyer (*286*) discuss liturgical aspects, and Bakere (*268*) suggests a range of sources. For a schematic comparison of the Cornish and English plays see Chambers (*23*, vol. II, pp. 321–3). On the Sethite legends (also in Cornish) see Esther C. Quinn, *The Quest of Seth for the Oil of Life* (Chicago: Chicago University Press, 1962) and *The Penitence of Adam* (Ann Arbor: Romance Monographs Inc., 1980). Latin texts of the Holy Rood are printed by Wilhelm Meyer, in the *Abhandlungen der philos.- philol. Cl. der Bayrischen Akademie*, Munich, 16/2 (1882), 103–66. The *Vita Adae* is translated in H. F. D. Sparks, *The Apocryphal Old Testament* (Oxford: Clarendon Press, 1984), pp. 147–67, and the *Gospel of Nicodemus* in Montague Rhodes James, *The Apocryphal New Testament* (Oxford: Clarendon Press, 1924), pp. 94–146. See also J. Caerwyn Williams, 'Ystorya Adaf ac Eua y Wreic', *National Library of Wales Journal* 6 (1949–50), 170–5.

6 On realism see James H. Marrow, *Passion Iconography in Northern European Art of the Late Middle Ages* (Kortrijk: Van Ghemmert, 1979). Cross (*271*) looks at the realism of Christ's torments from a different angle.

7 Nance (*295*) postulated an originally independent lyrical *Lamentactio Mariae* here worked into the play, but passages of high lyrical quality are numerous.

8 James, *Apocryphal New Testament*, pp. 157–9. See also Paull F. Baum, 'The Medieval Legend of Judas Iscariot and Pontius Pilate', *PMLA* 31 (1916), 481–632. On the drama, including Cornish, see Williams (*46*, pp. 9f.).

9 See John K. Bonnell, 'The Serpent with a Human Head in Art and in Mystery Play', *American Journal of Archaeology*, 2nd ser., 21 (1917), 255–91; Rothschild (ed.), *Mistére*, vol. I, p. 44; Arnold Immesen, *Der Sündenfall*, ed. Friedrich Krage (Heidelberg: Winter, 1913), p. 119.

10 In the Breton *Creation* the serpent claims to be an angel in a different shape; see Murdoch (*289*, pp. 167–9).

11 See Derek van Abbé, *Drama in Renaissance Germany and Switzerland* (Melbourne: Melbourne University Press, 1961) p. 26. There are many examples in a play almost exactly contemporary with *Gwreans an Bys*: see Jacob Ruff, *Adam und Heva*, ed. Hermann Kottinger (Quedlinburg and Leipzig: Basse, 1848). The Swiss Protestant has Noah preaching to the Cainites, something that John Gassner (ed.), *Medieval and Tudor Drama* (New York: Bantam, 1963), p. 188, finds unusual in *Gwreans an Bys*.

12 Marina Warner, *Alone of All her Sex* (London: Weidenfeld and Nicolson, 1976), pp. 44f.; Yrjo Hirn, 'La verrière, symbole de la maternité virginale', *NM* 29 (1928), 33–9. For Celtic examples see Andrew Breeze, 'The Blessed Virgin and the Sunbeam through Glass', *Barcelona English Language and Literature Studies* 2 (1991), 53–64.

13 The *Donation of Constantine* is in H. Bettenson (ed.), *Documents of the Christian Church*, 2nd edn (London: Oxford University Press, 1963), pp. 135–40. For

the *Golden Legend* see Theodor Graesse (ed.), *Jacobi a Voragine Legenda Aurea* 3rd edn 1890, repr. (Osnabruck: Zeller, 1969). There is an English version in Granger Ryan and Helmut Ripperger (eds.), *The Golden Legend* (New York: Arno, 1969). Although the *Legenda* was a major handbook, the borrowings need not have been direct. For the French play see Gaston Paris and Ulysse Robert (eds.), *Miracles de Nostre Dame* (Paris: SATF/Didot, 1876–94), vol. III, pp. 187–240.

9

PAMELA M. KING

Morality plays

INTRODUCTION

Only five medieval English morality plays survive: *The Pride of Life* (*85*, pp. 90–105), *The Castle of Perseverance*, *Wisdom*, *Mankind* (*83*) and *Everyman* (*86*, *87*), to give them their common titles, together constitute the entire corpus of an apparently influential native dramatic genre. The identification of the genre has been retrospective and depends largely on the perceived influence of these plays on the more abundantly surviving Tudor interlude. It is possible on the basis of the few surviving texts to construct a working definition of a characteristic dramaturgy for the morality play, yet their absolute cohesion as a group is bound to be questioned in any attempt to define that form in its individual manifestations and theatrical contexts, particularly as *The Pride of Life* is a corrupt Anglo-Irish text and *Everyman* a translation from a Dutch original.

What these plays have in common most obviously is that they offer their audiences moral instruction through dramatic action that is broadly allegorical. Hence they are set in no time, or outside historical time, though their lack of historical specificity is generally exploited by strategically collapsing the eternal with the contemporary. The protagonist is generally a figure of all men, reflected in his name, Everyman or Mankind, and the other characters are polarised as figures of good and evil. The action concerns alienation from God and return to God, presented as the temptation, fall and restitution of the protagonist. The story of man's fall and redemption presented in a cycle of mystery plays as an epic historical narrative is thus encapsulated in the morality play.

The dramatic variety this material offered was a direct product of the details of contemporary belief, particularly regarding the degree of control that the individual had in this world over his fate in the next. Orthodox Augustinian thought held that a person's endeavours towards the attainment of heaven were ineffectual without the direct intervention of God's grace through the Redemption. This was tempered by other currents of thought which held that man had absolute free will to choose in this world between vice and virtue and that those choices affected his fate in the next. The late fourth-century writer Prudentius's *Psychomachia*, an imaginative portrayal of the battle between vice and virtue for the soul of man, was most evocative of the latter line of thought.

The element of free will allowed to man in deciding his eternal fate led to an increasing refinement of people's imaginative perception of the forces of good and, particularly, evil, varying according to degree and kind. Popular schemes of vices and virtues abounded, the most prevalent being the designation of seven cardinal or deadly sins, corroborated by a body of visionary literature in which various witnesses, such as Lazarus of Bethany and St Patrick, offered first-hand accounts of how individual sins were punished in hell. Further categories of venial sins were identified for which self-help was possible in this world or, with the development of the concept of purgatory, in the next. Dante's *Commedia*, written at the beginning of the fourteenth century, is perhaps the best known and most widely influential developed imaginative vision of the entire other world in terms of crime, punishment and reward.

The believer faced both individual judgement when he died and final judgement on Doomsday when he would be relegated body and soul either to heaven or to hell for all eternity. He also knew that his encounter with a differentiated sin did not take the form of being snatched in an instant by some grisly mishapen 'bug', but was the matter of protracted struggle, demanding constant personal vigilance as well as the invocation of grace through the sacraments, particularly the sacrament of penance. In other words, against the variegated temptations to sin, he could invoke the fortification of Christ and the compensatory effects of his own good deeds. This struggle is the matter of the plot of an individual morality play, the whole dynamic of its action.

Although the action of a morality play is frequently described as allegorical, the term is used loosely to describe how action, character, space and time are related to the real world through a tissue of metaphor. The use of *prosopopoeia*, or personification, in creating dramatic characters involves a fundamental rhetorical separation between the play world and the real world, as players take on the roles of qualities, e.g. Mercy; supernatural beings (Good Angel); whole human categories (Fellowship) and human attributes (Lechery). The original audience's perception of reality was in any case different to that of a modern one (391), and it is not always clear what is an outside agent sent by God or the Devil and what an internal motive. Each role, as actualised in a theatrical context, is presented as a distinct consciousness and is, therefore, a dramatic character. The action can be seen securely only in terms of its own mimesis, as an instance imitating an eternal reality. What may seem abstract was, for the period when the plays were written, representative of true reality, transcending the ephemeral and imperfect world of everyday existence.

Later allegorical fiction, such as A Pilgrim's Progress, Gulliver's Travels, and Animal Farm, presents its audience with a sustained, developed literal story, structurally separable from the message for which it is the vehicle. The only literal storyline in the medieval morality plays is, however, the actualisation on stage of their moral 'sentence'. Hence the imaginative development of the situation or instance, constituting the plot of a play, is essentially thematic, rather than narrative, because it deals directly in eternal truths. To anchor their action in the world, the plots of these plays depend heavily on extended metaphor instead of a causal pattern of domestic events. In some instances this may be a battle, as at the climax of The Castle of Perseverance, where the forces of evil besiege the eponymous castle and are repulsed with a deluge of roses, a scene borrowed directly from the Psychomachia (316). Elsewhere in this play, however, the plot corresponds more nearly to a journey, or pilgrimage, from birth to death – another commonplace in contemporary literature for man's life, notably in Deguile-ville's Pélérinage de la vie humaine (321). Everyman also is a pilgrimage, but one which focuses on the end of the journey, as the protagonist confronts his death, whereas the unfinished Pride of Life appears to present the same journey interrupted by the untimely early arrival of death. Mankind employs yet another metaphor for fallen existence, the life of hard agri-cultural labour being equated with virtuous penitential living for the pro-tagonist. The more socially refined tone of Wisdom unites its highly complex theological argument by presenting the movement towards a hard-won final harmonious relationship between the soul and Christ in terms of marriage metaphors. What all have in common is an argument directed against a specific sin, based on a package of doctrine and illustrated through these systems of sustained metaphors, drawing on the received commonplaces of virtuous living.

As aspects of an argument intended for edification, time, place, plot and character are all morally directed. The same strategies extend to the spoken text. All the plays under consideration are in verse and employ clear rhe-torical markers. The speaker is instantly placed at any given moment on a scale between absolute good and absolute evil by the controlled choice of lexis, syntax and register, as well as by manipulation of stanza structure. The transformational nature of fall and redemption are both indicated in this manner: fall into sin is characterised by fragmented lines, blasphemy and nonsense. Virtue, on the other hand, is characterised by high-style, latinate structures, characters more usually talking in complete stanzas.

The rhetoric of theatrical communication must be unambivalent in a play that offers its audience prescribed doctrine. Although these plays are often described as didactic, that term also requires qualification. As is the case with the cycle plays, their orthodoxy serves to confirm and to celebrate rather than to argue. In fifteenth-century religious drama, the desired effect was concordance, achieved by a conspiracy of the verbal and the visual: diction, costume, placing and gesture all function as clear supportive signs of moral status. The dynamic nature of these plays lies not in internally contrived conflicts, but in the manner in which they generate pressure upon their audiences emotionally and physically, as well as intellectually. The precise manner in which these various effects are achieved is best explored by reference to individual plays. In what follows, the five plays are treated in an order that allows for a developed analysis of their form, rather than one determined by their strict chronology, which cannot be positively established in any case.

THE CASTLE OF PERSEVERANCE

The survival of the three fifteenth-century English morality plays may be attributed to the action of one East Anglian antiquarian. Manuscript V. a. 354 in the Folger Library, Washington D.C., which contains the only texts of *Mankind* and *The Castle of Perseverance* and the only complete text of *Wisdom*, is named for its first known modern owner, Cox Macro (1683–1767) of Bury St Edmunds. Hence the plays are edited and commonly referred to as 'The Macro plays' (*83*, *115*). The three Macro play texts bound together are in fact bibliographically discrete units of different dates. None is in the hand of the author, though *Wisdom* and most of *Mankind* were copied and owned by an East Anglian monk, Thomas Hyngham of Bury St Edmunds (see above, p. 196 and 239). All are written on paper and have been dated by their watermarks and handwriting style. The manuscript of *The Castle of Perseverance* is thought to date from around 1440, *Wisdom* from 1460–65 and *Mankind* from 1465–70. *Wisdom*, otherwise called *Wisdom Who is Christ*, or *Mind, Will and Understanding*, is the only one to appear elsewhere, in an imperfect text in another collection of plays, the Digby MS 133 in the Bodleian Library, Oxford (*84*).

All three plays are of proven East Anglian provenance. But the three plays are also very different in the theatrical auspices that they display and could, of course, exemplify peculiarly East Anglian tastes. The eastern counties of England were hardly typical of the country as a whole in the late Middle

Ages: the wool trade meant that the population was very prosperous but also persistently rural, no significant proportion gravitating to town life. Consequently, and because of direct links with the continent, the corpus of late medieval arts of all kinds is both rich and distinctive in character (253). On examination it becomes apparent not only that each of the three plays belongs to a radically different theatrical context and, consequently, audience, but also that all are related to other contemporary dramatic traditions.

The Castle of Perseverance is an extremely elaborate and expansive play. Briefly, it offers a package of orthodox biblical doctrine as armament against the sin of covetousness (318). Mankind (*Humanum Genus*), accompanied by his Good and Bad Angels, is subjected to various temptations by the forces of the World (*Mundus*), the Flesh (*Caro*) and the Devil (*Belial*). Backbiter eventually persuades him to join Covetousness, but he is retrieved by Penitence and Confession and enters the Castle of Perseverance. The forces of evil lay siege to the Castle, where Mankind is defended by an array of seven Virtues. Although the Virtues win, Covetousness tempts Mankind to leave the Castle, offering him material success in the form of possession of the now vacant Castle. Death comes and Mankind's riches are seized by the enigmatic I-wot-nevere-Whoo, while his Soul is carried to Hell. The Four Daughters of God – Mercy, Peace, Righteousness and Truth – hold a debate, which Mercy wins, freeing the Soul to ascend to Heaven.

The play draws on many commonplaces: the objectification of man's moral armament as a castle is familiar in sermons and also in the influential Anglo-Norman *Chasteau d'Amours* by Robert Grosseteste, which also contains a debate of the Four Daughters of God. Both elements disclose the medieval tendency to illustrate man's relationship with God through feudal and familial analogues (320). The battle between vices and virtues draws directly on Prudentius's *Psychomachia*. But the major thematic movement of the play depends on the presentation of man's life as a journey. Good Angel in the beginning sets up Christ as an example of poverty and a remedy against coveting the world's goods, citing biblical texts in Latin to support his argument. Despite these warnings, Mankind falls in trying to protect and retain his 'cupboard', which contains the goods he amasses through his temporal existence. The course of that existence is the play's whole action – a pilgrimage, from birth to death, synonymous with the progress from flawed innocence to experience, and represented theatrically as a physical journey through a landscape (317). The protagonist describes his own journey at the outset.

> Aftyr oure forme-faderys kende   *manner*
> Þis nyth I was of my modyr born.
> Fro my modyr I walke, I wende,

Ful feynt and febyl I fare ʒou beforn.
I am nakyd of lym and lende   *loin*
As Mankynde is schapyn and schorn.
I not wedyr to gon ne to lende   *I don't know*
    where to go nor to settle
To helpe myself mydday nyn morn.   (lines 275–82)

Shortly afterwards he reaches his first crossroads, the choice between earthly and heavenly reward:

Whom to folwe wetyn I ne may.   *know*
I stonde and stodye and gynne to raue.   *begin to go mad*
I wolde be ryche in gret aray
And fayn I wolde my sowle saue.
As wynde in watyr I wave.   *waver*
    (lines 375–9)

The moment of Mankind's fall to Covetousness is presented as a choice that centres on the journey motif:

ʒa, up and don þou take þe wey
Þorwe þis werld to walkyn and wende   *through*
And þou schalt fynde, soth to sey,   *truth to tell*
Þi purs schal be þi best frende.   (lines 2518–21)

Put that way, the choice between staying still in the Castle of Perseverance or moving on is as inevitable as it is fatal. Fixed points on the play's set, including the Castle, operate as ports of call on the journey, objectifying the moral state of the protagonist.

We know more about the set of this elaborate action than can simply be surmised from the spoken text because the manuscript of *The Castle of Perseverance* contains a diagram (see illustration 8). It shows centrally the castle itself, a structure on legs, with a bed below it from which Mankind will be born and from where, at his death some 3,000 lines later, his soul rises up to be judged. These are the only features that are actually drawn. They are enclosed by a double circle, outside of which, at the appropriate points of the compass, scaffolds are labelled, one for God in the east, the Devil in the north, the World in the west, and the Flesh in the south. Destroying the familiar symbolic symmetry of the rest, Covetousness has a scaffold of his own, in the northeast. As Covetousness alone among the comprehensive scheme of sins that assail the protagonist in the play is the one that he will find irresistible, the diagram is effectively a map of the play's action.

Attempts to reconstruct this playing space have, however, raised funda-

and Anima being presented as the recalcitrant bride. The sacrament of penance, which is the underlying focus of the play, is, therefore, represented within the action by another sacrament.

The play opens with a scene in which Wisdom and Anima explore their relationship, laying the foundation for later action. Wisdom's appearance, minutely described in the first of many elaborate stage directions, indicates that he is an embodiment of Christ in Majesty, but carrying the symbols of the whole Trinity, the cross of the Son, mounted on the orb of the Creator, and the sceptre of the sanctifier, the Holy Spirit. The iconography of his appearance is supported by what he says, identifying himself with the Trinity together, but with the Son 'properly', 'by reason'.

St Augustine's *De Trinitate* is the source which offers the quintessential explanation of wisdom as the entire Trinity, but especially the Son (326). Augustine founded his argument upon the text of John 1.14: 'The word became flesh and dwelt among us.' John's 'word', drawn from the Greek *logos*, is fused with the 'wisdom' bestowed on Solomon in Hebraic tradition, existing prior to the Creation, and God's most precious gift to man, defined by St Paul in I Corinthians 1.20–24:

> hath not God made foolish the wisdom of this world? . . . For the Jews require a sign, and the Greeks seek after wisdom: But we preach Christ crucified, unto the Jews a stumblingblock, and unto the Greeks foolishness; But unto them which are called, both Jews and Greeks, Christ the power of God, and the wisdom of God.

Augustine concludes that man's way to salvation lies through his participation in the wisdom of God, which amounts to a knowledge of God the Son. This is what Anima is urged to move towards by Wisdom, clearly established visually and verbally as the Trinity and the Son, three-in-one, God and man. As word-made-flesh, Wisdom also represents the essential duality of Christ as God and man, imperfectly mirrored in the soul. In the soul this duality is defined as reason and sensuality, thus the iconography of Anima's costume is explained – white and black to represent this duality, which is also her inherent instability, the potential of which will be realised in the ensuing action.

One of the properties of the fallen condition of man is his subjection to time and change. Hence, when the soul is represented as its own trinity of Mind, Will and Understanding in the play, its aspects appear successively, separate but initially harmonious, singing tenor, bass and the 'mean' Anima's very vulnerability lies in her reducibility, which explains doctrinally why the central character is fragmented, even if this fragmentation appears dramatically injudicious.

The fall of the protagonist depends on an extension of the proposition of imperfect likeness into the realms of spurious likeness, disguise and deceit, as perpetrated by Lucifer. As each of the Mights falls, he, too, takes on a false likeness or disguise: Mind becomes 'Maintenance'; Understanding, 'Perjury', and Will, 'Gentle Fornication'. These distortions of identity are reflections of the nature of the temptation offered by Lucifer. In this play it is not one single sin which the composite protagonist is lured into, so much as an alternative way of life: Lucifer argues that the contemplative life is less pleasing to God than the mixed life, but what he puts forward as the mixed life is purely secular. Disguise, dissimilarity and distortion of person have their counterpart in the unreason of fallacious argument in the fall scene.

The doctrine of the play is Augustinian, therefore, but its means of expression through dialogue owes much to fourteenth-century contemplative writers, particularly Richard Rolle, Walter Hilton and the German Henry Suso (323, 327). The sustained metaphor of marriage in the play not only gives it intellectual coherence, but also allows for the relationship between Christ and the individual soul to be expressed in terms of love imagery, with an emphasis on the passionate and instinctive nature of that relationship. This play, therefore, rather than seeing the soul as a battleground between good and evil, draws on a tradition suggesting that the soul is the multifaceted object of contemplative exploration. All the strategies of the play, its careful placing of characters on its envisaged set, its elaborate symbolic costumes, its apportionment of role and its use of the marriage metaphor, substantiate this approach to the interrelatedness of the many aspects of the soul, in fact the psychology, that it promotes.

Placing so genteel and doctrinal a drama as *Wisdom* in a plausible milieu is tricky. Much of the topical reference material is relevant only to courtiers. Mind when he falls becomes Maintenance, or the practice of hiring surplus retainers who will bear arms on one's behalf in return for protection. He has a reciprocal relationship with Perjury, Understanding's fallen identity, as the chief protection offered in so-called bastard feudalism was protection from the law of the land, effected most simply by the bribing of jurors.

The tendency was to link the play with a London audience until Gail McMurray Gibson (324), on grounds of the external, casual evidence of manuscript marginalia, suggested reviewing its East Anglian connections and persuasively demonstrated several circumstantial links with the Abbey of Bury St Edmunds, Cox Macro's home town. The recent discovery that the scribe and earliest owner of the Macro copy was a monk of Bury (see above) goes far towards substantiating the suggestion. The subject matter, being a consideration of the relative merits of contemplative, mixed and secular lives, is well suited to an audience such as might be found in one of

the richest abbeys in England, one which, although nominally full of con-
templatives, also owned and ran the prosperous cloth-town in which it was
situated. It was also embroiled in national politics and frequently entertained the court. At the time around which it was likely that the play was
written, the Abbey was busy ingratiating itself with the Yorkist monarch,
Edward IV, having supported the defeated Henry VI. Kingship and authority are major themes within the play: Wisdom and Anima, although their
meaning is eternal, are clad in the manner of a contemporary monarch and
his consort, and the fall into sin within the play features contemporary
issues concerning the abuse of authority.

A view of the play that fixes it in a specific social context also illuminates
the play's strategies for involving its audience. The initial tableau of
Wisdom and Anima, if played at a banquet for the visit of the real monarch
and his consort, not only suggests a moral doctrinal truth, but substantiates
it with an intelligible visual mirror of the political circumstances in which the
action is set. The banqueters become loyal subjects of the king and Wisdom.
The fall of Will into the temptations of the flesh has a direct humorous
analogue with the banquet context, whereas the fall of Mind and Understanding into political corruption reflects more darkly the crimes to which
courtiers and their acolytes could be tempted in such turbulent times.

Once one begins to look at the way in which the stage picture in *Wisdom*
develops metaphoric connotations (322) it becomes apparent that visual
aspects of the play do rather more than support meaning as conveyed by
spoken text. Costume and set in particular open up other dimensions of
meaning in the play. In the opening scene Christ as king is seated centrally
and enthroned, suggesting not only an earthly monarch by his sumptuous
clothing, but Christ in Majesty at the Last Judgement as it can still be seen
in numerous paintings, especially the chancel-arch frescoes of the Judgement so common in East Anglian wool churches. It is inconceivable to
imagine the ensuing action without the kind of horizontal symmetry and
vertical hierarchy which that implies. In addition to symmetries and oppositions, there is change, another aspect of the play's moralised process,
which is visually and emblematically developed. Garment change accompanies change of name to indicate change in moral status and identity.
Appropriately, Lucifer, the prince of disorder, abuses this language by disguising himself as a goodly gallant whilst remaining unchanged in his moral
character. Hence visual expression is succinctly given through the language
of the theatre to his inherently deceitful and unstable nature.

Codes of appearance are given their most extravagant expression in
Wisdom in the non-speaking masque elements of the play. The Five Wits
belong to Anima in her incorrupt state and are consequently dressed all in

white, a supportive signal of the purity of the soul. All these disguisings embedded in the action are unambivalent and are removed and replaced when a moral change takes place. Hence the white robes, liturgical song and procession of the Wits are later replaced by the three masques of Maintenance, Perjury and Gentle Fornication. Mind/Maintenance's masquers are dressed in a livery which parodies the ostentatious traffic in badges that characterised bastard feudalism, and Understanding/Perjury's masquers wear double-faced masks, whereas Will/Gentle Fornication's masquers are all anonymously identical.

These non-speaking elements contribute to the play's meaning not only through their content but by reference to the other theatrical forms they represent. Liturgical procession and song are equated with good, whereas the disguising, the kind of entertainment courtiers expected at a feast, is equated explicitly with fallen virtue. Many later plays incorporate masque or mumming elements to enhance their properties as visual spectacle, but none gives it so potent and witty a semantic value as *Wisdom*. A normally morally neutral and celebratory theatrical form is set in such a way as to give it derogatory moral bias. *Wisdom* is a curious metatheatrical composite, in which the entire masque element is transposed as the play's antimasque, to be assimilated as order is confirmed. It therefore confirms orthodox Christianity, recommending the harmonious marriage of the individual soul with Christ and of the church with the state. It may also controversially insinuate that true authority and harmony can best be achieved by the submission of secular authority to modes of ecclesiastical authority. Despite its apparently arcane theological argument, *Wisdom* is intended to be visually sumptuous and demands that its audience bring to it not only an ability to understand its theology but an experience of contemporary theatrical forms, in order to comprehend its strategies and discover its range of potential meaning.

EVERYMAN

Although *Everyman* has long been seen as the archetypal moral play, the first medieval English play of any kind to be revived in modern production,[1] it is generally believed not to be a native English composition at all, but a translation of the Dutch *Elckerlijc*. The question of priority has been the subject of extended critical debate.[2] The Low Countries had an unbroken tradition from the fourteenth to the eighteenth centuries of urban theatrical activity institutionalised in guilds of rhetoricians, the *Rederijkers Kamer*. These held competitive festivals of drama, as well as publishing plays written by their members, under their own imprint. *Elckerlijc* was written for a Rhetoricians' festival in the 1490s in Antwerp. The surviving English tradition cannot match the Dutch either in proliferation or sophistication until the sixteenth century, but the survival of *Everyman* and its Dutch source testifies to a degree of cross-fertilisation that one could only expect in the case of two near trading neighbours. Although the English version varies slightly from its original, both show the influence of the current of continental reformist religious asceticism known as the *Devotio moderna*. *Everyman* survives in four printed texts, two printed by Pynson, two by John Skot, all undated; but the play in English may be as late as the first quarter of the sixteenth century.

It is another play about every man's journey towards death, but this time it begins in the last act, concentrating wholly on the preparation for death, or how to avoid dying like Hamlet's father,

> Unhousel'd, disappointed, unaneled;
> No reckoning made, but sent to my account
> With all my imperfections on my head.
> O, horrible! O, horrible! most horrible!
>
> (*Hamlet*, 1.5, lines 77–80)

It draws upon contemporary commonplace teachings on the subject, such as *The Book of the Craft of Dying* and particularly *The Mirrour of St Edmund*, by Edmund Rich, Archbishop of Canterbury. Its characters are personifications, its theme the salvation of the soul, expressed through the customary device of sustained metaphor, in this instance the reckoning of an account. Yet *Everyman* is very different from the Macro Plays, most assailingly so in its even tone of high seriousness. As the protagonist's fall into sin has taken place before the action begins, there is no conflict, no *psychomachia*, but simply an orderly progress towards a predetermined end.

The play's prologue sets up its didactic nature:

> This mater is wonders precyous;   *wonderfully*
> But the entent of it is more gracyous,
> And swete to bere awaye.   (lines 7–9)

It also makes the assumption that all its audience are sinners and employs no ruses which suggest that the play might be designed purely for diversion. They are required to listen 'with reverence' (line 2). The theme, which lies behind the action yet never takes place, is judgement. As Everyman himself is both a personification of the entire human race and an individual actor, he represents the fusion of one man and all men, so in him is conflated the judgement each individual will meet at death with the Last Judgement.

Judgement becomes pilgrimage as Everyman sets out in search of the most fitting companions to accompany him. Fellowship, Kindred, Cousin and Riches will not go with him, Good Deeds is too weak. This accords with the orthodox Augustinian doctrine of penance, which makes clear that salvation cannot be attained by good deeds alone. Everyman learns from Knowledge that the necessary grace comes from the sacrament of penance, which he approaches via Confession and the gown of contrition, thereby strengthening his good deeds. The parts of the sacrament of penance – contrition, confession, absolution, extreme unction and satisfaction – are all worked through in the play in some detail. At this point in the action he has overcome the first crisis. He then embarks on finding companions to accompany him yet again, and after unsuccessfully attempting to recruit Beauty, Strength, Discretion and Five Wits, he is finally left to face Death with only his Good Deeds, though Knowledge accompanies him to the graveside.

The play reverses the accepted morality play focus on defining evil so that the audience may better recognise and avoid it, and concentrates on defining the good. The resultant want of conflict between vice and virtue, of good and bad angels, clears the way for a different and poignant message about man's condition in the face of death, for *Everyman* is a play about abandonment, focusing on Everyman's want of a comforter. The central irony is that, in order to balance his account, Everyman must subtract, yet he persists in seeing his plight in terms of simple mercantilism, and he pathetically attempts to bribe Death.

Structurally the play deals in two sets of meetings, separated by a reversal of situation when the first four companions leave. The second attempt to muster companions can look like a senseless repetition, but is in fact a development. John Conley (337) identifies the first group as 'goods of fortune' that are external to the protagonist. These are tested according to the classical definitions of the good friend found in, for example, Cicero's *De Amicitia*, and are found to be wanting. A good friend is one who has been tested, who is eternal, who is virtuous and whose virtue is of supernatural origins, a gift from God. The tests are to be found in Proverbs 17 and in Ælred of Rievaulx's *De Spirituali Amicitia*. Only Good Deeds and Knowledge are fit to pass these tests. The second set of would-be friends are subjected to the same tests, but they are different in kind, being 'goods of the soul', attributes integral to the protagonist. These are not friends that Everyman has selected but those he has inherited, and their leaving him mirrors his movement through life. They are not vicious in leaving him, but merely reflect the limitations of human nature. Hence, although the play's action apparently begins at the end of life's pilgrimage, it has embedded within its second half the extended time scheme of Everyman's whole life, represented in his abandonment first by Beauty, then by Strength, Discretion and Five Wits. Once Everyman comes to self-knowledge in the middle of the play the pattern of his life, arranged in terms of the attributes associated in turn with Youth, Manhood, Middle Age and Old Age, passes before his eyes as a series of treacherous transient companions.

The play, therefore, has a most subtle time scheme, where the time of the action is the same as the stage time, as is the case with *Mankind*, but a further extended time scheme is conveyed by personification allegory. The play is also full of references to time and its inexorable passage. The message is a pessimistic one – life is unreal, death is the only reality. The audience is made aware of the inevitability of death, and death's finality; suffering and loneliness eclipse any sense of what may lie beyond. Everyman's companions are not false vices, they are simply irrelevant, existing on a superficial plane. By extension, it suggests that life's companions are delusory, that the fallen condition is one of perpetual abandonment. Most strikingly, as Everyman cannot be redeemed this side of death, the focus of this play alone approaches the tragic, whereas all the other native morality plays, in their final spiritual optimism, conform to the resolution of a comic ending.

Everyman is a relatively complicated play in several respects, certainly reflecting the sophisticated and competitive context of its original. The suggestion that death is the final reckoning, requiring the balancing of an account, is apt in the mercantile urban world of the *kamers*. Rhetorically the play adopts a middle style, with sections of lively dialogue between Everyman and his companions. He then moves up into a higher style in soliloquy, his language becoming increasingly biblical as he moves towards death. As far as the play's staging is concerned, at least seven actors are required to play on a set which has to include a raised place for God as well as houses for the friends. A fixed set with several scaffolds seems most probable.

THE PRIDE OF LIFE

The fear of confronting death unprepared is also central in the one text that remains to be discussed. The problematic 502-line fragment known as *The Pride of Life* is probably the earliest surviving text in English that conforms to the criteria defining the morality play. The manuscript version of the play was written in cramped columns on the reverse of account rolls from Holy Trinity Priory, Dublin, dating from 1337–46, and was lost in 1922 in an explosion at Four Courts' Building in Dublin. Subsequent editions have depended on the description and edition made by James Mills for the Royal Society of Antiquaries of Ireland in 1891, which included an image of one page of text made by photozincography (85, plate 3). The play was clearly copied later than the accounts in the manuscript, but beyond that it has proved hard to establish a date. The extant copy has been placed in the early to mid fifteenth century because of its apparent generic relationship to the Macro plays and, for similar reasons, an English original has been suggested. More tangible relationships to non-dramatic Anglo-Irish poetry, notably in the early fourteenth-century Kildare manuscript, in the area of metrics and scribal practices, must permit the possibility of a fourteenth-century date and Irish provenance for this play.

The general outline of the play's action can be cautiously constructed from its long prologue, equivalent in function to the banns of *The Castle of Perseverance*. The protagonist, the King of Life, is introduced, royal of birth, haughty and afraid of no one, particularly,

⟨He⟩ dredith no deth for to deye.

He is warned to prepare for death by his queen, then – when this has no effect – by a bishop. He then sends his messenger, Mirth, to issue a challenge to Death. At this point the text breaks off, but the Prologue indicates that the King dreams of Death taking everyone. On waking, he fights with Death and loses, so his soul is conveyed to Hell. It is then saved by the Virgin Mary, who prays to her Son to intercede.

To the literary critic the most striking characteristic of this play is the plethora of analogues – dramatic, pseudo-dramatic and non-dramatic – suggested at every turn. In terms of its overall plot structure, concerning life, death and salvation, it is typical of the morality play as observed so far. There is no developed *psychomachia*, as the potential for damnation is integral to the character of the protagonist from the outset rather than being externally imposed as part of the action of vice figures operating on him: Fortitudo and Sanitas, his two guards, serve to corroborate the King's erroneous moral stance rather than to construct it. Mirth, the messenger figure, is more agent of misrule than vice, part commentator, part court fool. The movement towards death and the failure to prepare for death adequately are, however, reminiscent of *The Castle of Perseverance*, as is the last minute retrieval of the soul from hell by the power of grace. The roles of the Queen and the Bishop construct a pattern of action reminiscent of *Everyman*, where the protagonist proceeds on the path to self-destruction in the face of increasingly emphatic warnings from the play's other characters. If the Prologue is to be accepted as an accurate description of the play's later action, and there is no reason to suppose otherwise, the last scene involved first the appearance of devils to carry off the soul, then the appearance of the Virgin Mary to plead for the soul's salvation (342).

If the play is accepted in this way as a straightforward analogue to

Wisdom or *The Castle of Perseverance*, however, it is theological nonsense, for there is no pattern of repentance in the protagonist. Even allowing for the most extreme Augustinian belief in the primacy of grace, the play read in this manner carries a rather suspect didactic message. The protagonist of *The Pride of Life* is radically different from that of the other plays studied so far, for he is not a representative of all mankind in the face of death, but a personification of the life-force itself and, therefore, the natural opponent of death. The absence of a pattern of *psychomachia* does not lead to an absence of conflict from the plot as it does in *Everyman*; rather that conflict is presented as the more primeval combat between life and death (311, pp. 14–15). This aspect of the play may be related to the more nebulous area of sub-literary dramatic activity assumed to have persisted throughout the Middle Ages in the form of folk rituals associated with the agricultural year. That death should prove not a problem to be overcome, but the solution to the regeneration of the life-force, may be associated with the harvest in which the grain must be cut down before it can bring forth new life. We have already noted in the context of *Mankind*, how, in recent versions of mummers' plays, the quack doctor character as a cure for the headache offers to cut off the head of the afflicted and set it on again. Beheadings leading to regeneration are frequent, particularly in Irish folklore.[3] The literary critic must proceed with a certain circumspection in these areas, but the general area of connection with what is understood of such rituals appears assailing. The opening speeches of Fortitudo and Sanitas are also insistently reminiscent of the many variants on the character called Slasher in recent mummers' plays. There is one parallel in literary drama, in the N-Town play of the Death of Herod, which seems also to be influenced by the idea of a struggle between the kings of life and death.

The confrontation between the King of Life and Death in the play is preceded by the King of Life's dream, described in the Prologue:

> Deth comith, he dremith a dredfful dreme –
> Welle aʒte al carye;   *ought, be anxious*
> And slow fader and moder and þen heme: *slew, him*
> He ne wold non sparye.   *would not spare any*
> (lines 81–4)

This description suggests that the action of the King's dream was performed on stage, perhaps as a dumb-show in which Death struck down the King's father and mother, and perhaps others. There is sparse evidence, but clearly a dramatic opportunity here for the inclusion of a miniature Dance of Death, the familiar textual and pictorial tradition of the late Middle Ages in which a personification of death seized representatives of different ranks in society, demonstrating, as the play does, the inevitability, unpredictability and socially levelling properties of death.

It should also be observed that the play, being given a court setting in which the characters include a king, a queen, a bishop and two knights, not only demonstrates the levelling properties of death in the traditional Dance of Death manner, but takes the form of another feudal allegory, where man's relationship with God is explained in terms of a contract of rights and duties. More specifically, however, the action of the whole play, but particularly the Queen's attempted protection of her King, is assailingly suggestive of the game of chess, not uncommonly employed in medieval didactic allegory, notably in the protracted complaint of the Man in Black in Chaucer's *Book of the Duchess*.

The Prologue does not make clear whether the King of Life's own combat with Death was part of the dream – played out in dumb-show possibly as a Dance of Death or as the denouement of a game of chess, or a combination of the two – or followed his waking. After the King's death, however, it is clear that a separate character, representing the King's soul, entered the action. The corrupt nature of the text again means that it is not clear precisely what form the ensuing action took, but there was some exchange at this point between the body and the soul. Again there is a rich field of possible analogues in the popular body and soul debates of the later Middle Ages. If the play did not contain an actual disputation, it probably at least included a complaint of the soul to the body, such as occurs near the end of *The Castle of Perseverance*. Dramatic poems in which the soul bewails its fate accusingly to the body are a recognised sub-group within the body and soul debate tradition as in, for instance, the Anglo-Saxon *Address of the Soul to the Body*.

The play, in short, suggests analogies with a large number of medieval literary and sub-literary traditions concerning the coming of death, the major of which have been indicated above. The popularity in the late Middle Ages in northern Europe of literary, didactic and visual materials exhorting the Christian to prepare for his own death is well attested. Within the play, the Bishop's sermon directed at the King of Life, but, of course, also at the play's audience more directly, is an embedded standard complaint against the abuses of the age, in which all the things of this world are presented as corrupt and empty, and the only certainty impending death:

Ricmen spart for no þing	*spare*
To do þe por wrong;	*poor*
Þai þingit not on hir ending	*think*
Ne on Det þat is so strong.	(lines 363–6)

Despite the physical problems presented by the text of *The Pride of Life*, which limit the amount of weight it can be given, the play serves admirably to demonstrate the inherent dangers central to any study of the English medieval morality play. The criteria by which the genre is defined are extremely general and permissive, particularly in the area of theme. Central to all the plays discussed is the nature and brevity of the life of man, the nature of death and the necessity of making suitable spiritual preparation for death: this might be said of the vast bulk of late medieval religious writing. There are undeniably features that these plays have in common in the treatment of these themes as dramatic text, particularly in the devising of dramatic character and the presentation of man's potential for damnation and salvation as a temporal process. As soon as one examines their dramaturgy more closely, however, their debt to other dramatic and pseudo-dramatic forms becomes apparent.

CONCLUSION

The five plays that constitute the corpus of medieval English moralities do not really supply adequate evidence of a coherent 'movement' within the development of native theatre. For this reason, one must be very careful in privileging them corporately as the nursery of Renaissance drama. To persist in imposing that retrospective burden on these plays also seriously distorts and underrates many of their own characteristics. Each play, far from representing a beginning, demonstrates an allusive, self-conscious theatricality. The texts show a variety of ways in which their authors manipulated the boundary between the play world and the real world, often addressing the audience directly and using the varied communication codes of the theatre to draw them into the action of the play. The assumption within the texts of audiences sufficiently competent and experienced in the workings of theatre to comply with such strictly metatheatrical devices again seems to bear witness to the maturity of the form.

Such devices are arrestingly exploited in Henry Medwall's *Fulgens and Lucres* (88), written in 1497. The play is not a morality play, but a dramatisation of a humanist treatise on the nature of true nobility. It is both the earliest surviving English secular play and a tour de force of theatrical manipulation, suggesting a strong but now lost tradition of play writing in this mode. The play has a sub-plot, in which two characters, A and B, emerge from the audience, become servants of the two suitors of Lucres, and unsuccessfully woo Lucres's maid, Joan. In their early banter, A cannot determine whether B is a player or not. As B denies that he is other than just a member of the audience, A complains, with heavy irony, that it is difficult to tell a player from another man. Later, when B is determined to become Cornelius's servant, A says,

> Peace, let be!
> By God! Thou wilt destroy all the play.

His companion retorts,

> The play began never till now.

Medwall was writing for an elite London audience, but such self-conscious devices are not so very far removed from the manner in which *Mankind*'s author manipulated an audience which has always been designated strictly rural.

Aspects of the dramaturgy of our five morality plays do turn up in the sixteenth-century interlude with a coherence that argues more strongly for the genre than do the individual surviving examples. The pattern of innocence, temptation, fall and redemption was exploited, in the protracted and turbulent years surrounding the Reformation, as an organ of political satire and religious propaganda. Skelton's *Magnyfycence* (90), written around 1520, has a protagonist who is a universal prince figure, preyed on by vices who are all too tangible as corrupt courtiers and bad counsellors, and who adopt false names and identities in order to bring about the fall. The political, religious and historical are combined in John Bale's *King Johan* (94), written under Henry VIII and revived under Elizabeth, in which the vices are scions of the Roman Catholic faith. In this very complex play, the vices, in addition to disguising themselves as good counsellors, have historical aliases which suggest an analogy between contemporary circumstances and the period of the reign of King John. John is the protagonist of the historical layer of the plot, whereas the state, represented by the estate figures of Nobility, Civil and Clergy, takes on the role of protagonist of the political morality. *Respublica*, probably by Nicholas Udall, was written for the first Christmas of the reign of Mary Tudor and, consequently, reverses the argument, creating vice-figures who are presented as self-seeking protestants. As the subject of these plays was not the reform of the self, but of the state, a new figure, representing the people, the victims of misgovernment, entered the cast of characters. He saw his apotheosis in John o' the Commonweal in Sir David Lindsay's play *Ane Satyre of the Thrie Estaitis* (96), a large-scale political morality play, written in Scotland for outdoor performance in the 1560s.

Plays continued to be acted by both amateurs and professionals, with many, showing the economy of characterisation of *Mankind*, probably written for touring troupes. Many of the plays written for the court were, however, performed by schoolboys. Although a lot, like *Respublica*, were designed for an adult audience, there are those that employ the admonitory plot-structure and themes of the morality play to offer homely education suitable for a youthful milieu. Many have proverbial titles, such as *Enough is as Good as a Feast*, and *The Longer thou Livest the More Fool thou Art*. Educational themes were dealt with in plays written for and by those interested in the new humanist learning, particularly John Rastell, whose *The Four Elements* (91) is a vehicle for material about the New World, but has characters that bear vestigial hallmarks of the traditional Vice and Virtue. The Vice was particularly persistent, even in plays of an entirely different order, especially comedies, in which he became a harmless agent of misrule, rather like Mirth in *The Pride of Life* (307).

The seventy or so surviving interludes written between the period of the medieval saints' plays, cycle plays and moralities and the construction of the first Elizabethan theatres represent a major period in English theatre history in their own right. In the present context, they are important in suggesting that there was some consensus about the morality play form, a form which was adapted for the changed perceptions of the world that developed during the sixteenth century. It is a form which is imperfectly attested by the five extant English medieval moralities, not because they are in any sense crude or ill-fashioned, but precisely because each demonstrates an individuality and inventiveness which in turn bears witness to its own place in a sophisticated, varied and thriving theatrical tradition.

NOTES

1 The first modern production was in the very influential adaptation directed by William Poel in 1901 (see *311*, pp. 1–5), the text of which is preserved in the Victoria and Albert Museum, London.
2 See, for example, E. R. Tigg, 'Is the *Elckerlijc* prior to *Everyman*', *JEGP* 4 (1939), 568–96; Henry de Vocht, *Everyman, a Comparative Study of Texts and Sources* (Louvain: C. Uystpruyst, 1947); Jan Pritchard, 'On Translating *Elckerlijc*, Then and Now', *Dutch Crossing* 22 (1984), 38–48.
3 For examples see Elisabeth Brewer, *From Cuchulainn to Gawain: Sources and Analogues of Sir Gawain and the Green Knight* (Cambridge: D. S. Brewer, 1973), pp. 9–44.

10

DARRYLL GRANTLEY

Saints' plays

Any attempt to consider medieval saints' plays as a genre is fraught with difficulty because of the paucity of extant examples, the ambiguity or incompleteness of records relating to auspices and to lost plays and the inherent difficulty of arriving at some sort of definition of form. A number of theorists have attempted to define this drama. J. M. Manly, in presenting a challenge to the evolutionary theory of drama, saw the saint's play as a spontaneous coming together of the drama and the saint's legend, which was a regular feature of the church sevice (32, pp. 585–6). The legend was defined by G. H. Gerould as:

> . . . a biographical narrative, of whatever origin circumstances may dictate, written in whatever medium might be convenient, concerned as to substance with the life, death and miracles of some person accounted worthy to be considered a leader in the cause of righteousness; and whether fictitious or historically true, calculated to glorify the memory of its subject.   (345, p. 5)

Manly defined the miracle play as:

> the dramatization of a legend setting forth the life or the martyrdom or the miracles of a saint.   (32, p. 585)

Karl Young, with particular reference to the St Nicholas plays, suggested that this definition be narrowed to exclude those saints who have a place in the narrative of the New Testament, such as the Virgin, Mary Magdalene, Lazarus and Paul (69, vol. II, p. 307). More recently Mary del Villar has provided a simpler and more comprehensive definition:

> A saint's play is a play that has a saint as its protagonist or a miracle as its main action.   (350, p. 84)

Del Villar sees English saints' plays as falling into the same types as continental ones, categories which overlap a great deal and which simply help to handle the material. These are: (1) Plays dramatising the entire life of a saint; (2) plays dramatising the entire life of a saint, based on historical sources; (3) plays dramatising only part of a saint's life, generally a crucial or emblematic episode; (4) plays that present a miracle of St Nicholas, the Virgin, another saint or the Host; (5) plays centering on martyrdom in which all, or the greater part, of the action involves torments; (6) romantic plays using the convention of saint's drama (e.g. miracles, counsel by angels) to dramatise legends about pious people (*350*, p. 87).

These definitions relate to subject matter rather than form, and it is appropriate that they should do so since the plays, lost and extant, that might be considered to constitute this category extend across a range of early dramatic forms, from liturgical drama to moral interlude. In the course of this discussion an attempt will be made to discern what common ground there is in this drama that might help to establish an idea of the genre, and a number of characteristic preoccupations will be identified and discussed, but these are based on the small number of extant plays and can only have conjectural application to the genre as a whole. Similarly, there is no one mode of staging which can with certainty be identified with the saint's play, though the few extant works do show some elements of similarity in their staging requirements.

Given the diversity of the few extant examples of saints' plays in Britain, it is useful to approach these with some idea of the dramatic tradition to which they belong, if any such tradition can be said to have existed in formal terms. The references to saints' plays extend over several centuries and the earliest extant mentions of such plays in England are to a St Katharine play from the twelfth century and a St Nicholas play from the thirteenth century, possibly liturgical plays.[1] The following is a list of further lost plays from the fourteenth to the sixteenth centuries: *St Thomas the Martyr*, King's Lynn, 1385–6; *St Katharine*, London, 1393; *St Clotilda* at court, Windsor, 1429; *St Laurence*, Lincoln, 1441–2; *St Susannah*, Lincoln, 1447–8; *King Robert of Sicily*, Lincoln, 1447–53; *St Dionysus*, York, 1455; *St Clara*, Lincoln, 1455–6; *St George*, Lydd, Kent, 1456; *St Katharine*, Coventry, 1490–91; *St George*, New Romney, 1490–97; *St James*, Lincoln, fifteenth century; *St Mary Magdalen*, (mentioned) Thetford Priory, 1503–4; *St Christian*, (mentioned) Oxford, 1506; *St George*, Bassingbourne, 1511; *SS Feliciana and Sabina*, 1516; *St Erasmus*, Aberdeen, 1518; *St Christina*, Bethersden, 1522; *St Swithin*, Braintree, 1523; *St Andrew*, Braintree, 1525.[2]

Since what remains of the overwhelming bulk of early saints' plays in Britain is simply this list of titles, with few other records besides, it is necessary to look elsewhere to provide an artistic context for those plays that are extant, and this makes Manly's connection of the saint's play with the saint's legend all the more important, as we may gain some insight into the largely lost dramatic tradition through this related area of literary production, written equally for public consumption. The saint's legend was one of the most important and enduring of literary forms from the Conquest to the Renaissance in England, despite the fact that now little attention is paid to it (345, pp. 1–16). This prominence was ensured by the position of saints' legends within the institutional processes of religious practice, as adjuncts to the homiletic and biblical literature in ecclesiastical use. These legends were usually assembled in collections along the lines of Jacob da Voragine's *Legenda Aurea*, itself appearing in an English translation by Caxton in 1498. The most notable of the English legendaries was the *South English Legendary*, which is to be found in two forms dating from the thirteenth century and exists in numerous manuscripts, the locations of which indicate a widespread use in various parts of England.[3] Other extant legendaries include Mirk's *Festial*, Osbern Bokenham's *Legendys of Hooly Wummen* and the Scottish legendary attributed to John Barbour.

Hagiographical prose and verse literature can be identified as having certain recurrent characteristics relating to the ideological function it is intended to fulfil. Pre-eminent among these is the motif of conversion, either that of the saint himself or herself or the saint's conversion of others. This more often than not gives rise to the creation of strong binary oppositions in the narratives between diabolic and divine power, to heighten the significance and dramatic effect of conversion. The oppressive forces of paganism are often emphatically drawn, both through the rhetoric of the pagans and the excess of their displays of power and cruelty. If the demonstrations of diabolic power are striking in these narratives, then equally the power of God in the face of these displays is what this literature is all about, and this is manifest in a number of ways, from miraculous cosmic events, angelic visitations and destruction of pagan shrines, to miracles surrounding the martyrdom and relics of saints. The element of miracle thus becomes another prominent motif. At the centre of most hagiographical narratives single or multiple miracles are to be found, serving a significant function in illustrating the power of God in a spectacular and easily comprehensible way, one that had far more earthly immediacy than any theological arguments about the afterlife. This went hand-in-hand with a certain sensationalism that characterises this literature, and that resides, too, in the graphic descriptions of the torture that many saints undergo.[4] The final major recurrent motif that might be identified in hagiographical narratives is the defiance by saints of the power of paganism. Saints are represented confronting this force in a number of ways, from the passive though resolute endurance of torture to displays of supernatural power as they become agents of God. Though the saints themselves are often drawn from the upper echelons of society, they nonetheless would have presented to a broad audience a satisfying picture of Christian radicalism triumphing over secular tyranny. Many of these legends represent the debates between saints and tyrants in dramatic dialogues of some force.[5] Since the pagans are invariably represented as being in positions of political and military authority, the ultimate triumph of their victims, in whatever terms, was probably a major part of the attraction of this literature for its audiences. As in secular legend literature, the narratives of saints' legends are constructed of certain repeated and popular motifs which are easily transposed from one legend to another, so that it is essentially formula literature (345, pp. 35–6). All this adds up to a literature essentially for popular consumption and with a particular and recurrent line of argument to advance.

The motifs and characteristics discussed above, consistently found in non-dramatic hagiographical literature, are also to be found in varying measures in the drama that is derived from this tradition. Since the number of extant saints' plays is so small, in order to place these in any larger context of genre it is necessary to view the non-dramatic literature as a sort of parallel genre which can be considered to share many of the attributes of the saint's drama. Conversion is certainly a predominant idea in all the extant plays included in this discussion. The oppositional forces implied in the choice involved in conversion are to be found here too, represented in various ways. Miracle is, if anything, an even more important element in a medium that is essentially visual and was able to draw on a variety of stage tricks both to attact audiences and to further the persuasive ends of the texts. Another feature of the prose and verse legends that could be considered to be even more appropriate to the dramatic medium is their sensationalism. Tortures and executions lend themselves to striking visual images which are often exploited in the pictorial representations of saints' lives.[6] Clearly, drama that was aimed at a popular audience would have been unlikely to pass up the opportunity to include these sensationalistic elements.[7] The spirited dialogues found in these legends also indicate the likely relationship between this literary form and the drama, since the narratives at these points become semi-dramatic anyway.

Another form of narrative to which saints' plays can be thought to be connected is the tradition of church window and wall illustrations. These pictorial cycles often represent the lives of saints, and it is precisely their visual nature which makes them especially interesting to the student of early drama. The most comprehensive study of these cycles in relation to the drama has been done by Clifford Davidson, principally in order to try to reconstruct a picture of a lost dramatic tradition, but also to provide an iconographic approach to the understanding of the extant plays (344).

Another useful area of comparison for early saint drama in Britain is the French tradition of saints' plays, which is, in terms of the extant works and of the documentation and records, the most extensive in Europe, and presents a much more complete picture than we could hope to build up on the basis of surviving British plays and records.[8] Saints' plays are found among French liturgical plays, and Jean Bodel's *Jeu de St Nicolas*, dating from around the turn of the twelfth and thirteenth centuries, is among the earliest vernacular plays in France. This play does not deal with the life of Nicholas but instead with the posthumous miraculous power of the saint. It is one of a number of French saints' plays that centre upon miracles rather than the biographies of saints, including Rutebeuf's *Miracle de Théophile*, from the latter half of the thirteenth century, and a large number of *Miracles de Nostre Dame* from the fourteenth century. Another group of plays deals with the apostolic saints, most notably the Gréban brothers' *Actes des Apôtres* from the sixteenth century. This play is particularly interesting for its documentation of the special effects that are so characteristic of the saint's play. Perhaps the most important group of saint plays in France, however, are those that depict the lives of local saints. These include saints who had a local connection such as patronage of guilds, saints whose relics were lodged in the vicinity in which their plays were produced, and other nonbiblical saints who had less specific local connections but whose lives were dramatised for other reasons. These plays, which include the immensely long *Ste Barbe* from the fifteenth century, provided considerable opportunity for the exploitation of popular interest. Apart from playing to the loyalty of communities to specific saints, these plays also often involved martyrdom and provided the opportunity for extended and sensational scenes of torture, as well as stage tricks. Plays in all these categories manifest the hallmarks of strongly popular drama. As well as the features already mentioned above, they characteristically include comic elements centered upon a *fou*, *stultus* or *vilain*, often with contemporary satirical targets. The tradition of saints' drama in France provides many interesting points of reference in a conjectural reconstruction of the tradition in England. Several of the elements typical of the French plays are to be found in the surviving British plays, and all three categories of the French drama are by chance represented in these plays: *St Paul* and *Mary Magdalen* are lives of biblical saints, *St Meriasek* concerns a local non-apostolic saint and the Croxton *Play of the Sacrament* is a sacred miracle. What is not represented among these is a martyrdom, but many elements characteristic of martyrdom plays are to be found in them.

In the absence of a large-scale survival of British hagiographical drama, the most immediate and accessible context for the extant saints' plays under

consideration is the contemporaneous non-hagiographical dramatic traditions of allegorical moral drama and scriptural drama. If an argument is to
be made for the distinctness of saints' plays as a genre, some examination
needs to be made of their relation to these other forms. It could be argued
that the ideological ends of scriptural drama are served pre-eminently
through the presentation of character as figure within a larger process,
hence the structural and philosophical devices of typology and prefiguration
in the cycles. In the moral plays the interest is arguably more biographical
since, although the central figures are fictitious and wholly or partly constructed along allegorical lines, the audience's engagement is with the actual
course of those characters' lives and fortunes, especially in plays like *The
Castle of Perseverance* and *Mankind*. Furthermore, while the narratives in
the scriptural plays are predetermined and known by their audiences to be
so, in the allegorical plays an important part of the writer's art lies in narrative invention, even though the format may be formulaic. In the case of the
saints' plays, the picture is more complicated. Where biography is involved,
the focus of the interest is squarely on that and although, for instance, St
Paul and St Mary Magdelene may be scriptural figures, their position in the
narrative is not that of the figures in the scriptural plays. In the case of the
latter, her appearance in the cycles as well provides a useful point of comparison. Whereas in the cycles in which Mary Magdalene appears, she is
presented uniformly as a figure of contrition for sin and in a sense is part of
a figural representation of Christ's love for the penitent human soul,[9] the
role or roles that she occupies in the saint's play disclose a much more
complex picture, quite aside from the effects of cumulative audience
engagement with the character over a protracted biographical narrative. As
I hope to show in the more detailed discussion of the Digby *Mary Magdalen*, she has a succession of fairly distinct identities which are held
together by a number of structural devices, not the least of which is her
centrality in what is otherwise a moving tapestry in which most characters
appear briefly, never to be seen again. The saint's play shares with the allegorical plays the interest in keeping to the very forefront of the action the
moral dichotomies that are the natural product of conversion drama, but it
differs from them in that its characters are perceived to be historical, and
these moral dichotomies have necessarily to be presented in historical terms.
This does not prevent the writer of *Mary Magdalen* from including allegorical characters, however, or presenting the conversion of Mary in terms
of an allegorical *psychomachia*. This indicates the greater degree of freedom
for narrative inventiveness which the saints' plays have over scriptural
drama, particularly where apocryphal legend is involved. The extensive
transposition of narrative elements from one legend to another in the prose

and verse legends evolves a sort of formula within the parameters of which a significant degree of freedom to shape and invent exists, and this is carried over into the drama. French hagiographical drama shows considerable evidence of this, as do the extant British examples, and it gives us some idea of the kind of dramatic writing that has been lost through the non-survival of the numerous saint plays that constituted the English tradition of such drama. It might even be asserted that their loss has distorted our view of the evolution of Tudor drama, in which the allegorical moral play is usually credited with such pre-eminence.[10]

Apart from the difficulty of establishing an artistic context for the surviving saints' plays, the lack of records makes it extremely difficult to determine under what auspices this drama was produced, and indeed whether it was typically produced under auspices specific to the genre at all. In his conjectural reconstruction of the saint's play tradition, Clifford Davidson has suggested several possible connections between certain lost plays and guilds dedicated to specific saints, but no consistent or convincing pattern of evidence emerges to establish these guilds as the usual auspices for the plays (344). Other suggestions that he makes include churches and the Franciscans, but none of these is established as being regularly responsible for the production of saints' plays. Glynne Wickham has conjectured that the production of much of this type of drama may have been associated with the constant need to raise funds for church expenses (352, p. 103).

Much of the difficulty comes of course from simple paucity of records, but the fact that even the extensive work of the *REED* project has so far been unable to establish any suggestion of a consistent institutional connection for saint's play production suggests that there may be no such traditional auspices to uncover. It may be of some use to turn again to the example of France. Here the principal stagers of saints' plays appear to have been the civic authorities, and guilds or *confréries*, and the popularity of this type of drama owed much to the cult of saints, especially local ones or patron saints of particular trades (349, pp. 140-2). It seems perfectly logical to assume that typically the promoters of saints' drama in this country would also have been those institutions who had an interest in keeping the profile of a particular saint high, as an emblem or patron. It is, however, probably a testimony to the popularity of this form of drama that its production does not seem to have been confined to these institutional auspices.

No records survive for the earliest production of *The Conversion of St Paul*, but the directions and staging possibilities of the original text and the changes resulting from additions to the text, as well as the putative textual history of the play, suggest that it might have started as a travelling play in Cambridgeshire and East Anglia and subsequently become a town play in

Chelmsford.[11] The location and original production circumstances of *Mary Magdalen* are equally obscure, and a number of places in the eastern counties (Lincoln, Lynn, Ipswich, Newark) have been suggested over the years. Wherever it was originally composed or first seen, there is now no doubt that the extant copy was made by a scribe brought up or trained in southern Norfolk (238, p. 101, map). Later in the sixteenth century, along with other plays in the Digby group, it was in the possession of Myles Blomefylde of Chelmsford, Essex, and may have had a second career there (242: see chapter 7, pp. 194–5 above). It is a play that requires very elaborate staging, involving some twenty-three actors and multiple doubling, and, as the recent EETS editors have indicated, is unlikely to have been a travelling production (84, p. xlviii). The question of the theatrical auspices of these and other East Anglian plays remains open, and their context within what D. C. Baker has called that region's 'community of drama – various, extremely flexible and adaptable, perhaps drawn from common sources' (234, p. 32) is the subject of current investigation (253, 265). The auspices of *St Meriasek* are also unknown and a matter for conjecture. The location of the play has been suggested as Penryn in west Cornwall, which was a centre for miracle play production, and specifically the collegiate church of Glasney (300, p. 23). There is some support in the text for a general ascription to west Cornwall but nothing more specific than that. Like the *Mary Magdalen*, the play is very lengthy, with technically complex staging arrangements, and is therefore not likely to have been a touring production. The general tenor of the work and Meriasek's identification of a parish church near St Mary's of Camborne which is to be dedicated to him indicate that the play may have been written to establish him as a patron saint in the area (300, chapter 2). The *Play of the Sacrament* is, by contrast, clearly intended for touring, as is indicated not only by the declaration in the banns that the play is to be performed 'at Croxston on Monday', but also the colophon at the end of the manuscript – 'Ix may play yt at ease' – and the play was probably the property of a large itinerant company. The range of size and implied staging arrangements of these extant plays do nothing to confirm any conjecture about guilds, religious orders or civic authorities constituting the typical auspices of hagiographical drama and, on the contrary, they suggest rather that this type of play would probably have been produced in a variety of circumstances by different sorts of company and, by extension, for a range of different purposes.

The variety of their staging requirements is something which adds significantly to the interest of saints' plays as early theatre. One reason is that even the few surviving pieces manage to encompass most of the principal forms of staging known to have existed in the period. A great deal of interest has been aroused by the staging of *The Conversion of St Paul*, centering principally upon some ambiguous stage directions in the text at the end of the first section of the play – 'Finis istius stacionis et altera sequitur' (The end of this station and the other follows) – and at the end of the second – 'Finis istius secunde stacionis et sequitur tercia' (The end of this second station and the third follows). At the end of the first section, *Poeta*, a narrator figure asks the audience to 'folow and succede / Wyth all your delygens this generall processyon'. It is the interpretation of the terms 'station', 'follow', 'succeed' and 'procession' which has given rise to speculation. An early view was that the play was presented on wagons which moved around with the audience (Furnivall, in the first EETS edition) and a later one that the audience moved from station to station (25, p. 313). The latter view has gained the widest currency (415, 358, 84, p. xxvi). Another view advanced by Glynne Wickham was that the play was produced in a market square and that it used two carts representing Jerusalem and Heaven, which moved into the playing area according to the scene being played (352). These models are all based on a literal interpretation of the terms quoted above, but Mary del Villar has argued that 'to folow and succede' should be taken to mean 'pay attention to' and 'this generall processyon' refers to the story (359, 404, p. 33). Although some of these arguments make highly plausible points, there is ultimately no conclusive proof to support any one exclusively. The play's later editors sensibly appeal for an open mind on the staging, as the play might have had different phases in its life, particularly in view of the later additions to the text (84, p. xxviii). It is apparent from several of the stage directions that considerable use is made of 'the place', whether this be a well-defined *platea* or an open space in the streets around the pageants that might be considered to form the visual focus of the play. Saul rides into and around the place and clearly several pageants are located there. What becomes immediately apparent is that this is not a play in which the action is entirely or even largely confined to scaffolds or pageant wagons,[12] and a recent production, described below (chapter 11, pp. 305–6), shows how much new light can be derived from practical experimentation when scholars and critics have reached an *impasse*.

The other Digby play, *Mary Magdalen*, is probably from the point of view of its staging the most complex and interesting play in the whole repertoire of early English drama. Despite the fact that Furnivall regarded it as having a pageant-wagon production, it was fairly obviously written to be presented in a place-and-scaffold type of staging. The problem of the staging of *Mary Magdalen* has given rise to a great deal of speculation. Earlier critics postulated an all round production, as is commonly assumed for *The*

Castle of Perseverance, their solutions differing mainly in the number and type of scaffolds used. Of the more recent commentators, only David Bevington has stuck exclusively to the all round form (62, p. 688). Glynne Wickham rejected full round staging in favour of 'some other form of staging' and suggested a parallel with the *Mystère des Trois Doms*, with the audience facing the acting area on one side only (352, pp. 111–15). D. L. Jeffrey also rejected the idea that the play was for production exclusively in the round, and he further suggested the doubling of scaffolds. He also paid some attention to the play's visual symmetry (348, pp. 85–6). The most recent and comprehensive study of the staging of *Mary Magdalen*, however, has been by M. K. L. Jones, who suggested a variety of staging arrangements on the assumption that the play might have been a travelling production (355). She provided schemes for a full round production, a half round setting of scaffolds with the audience and actors sharing the circular *platea*, and the setting of scaffolds in a horizontal line facing the audience. Jones's ideas have the advantage of flexibility and approach the problem of staging from a thematic point of view, representing Mary's pilgrimage from hell to heaven. The problem with her postulations is that, although she accepted the possible use of doubling to reduce the number of scaffolds, she did not work out doubling schemes. Her resultingly elaborate plans make her already rather dubious suggestion of a touring play all the more implausible. There are also problems of visibility, as she herself recognised, and it is interesting to note that her own production of the play did not follow any of her three staging plans. The multiplicity of solutions offered is testimony to the difficult staging problems that arise from the sheer size and technical complexity of the play, the stage directions of which, though often full, give no indication of the approaches used in the original presentations of the piece.

Mary Magdalen was regarded by early critics as having been designed for performance in two halves. More recently, J. C. Coldewey has supported this division and suggested that the play may even have been regarded as two separate plays (242). He argues that the appearance of the king of Marcyll midway through the play, with a boast much like those at the opening and with the same ceremony of wine and spices, indicates the beginning of the second half, and he supports this by pointing out that the only characters from the first half who appear in the second are Mary, one devil, one good angel, Christ, Pilate, Pilate's messenger, Herod and the Emperor. However, although in a play of this length there may have been breaks in the performance, several objections can be made to such a division. It seems likely that the boast of the king is placed where it is to allow time to elapse between the departure of Christ in line 923, s.d. and the *visitatio* sequence, for the crucifixion to have taken place offstage. There appears otherwise little reason for placing the boast so inappropriately in the midst of the Passion drama. If the play were to be played in two halves, there would be no need for this as the interval between the performances would suggest sufficient time for the events of the crucifixion to have occurred. Coldewey suggests that Christ's words, 'Vade in pace' just before the supposed break confirm the ending of the first half, but the stage direction following this contradicts this suggestion:

> Here devoydyt Jhesus wyth hys desypyllys; Mary and Martha and   *exits*
> Lazare gon hom to þe castell, and here begynnyt [þe Kyng of Mar-
> cylle] hys bost   (line 924, s.d.)

The non-reappearance of many of the characters can be explained by the episodic nature of the play, and doubling can take care of the sheer number of characters. Similarly the re-use of stages could easily be effected without the division of the play. Most of the locations can be left without distinguishing characteristics as the characters themselves frequently indicate the locality to the audience. Coldewey also bases his argument on a number of narrative parallels in the play, but it could be argued that these are part of a larger pattern of parallels, several of which do not provide echoes of the first half in the second. Finally Coldewey's argument that the division reflects the two aspects of Mary's life – the private life and the role of saint – does not stand up to close analysis. The development towards sainthood is gradual throughout the play and much of it comes through her close association with Christ, which is depicted in the first half.

St Meriasek is another play which demands a place-and-scaffold type staging. Here there is clear evidence that the play was split into two halves in performance and we have the benefit of two diagrams, one for each of the two days over which the play was intended to be staged, found in the manuscript of the play and reproduced by Whitley Stokes in his edition (*100*, pp. 145, 266). This indicates thirteen scaffolds placed in a circular arrangement, with a central chapel for the first day. The play was very probably designed to be played in a Cornish round or *plen an gwary* (*421*, pp. 60–69). Each scaffold is identified by the name of a specific character, those characters who appear only on the first being replaced by those appearing only on the second, with the others retaining the same scaffolds on both days. There are strong indications in the text that action took place on the *platea* rather than on the scaffolds: the large number of directions for characters to descend and the numerous actions that clearly needed more space than the scaffolds could provide. The sheer number of scaffolds is another consideration. Given that there are thirteen in all, really large playing stages would have required an impractically large space. The fact that each scaffold has the name of a character suggests rather that they were intended as identi-fying structures rather than anything else. Named locations such as Meriasek's hermitage have no scaffold, and there is none for the saint at all. Most of the major characters parade (*pompare*) before engaging in the action. This consists of a self-identifying boast, probably delivered on the scaffold before the descent to the *platea*.

The *Play of the Sacrament* appears to have been designed for a place-and-scaffold production, with three scaffolds representing the merchant's house, the church and the Jew's house. It is not clear how big the scaffolds needed to be except that the Jew's house has to accommodate a table, though this could have been placed in front of the scaffold. That most of the action does take place on the scaffolds is indicated by the directions for entry into these. Several other items around which action takes place are not attributed in the stage directions to any specific location, but the technology required for the miracles associated with these objects makes it likely that they would have been placed at least adjacent to a scaffold, specifically that of the Jew's house, which may have been the central scaffold of the three, being the focus of most of the dramatic action. That at least some of the action takes place on the *platea* is indicated by some of the stage directions clearly indi-cating movement not confined to the named locations, such as 'Her he renneth wood [mad], with þe Ost in hys hond' (line 503, s.d.) and 'Here shall the lechys [doctor's] man come into þe place sayng:' (line 524, s.d.). Apart from the technology required for the miracles, the staging arrange-ments seem fairly simple, as befitting a travelling play.

Besides a presumed tendency to a place-and-scaffold arrangement, highly doubtful in the case of *The Conversion of St Paul*, there is little in the staging arrangements of the extant plays to suggest a consistent pattern which could be regarded as typical of saints' plays. In terms of length, narra-tive elaborateness and number of players, these works differ greatly despite their numerical paucity. What they do share and what is, from a technical point of view, particularly interesting about saints' plays is their consistent need to represent miracle. This places them among the most challenging and problematic examples of early drama from a technological point of view, as these miracles often face us with the problem of how they were first staged and what this indicates about currently available technology, particularly since details of these skills are not provided in the directions. Many of the miracles that occur in the plays are, of course, easy enough to stage through acting alone, such as the numerous acts of healing and resurrection which occur in all the pieces under discussion. However, all these plays contain other miracles in which *trompe l'œil* technology is required, such as the flash of lightning in *The Conversion of St Paul*; the burning of the pagan temple, the disappearance of the pagan priest and acolyte and the raising of Mary to heaven in *Mary Magdalen*; the appearance and taming of the dragon and the summoning of the fountain in *St Meriasek*; and the many miracles requiring staging in the *Play of the Sacrament*. The dramatisation of miracle is central to a form of drama that is concerned to represent the manifest power of God on earth and the audience's astonishment at the stage devices is arguably integral to the dramatic process of persuasion. It is mainly by analogy with contemporaneous continental practice, the technology of which is somewhat better known, that we are able to deduce the methods that might have been used to stage these miracles. This is effectively beyond the scope of the present chapter however, and is something that I have discussed in some detail elsewhere (346).

Although some of the identifying qualities of saints' plays might be seen to emerge from aspects of their staging, it is necessary to subject these plays to broader critical examination in order to discover the extent to which they could be seen to reveal a consistency in their ideas and their approach to the dramatisation of conversion and the role of miracle in hagiographical narratives. For instance, it could be argued that the central motif of conversion leads to an emphasis on structures of competing and conflicting authority systems in the plays, to and from which the subject is converted. To what extent this affects the structuring of the plays needs to be examined. The other dominant motif, miracle, also needs to be considered for the emphasis it places on the role of saints as the earthly manifestations of divine power or, more broadly, the earthly loci of cosmic conflict.

The Conversion of St Paul is narratively a fairly simple play. The principal features that characterise a saint's play – conversion and miracle – are already provided by the scriptural account of the conversion of St Paul and the playwright needed only to flesh out the story. The elements of dichotomy, contrast and conflicting claims to authority, which might be regarded as endemic to the dramatisation of a saint's legend, are here constructed in terms of the conflict between the authority of the Jewish priests, Caiaphas and Annas, and that of God, whose presence is manifest on the stage and whose power is also represented by Ananias. At the beginning of the play Caiaphas and Annas are the givers of the law which Saul pledges himself to carry out, and they speak in the same characteristically threatening language that Saul himself uses. After Saul is struck blind by lightning and God addresses him, divine power dominates until the end, not only in Saul's changed allegiance, but by God's direction of Ananias to perform another miracle in the restoration of Saul's sight, and in the appearance of the angel who warns Saul to escape persecution. After Saul's conversion,

Caiaphas and Annas appear only once more, towards the end of the play, to express their dismay and desire for vengeance, thus confirming their status as losers of a battle. An episode involving the demons Belial and Mercury has been added in the manuscript in a later hand, clearly principally to add some dramatic spice to the play, but this fits in well with the implicit argument since it, too, deals with diabolic disappointment and rage at the loss of a sinner's soul to God. This episode might be compared to the similar scene of diabolic rage in *Mary Magdalen*. The construction of the figure of Saul himself also contributes to the representation of the conflict of authority in the play. On entry Saul identifies himself by means of an elaborate boasting and threatening speech conventionally used to characterise pagan tyrants, and his subsequent speeches before his affliction continue in much the same vein, making recurrent reference to the pagan laws he upholds and the oppression of his Christian enemies. After his blinding he moves through terror and sorrow to a mood of contemplative resignation and thanks to God, and his development towards spiritual authority culminates in a sermon he delivers on appearing 'in hys dyscyplys wede' (line 502, s.d.). (Compare this with the entry in an apostolic role of Mary in *Mary Magdalen*, line 1335, s.d.) In this way the playwright quite economically depicts the change from Saul's claims to pagan authority and power, through a process of suffering and contemplation to the ultimate demonstration of his spiritual authority. The conflict of power and value systems as located in the subject is encapsulated in the fact that in the end Saul is the potential victim (though given angelic protection) of those very forces whose pagan laws he had been instrumental in enforcing at the outset. In this potential persecution there are elements of martyr narratives in both the threats of the Jews and the divine support of Saul. Stage spectacle in the form of pyrotechnic displays is also used quite effectively in the representation in manifest terms of the cosmic powers: the first is the 'feruent, wyth gret tempest' (line 182, s.d.) which strikes Saul down, the second comes at the beginning of the interpolated episode when the devils enter 'wyth thunder and fyre', and there are two more fiery events, including the disappearance of the devils 'wyth a fyrye flame, and a tempest' (line 501, s.d.). The same device is clearly used on all these occasions, giving rise to an implication of comparison: where fire demonstrates divine power in victory, it signifies empty fury in the demons.

Mary Magdalen also has as its subject a scriptural saint, but this play ambitiously deals with both the scriptural and the legendary life of its central character. It depicts Mary's fall into sin, her repentance and approach to Christ at the house of Simon the Leper, the resurrection of her brother Lazarus, Mary's sorrow after the crucifixion and her meeting with the risen Christ in the garden, her legendary disciplehood during which she converts the kingdom of Marcyll, her last years spent in hermitage in the desert being fed by angels and her final assumption into heaven. It is a large play with an extended list of characters and it has often been regarded as formless and sprawling. Certainly, it is episodic and Mary is the only character who is seen from the beginning to the end of the play, many having been discarded after one or two scenes. Moreover, the play combines not only apocryphal legend with scriptural account, but also allegorical with historical modes of representation. The work is, however, far more intricately structured than at first appears, and several principles of organisation might be seen to be at work here. The play can be regarded as having a double plot structure – the drama of the Passion and the drama of Mary – and the two are ultimately fused to enhance the sainthood of Mary. Tiberius, Herod and Pilate, who are all tyrannical figures concerned with the persecution and crucifixion of Christ, open the play, but Mary never comes into contact with them. Many scenes are involved exclusively with the drama of the Passion and appear to have little to do with the dramatisation of the life and career of Mary. However, the Passion drama is not simply tacked on to the story of Mary: the writer stresses those aspects of Christ's life and ministry that pertain especially to Mary, while omitting many aspects normally dramatised in other plays dealing with the subject, such as the trials before Pilate and Herod and the buffeting of Christ. Even the crucifixion takes place offstage. The presence of Mary herself is an important unifying element in the play. She makes her appearance very early, there are never more than three scenes together without her physical appearance onstage, and she is given just under a quarter of all the lines spoken. The structure of the work depends to some degree on keeping the focus on its central character, and since what it purports to do is depict the life and beatitude of that character, its structure is successful to the extent that it achieves that focus. The construction of the figure of Mary is particularly interesting for the adeptness with which it is done. We see Mary first not as a sinner but as a virtuous young woman. Her fall into sin is represented by means of an allegorical sequence in which she is besieged by sins during a period of grief for her father's death, which makes her vulnerable. The period of life in sin is extremely short and the writer avoids any salacious details, stressing Mary's naivety throughout. Her bitterness and contrition for her sins get much fuller treatment than her brief enjoyment of them. Her development through the play is from a position of passivity to one of active spiritual authority. She is at first dependent on her father, then led by the allegorical figures of sin, even literally in a dance at one point. On her conversion she transfers to a relationship of dependence on Christ, illustrated by her gratefulness for her personal salvation, her appeal to Christ when her brother dies and her sorrow after the Crucifixion, again relieved by Christ. Her growth out of this stage comes after the Ascension, when she enters with a disciple of her own. She talks authoritatively about the Ascension and the dispersal of the apostles. The next stage comes when she is sent to convert Marcyll. The legend has her fleeing persecution by the Jews and being set adrift in a boat with a number of others,[13] but in the play the writer emphasises her apostolic function by depicting her making a deliberate journey to undertake an evangelical mission and going alone. At this stage in the play she starts to preach sermons, at one point holding the stage for forty-five consecutive lines. Like many characters in the prose and verse saints' legends, she engages in debate with the pagan king. She also gains the ability to work miracles through prayer, which confirms her spiritual authority. She gives protection to the king and queen of Marcyll and effectively completes the move from being a protégée to a protector. The final stage of her spiritual development comes in the desert section of the play. Here her whole life becomes a miracle with her daily elevation by angels and feeding with manna. She becomes an object of devotion herself, and a priest enters to revere her. At her death, her assumption into heaven is very reminiscent of dramatic Assumptions of the Virgin, the culmination of a number of points in the play at which an association between Mary and the Virgin is implied.

Although the playwright manifests a strong interest in the spiritual biography of the saint and her development in terms of religious authority, this does not preclude him from representing her as a locus of cosmic conflict. Claims to sovereignty abound, and the idea of 'domynacyon' occurs throughout the play. An important study by J. W. Velz shows a fundamental conflict between rival claims to sovereignty: on the one hand the false ones of man, particularly in the figures of worldly magnificence whose boasts open the play, including Syrus the virtuous pagan father of Mary, and those of the three chief allegorical powers – the World, the Flesh and the Devil – and on the other hand the true claim of Christ (357). A later study of the images of the play identifies several references to and actions involving feeding and nourishment, and argues that food serves the double purpose of representing worldly preoccupations and conflicts, while providing images of spiritual nourishment (353). Both of these analyses are based on the dichotomies between worldly and spiritual or diabolic and divine, which are fundamental to this work, and indeed to any saint's drama concerned with conversion. The play moves from the ascendancy of worldly powers dramatically represented by the rants of Tiberius, Herod, Syrus and Pilate, all of whom make claims to wealth and power, to a deeper and more insidious level of evil in those of the World, the Flesh and the Devil, until the entry of Christ. This parallels Mary's entry in the context of worldly magnificence and comfort in her father's castle and, when that comfort fails her at her father's death, her move into the sphere of hell until she is redeemed. Thus the conflicts, both worldly and cosmic, have as their focus the soul of Mary herself: she is the battleground, and her fall and redemption are major battles in the war. The relationship between the human soul and the cosmic powers is one of dependence, and the play is replete with images of succour and sustenance. Despite the grandiose claims of the worldly wielders of power, the limitations of that power are shown by the two graphic portrayals of the deaths of Syrus and Lazarus and, more importantly, in the false consolation offered by the demonic powers to Mary in her grief. By contrast, Mary is not only the recipient of divine help at various points, but is herself a dispenser of such aid to the king and queen of Marcyll after their conversion. However, the most graphic illustration of the soul of Mary as a locus of cosmic conflict comes first in the allegorical siege of her castle by the Deadly Sins, and subsequently the *psychomachia* type scene of her conversion as she is asleep in the arbour. Although the Bad Angel is silent, he is present during the Good Angel's address to her. In terms of this conflict, the inclusion of the whole allegorical episode of the Seven Deadly Sins into a basically historical play can be justified as a precursor to the dramatisation a little further on of Christ's casting seven demons from Mary after her conversion, an episode which is scriptural. Here the demons are clearly to be identified with the Sins. The conflict of the cosmic powers is represented iconographically in the play, too. At the outset the focus is squarely on the scaffold or scaffolds used by the worldly and cosmic figures of evil. The final episode of the play takes place directly before and on the Heaven scaffold, whence Mary is winched to glory at the end.[14]

  Both parallels and contrasts are liberally used in the play to reinforce its unity and to articulate ideas. Some of these are inherent in the legend, while others are introduced by the writer. Some of these parallels are in actions, such as the conversions of Mary and of the king and queen of Marcyll, made more pointed by the writer's presentation of them, or the resurrections of Lazarus, Christ and the queen of Marcyll, for which it is quite possible to use the same stage locations. Some parallels are in forms of rhetoric. All the major pagan characters, as well as the allegorical figures of the World, the Flesh and the Devil, are introduced by means of self-glorifying boasts. The triumvirate of Tiberius, Herod and Pilate, the chief enemies of Christ, is thus associated with the diabolic trinity. Syrus, the father of Mary and the king of Marcyll are introduced in the same way, enabling the audience immediately to place them in the appropriate focus and integrating scriptural, legendary and allegorical characters in one mode of dramatic presentation. Important locations might also be paralleled in the play: the arbour or garden where Mary waits for her lovers becomes a powerful symbol which appears at important points in the play. In this scene it represents a garden of lust; in the *hortulanus* sequence the garden is reinterpreted allegorically by Christ in his speech to Mary:

> Mannys hartt is my garden here.
> Þerin I sow sedys of vertu all the ȝere.
> Þe fowle wedys and wycys I reynd vp be þe rote!   *vices*
> Whan þat gardyn is watteryd wyth terys clere,
> Than spryng vertuus, and smelle ful sote.   *sweet*
>
> (lines 1081–5)

Finally there is a contrast when Mary enters the wilderness towards the end of the play. This is the garden of religion. Again, it is possible to use the same place for all three locations.

St Meriasek compares with *Mary Magdalen* in that it is a play of some length and complexity, dealing with the life of its saintly hero to its end, and introducing in its highly episodic structure a large number of other characters on the way, yet possessing a considerable degree of coherence and formal order (see above, chapter 8). The work might be seen as encompassing three saint plays: apart from the life of Meriasek, it has a life of St Silvester and a miracle of the Virgin. Though the narrative is liberally sprinkled with conversions and, especially, miracles, the principal interest is in Meriasek's hagiographical career, and much in the play suggests that it may have been written to advance the status of this local saint. There is no question here of the subject's conversion to faith as in *The Conversion of St Paul* or *Mary Magdalen* since the saint is already the son of Christian parents. However, this excessive early zeal and high birth allow the writer to introduce a debate (between the saint wishing to maintain a chaste life and his father and the king, whose daughter he is offered in marriage) of the type found in several saints' legends, particularly those of women, such as SS Katharine and Justina. In many ways, Meriasek is a formula saint, distinguished as a character not by any particular quality of his own, but by the accretion of conventional saintly attributes. His asceticism is established early in the play when he refuses to eat on Friday, and is continued to the end, where it is revealed after his death that he slept on straw and wore a hair shirt under his episcopal garments. His unworldliness is indicated by his pointed refusal to consider any material reward for the healing of a nobleman, Count Globus, his resolute retirement into reclusivity and his reluctance to take up the post of bishop. He is also given a number of ministering functions, such as healing the sick and clothing the poor. Quite apart from the miracles he performs, his arguments with various individuals throughout the play, such as his teacher, his kinsmen, the pagan Teudar and the ecclesiastical patron, the Count of Vannes, give him an authority and spiritual singlemindedness which mark Meriasek out. Like the heroine of *Mary Magdalen*, Meriasek is fed by angels with manna, an action which iconographically confers upon him what is possibly the pinnacle of divine recognition during his life of his position as saint.

It is worth noting that his actual presence in the play effectively mirrors the reclusive figure that is presented in the text, since a great deal of the action takes place without him. The life of St Silvester, which is interwoven with Meriasek's biography, functions as something of a parallel, many of Silvester's deeds echoing those of Meriasek. It is easier to understand this interweaving of two or more apparently distinct narratives when one bears in mind the transposition of narrative motifs that occurs in the construction of prose and verse legends; the principles that are at work here are not wholly different. The way in which the figure of Meriasek is threaded through a play replete with turbulent action achieves the dual purpose of creating a dramatically respectable piece out of the life of a basically dull saint, making this very lack of presence into the virtue of spiritual quietude.

Miracle and conversion are both significantly present as major recurrent events in the play. All the conversions follow or are connected with the exercise of divine power in the form of miracle, such as the conversion and healing of Constantine by Silvester, the conversion of the robbers after Meriasek has brought fire upon them and the conversion of the pagan magi after Silvester has tamed the dragon. However, this is not a play which deals with a conversion that leads eventually to sainthood, as its saint heroes are devout from the outset. Contrasts between piety and evil are represented much more in relation to the conflict between Christians and pagan evildoers, such as Teudar, than within the life histories of particular individuals. With the slight exception of Constantine there is no real exploration of the process of change of heart, no real psycho-moral crisis. Miracle in the play is used mostly as an indication of saintliness and is closely associated with the role of saints as the agents of divine power. The recurrent presence of heavenly figures – Christ, the Virgin, the apostles and angels – presumably all mounted upon or descending from the Heaven scaffold, helps to emphasise the function of miracles as expressions of this power. The contrasting lack of power of pagan gods is indicated at various points, most notably in the failure of pagan magicians to tame a dragon, something that St Silvester subsequently succeeds in doing. This episode, arguably of folk-play origin, is squarely in the tradition of contests of potency which can be found not only in the saint's play (compare the contest between Mary and the King of

Marcyll in *Mary Magdalen*), but in saints' legends as well. Most of the miracles are those of healing, which are able to be staged through acting alone, but a few involve theatrical feints and machinery. These are strategically placed through the play to add to the spectacle at regular points in the action: on the first day of the play's duration Meriasek causes a spring to burst up, he later tames a wolf and then brings fire on a group of robbers. On the second day the Virgin rescues a boy from captivity by firing the prison in which he is being held, and the even more spectacular dragon episode takes place a little later.

The *Play of the Sacrament* is not the biography of a saint and in fact contains no saint figure at all, but it is concerned with sacred miracles, which lead to conversion. Since it is the only play of its kind in English, it fits probably more comfortably into the genre of saint and miracle drama than into any other. It dramatises a legend that concerns the abuse of the Host by a group of Jews who buy a sacramental wafer from a Christian merchant. Their treatment of it provokes a series of miracles including the bleeding of the Host, the inextricable attachment of one of the men's hands to the wafer, the boiling over with blood of a cauldron into which they cast the bread, the riving asunder of an oven and the appearance of an image of Christ, who addresses the Jews. As a result of these experiences, they convert to Christianity, and the Christian confesses his treachery and is absolved. Also included is a rather redundant comic episode with a quack doctor and his assistant, which may be an interpolation. The story is an old one, existing in several versions on the continent, some of them dramatic. The legend of the desecration of the Host appears in a fourteenth-century Italian text, Giovanni Vilani's *Cronaca*, and is recorded in dramatised form in Italy, the Netherlands and France in the fifteenth and sixteenth centuries. Whereas the English play sets the action in 'the famous cité of Eraclea' in the forest of Aragon in 1461, the sixteenth-century French version places it in thirteenth-century Paris. The Jews in the French version are burned in the end and the Christian betrayer is a poor woman. The desecration of the Host episode is set in a longer narrative, and there are several other differences between the two. What the French play does not include is the episode with the doctor, which may have folk-play origins (85, p. lxxv).

The *Play of the Sacrament*'s commitment to the twofold aim of saints' plays, the representation of conversion and the depiction of divine miracle, is indicated early on in the manuscript, directly after the banns, when the play is announced as 'þe Play of þe Conuersyon of Ser Jonathas þe Jewe by Myracle of þe Blyssed Sacrament'. Conversion as the switch from one mode of life to another is not simply a process which takes place in the narrative, but is actually suggested by the contrasting rhetoric of the play.

While the centre of the play is taken up largely with action, the beginning and the end have long speech sequences. It opens with the self-identifying boast of Aristorius, the Christian merchant, and this is followed by that of Jonathas, the principal Jew. Both these speeches are alliteratively ringing and vauntingly self-aggrandising as well as containing an element of threat against those who oppose the speaker. While this is perfectly logical for characterising the 'pagan' Jonathas, it is curious that it is used for Aristorius too, as this type of boast is consistently used in early drama for the characterisation of pagan or diabolic characters. However, the rhetoric serves a dramatically and ideologically useful purpose here. Not only does it help to compromise Aristorius even before he has stolen the Host and done the deal with Jonathas, but it contributes to the weight of pagan rhetoric which dominates this section of the play. In the central section of the play, by contrast, most of the speeches are not in the form of long rhetorical passages but are concerned rather with the actions in hand, until the conversion of the Jews, at which point they become very formally devotional. This starts with the address to the Jews of the image of Christ and their contrite responses to it, all replete with Latin scriptural quotations. The rest of the play is dominated by the repentance of Aristorius and the ministration of the bishop, who enters for the first time at this stage to add to the representation of Christian authority. The language here is very aureate, quite aside from the liberal dosage of Latin quotation, and constitutes an interesting contrast to the alliterative bluster of the opening scenes. The dichotomy so characteristic of saints' plays and legends, between the power of paganism/diabolism on the one hand, and that of Christianity on the other, is consistently sustained by this contrasting rhetoric in the play.

The element of the miraculous is also very prominent as the central action consists, apart from (in narrative terms) a fairly irrelevant comic episode with a doctor and his boy, of a series of remarkable staged miracles, spectacular in their dramatic effects but also significant for the images they create. Redemption through the body and blood of Christ is the Christian concept that is challenged by the Jews who purchase the Host from Aristorius, and the emotive issue of the physical torments of Christ are also to the fore. Thus the physical presence of blood in the three most powerful of the miracles – the bleeding of the Host, the bloody boiling over of the cauldron and the sanguinary riving asunder of the oven, to reveal a bleeding image of Christ – helps to underline two of the major ideas in the play. The gore provides a sensational picture of the Jews' torture of Christ, and it is almost literally through the blood of Christ that the Jews are saved. The play thus successfully combines sensational dramatic spectacle with sound theology effectively popularised.

Each of these plays has a comic element to a greater or lesser extent, and, interestingly, these show certain similarities to each other. All are contained within specific episodes of the plays, often with little immediately apparent significance for the work as a whole. *The Conversion of St Paul* has a brief sequence involving banter between a servant and an ostler which is incidental to the narrative and necessitates a complete change of tone. Such banter is also found between two comic pairs in *Mary Magdalen*, a pagan priest and his acolyte, and a shipman and his boy, both pairs probably played by the same actors doubling. As in *The Conversion of St Paul*, vulgar insult is the currency of conversation here. In the case of the priest and his boy there is additionally a dog-Latin parody of the Mass which does help to illustrate the crudity and salaciousness of pagan worship prior to the exposure and disgracing of the pagan gods by Mary. *St Meriasek* has little that is straightforwardly comic: apart from the wry comments of Meriasek's teacher early in the play, there is only really a bit of a banter between the quack doctor called to heal Constantine and his apprentice, Jenkin. In the *Play of the Sacrament* it is again the doctor and his assistant who provide the comic sequence, apart from whatever comic potential is exploited in the discomfiture of the Jews. The somewhat extended appearance of this pair contributes little to the development of the narrative. In all of these plays, in fact, the comic episodes are provided by low-life figures who are extremely peripheral to the main action. Their inclusion may have been largely for the purposes of varying the tone and increasing the dramatic attractiveness of the plays, but in works which construct such stark dichotomies of good and evil they also supply a leavening element of unregenerate humanity, neither tyrannically evil nor saintly, but somewhat *hors de combat*. They also furnish some potential for satire on certain social and professional types. In all these respects the comic figures of these plays bear some relation to those in the scriptural drama.

In addition to the four plays that might be considered to constitute the extant genre of early saints' plays in Britain, one further work that could possibly be regarded as falling into this category is Lewis Wager's *Life and Repentaunce of Marie Magdaleine*.[15] This is a curious work which, if it merits inclusion in a discussion of saints' drama at all, does so only as the sole example of a type of Protestant saint's play. It was written in around 1566, about thirty years after the break with Rome, and it is a telling reflection on Mary Magdalene's status as an apostolic figure that a play with this title could be written at this time at all. The play, in fact, makes considerable concession to the new Protestant ethic in both its form and ideas. It dispenses entirely with the non-scriptural legend and insofar as it deals with her life at all it confines itself to those scriptural details that are narrowly relevant to the process of repentance, which is the central idea of the play. Consistent with Protestant ideas, the stress is on faith, and miracle is rigidly excluded. Although the play does, of course, contain scriptural characters, it is largely allegorical drama. The historical figures – even Christ – mingle freely with the allegorical ones and are themselves to a large extent allegoricised. Although it cannot be said to be in all respects a morality play, the piece does follow the traditional pattern of the moral play: temptation – fall – repentance – struggle – salvation.

The play opens with the Vice figure, Infidelitie, who makes his conventional self-revealing confession to the audience. When Mary enters she is shrewish and not the simple *tabula rasa* of the moral play Everyman figures. She is concerned about her garments and complains about her tailor, thereby proclaiming the worldliness of her preoccupations. The dialogue reveals her as a noblewoman and the owner of the castle of Magdalene, but there are no other biographical details. As in the Digby play, there is a conspiracy of the sins to corrupt her, which they do largely through the agency of Infidelitie. After a period in which she rhetorically embraces sin, Mary's conscience is pricked by a character called Love of God, and he is followed by another called Knowledge of Sin. The process of moral realisation is thus dramatised allegorically before the meeting with Christ, but when Christ enters he and Infidelitie oppose each other in debate about Mary, like good and bad angels in a *psychomachia* contest. The play is interesting for the way in which a specific scriptural episode is given an allegorical treatment, and specifically for the Protestant interpretation of the process of conversion. This work, however, signals fairly clearly the full stop that the Reformation put to English saints' plays in general, and more particularly the tradition represented by the four plays discussed here.[16]

These few extant early saints' plays in Britain constitute a tantalising sample of a largely lost dramatic genre which, to judge from the little evidence that is left to us, was exceptional in a number of ways. Ranging as it did over scriptural and legendary material as well as a great deal of invented narrative, it was a type of drama which was characterised by a considerable degree of narrative freedom and a great deal of variety in its subject matter. It was therefore perhaps more resistant than most other dramatic forms to any urge to conform to certain formulae of writing and presentation, as its capacity easily to encompass a juxtaposition of allegorical and historical modes of dramatisation suggests. The genre is also probably one of the most challenging forms of early drama as far as staging is concerned, since it not only includes works of enormous breadth and complexity, involving historical, allegorical, celestial and infernal figures, but often requires theatrical feints of a sometimes remarkable degree of sophistication to achieve its narrative and philosophical ends. The unfortunate fact of the extinction of the vast majority of plays of this type has resulted in an unjustified neglect of the position of the saint's play in early English theatrical culture, and it is only in recent years that scholarly work on saint drama has begun to redress this tendency.

NOTES

1 For the St Nicholas play (thirteenth century) see Carleton Brown, 'An Early Mention of a St Nicholas Play', *SP* 38 (1931), 594–601. The St Katharine play (twelfth century) is discussed by C. B. C. Thomas, 'The Miracle Play at Dunstable', *MLN* 32 (1917), 337–44.

2 Saints' plays to 1558 are listed, with further references, in Lancashire (4, *passim*). See also R. M. Wilson, *The Lost Literature of Medieval England*, 2nd edn (London: Methuen, 1970), pp. 209–33.

3 See Manfred Görlach, *The Textual Tradition of the South English Legendary* (Leeds: University of Leeds, School of English, 1974), especially the map on p. 305, showing the dialectal distribution of the manuscripts. On the *Legendary* as a form of drama, see K. Bjelland, 'Defining the *South English Legendary* as a Form of Drama', *CD* 22 (1988), 227–43.

4 Compare, for example, the legends of SS Barbara, Cecilia, Christine, Agatha, Lucy and Dorothy in the *Legenda Aurea*. Male saints who suffered torture include SS Denis (Dionysus), Sebastian and Lawrence.

5 Examples include the debates between St Barbara and the judge, St Agatha and Quintinianus, and St Cecilia and Almachius, in their respective stories in the *Legenda Aurea*.

6 For example the representations in paintings and manuscript illuminations of the tortures of SS Katharine, Lawrence and Denis; see the discussion of these and others by Davidson (344).

7 An interesting illustration of the dramatisation of such sensational torture appears in the miniature showing the martyrdom of St Apollonia in *The Hours of Etienne Chevalier*, painted by Jean Fouquet in *c.* 1455 (see above p. 58, and illustration 7).

8 Accounts of saints' plays in France will be found in 27 and 349, with list of examples, pp. 170–2.

9 One might compare here also the representation of Mary Magdalene in the two plays in MS Oxford, Bodleian, E Museo 160 (*c.* 1520), known as *Christ's Burial* and *Christ's Resurrection* (in 84). In these two short pieces her role is almost exclusively that of a highly emotional figure of contrition.

10 John Wasson (351), for instance, has argued that the saint's play rather than the morality play might be considered the proper forerunner of Elizabethan drama. Glynne Wickham has even suggested that saints' plays may have been 'the parents and not the children of the mysteries and moralities' (352, p. 101).

11 This is the suggestion of the recent EETS editors, who quote the insertion of the Belial episode as evidence that the play went through two phases in its life (84, p. xxvii). The ascription to Chelmsford derives from John Coldewey's argument that it was acted there in the 1560s (242).

12 Raymond Pentzell suggested that *The Conversion of St Paul* has not one *platea* but three: see his debate with Mary del Villar in *Theatre Survey* 14 (1973), 76–89.

13 Both the *Legenda Aurea* and the *South English Legendary* describe the flight and setting adrift of Mary, and other saints. Thus the former: '. . . when the disciples were departed, S. Maximim, Mary Magdalene and Lazarus her brother, Martha her sister, Marcelle, chamberer of Martha and S. Cedony . . . all these together, and many other Christian men were taken of the miscreants and put in a ship in the sea, without any tackle or rudder, for to be drowned' (*The Golden Legend or Lives of the Saints as Englished by William Caxton*, 3 vols., ed. F. S. Ellis (London: Kelmscott, 1900; repr., 4 vols., New York, 1973), vol. IV, p. 76).

14 A report on a modern production of the play at the University of Colorado, Boulder, brings out the iconographic significance of the movement of the action across the acting area in the course of the play: 'Our production showed us the central unity of the play, the unity of Mary's pilgrimage from sin to beatitude, a pilgrimage whose path is thematically reinforced by the acting area itself. At the beginning of the play, Hell dominates; in the middle, action spreads across the entirety of the 'place'; at the end, Heaven directs the action' (John R. Elliott Jr, 'Census of Medieval Drama Productions', *RORD* 21 (1978), 96).

15 Lewis Wager, *The Life and Repentaunce of Marie Magdalene*, ed. F. I. Carpenter (Chicago: Chicago University Press, 1902).

16 See, however, Peter Happé's discussion of the Protestant adaptation of the saint's play (347), and John Wasson's argument for 'secular' saints' plays in the Elizabethan era (351).

11

JOHN MARSHALL

Modern productions of medieval English plays

The casual reader of academic journals given over to medieval matters could be forgiven for thinking that more medieval drama has been produced in the twentieth century than was in its own time. Notices of future and reviews of past productions occupy a significant section of journals such as *Medieval English Theatre (METh)* and *Research Opportunities in Renaissance Drama (RORD)* in proper recognition of the current academic and theatrical interest in the performance of medieval plays.[1] Although the casual reader's impression is almost certainly false, created as much by the modern exercise of practical criticism as by the limited number of surviving medieval texts and records of performance, it is true that this century has seen an unprecedented interest in the revival of medieval drama. Indeed, the committed theatre-goer, as opposed to the casual reader, could probably have seen, within the last decade or two, a performance of almost every extant medieval English play text.

The occurrence of medieval drama revivals in the twentieth century may seem an historical phenomenon that encapsulates in time a single purpose, but it would be misleading to assume that the motives of revivalists were always the same, even though it may be possible to detect three generally distinct phases within the movement. The earliest productions of William Poel and Nugent Monck owed much to the antiquarian spirit of the time and the desire of these two actor/producers to extend their practical exploration of Elizabethan theatre texts and conventions of staging into what they and scholars of the time saw as the period of Shakespearean ancestry. Poel's Elizabethan Stage Society production of *Everyman* in 1901 was remarkable not only for its novelty (the first revival of a medieval play) but also for its commercial and partial critical success (311, pp. 222–5).[2] Various aspects of the production and cuts in the text, however, suggest that in spite of Poel's religious scepticism the informing principles of the production were essentially Victorian rather than medieval. Unfortunately Poel would not be the last director to allow a sense of decorum and an ill-conceived notion of audience expectation and response to obscure the nature and demands of a medieval text, leading to the compromise between authenticity and accessibility which rarely satisfies the interests of either.

If the initial impulse to revive was antiquarian and exploratory in nature, the movement – if it can be unified as such – was sustained by the early twentieth-century reawakening of interest in religious and verse drama, which found notable expression and critical recognition in the work of T. S. Eliot. Its influence on E. Martin Browne, culminating in the 1951 Festival of Britain production of the York cycle, was especially significant in the area of medieval drama revival. It was this performance that led to the cycle becoming the focus of the triennial York Festival. Enjoyed by a large number of people, most of whom will have no other experience of medieval drama, the play can be seen to fulfil one of its original purposes in bringing together a community of participants and spectators in celebration of both God and City. Given the coincidence of intention, it is, perhaps, a regret not just of purists that the production in the ruins of St Mary's Abbey on fixed staging bears such little resemblance to what is now known of the performance conditions in medieval and Tudor York. What is more, the success of the Festival productions has encouraged other cities keen to promote their heritage to imitate the style and form of presentation adopted at York, creating a popular impression of medieval drama which is somewhat detached from reality.[3]

This is not to underestimate the commitment and energy of those involved or to minimise some of the qualities and insights gained from such productions. Neither is it to insist that every production should take the form of an archaeological reconstruction serving the interests of research, but it is clear from the revival of drama from other periods that productions grounded securely in an understanding of performance conditions and conventions are, all other things being equal, only likely to benefit the quality of performance and experience of the audience.

In many ways it is the testing of this knowledge in practice that inspired the third and most recent phase of modern productions. Although an oversimplification of the case, the phase coincides with the establishment of drama departments in universities and colleges and a new recognition of and concentration upon the theatrical as well as the literary qualities of the plays. Reinforced by the research and publication of works such as Glynne Wickham's *Early English Stages*, with the more recent development of the *REED* volumes making available previously unknown or difficult to access records of performance, it has been possible to undertake productions in which staging, costume, masking and so forth are to some extent authenticated by evidence. Since the mid 1970s the emphasis on 'original staging' has principally encouraged production of the cycles where the evidence is fullest but it has also inspired attempts to reconstruct the performance of plays such as *Wisdom* and *Mary Magdalen*, where close attention to stage directions and the application of research findings in connection with other plays has resulted in significant discoveries (476).

Although research and academic interest has played a leading role in the recent revival of medieval drama it is by no means the sole factor responsible for its current popularity. The success of a theatrical event depends upon more than the satisfaction of academics seeing their research take practical form. It is undoubtedly true that they often constitute a fair proportion of the audience for these productions, but reviewers frequently remark upon the broad social and age spectrum of the audience and their level of engagement, particularly at street performances, which recreate the potential for casual attendance. There is clearly something in the nature and structure of medieval drama and its relationship with community and audience that generates popular appeal. In this context it is perhaps significant, rather than simply coincidental, that two of the major developments in theatre in the past twenty years seem to have much in common with some aspects of medieval drama. The community play, given focus by Ann Jellicoe and drawing on the skills of dramatists as renowned as Howard Barker and David Edgar, seeks to involve as many local people as possible, with enabling assistance from some professionals, in creating a play that celebretes the history and traditions of the community (473). Without being sidetracked into detail, it is possible to see very real connections between the purposes and processes of such undertakings and the production of medieval Corpus Christi cycles. The satisfaction to be derived from engaging in activity dependent upon cooperative skills and energy for its success and one in which corporate identity is reaffirmed has evidently not diminished as much in 500 years as some social critics and politicians would have us believe. What is obvious here but worth re-emphasising is that Corpus Christi plays were and modern community plays are undertaken largely by amateurs, with professional assistance sought only in areas essential for the technical proficiency of the performance.

In the case of fully professional performances connections can also be made between those companies that presented, among other things, moral interludes and some of the small-scale touring work of the alternative/fringe theatre movement since 1968. It is, for example, probably similar economic and practical, rather than artistic, factors which tend to restrict both types of company to five or six members, thereby making doubling a necessary theatrical convention shared by both. More fundamental, though, is the way in which the religious commitment and didactic intention of much medieval drama produces a type of theatre that echoes in the forms of more recent political theatre. John McGrath, one of the most influential exponents of the latter and founder of 7.84 theatre company describes, in his series of lectures on popular theatre, the styles, techniques and devices evolved from the tradition of working-class entertainment that characterise the company's work (475). He does this at one point by describing 'some fairly generalized differences between the demands and tastes of bourgeois and of working class audiences'. Recognising them to be highly contentious he nevertheless lists nine differences covering the areas of directness, comedy, music, emotion, variety, effect, immediacy and localism (of material and of identity (475), pp. 53–60). He provides examples of each difference and, while it is not appropriate to discuss them in detail here, it is remarkable that without reference to, and possibly even knowledge of, medieval drama he accurately identifies many of the features now recognised as being instrumental not only in the effective communication of the message of medieval drama but also in the popular appeal of the medium. This similarity of stylistic features in types of theatre separated by time and ideology is perhaps not as surprising as one might initially think. Both have clear and declared intentions which go beyond the mere distraction of their audience, and both are aware of the need to achieve their brand of 'profit' by means of popular 'pleasure'.

The realisation that medieval plays were not only popular in their own time but have the ability to entertain more than those predisposed by a sense of history, religion or scholarship has recently been confirmed by some professional productions which have not only received critical acclaim but have also achieved a degree of commercial success. The work of the Medieval Players in building up a large and loyal following for medieval and Tudor plays is the clearest demonstration of the wider appeal of at least some medieval drama in crossing national, social and educational boundaries.

Further justification for placing medieval drama in the popular category came with the enormous success of the National Theatre's production of *The Mysteries* (see illustration 22). Starting life as an Easter Saturday performance of the *Crucifixion* episodes on the National Theatre terraces in 1977, the project grew to encompass separate performances of *The Passion* (1977), *The Nativity* (1980) and *Doomsday* (1985) before being presented in sequence at the Cottesloe Theatre in 1985 and subsequently being transferred to the Lyceum Theatre, where it was also filmed for Channel Four (487). Whilst one may not entirely agree with translator and adapter Tony Harrison's remark that 'these are local northern classics that have been taken away from northerners and betrayed, made genteel' (474, p. 6), it was clear to those who attended the performances that the resources and skills of a major professional theatre company contributed immensely to the realisation

22   The York *Crucifixion* from *The Mysteries*, National Theatre, London, 1977–85.

of the plays' theatrical energy and brilliance to an extent perhaps not seen before in modern times, and justifiably making *The Mysteries* one of the most significant and talked-about theatrical events of the 1980s.[4]

If Tony Harrison and director Bill Bryden were not entirely responsible for rescuing the cycle plays from genteel betrayal their production did raise important questions about the limitations of some original-staging, predominantly amateur performances. While the professional performances provide ample evidence that medieval drama still works in performance for more than a coterie audience, it is apparent that the vast majority of modern productions are the work of non-professionals, either local amateur groups contributing to a cycle production or student productions. Because these productions are often initiated by those engaged in research, it is from them that much can be learned, but they are not without their problems. In the case of large-scale cycle productions the situation often requires groups of varying interest, enthusiasm and experience to participate on the original guild model of taking responsibility for an individual pageant. Such arrangements have much to commend them but the organisation of these events is awesome, and resources rarely extend to the provision of individual specialist assistance. Consequently standards of production and acting vary considerably and so, potentially more damagingly, do levels of understanding. Compounded by limited funds, some of the presentations, whilst fun for the participants, and no less valuable for that, can be almost counter-productive in reinforcing erroneous notions of naivety and primitivism. This may seem harsh, but records relating to the organisation and preparation of civic drama clearly indicate that the cycles were undertaken with enormous care, adequate finance and an almost frightening degree of quality control – circumstances increasingly difficult to reproduce in an amateur or academic context. This is not to suggest in any way that much that is good has not come out of revival productions, since for the most part they are thoroughly enjoyable occasions in which important questions are raised, new ideas stimulated and speculation confirmed or challenged. But it is noticeable that the quality of performance is often the most persuasive factor affecting the reception of an idea. In a related way, student productions, when part of a curriculum, necessarily give priority to the educational needs and development of the participants, which may conflict with the more straightforward task of maximising an audience's enjoyment or of proving a point.[5]

There are, of course, other problems in presenting medieval drama in the twentieth century in the hope of learning more about how the plays worked when originally performed. Not least is the question of text and language. Even the most ambitious projects have found it necessary to edit or more ruthlessly cut passages or whole pageants. In some cases this is simply a matter of expediency and practicality. Few modern audiences, without some vested interest, are prepared to sit through *The Castle of Perseverance* in its entirety or commit a whole day to the performance of a complete cycle. Cuts of a different order, such as Poel's excision of references to 'Fellowship's offer of a woman to Everyman, and the allegations of Knowledge regarding the illegitimate children of sinful priests' (311, p. 222) and the deletion of all anti-Semitic references from the Towneley text for the Toronto production in 1985,[6] owe more to changes in attitudes than in stamina. Cuts in the text for reasons of reduction to manageable length, where they are not detrimental to the structure or meaning of the plays, may be excused on the grounds of modern levels of physical tolerance and concentration and, kept within reason, probably do not dramatically alter the experience of the plays. Having said that, it is important not to underestimate an audience's staying power or to ignore the lesson to be learned from cycle reconstruction of the quality of endurance: the sheer scale of witnessing a day-long performance produces a sensation quite unlike any other theatrical experience and distinctly transforms for the audience the relationship between spectating and participating. Furthermore, as Sarah Carpenter has pointed out, the playing of a whole cycle has 'the effect of reducing the focus on any single play, and bringing out the powerful connections between different plays in the cycle' (480, p. 49). Inevitably this, and much else, is lost where cutting involves reducing a cycle to the convenience of a three-hour evening performance or disregards essential elements of the narrative.[7]

The question of whether to modernise the pronunciation or idiom of the original text or to attempt a reconstruction of medieval speech is one that concerns all directors of medieval plays (477, pp. 250–52). For plays with relatively uncomplicated plots which are conveyed as much through action as by speech, the use of original pronunciation does not seem to inhibit enjoyment or understanding. In other circumstances where speeches are long and theologically complex and where characters tend to stand and speak at rather than to each other the desire for authenticity can be at the expense of comprehension. Almost every alternative imaginable has been tried at some time but the solution to the problems of length and language most commonly adopted is that succinctly described by David Mills in a review of *The Castle of Perseverance* at Manchester: 'the text, shortened and modernized was an intelligent compromise, retaining the rhythms of the original and communicating efficiently at the expense of occasional and probably inevitable stylistic incongruities'.[8]

The distance between a modern audience and the original performance of medieval drama is not just one of vocabulary and pronunciation. It is also one of context. What distinguishes medieval drama from that of our own time as much as anything else is its religious sense of festive occasion. No amount of carnival trappings is going to reproduce the essentially spiritual dimension of the original performances and one must accept that this represents a major omission from even the most rigorous recreations of original staging. Unavoidable and regrettable as this loss may be, it probably does not constitute such a serious distortion of the plays as some of the directorial responses to the loss of relevance of the play's religious content. Undeniably, religion plays a less significant role in the lives of a modern audience than was the case when the plays were written, but this discrepancy is not dissolved by simply humanising the issues, contemporising the setting or over-exploiting the comedy.[9] This is a quite different issue from that of modern-dress production, which can be quite successful but seems to be a consequence of directors either underestimating their audience or failing to trust their material. This is not meant to sound like a plea for undue reverence or the suppression of innovation and experiment – far from it – rather it comes from the simple belief that a production of medieval religious drama must treat its audience as intelligent Christian adults, whether they are or not. By starting from such a premise it is unlikely that directors and actors will be tempted to achieve spurious relevance though acts of gimmickry. An alternative approach to the question of context – but as damaging to enjoyment as gimmicks are to intelligence – are productions in which bogus authenticity substitutes for considered reconstruction. Though less common than meretricious productions, they are nevertheless just as thoughtless and insulting to an audience. Attempts to recreate a formal manner of delivery only by the use of bold and mechanical gesture with exclamatory speech patterns while ignoring other more intimate and subtle demands of the text simply alienates an audience in the 'I wish I was somewhere else' sense rather than the Brechtian use of the term.[10]

Location is a further aspect of the context which separates modern revivals from original performances. If the sense of occasion was a more essential feature of medieval drama than it is today then so, too, was the sense of place. Even for modern productions the playing of Chester at Leeds, or York at Toronto is an away game, and with all the advantages to be gained from being at home, and in spite of considerable efforts, it has still not been possible to present a complete cycle in the circumstances of time and place approximating to the original performances. This has to do with the bureaucracies of local government rather than the convenience of those organising the cycle revivals. It is, for example, quite surprising, given the pride with which York promotes its heritage, that the authorities have not yet given permission to close the appropriate streets to traffic for twenty-four hours in order to present a fully processional performance on wagons along the original route.

A first attempt at achieving the right plays in the right place was the presentation of eight pageants from the Chester cycle in the city streets in 1983. Although this proved an illuminating and rewarding experience, even here the twentieth century imposed its own unique limitations on reconstruction, with traffic noise turning speech to shouts and parked cars preventing the full use of what, even without them, would have been a

23–25   The York *Crucifixion*, wagon production at the Minster Gates station, York, 1992: raising the cross, placing the cross in the mortice, Christ crucified. Players from Bretton Hall College, Wakefield, directed by Philip Butterworth.

26   The York *Harrowing of Hell*, wagon production at the station in Low Petergate, York, 1992.

27   The York *Resurrection*, wagon production at the station in Stonegate, York, 1992. Joculatores Lancastriensis, directed by Meg Twycross.

28   Masked actor (Christ, holding the soul of the Virgin) from the wagon production of the York *Death of the Virgin*, Low Petergate, York, 1988. The Unicorns of Copenhagen, directed by Lene Christensen, Dennis Omø and Birgitte Lomborg.

29   The York *Coronation of the Virgin*, wagon production at the station in Low Petergate, York, 1988. The York Lords of Misrule, directed by Paul Toy.

truncated route.[11] There are many aspects of medieval drama concerning which lack of evidence sets a limit on knowledge, but one of the few things about which there is a degree of certainty is the pageant route at York (*170*, *174*) and, to a lesser extent, Chester (*185*). Recent opportunities (in 1988 and 1992) to produce parts of the York cycle along a section of the original processional route have thrown up a wealth of new ideas, problems, and pleasures (see above, chapter 3, pp. 98–100; *478*, *479*, *488*, *490*).

Perhaps the difference between outdoor and indoor performance has an even more fundamental effect upon an audience's experience than the accuracy of location. Commerce and climate may be the main reasons for giving outdoor plays in indoor venues, but the implications for changes in performance are quite considerable. The effects of such change are particularly noticeable when the weather is responsible for making the transition in mid-performance, as it was at Leeds in 1983 for the production of the Chester cycle. The intention was to perform the cycle over three days, as in the sixteenth century, on decorated wagons at three stations in the university precinct. The first day saw the realisation of these ambitions, but for the second and third days rain drove plays and audience indoors, where the former became 'leisurely and emotive' while the latter behaved with new-found reverence. It seemed that the actors took their tonal cue from the conditioned response of the newly-enclosed audience in becoming 'slower, more expansively self-indulgent'.[12] It may be that professional actors would have been less intimidated, and indeed less disappointed, by the change in atmosphere brought on by a change in venue, but it is clear from such experiences that audiences behave quite differently watching a play inside than they do when part of an outdoor event. It is also the case that texts intended for outdoor performance contain within their structure and in their devices an acknowledgement of open-air scale almost impossible to give full expression to in the more intimate surroundings of a theatre or hall. This does not mean that indoor performances of outdoor plays are always negative affairs. On the contrary, they can offer new and different insights into the play. Meg Twycross identifies some of the different qualities, when comparing the outdoor Toronto performance of *The Castle of Perseverance* (1979; see illustrations 30–32) (*483*) with the indoor production of Philip Cook's at Manchester (1981):

> it [Toronto] was spectacular, sweeping . . . on the whole declamatory, declarative and flat; while Philip's much smaller-scale indoor production was more subtle, the characterization stronger and more detailed, and the climaxes better engineered, but missed out on the grand-scale pomp and pageantry.[13]

What this all, rather obviously, points to is that choice of venue is a highly

30 *The Castle of Perseverance*, Toronto, 1979. Poculi Ludique Societas, directed by David Parry.

31 *The Castle of Perseverance*, Toronto, 1979: Hell scaffold.

32 *The Castle of Perseverance*, Toronto, 1979: Death.

significant feature in the sympathetic or otherwise realisation of the medieval text and will be an important contributing factor in the audience's reception of and response to the performance.[14]

The twin problems of furnishing an appropriate religious and location context for the revival of medieval drama often find a compromise solution in the selection of a church or cathedral for the performance, although initially satisfying in seeming to provide ready-made compensation for the lack of religious occasion, it rarely is the right location either in terms of historical accuracy for most of the surviving English plays or in terms of atmosphere and actor–audience relationship. If being in a building reduces audiences to reverential voyeurs responding with polite applause at conventionally acceptable moments, then the even more powerful conditioning of the church elevates this to a form of worship. Whilst for some plays like *Wisdom*, for example, the liturgical and processional associations of church performance can be a useful gain, for others it can negate more than it offers. A specific problem associated with performances of modern pronunciation texts in churches is the acoustic tendency they have to enhance and solemnise the sung Latin word and to jumble and distort the spoken English. Again, for plays in which processions or splendour of pageantry are dominant features this may not matter too much, but for plays in which character and spoken idea are paramount lack of verbal comprehension is a serious defect. In passing, though, it might be worth speculating on how influential the factor of acoustics was in the complex development of vernacular drama and the church.

It may seem from the discussion so far that modern productions of medieval drama are fraught with potential pitfalls and more inclined to failure than success. Such an impression would be an unfair distortion of a reality where some unfortunate misjudgements are more than outweighed by the excellent work of the Medieval Players, Poculi Ludique Societas, Joculatores Lancastrienses and countless untitled ad hoc groups. But it does give an indication of some of the very particular problems encountered by both original-staging and modernised productions of medieval drama. There has been an inevitable element of learning from mistakes, but production in the twentieth century has also provided answers to questions unlikely to have been resolved in the study alone. This is certainly true of the whole area of staging, where production helps to flesh out limited evidence, test hypotheses and settle conflicting interpretations. It was in many respects for these reasons that one of the first original staging productions, of the York cycle at Leeds in 1975, came into being. In part it was a practical response to Alan Nelson's vigorous questioning of the entire validity of processional staging at York and elsewhere (34). In retrospect his heterodoxy may have been just the impetus the production of medieval drama needed. It certainly provoked heated debate, and ultimately it was the success of productions like Leeds, as well as the weight of accumulating evidence, that was to convince most doubters that not only was processional staging feasible in practical terms but also that the mode of staging was crucial in more ways than simply meeting the demands of a particular dramatic form. The production did confirm the expectations that a cycle structured as a sequence of short, separate but related episodes demands the definition of serial production offered by processional wagon staging and that much of their power and interest is eroded when conjoined for the convenience of continuous performance on fixed staging. What was less expected was the significance of the non-textually related aspects of processional staging; the sheer spectacle of even moderately dressed converted farm wagons accompanied in procession by costumed and masked actors, some with musicians, approaching an expectant audience is unparalleled in English theatre, though it has much of the excitement if less of the brazenness of Notting Hill Carnival. Productions like the one at Leeds have revealed a wealth of information about the practice and mechanics of cycle production, which can hardly have altered very much since the original performances. The fact that as a member of an audience it was possible, if not essential, to leave the performance at certain times without any substantial sense of loss and either pick up where you left off at a different station or simply give an episode a miss was something of a revelation, certainly something one could not have discovered from reading the text. This seemingly non-compulsory aspect of the relationship with the performance can be strangely liberating, creating a far greater active ingredient in the act of spectatorship than modern audiences are accustomed to. Far from inhibiting concentration, it actually sharpens it by allowing for self-determined breaks. It also carries with it, of course, the potential for the cruellest of all acts of criticism. The plays seem to be structured to accommodate this feature of performance in that dramatic climaxes occur at fairly frequent intervals and important narrative points are subject to repetition. This may sound like the blueprint for a soap opera, but it is further evidence of the dramatist's acknowledgement not only of the mode of staging but also of the nature of the event. It also meant in the circumstances, at Leeds at least, that an early repeat of a particularly enjoyable pageant was always possible. For a quite different reason I seem to remember for the Chester production at Leeds in 1983 *Adam* having built up quite a following by the third station.

A feature of station-to-station presentation that had always been foremost in criticism of it was the problem of scheduling a sequence of pageants of unequal length (34, pp. 15–33). Although the Leeds production could not have been expected to answer questions relating to the effect of interval accumulation on the whole cycle playing time it did demonstrate that inequalities of length causing delays between pageants was of no real concern to the audience, who were free to wander off for refreshment, craft stalls or a pageant elsewhere. It is also the case in these, and presumably was in the original, productions that the actor–audience relationship is enhanced by the former making up a considerable part of the latter. There are few other events where it is possible to experience both in the same day. This genuine sense of sharing the occasion engendered by the particular organisation of the plays and the effect they have of drawing a wide audience from a variety of interests reveals something of the social dimension of the original performances.

Something else that had been suspected but could only be confirmed in practice was the effect different actors playing the same character had in emphasising the non-illusory nature of this theatre, and that performance requires acts of presentation rather than identification (*480*, p. 50; *476*, p. 94). In this and other respects it would be fair to say that as much as anything else original-staging productions have challenged preconceptions derived from a twentieth-century experience of theatre-going rather than a medieval imagination.

Another consequence of the original-staging production of cycles has been the cutting down to size of the pageant wagon. Partly because of the limited evidence there has been a tendency to go along with M. James Young and his proposition that the wagons at York, and by implication elsewhere, were 'a maximum size of ten feet by twenty feet' (*175*, p. 13). He arrived at this figure in recognition of practical and aesthetic demands for compactness but may still have overestimated what was required. Albeit on the flimsiest evidence of pageant-house dimensions in Chester it is possible to propose a wagon of no more than twelve feet by seven feet six inches (*185*, p. 34). This size having been arrived at independently of practice and almost rejected for being impractical, it was illuminating to see that it approximated to the size of the farm wagons adapted, out of necessity, for performance at Leeds (*476*, p. 92). I am not for one moment suggesting that at York and Chester farm wagons were converted for use in performance: on the contrary, the evidence suggests that not only were carts in more frequent agricultural use, but that the pageant wagons were purpose-built. What is of particular interest is that the experience of stages this size did not, as had been feared, impair performance or limit theatrical possibilities. Rather, in the case of pageants like the *Last Supper*, it forced a visual arrangement pleasingly reminiscent of medieval manuscript illuminations of the scene and provided a framing of view that could be encompassed whole by the human eye at a moderate distance, which more expansive staging cannot achieve. The condensing of image and action is a formal feature of the plays which staging of this type and size enhances rather than promotes.

Modern productions have not only helped resolve conflicting interpretations of the records, they have also provided insights where no other evidence but the text exists. Such an example is *The Conversion of St Paul* and the question of whether it was intended for peripatetic or fixed staging (see above, chapter 10, p. 273). The confusion centres on the proper meaning of the Poet's instruction to 'folow and succede / Wyth all your delygens this generall processyon' (lines 156–7) and what precisely is meant by the same character's reference to 'thys pagent at thys lytyll stacyon' (line 363). Semantics has played no little, if inconclusive, part in this issue. It convinced F. J. Furnivall, one of the first editors of the manuscript, that the play was performed at a series of three stations with the audience following the actors and their wagon from one to the other. Much later Mary del Villar argued that 'this generall processyon' meant 'this story' and that the play was produced in the place-and-scaffold mode (359). At around the same time Glynne Wickham also contested the case for a perambulatory audience and proposed instead a fixed arena into which successive pageant wagons were brought, representing the required locations (352). If arguments about the meaning of words like 'processyon' in the late fifteenth century failed to resolve the problem, then perhaps production could. This was one of the reasons behind the performance at Winchester Cathedral in 1982.[15] Making use of architectural features and church furnishings for the setting, the play was performed in three separate locations: the north transept, the nave (with all chairs removed) and the south transept. The audience followed the Poet's instructions and Saul's journey in the most natural commingling of spiritual theme and physical action. If the play lacks the implicatory devices characteristic of moralities like *Mankind* it more than makes up for the sense of audience complicity in the action by making them literally followers of Saul. For this production it was also decided to realise the stage directions to 'daunce' between the stations, even though they are later additions to the manuscript. It may well be that the 'daunce' directions are connected with the 'si placet' option recorded in the right-hand margin of the manuscript against the Poet's concluding speech at the first station. The omission of this speech removes the reference to following the general proession and could be a way of acknowledging that processional performance was not in all circumstances either possible or appropriate. The dances may then have provided an effective alternative means of demarcating the three distinct sections of the play (cf. 234, pp. 21–4). However, the Winchester production chose to make them an integral part of the movement

33 *Wisdom*, staged in Winchester Cathedral, 1981. Players from King Alfred's College, Winchester, directed by John Marshall. The Dance of Lechery.

process, suggesting that their addition to the play might have been a further and deliberate exploitation of this type of staging rather than a substitute for it. Used to comment on the action and reflect the atmosphere by changes in tempo and costume, the dances led the audience in masque-like fashion from one station to the next, producing a spectacular effect entirely in keeping with the tone of the play but one that far exceeded any expectations one might have had from the appearance of 'daunce' in the text. What the production 'proved' was that *The Conversion of St Paul* really does benefit from performance at separate locations with the audience encouraged by processional dances to follow the action physically. But there is little doubt that it is perfectly possible to present it with perhaps less audience involvement at a single site, with or without the dances. Unlike processionally staged cycles like York and Chester, where there seems to be an intimate relationship between play and stage, it appears that performance flexibility may have been an essential characteristic for many of the non-cycle plays. Given that manuscripts of plays for which it is not possible to provide a specific location were, in many cases, probably intended for performance in a variety of places, either as the property of a professional touring company or as a text for hire, it is not surprising that their staging requirements

34   *Wisdom*, staged in Winchester Cathedral, 1981: the final procession.

should be relatively flexible. Paradoxically, the very specific demands of *The Castle of Perseverance* may explain why this apparently touring manuscript uniquely has a staging plan attached to it.

Production of the non-cycle plays does more than confirm their potential for a varied and flexible performance history; it also gives prominence to the non-verbal dramatic elements of the plays. In the case of *Wisdom*, which conveys meaning as much through the actualisation of visual metaphor as through words, production has played an important part in rescuing it from the prevailing critical view expressed by its most recent editor: '*Wisdom* is too intent on teaching moral virtue to have much concern with dramatic virtues' (83, p. xxxvi). Dramatic virtues that engage the eye, such as signification through costume, liturgical resonance through procession, as well as song, and the emblematising of spiritual condition through dance require either a vivid theatrical imagination or performance in order to be fully appreciated. It is these virtues which particularly characterise *Wisdom*, and recent productions have done much to alter critical perceptions of this – perhaps more than in the case of any other medieval play – and help redefine it, if somewhat anachronistically, within the genre of the masque (see illustrations 33–4).[16] Earlier critical neglect of visual and non-verbal potential within the plays has certainly been rectified, at least in part, by the attention drawn to it by performance. Music, costume and masking are now taken much more seriously as essential components of the whole experience of medieval drama. Deserving of similar attention is the area of dance. Production of *Wisdom* has demonstrated how imperative the three dances are to the meaning and structure of the play even though a marginal note in both surviving manuscripts indicates that they may be omitted. Less obviously structural in their purpose are the dances added later to *The Conversion of St. Paul* discussed above. Incorporated in the text of *The Killing of the Children* for reasons of 'solas' for the people and 'reuerens' to God are three dances by 'virgynes, as many as a man wylle' following the Poet's prologue and before and after his epilogue. What makes these three examples of dance in medieval drama particularly intriguing is that they occur in the three shorter plays collected together in Bodleian MS Digby 133. The other play in the collection, *Mary Magdalen*, is much longer and seems to require a form of staging that distinguishes it from the others.[17] It does, however, include a dance but, unlike the group dances of the other plays, it is undertaken by two characters, Mary and Curiosity, as part of the seduction plot. My own involvement in the production of the three shorter plays in successive years in the same venue convinced me that the dances are not merely diversionary afterthoughts but have a real contribution to make to the feeling and understanding of the plays. Their significance in performance seemed to be so out of proportion to the minimalism of their reference that it raised the question of whether it is their inclusion of dance that explains the collection of what is otherwise a disparate group of plays. It is perhaps the most obvious feature that connects them. Their collection could represent common ownership by a company with regular access to a group of professional dancers, although the eighteen required by *Wisdom* and the variation in number allowed for by 'as many as a man wylle' at the end of the *Candlemas Day* play makes this somewhat unlikely. More speculative but in many ways more interesting is the possibility that the dances make provision for a highly innovative form of prepared audience participation, whether at the aristocratic level of disguising incorporated into *Wisdom*, or the festive engagement of local people, probably young women, in the celebration of St Anne's Day, to which the Poet dedicates the performance of *The Killing of the Children*. This is, perhaps, not as improbable as it might first appear. In a context where 'dancing is the characteristically medieval form of rejoicing and self-entertainment, appropriate to secular revels, seasonal festivals and Church feasts' (22, p. 47), it would not be incongruous for drama which shares a similar impulse to accommodate this popular form of expression within performance. The plays with their different levels of integrating dance within drama may, then, be indicative of a theatrical tradition more common than the limited survival of texts would otherwise seem to suggest. The spirit of the dances that concluded *The Mysteries* at the National Theatre may not have been as removed from the truth as twentieth-century feelings of embarrassment implied.

Recent productions have done much to re-emphasise the dramatic virtue and theatrical quality of features such as costume, music and dance and provide a modern audience with a genuine opportunity to share in the pleasure of spectacle that was clearly part of the plays' original attraction. In such instances the interests of research and audience coincide; discovery of what delighted a medieval audience is seen to be not so very different from what is theatrically pleasing in the twentieth century. Not all theatre conventions travel so well however and their restoration in performance, whilst academically valid, can actually distance a modern audience from a sense of shared experience. Such is the case with attempts to recreate the effect of all-male casting. All the English evidence confirms the exclusion of women from medieval performance, although they may have been involved in some of the dances and were at Chester, as 'wyffys of this towne', responsible for the organisation of the *Assumption of Our Lady* pageant. Meticulous reconstruction of a medieval performance should, then, include the casting of men and boys in women's roles. The experiment conducted by Meg Twycross of having men play the parts of Anna and Mary in the Chester *Purification* (485) promoted necessary and valuable discussion to do with the implications for performance style and the encouragement of expectations of non-realism which has been well documented.[18] Without detracting from the importance of the experiment or minimising the extraordinary care with which it was executed, it did seem that much of the general and critical response was governed by the sense of difference that men playing women engendered amongst a modern audience. The appropriate element of alienation produced by the convention was formed as much by the fracturing of modern expectation as by any inherent potentiality. In these circumstances closeness to the original practice may actually distance the sharing of the original experience. For what to the medieval audience was presumably an accepted custom, validated by tradition, today raises questions of sexuality and gender that transform a convention into a theme.

In many ways this encapsulates a predicament faced by all modern revivals of medieval drama: their place on the 'reconstruction' to 'reinterpretation' production scale. That the balance so far tends to tip in favour of reconstruction is not surprising when so many of the plays have only comparatively recently received either their first revival or the benefit of a researched production. In these circumstances accuracy of original detail may seem more important than the more speculative comparability of audience experience. As knowledge through evidence and practice grows it seems probable that medieval drama will increasingly inhabit the tradition of living theatre and receive reinterpretation though modernised production in the manner of some current performances of Elizabethan and Jacobean drama.[19] The success of such productions, though, will depend in no small part on the understanding of text and performance derived from dedicated reconstruction. Whatever directions future performances take it is clear that recent revivals have done as much to inspire scholarship and re-assess criticism as research has to encourage performance. This is a positive and fruitful relationship not unlike that of a laboratory science where theory and practice inform each other. And like the best of humane science it is rewarding for those concerned with medieval drama when the fruits of endeavour are enjoyed by the widest possible audience, 'In such order and sort as they haue byn acustomd'.

NOTES

1 These two journals provide the most comprehensive coverage of recent productions, and *RORD* 13–14 (1970–1), 259–66 contains John R. Elliott Jr's list of earlier productions; this also forms the basis of the list given by Glynne Wickham in *The Medieval Theatre* (London: Weidenfeld and Nicolson, 1974); repr. Cambridge: Cambridge University Press, 1987), pp. 221–6. For discussion of modern productions based on reviews of plays produced between 1965 and 1980, see Neuss (477), and, for a more general survey of the phenomenon in the twentieth century as a whole, Elliott's *Playing God: Medieval Mysteries on the Modern Stage* (472). A number of the productions discussed above and in these publications are available on videotape (483–490)

2 Early revivals of medieval plays are discussed by Elliott (472), and in the context of editing the texts by Lancashire (103).

3 For an unfortunately typical view of the York Festival productions in recent years, see the following selection: John R. Elliott Jr, 'Playing the Godspell: Revivals of the Mystery Cycles in England 1973', *RORD* 15–16 (1972–3), 125–30, and

'The York Mystery Plays', *RORD* 27 (1984), 187–8; David Mills, 'The York Mystery Plays at York', *METh* 10 (1988), 69–72. A similar problem elsewhere is touched on by William Tydeman, '*N-Town* Plays at Lincoln', *METh* 3 (1981), 131–4.

4 For an example of non-medievalist enthusiasm, see the review by Bernard Levin, 'When Mystery was an Open Book', *The Times* (London), 19 April 1985.

5 On this point in practice see the review by Peter Meredith, '*The Conversion of St Paul* at Winchester Cathedral', *METh* 4 (1982), 71–2.

6 Martin Stevens, '*Processus Torontoniensis*: A Performance of the Wakefield Cycle', *RORD* 28 (1985), 189–99 (197).

7 On these points see Tydeman, '*N-Town* Plays at Lincoln', 131–2, and David Mills, 'The *N-Town* Pageants', *METh* 10 (1988), 63–9.

8 David Mills, '*The Castle of Perseverance* at Manchester', *METh* 3 (1981), 55–6, (56).

9 It is perhaps unfair to single out particular examples, but each of the following reviews is generally favourable except in respect of the responses identified in the text: Patricia S. White, '*Everybody*: On Stage in New York', *RORD* 29 (1986–7), 105–7; David Mills, 'Part Two of Medwall's *Nature*', *METh* 6 (1984), 40–2; Diana Wyatt and Pamela King, '*Chanticleer and the Fox* and *The Shepherds' Play*', *METh*, 6 (1984), 168–72.

10 For an example of such a production, see Pamela King and Jackie Wright, '*Rex Vivus* at Southwark Cathedral', *METh* 4 (1982), 61–3.

11 Meg Twycross, 'The Chester Plays at Chester', *METh* 5 (1983), 36–42; also Meredith (476, pp. 68–73).

12 Sarah Carpenter, 'The Chester Cycle at Leeds', *METh* 5 (1983), 29–35.

13 Meg Twycross, 'The Toronto Passion Play', *METh* 3 (1981), 122–31 (126).

14 For an interesting experiment in performing the same text, the morality *Wisdom*, both indoors and out see Riggio (330).

15 For reviews of this production see Peter Happé, '*Conversion of St Paul*', *RORD* 25 (1982), 145–6, and Peter Meredith, '*The Conversion of St Paul* at Winchester Cathedral', *METh* 4 (1982), 71–2.

16 On the production of *Wisdom* at Winchester see Avril Henry, '*Wisdom* at Winchester Cathedral', *METh* 3 (1981), 53–5, and Happé (325); on the production at Hartford, Connecticut, see Theresa Coletti and Pamela Sheingorn, 'Playing *Wisdom* at Trinity College', *RORD* 27 (1984), 179–84, and Riggio (330).

17 On the staging of Digby *Mary Magdalen* see above, chapter 10, pp. 273–5; Meg Twycross and Peter Meredith, '*Mary Magdalen* at Durham', *METh* 4 (1982); McKinnell (482).

18 On this topic see Happé and others (403), Twycross (424), and Rastall (418).

19 See Stevens, '*Processus Torontoniensis*', p. 198.

12

PETER HAPPÉ

A guide to criticism of medieval English theatre

CRITICAL APPROACHES

NINETEENTH- AND TWENTIETH-CENTURY OUTLINES

The English drama that preceded Shakespeare was held in such disrepute for four centuries that it has been necessary for the twentieth to invent the concept 'medieval drama'. Both words show the needs and aspirations of our time, the adjective reflecting a concept of medieval society which need not be either romanticised or patronised, and the noun embodying the profound experiences of the twentieth-century theatre. The latter have been influential in both the performing of the early plays and the redefinition of drama.

The invention of the term 'medieval drama' cannot be attributed to one person, but it is the business of the first part of this guide to consider a number of authors whose work forced a revaluation of the plays and made them seem, as they now do, one of the riches of English culture in spite of their rather chancy survival. The second part deals with a number of special topics indispensable to the study of the plays, and embracing in differing ways the changing corpus of ideas which forms the basis of our understanding and appreciation of the early plays.

Writers before the twentieth century were often antiquarian in stance, and as such they left us much valuable material; often they were so overpowered by Shakespeare, and indeed so 'literary', that they condemned the material before them even as they studied it. However, the judgement of Robert Dodsley (64) upon the moralities and interludes was not shared by William Hone (30) and Thomas Sharp (39), whose work remains indispensable to the study of mystery plays. As J. W. Robinson (37) noted, Hone, a bookseller interested in popular art, became embroiled in a charge of blasphemy because of parodies he had published, but defended himself by showing that parody does not debase its subject. The 'mysteries' of Coventry and Chester were part of his evidence. Like Sharp, he erroneously believed *Ludus Coventriae* (now known as the N-Town plays) was true Coventry, but he initiated the modern study of sources by printing parallel passages from the manuscript with excerpts from the Apocryphal New Testament. He also suggested that the York cycle was typical of arrangements in other cities, and suggested that the 'Coventry' plays were created by the Franciscans to counteract the labours of Wycliffe.

Sharp's *Dissertation* was a more comprehensive attempt to envisage the Coventry performances. He anticipated both the *Records of Early English Drama (REED)* project and the work of the Early English Text Society (EETS) by printing extensive records, particularly for the Smiths', Cappers' and Drapers' pageants, and by including the text of the Shearmen and Tailors' Play. Because of subsequent losses through fire in 1879 and air raids in 1940, his transcriptions of some of the records and of this pageant have become the sole authority. Information he gave about characters and costumes in other pageants is also unique, since only two Coventry pageants survive. He was deeply interested in the subject of medieval drama at Coventry and well-informed enough to adduce information from Chester, Newcastle, London, Dublin, Edinburgh and Lisbon, as well as the diagram from *The Castle of Perseverance*. Where his work can be checked it has been found accurate (51).

There is no doubt that E. K. Chambers (23) is the first important modern critic of medieval drama, even though he saw it as a forerunner of Shakespeare and worked under the influence of Frazer's anthropological ideas in *The Golden Bough*. On the one hand his interest was that of a scientific historian gathering data and hoping to follow an evolutionary model characteristic of his time. He was preoccupied with relating the medieval plays to classical precedents by means of the continuity of the acting traditions, to the medieval Church as an adjunct of its ritual and to the survivals of folk ceremonial that embody anthropological data. Much of the vast amount of English and European information he accumulated from plays, or from associated records and descriptions, was diffused in the text of his argument. But he did not actively treat the nature of drama or address the texts as dramatic works. The Appendices to his work were an invaluable guide to the material that has survived, especially on the topics of prohibitions, on the provenance of existing plays and records, and upon details of texts and editions. Chambers worked so efficiently on these matters that it is still hard to better him. He also wrote a separate work on *The English Folk Play* (367), which again pursued anthropological objectives.

Anna J. Mill, working on Scottish drama (57), followed much of Chambers's method, but eschewed comment, or indeed theory on evolution. Instead she concentrated upon detailed records, and moved significantly along a road of investigation which has more recently become central with the *REED* project. She concentrated upon processional entries, and upon records of folk ceremonial, to clarify the social nature of the early drama of Scotland.

In G. R. Owst (35) we have a historian whose work on sermons illuminated much in medieval drama, even though he denied the quality of morality plays (p. 545). The dismissal is of interest because it suggests that he had not seen any of them performed, and that he was applying inappropriate 'literary' criteria. But Owst was deeply sympathetic to medieval civilisation, especially as manifested in the sermons, and he was able to illuminate many conventional ideas that were common to both sermons and plays. In the sermons he found characterisation, social satire – including Cain as a bad husbandman and Mrs Noah as a shrew – the Hot Cockles game at Christ's Buffeting and many details of devils and hell. He suggested that the playwrights were partly anticipated by dialogue in sermons, and thus questioned their originality. He rightly showed the importance of motifs such as the siege of the castle of virtue, the Coming of Death, and Death as God's messenger. In considering these, Owst began to demand the serious appreciation of what medieval sermon literature was about, and its shaping influence on other genres.

As a Jesuit, Father H. C. Gardiner (129) contributed a point of view which did much to change the appreciation of the early dramas into a more positive direction. He had two main objectives. He showed that the disappearance of the mystery cycles occurred not because they were effete and out of date, ready to be replaced by the new Renaissance theatre, but rather because the Protestant authorities after 1575 found it expedient to suppress them as dangerous relics of the old religion. He noted that the cycle plays were particularly popular in the North (p. 71), where concerted action was threatening to Elizabeth I. His second objective is implied by the first: the plays were popular and much liked not because of their humorous content, but because they were 'still a *religious* drama'. His assertion of quality was invaluable even though some aspects of his suppression theory have been subsequently challenged (127). It is true that he did not analyse the qualities noted, resting chiefly upon a wish to appreciate the religious virtues. He thought that the moralities were as popular as the mysteries.

An appreciation of rather a different kind comes from A. P. Rossiter (38), a critic rather than a scholar. He had a taste for what he called Gothic drama – a genre which he conceived as having a grotesque comic appreciation of the serious business on hand. His critical stance did not imply the serious piety of Gardiner so much as the notion that the plays embodied a comic truth about human nature and the human condition. It is clear that he was much impressed with the inheritance arising from ritual:

> a ritual of defamation sometimes reaching an adumbration of the undermining negatives which threaten all human values and respects, regards and venerations, is the true basis in the English legacy of the clashing comic contrasts of Gothic drama. (p. 80)

Rossiter was a colourful and impulsive critic, and one always has the feeling that he liked to surprise his readers by championing the unlikely – and it *was* unlikely that the medieval drama had positive qualities of its own in 1950. To some extent his views have been revived by Gash (28).

In the enthusiasm of F. M. Salter (*191*) for the Chester plays, a number of qualities were blended. He was interested in the history and development of the medieval plays, suggesting that folk drama had been formative. He saw that the Church took a teaching role through the plays, but that this was combined with civic pride. The craft guilds, he observed, were semi-religious organisations and as such could help in the achievement of both aspirations. His interest led him to an extensive study of the Chester records, from which he deduced much about how the cycle was produced and performed. He asserted the value of dramatic rather than literary criteria, though he was strangely out of tune with the versification (p. 84). Alongside these scholarly concerns ran his enthusiasm for the success in performance, and he was keen to articulate this:

> entertainment, beauty, representations of human life, the power to grip and hold an audience and – above all – meaning or significance, or, if I may say so, moral value. (p. 84)

The playwrights 'never forgot their sacred mission' (p. 96), and in this way, like Gardiner, he saw the religious concern as an asset, rather than a weakness. A great deal more work has been done subsequently on the Chester records and manuscripts, but the appreciation he shows for the plays adumbrated many features of later critical thinking.

T. W. Craik (*304*) addressed the problem of the definition of interludes of the mid-sixteenth century, largely outside the scope of this *Companion*. But the continuum of moralities to interludes shows many common features, and Craik included the fifteenth-century moralities, as well as making much of such plays as *Fulgens and Lucres*, *Hick Scorner* and *Youth*, and the plays by Heywood, Redford and Bale. Professor M. C. Bradbrook, in her Foreword, remarked that the quality of a play

> must be recreated from all the data by scholarly insight before an act of sympathy can reclothe the lines with the depth of colour, movement, and vivacity that they ought to convey. This ... is a learned skill. (p. vii)

Craik gave attention to aspects of performance, the central concept being that the interludes were indoor plays which relied firstly upon a *place* for performance but operated by establishing an intimacy with the audience. This was constantly renewed by such devices as direct address, or planting actors among the audience (as in *Fulgens and Lucres*). The Tudor hall in its entirety thus became a performance space. Craik further considered technical matters such as doubling, the place of the Vice as the hub of the action and the use of song. He discussed costume and its emblematic significance, and considered the importance of changes of costume: the symbolic use of attire, he made clear, ran through the continuum.

Craik's emphasis upon the skill of the performers implied a skill also in the original conception and development of the plays by their authors. In a work complementary to Craik's, David Bevington (*303*) considered both actors and authors. He studied the size of the early acting companies, which were gradually to become professional. Though his division of plays into elite and popular is suspect, he demonstrated that the small size of the companies placed a constraint upon plays. Yet this constraint the authors turned to advantage as they learned to structure their work to give maximum scope to the acting skills of the performers, making the most of these by the doubling which became virtually ubiquitous by the mid-sixteenth century. Within the companies Bevington identified the role of the most skilful and versatile actors, and thus he showed the importance of the interrelationship between the leading character and the Vice. His recognition of professionalism in the interludes embraced success in the writing of dialogue, and in the interplay of action, gesture and movement. The determined and scholarly exposition of the texts on the grounds of structure and technique exhibited by Craik and Bevington virtually put an end to the poor opinion that these early plays had acquired, and it must be said that by the time these critics appeared in print there had also been sufficient practical demonstration of skills to make the fruits of scholarship beyond doubt (see chapter 11).

Glynne Wickham pursued a number of distinctive issues, stressing the continuity of theatre development from the medieval period to the Restoration. He considered that the medieval Church created a theatre of worship as well as one of social recreation, and the two interacted. With the eye of a practising director, he drew upon a wide range of material embodying an inheritance of Christian and pagan mythology. He linked the pageantry at Court and the civic processions in the early fourteenth century with the genesis of the mystery cycles (*430*, vol. 1, p. 122) and suggested 'a progressive adaptation by the Church to its own ends of those principles of secular stagecraft that answered to its own needs' (*430*, vol. 1, p. 126). He drew a parallel between the Corpus Christi processions and the royal entry and the

Lord Mayor's Show, all sharing what for him was an essential to drama, the spectacle. In this he may have been more successful in altering perspectives on medieval drama than in offering proof.

His reconstruction of the pageant wagon (430, vol. 1, 173–4) stressed the richness of the furnishings, related to the elaborate materials and settings used on civic occasions. He attended to indoor performances, which he connected with mummings and disguisings. In his third volume he pursued in visual and verbal terms the idea of 'device', the imaginative invention by playmakers that enabled the plays to work upon the stage. He also turned his attention to the Christian calendar and its influence upon festivals, which contributed to the richness of staging.

The combination of theatrical qualities and religious doctrine was seen by Eleanor Prosser (133) as the heart of the mystery cycles. She treated doctrinal aspects, especially those concerned with repentance and mercy, denying that 'didactic urgency eliminates the possibility of dramatic effectiveness' (p. 189). The feast of Corpus Christi implied both repentance and the mercy of God, and she showed how there is a sense of a new-made person emerging in the individual plays, especially for Joseph, Mary Magdalene and Thomas. She made a comparative study of the treatment of selected episodes in the five English cycles. She looked especially for dramatic conflict, and praised most the plays where she discerned this – though it was hardly an objective criterion. In spite of her avowed interest in performance characteristics there were some surprising judgements upon individual plays, especially the Wakefield *Mactatio Abel*, whose dramatic success she gravely underestimated. It is clear, though, that she shared with other critics of the fifties and sixties both a sense of the theatrical vigour of the plays and an awareness that the Church's didactic intentions helped positively in the development of the drama.

FOUR INFLUENTIAL ANALYSES

In this historical review of the development of the twentieth-century conceptions of medieval theatre, we come now to four books that have been more influential than most. They do not necessarily speak with one voice, but there is no doubt that most critical thinking cannot now take place without noting them. O. B. Hardison Jr (29) and the Taylor-Nelson collection of essays (21) exhibited an ideological change which operated by setting out to alter assumptions about criticism itself, as well as adducing fresh material for discussion. V. A. Kolve (130) and Rosemary Woolf (138) were not so much ideologues, being more traditional in their outlook, but they brought a depth of medieval scholarship, often from non-dramatic sources, to the interpretation of the Corpus Christi plays. These books all carried forward the tradition of scrupulous scholarship established by Chambers, but their critical view of what they collected was determined more specifically than before by the understanding of religion expressed in aesthetic form, and a deep sense of the value of the drama.

O. B. Hardison's first essay 'Darwin, Mutations and the Origin of Medieval drama' contained an analysis of the work of Chambers, together with Karl Young (69) and, to a lesser extent, Hardin Craig (25). He saw a number of influences at work upon Chambers, especially a late Victorian scepticism about religion, and closely associated with it, a Darwinian model for the development of drama. Early drama was seen to be a classic example of evolution in the form of a literary genre. It represented a primitive or barbaric stage which, because of some perceived qualities, especially successful comic effects, would eventually develop into the Shakespearean climactic. After Shakespeare would come a decline through the Jacobeans to the closing of the theatres in 1642. The methodology of Chambers was designed, according to Hardison, to collect a wide range of material that would substantiate the evolutionary model. Ultimately the attempt was a failure, as the empirical approach limits the kind of question asked – 'what?' rather than 'why?'. Because of this limitation Chambers did not come near to an understanding of the nature of drama, and indeed never approached a critical consideration of it. The weakness, besides failing through the nature of its method, also shows in that evolutionary ideas could not be properly used to deal adequately with artistic matters. Moreover Chambers subsisted on a theory of drama which, following J. M. Manly (32), posited action, dialogue and impersonation as characteristics of drama – externally observed and not intrinsically part of the experience of drama. In the case of Young, Hardison saw a somewhat broader view of drama, but essentially he was concerned to show that there was a fundamental failure to observe the continuity of the dramatic tradition through the moralities to Shakespeare. The force of identification between actor and role is one of the essential features of drama which Hardison felt had been regrettably overlooked.

This systematic assault upon the established scholarly citadel was as refreshing as it was effective. There is no doubt, as Hardison conceded, that the collections of material by Chambers and Young were made with admirable thoroughness and skill, but Hardison's proposition that, in spite of this hoard of riches, the collectors actually missed the point of the exercise is engagingly iconoclastic, and it went a long way towards explaining two reactions that must be commonly felt: that Chambers and Young said little about what plays were actually like, and also that their work may be ceaselessly referred to, but it is rarely read for the continuity of its argument.

Most of the material Hardison used was liturgical. His chief opinion was that 'Religious ritual *was* the drama of the early middle ages and had been ever since the decline of the early theatre' (p. viii), and he made much of the proposition that boundaries between drama and ritual did not exist. Ritual indeed became representation, and he traced the process in the Mass as a whole, which is timeless and recreates itself in the present, whilst at the same time it must recreate the past events which underly it. He furthered this argument by considering the Lenten Agon, which in the Mass recreates the original sacrifice, and the Resurrection, which shows a change from *Tristia* to *Gaudium*, a *peripeteia* in the Aristotelean terms underlying Hardison's conception of the drama. There is perceivable in these propositions a notion of the organic force of the Mass, which by its timelessness completely absorbs participants (active as well as passive) in the action that takes place. Apart from the change in perspective we have noted, this concept seems to be the most important and valuable idea Hardison offered. The problem of the relation of the early rituals with the Corpus Christi plays or the moralities remains a very complex one. It is partly cultural, turning upon what participants might have experienced inwardly, and partly one concerned with the definitions of ritual and drama. Though the experience of the medieval audience at York may have had something in common with the participants at the Mass in the religious awe felt by both, such a parallel comprises only part of the experience for those at the Corpus Christi plays. It is evident that the data relating to direct development from liturgy to play is somewhat tenuous – though there were liturgical elements in the plays, especially the music. But these elements are limited. The explanation of the similarities may lie elsewhere than in linear development. Hardison's work seems to propose the problem without actually investigating it. Nevertheless the sympathetic perception of the nature of the Mass and of the drama it embodied is the most revealing aspect of the critic's work.

The question of the medieval audience's response to the Corpus Christi plays was taken up by V. A. Kolve (*130*), and therein lies an important difficulty in the appreciation of medieval theatre. On the one hand, by means of the 'learned skill', it is possible to develop a modern reader's appreciation, but the point of perfection will never be reached. The modern remains in his time, however much is known about medieval persons, and the assumptions of today cannot be shaken off. Similarly the revelation of much that was available for the medieval person will never give us a medieval consciousness. Kolve, sensitive to the problem, pointed out that much of the machinery of learning that he assembled would be understood by a medieval person, but probably not consciously known (p. 265). Nevertheless Kolve created a structure of theological ideas which helps us to see what might have mattered, and he was very preoccupied with the objective of placing the plays in their time, chiefly by parallels and sources from non-dramatic theological writings. These were made to illuminate certain concepts about the world and to suggest a positive interpretation of it. Medieval time and place reflected the divine participation in the world. Kolve investigated what made the Corpus Christi plays different from non-dramatic theological writing, with which they share many assumptions. His answer was that the drama by its economy forces single-minded attention upon the essence of human experience and human nature, and he noted that the plays do not for the most part show humans as wholly good or wholly bad. His second purely dramatic criterion was that the Corpus Christi plays were part of a celebration, a festival of love and redemption. Though there is criticism of human beings their potential to be loved is affirmed. Behind these ideas lies an awareness of the contract between audience and actor: 'It is with the spectator ... that theatrical communication begins and ends' (26, p. 97).

Kolve drew upon medieval ideas in investigating what he describes as the 'generic self-awareness' of the Corpus Christi drama (p. 11). He came to a theory of the theatre as game, and relates this to Brecht, Ionesco and Beckett (p. 23). It is a matter of both festival and contract. Semiotic exploration of the theory of drama in our own time has come to much the same view, and it could be supposed that what happened was that Kolve rewrote medieval theory in a modern image. However, his evidence was partly linguistic and partly observation of the nature of theatrical action. He rejected illusionist theory and said of the Expositor figures:

> Their function is to enclose the action, whether natural or mythic, in a frame of commentary which puts the playing unmistakably at a distance from reality. The *Chester* Expositor, for example, really does control the game – hurrying here, moralizing there, now briefly narrating a story that cannot, because of time, be played, and occasionally stepping forth to address the audience directly on what they have been watching together.   (p. 27)

Kolve went on to argue that the concept of game creates a need to forgive the *tortores* in the Passion plays, where an indirect emotional concern keeps feelings under control (p. 180). He treated comic actions as of value in themselves (rather than as anticipations of Shakespearean comedy) in that they 'concentrate and define the Flood or Nativity moment. They are like mirrors arranged in a circle around one center' (p. 174).

Like Hardison, Kolve was concerned with the eternal in the present and he perceived that the origin of the cyclic form was directly related to the urge to contemplate and celebrate the whole story of God's intervention, but to do it outside the narrative structure of the Church's year, which runs from Advent to Pentecost. He noticed the interrelationship of *figurae*, which is a dramatic device of anticipation and retrospect by means of symbol (p. 85), and he relied heavily upon a Seven Ages theory to explain the popularity of the narrative elements common to the cycle (challenged by L. M. Clopper, *180*). He tried to justify the structure and scope of the cycles, which is surely a fundamental desideratum. Characteristically he minimised the limitations of the medieval stage (though he admitted that the cycles 'vary from the superb to the perfunctory', p. 271), and affirmed their effectiveness in bringing the divine into medieval streets.

The feel of Rosemary Woolf's criticism (*138*) is distinctly literary, as she seems keen to apply standards derived from medieval poetry to the works. However, there was a careful consideration of the cycle form in the Corpus Christi plays in relation to origins, and a number of useful comparisons were made with continental biblical drama which serve to clarify the distinctive nature of the English cycles. The bulk of her book was a comparative review of each of the episodes of the cycles. She perceived a close relationship between the Corpus Christi processions as distinct from the plays, and settled for co-existence rather than a development of the one from the other. She saw the impulse of Corpus Christi as more didactic than devotional. An unresolved argument explored the penitential nature of the Judgement plays, and she questioned why, in a series that was meant to celebrate, this was the concluding note. The difficulty she observed is related to her analysis of structure and sequence, and at the end of her book she judged the discontinuity of the cycles as obstacles to literary appreciation.

She thought that the visual conventions from iconography affected the drama, and she suggested that the wagons provided a picture frame for iconic effects. Some modern reconstructions have certainly followed this suggestion with stunning effect. In general she was rather cautious as to how far iconography influenced the plays, but she was right to make the link.

It is not possible here to examine all the details of the comparisons of treatment of episodes, but some of her comments on the Passion sequences (pp. 238–268) may illustrate her major preoccupations. There was a strong interest in characterisation – even though she commented on the lack of 'inwardness' because of the open-air setting (p. 99) – centering on emotional characteristics, with particular reference to villains and betrayers. These are powerful dramatic figures, and Woolf was interested in showing how the dramatists exploit contrast between them. She supported her observations by comparison with continental equivalents: Pilate, for example, never becomes the almost holy figure trying to resolve a dilemma of justice as he does in Gréban. But she noted that the Towneley Pilate is uncharacteristic of Christ's enemies in that he takes no relish in what he does (p. 246). She showed how closely Christ's gospel utterances are incorporated in the plays. The laments of the Virgin in Towneley were compared in style to meditative lyrics. The authors were sensitive to other literary genres, and in many instances, together with the iconographic dimension noted above, the effect is to direct attention to the enrichment of texture.

Woolf was prepared to condemn the plays for aureate diction, and she observed that no major poet contributed to the cycles. Her view was that the coherence of the tradition allows poets of lesser rank to operate with some effectiveness. But the test of performance and onstage interpretation suggests that these strictures may have been misplaced.

The Introduction by Jerome Taylor to the collection edited by himself and Alan H. Nelson (21) set the critical principles involved. Though plenty of scope was allowed for the individual judgement of the contributors, there was an underlying need to justify the demand for a historical criticism of the early drama. This manifested itself partly in avoidance of the evolutionary model exposed by Hardison, and in the embracing of a more flexible approach:

> a less partial interpretation and more plausible history of medieval English drama than those offered in interpretations and histories still widely read.
>
> (p. 6)

These objectives were actively involved in discussion of ritual and drama, the Introduction anticipating fuller treatment in several of the following essays devoted to the Latin liturgical drama. The distinction between ritual and drama is hard to make since it is, as Taylor pointed out, necessary to consider internal material as well as external characteristics. Nevertheless there was a closely argued account of how the liturgical dramas, with elements of action and gesture, still retained an essentially iconic function, which means a function of worship. This iconic function, which is entirely appropriate to worship, affected the nature of drama by limiting the development of character, even though, in Taylor's terminology, the icon can be moved through a dramatic action involving a *peripeteia*, a change of spirit, from anxiety to exultation in the case of the Maries, for example (p. 9). Thus the ritual was dramatic because of the psychological development in the action involving the icons' effects upon the audience, but it was only dramatic so far, and there is much that drama would add in a fuller range of gesture, movement and action.

The perception of a historical view was carefully circumscribed in two ways. Taylor was keen to prevent the characteristics of drama in later periods being used to misinterpret what is actually present in medieval drama, a form of critical metonymy he felt was misleading. A particular risk was noted in the attempts to identify embryonic tragedy and comedy in medieval plays. Secondly, in a further reaction against the evolutionary or 'germ' theory, he urged that comparison and identification were sufficient:

> Classification and comparison of themselves need imply no causal-sequential line ... no exchange of influence even were chronological pinpointing possible, can generally be more than guessed. (p. 16)

The concern should be not how plays were developed, but that they developed.

Later material in the book emphasises the symbolic effect of elements in various genres. The investigation of the signification of design and staging in N-Town (415), of the way created things inevitably represented the spiritual mystery (211), and the metaphoric significance of wealth and the journey in *Everyman* (339) were part of a systematic approach to the understanding of medieval drama, and it seems likely that the essays dealing with such topics had a significant effect upon the way critics look at the drama, sensitive to its specifically medieval cultural resonances.

HISTORICAL PERSPECTIVES

Historical perspectives are continually changing, not least because of the changing standpoints of their authors. Robert Potter (311) dealt with the idea of the morality play from its earliest beginnings up to modern developments, including twentieth-century revivals. His treatment of the medieval morality took account of its relationships with sermons and penitential literature, which contributed to the formulation of 'repentance drama', as he designated it. He was interested in ritual rather than in the traditional view that allegory was the sustaining force of the moralities, and he described these plays as 'a didactic ritual drama about the forgiveness of sins' (p. 57). He placed special emphasis upon penance, and suggested that the coming of the Dominicans and Franciscans introduced a style of preaching strong on doctrine and realism which influenced development (p. 20). He also noted the possible relationship between the moralities and the Dance of Death, the Seven Deadly Sins, the Paternoster plays and some continental analogues. He saw this drama as a drama of ideas, 'analogical demonstrations of what life is about' (p. 33). He concentrated particularly upon the nature of man (pp. 37–47), and stressed his need to seek forgiveness. Extending his study historically, he considered the morality of state as practised by Medwall and Skelton, which turns upon the figure of the king. The Reformation also developed the morality for polemical ends, as he showed in his consideration of Lindsay, Bale and Udall.

Though the historical perspective offered by Richard Axton (22) was European in scope, it reflected directly upon both the English mystery plays and the moralities. He described the complexity of the dramatic traditions and indicated that the liturgical drama should not be seen as the sole ancestor of the English vernacular drama. In considering the diversity of its inheritance he considered the tradition of mimicry in the secular acting styles carried on by the *mimi* and their congeners. The folk drama was another independent tradition manifesting itself in the mock battle, the wooing and the resurrection. He also considered aristocratic and popular games about love. Against these lively genres, he noted by contrast that the church ceremony was not really dramatic so much as offering a participatory experience. These ceremonies dissolved chronological time, and offered a simultaneous apprehension of the sacred events portrayed. Instead of being mimic historical persons, the actors in the liturgical dramas were iconic aids to worship.

Besides an illuminating consideration of the social aspects of the plays of Arras, the work contained some important observations about the earliest English drama in the vernacular. Indeed the emphasis upon the vernacular drama forms an important motif throughout the book. The English cycle plays do have some links with the liturgical drama, but they are separated from it in matters of belief and didacticism. There was also an exploration of folk-play elements in the *Mactatio Abel* and in other parts of the vernacular cycles. The treatment of the Shepherds showed how closely they are related to folk drama, as well as to social problems. Finally some of the moralities were seen as capable of developing into a new portable drama as the conditions of actors changed in a new age.

Axton's approach depended upon a very sensitive appreciation of many different and interrelating strands of dramatic experience, and a sympathetic and detailed consideration of a number of specific plays. Its usefulness and influence are continually in evidence in the work of many other critics.

The *REED* project is to publish all the records of drama, ceremonial and minstrelsy in the United Kingdom and Ireland. So far ten volumes have appeared and already they are having a significant effect upon thinking about the early drama. The editorial procedures are strictly conceived in terms of fidelity to the originals, and also in the intention to avoid commentary so as to make the documents available to objective consideration of all kinds. It is discernible already that the volumes are different in scope in that the city volumes such as York (158), Chester (179) and Coventry (51) dealt with close communities and in fact a rather limited range of drama, whereas the county volumes such as Devon (61) showed much variety of size, scope and distribution. The *Cambridge* volumes (59) show yet another context, in the interrelationship between town and gown.

A number of assumptions about the early drama have been brought into question, particularly the universality of cycles like York's. Even within the cities the picture which has emerged is one of ever-changing circumstances and locations, and many intriguing questions remain about how to relate the performances as recorded to the extant texts. Nevertheless the abundance of detail is welcome and exciting, giving scope for increased understanding of such matters as the payment of players, the materials and colours of costumes, the continuing difficulties over financing, the routine and frequency of rehearsals and performances, the copying of parts and the locations used. The varying fortunes of the guilds are particularly well reflected. The decision to include references to music has proved invaluable, though the actual interrelationship between data about music and that about drama will need careful interpretation. There is also an interesting quantity of material about processions and shows for important visitors, including royalty. Once again the interpretation of this in relation to drama needs careful handling.

The publication of records does make them available more generally, and it reduces the risk of disappearance of priceless information: for example, the Coventry volume is in part dependent upon the early nineteenth-century work of Sharp (39), who quoted from records since destroyed. But survival is not uniform and, grateful though we must be for the enormous success of the project, our knowledge of the early drama will still be patchy because of the arbitrary nature of the texts and records that have survived.

A more fundamental criticism of the project is offered by Theresa Coletti (47a) who seeks to identify its historiographical limitations. Seeing the objective as a pursuit of facts, following the tradition of earlier antiquaries, she notes the risk of separating factual information from its social and cultural context. Not only is the value of this information limited by the uncertainty of survival, it is also subject to selection criteria based upon a neutrality which she does not think can be countenanced by an understanding of historicism. For her the prevailing image is that of the 'interim report' (p. 284), awaiting a conclusion which must be derived from other directions, especially the dramatic texts themselves.

SPECIAL TOPICS

TEXTS AND EDITIONS

The development of textual scholarship is closely associated with the development of critical thinking about the plays. Initially there was little attention to dramatic values, and editors were primarily concerned with a comparative study of manuscripts where parallels existed, and with the study of language. The latter may well have been out of respect for the linguistic inheritance, and it was no doubt closely associated with the *New English Dictionary*. These preoccupations gave rise to the Early English Text Society editions of 1892 and 1916. The Introductions had no shared objectives, and they were remarkably unsystematic. There was usually a discussion of manuscripts, and their provenance and interrelationship. An attempt was made to deal with sources in *Ludus Coventriae*, and with records in *Two Corpus Christi Plays*. There was attention to glossary, though the style of glossing was very brief. R. L. Ramsay's edition of John Skelton's *Magnyfycence* (1909) became a reference point because of his comprehensive account of the structure of morality plays. Even though these early editions made the texts available in a fairly reliable form the major drawback was the consideration of text as essentially a written phenomenon. The shortcomings in scope, and doubts about the need for a more systematic study of manuscripts, particularly in comparative terms, led to a programme of revision beginning with *The Macro Plays* (83), followed by *Non-cycle Plays and Fragments* (85), the Lumiansky and Mills *The Chester Mystery Cycle* (73), with accompanying volume of essays and documents (182), *The Late Medieval Religious Plays of Bodleian MSS Digby and E Museo 160* (84) and *The N-Town Play* (78). The newer texts are in old spelling following the Society's tradition, but the appearance of the text on the page is clear and uncluttered.

The discipline involved in these revisions gave a more balanced view of the texts, and clarified the difficulty of deciding upon a definitive text when the uncertainties of scribal error, selection and development are considered. There is an uncertainty about whether the pursuit of an original in one finite form is practicable, as Mills suggested:

> Choice and change were built into the cycle-form, so that the civic authorities may have had an extensive range of decisions before them in deciding what form of the cycle should be played. (182, p. 41)

The Malone Society offered a stricter uniformity than the EETS, but was maintained by attempting less in the way of supporting material since the policy was to reproduce many peculiar or special features of manuscripts, and to account for every detail of the printed texts by a system of literal or type facsimiles. This does of course allow the introduction of editorial error, however high the standard of accuracy, and also a much more subtle problem of editorial interpretation, which may show in many decisions about type, layout and presentation. However there has been some outstanding detective work in establishing the nature of the manuscripts, as for example the Pafford and Greg edition of Bale's *King Johan* (1931). The Society has been responsible for preserving a number of important fragments in its *Collections*. In recent years a policy of issuing photographic facsimiles has given a closer visual impression of the original layout, and has eliminated transcription errors. One further positive achievement by the Society has been printing of records of early drama, anticipating *REED*, especially of the livery companies (*60*), plays and players in Kent (*48*), Lincolnshire (*54*), and Norfolk and Suffolk (*252*), Greg's '*The Trial and Flagellation*' *and other Studies in the Chester Cycle* (*181*) made an important contribution to the information about the development of the cycle.

A third major effort has been the gradual development over the last hundred years of photographic facsimiles, and these are now perceived to be an indispensable tool for modern scholarship. The earliest significant attempt was by J. S. Farmer, who in 143 volumes of his Tudor Facsimile Texts (*118*) provided generally acceptable versions, mostly of interludes, though he did issue *Mankind*, Medwall's *Nature*, *Hick Scorner*, *Youth*, *The Four Elements* and *Mundus et Infans*. A facsimile of *Macro Plays*, edited by David Bevington (*115*) included a face-to-face transcription in modern type. Facsimiles published by the Leeds Centre for Medieval Studies under the general editorship of A. C. Cawley, S. Ellis and P. Meredith have provided detailed introductions incorporating modern standards of scholarship in handwriting, paper, watermarks and binding (*109–114, 116–117*).

The editorial projects so far considered have in general been primarily concerned with accuracy of text, mostly in purely textual terms, without much attention to dramatic qualities, or indeed to practical considerations of theatre. These important areas of scholarship are essentially interpretative, and as such give rise to a wide variety of editorial material, and even within series of apparent uniformity give rise to editorial deviation. J. S. Farmer's second major contribution to drama scholarship appeared under the somewhat obscure umbrella of the Early English Drama Society (*65*). Unfortunately his transcriptions were not accurate, and he modernised spelling to such an extent that his texts cannot be used for many scholarly purposes. However, his editorial material gathered in alphabetical notebooks in each volume contained much useful information, though not all was reliable.

The Tudor Interludes series (General editors Richard and Marie Axton) aimed at a much higher standard of textual accuracy and a concern with the appearance and practicability of each volume. The plays were in old spelling, with modernised letters. They included a number of important early plays, including *Gentleness and Nobility*, *The Four Elements* and *Calisto and*

Melebea (91); *The Plays of Henry Medwall* (88); *Three Classical Tudor Interludes* (93); *The Complete Plays of John Bale* (94) and *The Plays of John Heywood* (92). There was a particular emphasis upon language, and also upon circumstances of performance and stage technique.

In the Revels Plays two volumes of early drama, *Magnyfycence* edited by Paula Neuss (90) and *Youth* and *Hick Scorner* in *Two Tudor Interludes* edited by Ian Lancashire (89), gave close attention to the provenance of the plays, the nature of the text and the historical circumstances of composition and performance. However, they raised again the problem of modernised spelling, which still divides scholars and teachers. The compromise in these Revels plays of modernised text and highly original scholarship is an uneasy one. The same may be said of the equally discriminating edition in the New Mermaids of *Three Late Medieval Morality Plays* by G. A. Lester (68), which includes *Everyman*, *Mankind* and *Mundus et Infans*.

One of the earliest and most long-lasting editorial achievements was Lucy Toulmin Smith's edition of *The York Plays* (72). This was in old spelling, drew extensively upon records and firmly placed the plays in relation to the guilds that produced them. A reworking of the text by Richard Beadle (70) produced a good deal more information, especially about the nature and purpose of the manuscript, and some new ideas, about the scribes and about the presentation of the plays. Beadle and King (71) made a selection based on this edition.

A. C. Cawley's *The Wakefield Pageants in the Towneley Cycle* (76) did much to identify the work of the Wakefield Master. The edition was particularly strong in its treatment of Middle English and local detail, and upon a consideration of the context in which these plays were written. Martial Rose's *The Wakefield Mystery Plays* (77) was conceived largely as a text actable by modern performers – a very new idea in its time, and one based upon his own practice. He addressed the questions raised by the cycle form, and worked out aspects of staging based upon the assumption that the plays were not played on wagons.

Everyman has been well served, appearing in a number of popular anthologies, especially Cawley (63) and Bevington (62). However, the most searching editions were those by Cawley (87), which is a rigorous examination of the text, and by Cooper and Wortham (86), which was close to Cawley textually but included a far more detailed examination of sources and analogues, a broadly interpretative approach and consideration of staging and stage history.

Original works of scholarship in connection with the editing of texts included K. Young, *The Drama of the Medieval Church* (69), an unrivalled source for the liturgical plays, although his theory of development has been somewhat questioned (29). D. Hamer's edition of the texts of Lindsay's *Ane Satyre of the Thrie Estaitis* (95) remains an example of thoroughness, giving much insight into the background of the plays and their context in the political world of mid-sixteenth-century Scotland. Further editions have followed by Happé (67) and Lyall (96). Similarly much is owed to Edwin Norris's edition of the three parts of the Cornish cycle, *Origo Mundi*, *Passio Domini* and *Resurrexio Domini* (97), which gives Cornish text and a translation, and remains the standard edition. Paula Neuss produced an edition and translation of *The Creacion of the World* (98) with notes.

In addition to the popular anthologies mentioned above, the following have several plays in old spelling, though with various degrees of modernisation in the presentation of text: Peter Happé, *English Mystery Plays* (66), including the pre-Reformation Chester Banns and thirty-eight plays, and *Four Morality Plays* (67). Peter Meredith's *The Mary Play from the N. Town Manuscript* (79) proposed that the five episodes in the cycle existed as a separate entity, an exercise in disentangling an earlier layer from the manuscript; it has lately been joined by his *The Passion Play from the N. Town Manuscript* (80).

A number of scholars discussed the principles underlying the editing of the early drama. Ian Lancashire (103) reviewed the history of editing, including its nineteenth-century genesis, and advocated fully-developed editions with variants, and a consideration for dramatic contexts. S. J. Kahrl, addressing the problem of 'Editing Texts for Dramatic Performance' (102), required editors to give readers' imaginary productions as much help as possible, but saw the need for a clear and authoritative text, acknowledging the right of directors to depart from it. David Mills discussed the stage directions in the Chester cycle and what could be deduced from them (187). Peter Meredith (104) also raised questions about the nature of early stage directions, and showed how manuscripts may reveal the process by which a play came into being, pointing out that the extant manuscripts have sharply differing relationships to original versions. This theme was taken up by Alexandra F. Johnston (155), who noted that the records force us to take account of the very different circumstances in which the cycles were performed, and add force to the view that the cycle of plays is an unreliable concept, depending very much upon circumstances and occasions. The Chester MS was seen as a collage with blurred components, while the York MS was 'a sharply focussed snapshot'.

Other contributions in the volume edited by Johnston (17) included an assessment by David Bevington of the ways that well-known anthologies have shaped and limited the interpretation of medieval drama (101), and two discussions of material extraneous to play texts but closely associated with them. David Parry considered the Latin lines in *The Castle of Persever-ance* (*108*), and Peter Meredith, pursuing stage directions, found them 'many layered' in their complexity (*105*). He noted that even texts which are reading versions, some way from actual performance, might still contain information about performance (p. 78).

The problems of the varying state of the York cycle are further con-sidered by Richard Beadle (*143*), who makes an urgent plea for setting aside the traditional separation of textual study and critical enquiry. Working through a number of apparently minor aspects of the York text and of records about it, he underlines the difficulty of determining what the cycle actually was. Even though we have the Register of 1463–77, he shows that there are great uncertainties about why that particular manuscript was compiled and what its relationship was to the year-by-year performances both before its creation and afterwards. There is a complex and dynamic relationship between the manuscript and the text it contained. Such a per-ception should make us more inquisitive about what the surviving docu-ments actually represent, and it points to a major task of revision and reva-luation of the whole corpus of medieval drama texts, a process which has barely begun outside the work on the play cycles. Such work, though daunt-ingly complex, must be easier in Chester and York, where there are accumu-lations of extra-textual information to aid enquiry. Other shorter plays, and ones more isolated in time and circumstance, offer further challenges.

STAGE AND STAGING

A great deal of information is available about the staging of medieval drama. It can be found within the actual speeches of the plays, in the stage directions – whether they be considered as instructions to performers or retrospective notes about what had happened – and in the records about performances from other sources, usually matters of expenditure. In addi-tion, the modern exploration of the texts by performance has revealed their dynamics, even if the context of modern ideas about staging drama differs radically from the medieval one. Nevertheless this accumulation of infor-mation is a jigsaw in which the pieces do not fit conveniently together. Some advances in knowledge have taken place amid much controversy: two of the most resonant have been the 'in the round' staging proposed for *The Castle of Perseverance* and the nature of the processional performance of the mystery cycles.

Richard Southern's theoretical reconstruction of *The Castle of Persever-ance* (*421*) 'in the round' came at a time when such staging was extremely fashionable with amateurs and professionals alike, and the notion had implications for ideas about the staging of other medieval plays, especially the Digby *Mary Magdalen*. From the manuscript drawing Southern evolved a design which required a circular mound around the outside of the audience with the ditch shown on the drawing circumscribing the mound as a means of controlling entrance to the arena. Hence the ditch could not play any part in the stage effects, and this was one of the chief objections to Southern's theory. Schmitt (420) associated the ditch with symbolism of the castle itself, and offered both practical and textual support for its relocation within the acting area. The quantity of earth to be moved following Southern's scheme and the loss of the ditch as symbol were critical objections, though Belsey (315) saw some allegorical advantage in retaining it outside. Nevertheless, Southern brought the play to life, and he positioned the audience in close proximity to the scaffolds and the actors moving between them. In his reconstruction, the scaffolds were used entirely convincingly, both as separate locations for action and in terms of their reaction upon one another.

His work illustrated a further theoretical aspect: the choice between localised stages, usually booths or platforms with a specific identity defined within the dynamics of the play – God's scaffold diametrically opposed to that of Mundus – and the flexible acting area which could be used for all sorts of purposes and was often a means of transition from the localised areas. This distinction between *locus* and *platea* was explored by Tydeman (41, p. 57) and Nelson (415, pp. 117–18), especially in relation to the N-Town cycle.

Using an analogy from tournaments, Pederson (416) noted that on the plan the ditch is an alternative to some kind of barrier. At lists and tournaments the spectators were defended by barriers. Moreover the central space was used for fighting, and 'stytelerys', or stewards, might also be necessary. This tournament tradition could provide a context for the dramatic encounter. Though it would require some preliminary setting up in the arena, it would be less demanding than the earth-moving required by Southern.

Theories about the processional staging of the Corpus Christi plays, with performances at fixed locations in a sequence through a city, had no doubt been derived from Sharp (39). The idea that the Coventry arrangements could be taken as a norm was vigorously challenged by Rose (77, p. 24). He was doubtful whether the Wakefield plays could be staged in a manner corresponding to that postulated for York and Coventry, particularly as the size of Wakefield did not lend itself to elaborate support from the guilds. Fixed stages might better accommodate some of the Wakefield texts, and he began the important task of separating the notion of the Corpus Christi plays from that of the Corpus Christi procession. Though this separation definitely existed, it is sometimes extremely difficult to determine whether surviving evidence points to the one or the other. Nelson (*413*) placed greater emphasis upon the procession at York at the expense of the traditional view of processional staging. He added a calculation of the time required to move forty-eight pageant wagons through the known route, with twelve stations, and noted the difficulty of coordinating plays of different length. Instead he suggested a procession with a single performance for the mayor and corporation at the Common Hall, an idea later confuted by Tydeman (*41*) because of the impracticable complexity of such a performance in a confined area. Stevens (*423*) supported Nelson, suggesting a single performance at the Pavement. However Dorrell (*150*) argued that evidence from the York records substantiates that there was processional staging at York, whatever the difficulties. One important offshoot of Nelson's hypothesis was that the traditional idea of a uniformity of performance for the four extant English cycles became untenable, and scholars looked more closely at local details to generate an accurate and unique picture of the staging of each. The discovery of the Mercers' indenture at York revealed detail about the preparation of their play (*156, 157*). Further work on the York pageant wagons was done by Butterworth (*144*) and Meredith (*160*). The stations at which the plays were performed were discussed by Mill (*164*) and Twycross (*170*), and by White (*174*), who examined the problems of placing the wagons in each known location in the streets of York.

Controversy regarding Chester has been less intense because three days seemed ample for the performance. However, there has been uncertainty about the stations (*177, 185*). Tydeman (*41*), Wickham (*430*) and Nelson (*414*) gave thought to the structure and size of wagons generally, though here, too, uncertainty remains. There is no information about wagons at Wakefield, and the arrangements for mounting the plays there were considered by Rose (*77*), Stevens (*212*) and Nelson (*34*), the consensus being for a single location, perhaps with wagons introduced.

Once separated from the idea that it was associated with Coventry, it became clear that the N-Town cycle was evidently not suited for processional performance. The stage directions put it beyond doubt that different *loci* were used simultaneously, with an adaptable *platea* in the middle (*221, 226, 77*). However, the assumption that fixed staging of the kind was necessarily 'in the round' was questioned by Nagler (*412*, p. 10), and a semicircular arrangement of scaffolds was offered by Kahrl (*31*, pp. 59–69).

The two major controversies so far discussed have had effects upon ideas for staging other plays. However, there seems little doubt that the *plen an gwary* or 'round' was used for the Cornish plays, as described by Nance

(294). Dramatic applications were developed by Denny (272) and Bakere (268) for the *Ordinalia*, Wickham (352) for *St Meriasek* and Neuss for *The Creacion of the World* (98). Diagrams accompanying these plays showed eight stations for the three days of the *Ordinalia*, thirteen for both days of *St Meriasek* and three for *The Creacion* (411). Neuss made it clear that the stations differed in use and configuration. The work of these critics, together with Bakere, who also dealt with costume, gesture and action, and Denny was particularly concerned to show that simultaneous action on different scaffolds was more extensive than with N-Town and noted that the cross-cutting is more complex.

The importance of the Tudor great hall for staging was recognised by Craik (304) and Southern (422). The latter gave special consideration to *Mankind, Nature, Fulgens and Lucres, The World and the Child, Hick Scorner, Magnyfycence* (especially the stage directions) and *The Four Elements*. Similarly Tydeman (42) looked for typical settings in *Mankind*, the Croxton *Play of the Sacrament* and *Fulgens and Lucres*. Much attention has been given to a few individual plays. Riggio (330) discussed the intimate nature of the performance of *Wisdom*, and the juxtaposition of ecclesiastical procession and masking; see also Happé (325) and Bevington (322). Some of the Digby plays have caused controversy. *Mary Magdalen* may have been produced in the round (Bevington (303), Hosley (404)) but Wickham (352) and Nagler (412, p. 53) were both sceptical, proposing 'half round', a solution adopted for practical reasons by McKinnell (482) and fully evaluated in his account of his own production. *The Conversion of St Paul* has been considered as processional, or in the round, using five scaffolds as proposed by Villar (359). Pentzell (358) opted for a kind of street theatre in line with a processional mode.

Twycross (171) discussed the relationship with the audience for the York *Resurrection*, and also the importance of emotional elements. Critical consideration of the *Thrie Estaitis* has turned upon the complex evolution of the texts, but there is a good deal of evidence to help differentiate the places for production inside Linlithgow palace and outdoors on hillsides at Cupar of Fife and the Greenside at Edinburgh in Hamer (95), Mill (57), Wickham (352) and Happé (67).

More general aspects of staging in terms of costumes and properties have been considered by Tydeman (41), Kahrl (31) and Happé (402). Twycross and Carpenter (428) produced an exceptionally well-documented account of masks with illustrations. Theatrical space was reviewed by Cowen (401) and King (406). Continental practice was shown by Meredith and Tailby (409) in a volume rich in detail on payments, dance and mine, wigs, dummies, trapdoors, fireworks and the performers. The actors also received attention from Robinson (*419*), Wasson (*429*) and Wierum (*431*). Marshall (*184*) showed that the players in the Coopers' pageant in the 1570s were guildsmen, and not professional actors. Doubling was discussed by Craik (*304*), Bevington (*303*) and Happé (*67*, pp. 677–83, and *94*).

Special mention ought finally to be made of the work on tournaments by Wickham (*430*), and on pageantry and royal entries by Anglo (*397*), Bergeron (*398*), Kipling (*407*, *408*) and Withington (*432*). These aspects have had an increasing influence upon ways of seeing the staging of the early drama in its social context, and also in relation to the actual processions and performances that were for centuries part of these public ceremonials and contemporary with medieval drama and its staging.

CHARACTER

The nature and function of character in medieval drama is far from settled. In the moralities human beings appear alongside abstractions. Potter (*311*, pp. 37–47) suggested that this had effects upon both. On the one hand humans are caught in a predicament between being made in the image of God and being corrupt and subject to mutable conditions. The abstractions, on the other hand, must be self-demonstrative, whether good or bad, though this, as Carpenter pointed out (*384*), does not mean that self-presentation and self-knowledge are the same thing. The key to morality characters must be their place in the moral design, and Kantrowitz (*388*) suggested that, this being so, abstractions in allegorical settings were indifferent to their auditors. Her discussion illustrated the related problem of defining the nature of allegorical characters as such, an issue also treated by Schmitt (*391*).

The problem changes somewhat in the mystery plays, where named people are usually the protagonists. Mills (*389*) rightly questioned whether the notion of 'character' existed in medieval times, and it is likely that character was in fact tropological, and operated in a rhetorical mode. Studies of Herod and Pilate have extended this further, especially in the case of Clopper (*385*). Non-dramatic traditions for both these characters were suggested by Parker (*390*) and Williams (*396*). Consistency has been a concern, especially as they appear in more than one pageant within individual cycles, but this leads back to the issues of function and realism. Brawer (*383*) reconciled the apparent contradictions in the York Pilate by demonstrating that anxiety about sovereignty explained the varieties of mood. Auerbach (*382*) was also interested in the realism of the mystery cycles, which he thought should be seen as different in kind from the classically oriented rhetoric of the Renaissance. Nevertheless the 'demonstrative mode' proposed by Carpenter (*384*, p. 22) for the moralities does seem applicable in part to the mystery plays. This is especially evident in the diabolic figures. There is no full study of the devil in the English medieval drama, though Walter (395) did offer some general characteristics in his account. Although from time to time they take part in action with humans, especially Satan in N-Town, devils must remain immutable in order to be antagonists for Christ.

A useful way of looking at characters comes in the possible analogy with Brecht's concept of the actor mediating between character and quality (389, 384, 394). Brecht was questioning the issue of consistency and realism, and his ideas seem pertinent even if he did not know the medieval English plays. Extensive studies on the Vice (386, 312) have shown that this character remains essentially a didactic showman rather than a realistic character, and yet he proves dynamic to plot and action.

<h2 style="text-align:center">MUSIC</h2>

The *REED* volumes specifically set out to include references to music even where there is not much obvious connection with drama. This has proved a benefit because the material collected makes it clear that the culture of medieval England was rich in music, and that it played many important roles in social life. The evidence from the plays supports this. In all probability there was a musical dimension in very many dramatic performances, perhaps indeed in a majority.

The general background of medieval music was considered by Hoppin (439) and Harrison (438). The information from the plays themselves, in the form of stage directions, references in dialogue, words of songs – whether titles only or full texts – and written music, has been systematically collected only in very recent times. It does seem essential to have adequate reference lists which show the extent of what we can regard as certain, and which also allow comparisons. Such a task has been completed by JoAnna Dutka (435), for the mystery plays, and gives an index of songs in Latin (fifty-five items) and in English (nine), with a commentary, a glossary of musical terms and an index of musical instruments in the cycles and in supporting account books. She listed nine songs which have music available. Happé (437) in a parallel study of the songs in the moralities and interludes, gives an index of songs, burdens and titles (146 items), as well as the literary texts. In these plays there are only three settings, though there are some more where the name of the tune suggests a possibility. This information has led to a number of conclusions about the frequency of songs and the most common number of singers, as well as some evidence about the instruments often used.

The provenance of the music lies mostly outside the vernacular drama itself. The chief musical source is the liturgy. The liturgical drama is largely beyond the scope of the *Companion*, but it is relevant to mention certain important works that help to show the background available for vernacular playwrights. Young's collection (*69*) remains indispensable, though it is more continental than English. It should be considered in the light of Hardison's reinterpretation of the significance of the subject (*29*), and of Wasson's retrospect (*45*). These may be supplemented by Smoldon's controversial *The Music of the Medieval Church Dramas* (*444*), which dealt in detail with musical aspects of the Church's own Latin drama, as distinct from the vernacular. Further information will be found in bibliographies printed in the *EDAM Review*, which, since volume 10.1 (1987), has been running a separate section on 'Music, Music-Drama, and Liturgy'. With regard to the early Tudor drama, John Stevens (*446*) made it clear that popular music must have been incorporated as settings for songs, and well-known carols were possible sources for playwrights; see also Greene (*436*).

Richard Rastall (*442*, *443*) pointed out that music in the Corpus Christi plays has two main functions. It is used as a means of indicating character, particularly in terms of the divine harmony inspiring angels and the consequent response of good men, and also for evil characters, where the music may well be a cacophony. It has structural functions, being used for entrances, exits, transitions from location to location, for passing the stage time and for contrasts. He noted the importance of supplementing evidence about music in the plays by reference to banns, accounts and other records. Stevens discussed the dramatic usefulness of music (*446*, pp. 252–9), and noted that it is used in interludes to suggest various degrees of depravity, often with dancing. The dance, however, has received little attention. Stevens commented briefly upon its instrumental accompaniment in *The Four Elements* and *Fulgens and Lucres* (where it is extensive), and it is a prominent feature of *Wisdom* and *The Conversion of St Paul*. There is a survey of dance manuals by Ingrid Brainard (*434*).

Several scholars have noted that in some sections of the cycles musical activities are very concentrated, so that plays rely heavily upon them for dramatic effect and mood. Carpenter (*195*) discussed celestial and earthly vocal styles in relation to Mak, the shepherds, and the nativity in the *Secunda Pastorum*. Meredith (*79*) made a special point concerning the use of liturgical music in the N-Town *Mary Play* (p. 21). A special emphasis on vocal music was also observed by Wall (*172*) in regard to York XLVI (now XLV) – Rastall (*165*) gave a full account of this music reproducing the text in coloured facsimile. Meredith and Tailby (*409*) translated the texts of musical set-pieces appearing in Chester Play 20 and the Bodley *Resurrection* (text in *84*).

ICONOGRAPHY

A consideration of the study of iconography and its relationship with the medieval drama has to engage with two large structures of knowledge: the increasingly well-informed and comprehensive accumulation of information about Christian art which began, like so much modern scholarship, with the nineteenth-century impulse towards the systematic growth of knowledge, and the development of an understanding of the drama itself. Of the former it is probably significant to note that the work of Didron (457) has continued to be an indispensable guide to the corpus of medieval art, even though it is not arranged as a reference catalogue. There can be perceived in it the uniformity of many artistic presentations of Christian ideologies. In more recent times this has been sustained by Réau (467) and Schiller (469). E. Mâle, whose pioneering work in the field of iconography concentrated on French art, especially the sculptures at the cathedrals, was emphatic about the didactic nature of Christian art and looked, quite rightly, for an adequate base of Christian learning to interpret it (461, pp. vii–xv). He saw medieval art as a sacred script (pp. 1–3), and one which, like a code, required an interpretative key: 'Position, grouping, symmetry, and number are of extraordinary importance' (p. 5). He accepted the *Speculum maius* of Vincent of Beauvais (printed at Douai in 1624) as his theological guide. This raised the difficulty that all perceptions of medieval art and drama do have their limitations precisely because we have to look at them through a 'glass'. Much later, Panofsky (464) identified the important principle in the study of iconography that it concerned itself with subject or meaning of works of art as opposed to their form. He further suggested that iconography was largely concerned with conventions of subject matter, which involved a study of written and oral traditions (pp. 3–17). Ross (211) has discussed the Wakefield Master's use of allegorical traditions.

Mâle believed that medieval art was directly affected by the drama since it recorded many aspects of production, and that it could in consequence be a source of information about many visual aspects of the plays, as well as their interpretation. This idea has continued to be an important topic, especially in the work of Hildburgh (459) and Anderson (449). It has also been extensively challenged, as we shall see, but none of the proponents of the priority of drama's influence on art urged it uncritically. Hildburgh, for example, in his treatment of the idea that Christ's stepping on the back of a soldier comes from stage business admitted to changing his mind twice (pp. 91–2). He was thus not categorical, recognising that both the alabaster tables and the plays may have a common source in the Gospels (p. 54). He suggested that, although there is fairly frequent reference in records to replacing or repairing stage costumes, the fashions concerned might well have been conservative. This might account for the uniformity of armour in many English alabasters. He gave plenty of parallels which may well illuminate our understanding of stage practices. For example, he suggests that *nimbi* and *mandorlae* were supported manually by surrounding angels as in some alabasters (pp. 66–7). He noted, among many other items, the gilt hair of God and Christ (pp. 77–9), the lamp carried by Malchus (p. 77), and the mace carried by one official at the Scourging (p. 81). Whatever the causal link between these parallels, they can give valuable clues for staging, and also for the interpretative process that lies behind them. As P. Sheingorn pointed out, 'iconography allows us to attach verbal meaning to visual symbol' (470, p. 102).

Mâle, Hildburgh and Anderson, for all the chronological and regional uncertainty their work generates, are still valuable for the scope of their detailed information. This is particularly true of Anderson's treatment of the Norwich Cathedral roof bosses, in which her information about costume might give clues about what contemporary actors might have worn. Conventional details such as Herod's crown and the appearance of the Devils may well help us to envisage the drama. The information offered is unfortunately limited in value in that the complete Norwich Corpus Christi plays have not survived, and their date and scope are largely a matter of conjecture: one is left disappointingly with only a possibility. Similarly there were many details in Hildburgh's account of the alabasters which must relate to a particular period, seen in two phases, 1340–80 and 1380–1420, when the Corpus Christi plays were emerging. However, both Anderson and Hildburgh, in spite of caveats, made assumptions about the priority of the drama which they did not substantiate. The truth of the matter probably lies in an interpretative tradition that is common to both drama and art, and the chicken and egg argument is unresolvable. Nevertheless the controversy is intriguing, not least in Hildburgh's note that the alabaster carvers might not have had access to literary sources lying behind the plays, whereas they might much more readily have been in an audience.

A change of perception has come in the field of iconography itself largely centred on the work of Clifford Davidson, who as executive editor of the Early Drama, Art, and Music Project (EDAM) at Kalamazoo has been instrumental in collecting and publishing a large amount of data. The Princeton Art Index has also been valuable, as has the *Journal of the Warburg and Courtauld Institutes*. In launching the project Davidson made a number of proposals. One was to see that data about regional art must be collected in a systematic way. This has led to the publication of *York Art* (*148*) and *Chester Art* (*183*), volumes which are catalogues of any visual material relating to the subject matter of the medieval drama. A checklist of topics will be found in Davidson's introductory volume *Drama and Art* (*453*) with a supplement in *EDAM Newsletter* 4 (1982): 25–50. Davidson stressed that 'the medieval theater must be studied in terms of its dependency on the kinds of images found in the visual arts' (*452*, pp. 91–2), and he advocated careful handling of visual conventions. His purpose was to centre upon 'the entire visual display of the drama as well as the imagery present in the text of the play' (*454*, p. 11).

The problem of cross influence will remain, but from work on small sectors of iconography, in terms of locality and time, it is becoming more possible to place medieval plays in their iconographic context. It remains an intriguing task for scholarship to see what certainties can be arrived at, especially as the dates of the plays and sometimes their provenance are often moving targets. One of the facets of the *REED* project is that the written records tighten the net of certainty in some cases, and also create a greater web of probability.

For the scholar and the theatre director, both trying to recreate the circumstances of performance, iconography remains a highly suggestive way of prompting solutions. Such a process was studied by Coletti and Ashley (*481*), who reviewed the Toronto production of the N-Town plays and found that 'using the arts as guides to determining the visual effects for cycle productions' (p. 185) had a striking effect upon costume, gesture and properties. Iconography pushes us more and more towards a symbolic drama as opposed to a realistic one. In many modern productions, particularly that by Meg Twycross of the York *Doomsday* at York in 1988 (*490*), it has become clear that a visual effect, often momentarily static, is implied in the text.

A number of iconographical interpretations of the plays have proved illuminating. On the York play of the Nativity, Robinson (*168*) noted that the distinctive sequence about Mary and Joseph concerning the radiation of light from the crib, the dressing of the Child and his worship, as well as Joseph's fetching of light rather than the more traditional midwives, followed the *Revelations* of St Birgitta (*c.* 1370), substituting a meditative for a legendary tradition (p. 254).

In his treatment of the picture cycles (*222*), P. J. Collins suggested that sequences of iconography relate to the structure of Corpus Christi plays. He picked up a number of motifs such as the significance of fruit at the Creation and the Nativity, and the long sequence of the divine triumph over Satan during the Epiphany. His consideration of this and other themes counterbalances the static aspects of visual art. For example he showed illustrations of the Fall in which there are three apples: one on the tree, one in Eve's hand, and one in Adam's mouth (Figs. 2, 8 and 9).

There have been a number of other specific areas of investigation. Davidson investigated Doomsday devils (455), and the saints' plays (344). Nichols, addressing the regional question, confined herself to East Anglian art and the significant corpus of plays originating in that area (462); and Gibson (253) has recently explored the evidence in more detail, using the discoveries to point up methodology, an interest shared by Twycross (471).

A full bibliography of the genres of medieval art, including such items as glass, wall paintings, bosses, manuscript illuminations, carvings, misericords and church plate, cannot be attempted here, but Davidson's introductory volume (453) gives the essential material. If the systematic study of iconography he advocates is continued it is likely that more close connections between art and drama will emerge. Suggestive as a quantity of parallels may be, actual chronological and regional links will have a special authority where they can be identified exactly.

TRADITIONAL OR FOLK DRAMA

The alternative title illustrates an uncertainty in this field of interdisciplinary study deriving from the contrasting views of students of medieval theatre and folklore. Chambers (367), drawing upon the pre-1914 collecting of Tiddy (379), commented upon the similarities and the diversities of versions of the mummers' play and offered a normalised version. He was tempted to suggest that there must have been an archetype, though its nature was doubtful and he admittedly could not trace medieval evidence of the Mock Death, or the Cure. However, under the influence of Frazer's *The Golden Bough* he formulated

> a primitive nucleus in which skin-clad worshippers accompanied by a traditional Woman capered about the slain figure of a man who had been King of the feast. (p. 225)

This concept has been enormously influential upon drama scholars contemplating the social and dramatic context of medieval text and performance, but it has also been forcefully challenged. Empirically it has not been possible to prove that the mummers' play of the eighteenth and nineteenth centuries had medieval forebears, though, as we shall see in a moment, a considerable number of parallels between elements in medieval plays and the recorded versions of the later mummers' play have been described or proposed. A more serious challenge has come from sociological and cultural historians (who do not wish to be called 'folklorists'), opposing the evolutionary nature of Chambers's formulation and requiring that the whole concept of 'folklore' be seen as a manufactured rationalisation imposed on the data for ideological reasons by scholars and antiquarians unable to shed their own social assumptions.

One key problem is that if the mummers' play as recorded did not have recognisable medieval antecedents, it becomes very difficult to say whether it influenced and infiltrated medieval drama or vice versa. The appearance of some parts of *Youth* in the Revesby Play written down in 1779 (see 89, pp. 258–9) makes a development from folk survivals into drama proper highly problematic, and may well have led to the comment:

> The dizziness occasioned by sustained circular movement is a condition to which any student of early folk lore must sooner or later be accustomed.
>
> (Pettitt, 377, p. 20)

T. A. Green (370) insisted that much of the material in the recorded texts is specifically of the eighteenth century and may well bear the interpretation that what the early collectors found was actually a ceremony that offered both a protest against social links and structures and a means of generating income by way of the *quête* in times of hardship (see also A. E. Green, 369). There is a need to see the recorded text of the traditional drama in what T. A. Green calls its 'behavioural context' (370, p. 423). His definition, accepting the idea of a written text, moves into the sociological background:

> a scripted performance which incorporates mimesis and role distribution among two or more players and which adheres to the traditional aesthetic and communicative models of the performing community.   (p. 428)

This is sustained by Burson (365). Written texts have certainly not survived for all six types of mummers' play identified by A. E. Green (369, p. 141). This difficulty is somewhat offset by Pettitt's exposition of the *Fastnacht-spiele* (376), which are earlier than their presumed English equivalent, and his work is especially useful for its emphasis upon the mode of performance, an objective clearly identified by Axton (22).

We must surely welcome any attempts to study relationships between traditional drama and medieval plays that depend upon a rigorous enquiry. Nevertheless a considerable amount of information has now been accumulated that offers analogues between the medieval plays and the traditional drama. Specific verbal parallels may be somewhat less valuable than similarities between the two dramatic modes, which may help us to understand the dynamics of the medieval plays. The items that have attracted most attention are wooing, combat, beheading, the cure by the comic doctor and his boy, the *quête* and the revival. Moreover the idea that the folk play, whatever it does by way of plot, may be essentially a show which is consciously presented is traceable in the regular drama. Axton (22) saw a variety of survivals, particularly the combat and the dancing game, as contributing much to the earliest medieval drama, and he followed this through to the Towneley *Mactatio Abel* and other cycle plays (pp. 175–82), as well as looking in more detail at examples from a number of moralities and interludes. The plays he considered were the *Interludium de Clerico et Puella* and the related *Dame Sirith*, the *Robin Hood Plays*, *Mankind*, the Croxton *Play of the Sacrament*, *Youth*, Medwall's *Fulgens and Lucres*, Rastell's *The Four Elements*, *Calisto and Melebea*, Redford's *Wit and Science*, Heywood's *Play of the Weather*, Bale's *Three Laws* and *Thersites*. Further material is available on *The Pride of Life* (360), *Mankind* (336, 367, 335, 28), *Wisdom* (364, 377) and the *Croxton Play* (373). Though he centres upon an Elizabethan play, Renwick (378) offers a useful structuralist approach.

Less directly concerned with dramatic aspects, but still of interpretative importance, is the relationship of traditional elements to political and social aspects of the drama proper. Tydeman (41) considered the Church's attitudes, and Axton (361) the Reformation, which obliterated many earlier survivals and festivals. Weimann's analysis (380) of the popular traditions and survivals was concerned with parody and festive inversion, especially in terms of language. Laroque (372) has recently surveyed the relationship between seasonal entertainment and the professional stage in the early modern period.

Dietrich's bibliographical article (368) gave a very useful list of examples of traditional drama, and the *REED* volumes have reflected many instances where and when performances are now known to have occurred. Cawte, Helm and Peacock (366) is the standard source of information about geographical distribution of different types of folk play.

FUTURE DEVELOPMENTS

Sidney E. Berger's bibliography of recent criticism of medieval English Drama (1) covers the period from about 1970 to 1990, and contains 1,744 entries, which gives a vivid idea of the annual number of publications in the field. The flow of editions, books, articles, reviews, videotapes of productions and so forth, continues undiminished, and the most effective way of discovering which are the more significant items is to consult the *Modern Language Association of America [MLA] International Bibliography of Books and Articles on the Modern Languages and Literatures*, the *Annual Bibliography of English Language and Literature* produced by the Modern Humanities Research Association and *The Year's Work in English Studies* (*YWES*), produced by the English Association.

On the editorial front, the chief outstanding item is the Early English Text Society's fresh edition of the Towneley plays, being prepared by †A. C. Cawley and Martin Stevens. A significant desideratum is an extended commentary on the York cycle along the lines of those provided for Chester and

N-Town in the EETS editions (73, 78). Editions of the York and Chester cycles in modernised spelling (71, 74) have been found useful by students new to the field and groups involved in modern productions, and similar treatments of Towneley and N-Town are likely to appear.

Provided there is adequate financial support, new documentary material will be issued by the *REED* project at intervals for some time to come. Well over twenty volumes are said to be in active preparation (1, pp. 473–4), but it may be decades before critics and historians of the early drama have all the information relevant to their projects in print. The biannual *REED Newsletter* publishes interim findings and signals the new record volumes as they appear. More specific developments relating to art and music with reference to the drama appear in the *EDAM Review*. Modern productions of medieval plays will undoubtedly continue to flourish, and to explore the surviving texts in radical and fruitful ways. Many of them are reviewed in *Medieval English Theatre* (*METh*) and *Research Opportunities in Renaissance Drama* (*RORD*). The annual publication of *Medieval and Renaissance Drama in England*, edited by Leeds Barroll, contains some essays on medieval plays and also an extensive review section. This series, and *RORD*, have the special benefit of blurring the undesirable demarcation between 'medieval' and 'Renaissance' drama scholarship.

Select Bibliography

Compiled by Richard Beadle and Peter Happé

The bibliography is intended to serve two purposes: first, to support the system of brief reference used in the text and in many of the notes to the chapters; and second, to give a classified overview of the more important current work in the field of medieval English theatre. The arrangement of the bibliography is determined largely by the structure of the book and the likely needs of the majority of its users. Systematic bibliographies of medieval drama, general surveys, listings of documentary materials, editions and ancillary research works, such as facsimiles and concordances, are followed by a series of sections which reflect the bibliographical underpinning of the chapters on the plays themselves, in the order in which they appear. A series of special sections towards the end, such as 'Folk drama', Staging, Music and drama, Art and drama, and so on, answer to the topics discussed in chapter 12.

The bibliography includes all the works cited by bracketed serial number within the text, together with many other significant items, most of them published since around 1970. The detailed bibliographies in the first section provide ample reference to earlier work. For the editions of the plays cited within the text see pp. xviii–xix.

The sections into which the bibliography is divided are as follows:

1	Bibliographies	13	The East Anglian drama
2	Collections of articles	14	The Cornish drama
3	General surveys	15	The morality plays and early
4	Documentary materials, and their		interludes
	interpretation	16	Saints' plays
5	Editions, and editorial issues	17	'Folk drama'
6	Facsimiles	18	Character
7	Concordances and dictionaries	19	Staging: actors, acting, costumes,
8	Cycle plays: general		props, special effects etc.
9	The York cycle	20	Music and drama
10	The Chester cycle	21	Art and drama
11	The Towneley cycle	22	Modern productions of medieval
12	The N-Town plays		plays

1 BIBLIOGRAPHIES

1   Berger, Sidney E. *Medieval English Drama: an Annotated Bibliography of Recent Criticism.* New York and London: Garland, 1990.

2   Hartung, Albert E., ed. *A Manual of the Writings in Middle English 1050–1500*, vol. v. Hamden, Conn.: Shoe String Press, 1975. See *5,6,9*.

3   Houle, Peter J. *The English Morality and Related Drama: a Bibliographical Survey.* Hamden, Conn.: Shoe String Press, 1972.

4   Lancashire, Ian. *Dramatic Texts and Records of Britain. A Chronological Topography.* Toronto: University of Toronto Press, and Cambridge: Cambridge University Press, 1984.

5   Lindenbaum, Sheila. 'The Morality Plays'. In 2, 1357–81, 1599–1621.

6   Mill, Anna J. 'The Miracle Plays and Mysteries'. In 2, 1315–56, 1557–98.

7   Newlyn, Evelyn S. *Cornish Drama of the Middle Ages: a Bibliography* Redruth: Institute of Cornish Studies, 1987.

8   Stratman, Carl J. *Bibliography of Medieval Drama.* 2 vols. New York: Frederick Ungar, 1972.

9   Utley, Francis Lee, and Barry Ward. 'The Folk Drama'. In 2, 1382–4, 1622–9.

10 Watson, George, ed. *The New Cambridge Bibliography of English Literature.* vol. i: *600–1600.* Cambridge: Cambridge University Press, 1974, cols. 727–42 (by J.W. Robinson).

11 Wilson, F.P. *The English Drama 1485–1585.* Edited with a bibliography by G.K. Hunter. Oxford: Clarendon Press, 1969.

2   COLLECTIONS OF ARTICLES

12 Briscoe, Marianne G., and John C. Coldewey, eds. *Contexts for Early English Drama.* Bloomington and Indianapolis: Indiana University Press, 1989.

13 Davidson, Clifford, and others, eds. *The Drama in the Middle Ages: Comparative and Critical Essays.* New York: AMS Press, 1982.

14 Denny, Neville, ed. *Medieval Drama.* Stratford-upon-Avon Studies, 16. London: Edward Arnold, 1973.

15 Emmerson, Richard K., ed. *Approaches to Teaching Medieval English Drama.* New York: Modern Language Association of America, 1990.

15a Gilman, Donald, ed. *Everyman & Company: Essays on the Theme and Structure of the European Moral Play.* New York: AMS Press, 1989.

16 Happé, Peter, ed. *Medieval English Drama: a Casebook.* London: Macmillan, 1984.

17 Johnston, Alexandra F., ed. *Editing Early English Drama: Special Problems and New Directions.* New York: AMS Press, 1987.

18 Neuss, Paula, ed. *Aspects of Early English Drama.* Cambridge: D.S. Brewer, 1983.

19 Potter, Lois, general ed. *The Revels History of Drama in English.* vol. i: *Medieval Drama.* London and New York: Methuen, 1983.

20 Simon, Eckehard, ed. *The Theatre of Medieval Europe: New Research in Early Drama.* Cambridge: Cambridge University Press, 1991.

21 Taylor, Jerome, and Alan H. Nelson, eds. *Medieval English Drama: Essays Critical and Contextual.* Chicago: Chicago University Press, 1972.

3   GENERAL SURVEYS

22 Axton, Richard. *European Drama of the Early Middle Ages.* London: Hutchinson, 1974.

23 Chambers, E.K. *The Mediaeval Stage.* 2 vols. Oxford: Clarendon Press, 1903.

24 Coldewey, John C. 'Some Economic Aspects of the Late Medieval Drama'. In *12*, 77–101.

25 Craig, Hardin. *English Religious Drama of the Middle Ages.* Oxford: Clarendon Press, 1955.

26 Elam, Keir. *The Semiotics of Theatre and Drama.* London: Methuen, 1980.

27 Frank, Grace. *Medieval French Drama.* Oxford: Oxford University Press, 1960.

28 Gash, Anthony. 'Carnival against Lent: the Ambivalence of Medieval Drama'. In *Medieval Literature: Criticism Ideology, Literature*, ed. D. Aers. Brighton: Harvester Press, 1986, 74–98.

29 Hardison, O.B., Jr. *Christian Rite and Christian Drama in the Middle Ages: Essays in the Origin and Early History of Modern Drama*. Baltimore: The Johns Hopkins University Press, 1965.

30 Hone, William. *Ancient Mysteries Described*. London: n.p., 1823.

31 Kahrl, Stanley J. *Traditions of Medieval English Drama*. London: Hutchinson, 1974.

32 Manly, John M. 'Literary Forms and the New Theory of the Origin of Species'. *MP* 4 (1906–7): 577–95.

33 Muir, Lynette R. 'Medieval English Drama: the French Connection'. In *12*, 56–76.

34 Nelson, Alan H. *The Medieval English Stage: Corpus Christi Pageants and Plays*. Chicago and London: University of Chicago Press, 1974.

35 Owst, G.R. *Literature and Pulpit in Medieval England*. Cambridge: Cambridge University Press, 1933; repr. with additions Oxford: Basil Blackwell, 1961.

36 Potter, Robert. 'The Unity of Medieval Drama: European Contexts for Early English Dramatic Traditions'. In *12*, 41–55.

37 Robinson, J.W. 'Regency Radicalism and Antiquarianism: William Hone's *Ancient Mysteries Described* (1823)'. *LSE* 10 (1978): 121–44.

38 Rossiter, A.P. *English Drama from Early Times to the Elizabethans*. London: Hutchinson, 1950.

39 Sharp, Thomas. *A Dissertation on the Pageants or Dramatic Mysteries Anciently Performed at Coventry*. Coventry: Merridew and Son, 1825; repr. Wakefield: EP Publishing Ltd., 1973, with a new foreword by A.C. Cawley.

40 Twycross, Meg. 'Books for the Unlearned'. In *Themes in Drama*, vol. v: *Drama and Religion*, ed. James Redmond. Cambridge: Cambridge University Press, 1983, 65–110.

41 Tydeman, William. *The Theatre in the Middle Ages: Western European Stage Conditions c. 800–1576*. Cambridge: Cambridge University Press, 1978.

42 Tydeman, William. *Medieval English Drama*. London: Routledge and Kegan Paul, 1986.

43 Vince, Ronald W. *Ancient and Medieval Theatre: a Historiographical Handbook*. London and Westport, Conn.: Greenwood Press, 1984.

44 Vince, Ronald W., ed. *A Companion to the Medieval Theatre*. London and Westport, Conn.: Greenwood Press, 1989.

45 Wasson, John. 'Karl Young and the Vernacular Drama'. *RORD* 27 (1984): 151–6.

46 Williams, Arnold. *The Drama of Medieval England*. East Lansing, Mich.: Michigan State College Press, 1950.

4 DOCUMENTARY MATERIALS, AND THEIR INTERPRETATION

47 Anderson, John J., ed. *Records of Early English Drama: Newcastle-upon-Tyne*. Toronto: University of Toronto Press, 1984.

47a Coletti, Theresa. '*Reading REED*: History and the Records of Early English Drama'. In *Literary Practice and Social Change in Britain 1380–1530*, ed. Lee Patterson (Berkeley, Los Angeles and Oxford: University of California Press, 1990), 248–84.

48 Dawson, Giles E., ed. *Records of Plays and Players in Kent, 1450–1642*. Malone Society Collections, 7. Oxford: Oxford University Press, 1965.

49 Douglas, Audrey, and Peter Greenfield, eds. *Records of Early English Drama: Cumberland/Westmorland/Gloucestershire*. Toronto: University of Toronto Press, 1986.

50 George, David, ed. *Records of Early English Drama: Lancashire*. Toronto: University of Toronto Press, 1991.

51 Ingram, R.W., ed. *Records of Early English Drama: Coventry*. Toronto: University of Toronto Press, 1981.

52 Johnston, Alexandra F. 'What if No Texts Survived? External Evidence for Early English Drama'. In *12*, 1–9.

53 Johnston, Alexandra F. ' "All the World Was a Stage": Records of Early English Drama'. In *20*, 117–29.

54 Kahrl, Stanley J., ed. *Records of Plays and Players in Lincolnshire, 1300–1585*. Malone Society Collections, 8. Oxford: Oxford University Press, 1969.

55 Klausner, David, ed. *Records of Early English Drama: Herefordshire and Worcestershire*. Toronto: University of Toronto Press, 1990.

56 Lancashire, Ian. 'Orders for Twelfth Day and Night *circa* 1515 in the Second Northumberland Household Book'. *English Literary Renaissance* 10 (1980): 6–45.

57 Mill, Anna J. *Medieval Plays in Scotland*. St Andrews University Publications, 24 (1927).

58 Murray, John Tucker. *English Dramatic Companies, 1558–1642*. London: Constable, 1910.

59 Nelson, Alan H. *Records of Early English Drama: Cambridge*. 2 vols. Toronto: University of Toronto Press, 1989.

60 Robertson, J., and D.J. Gordon, eds. *A Calendar of Dramatic Records in the Books of the Livery Companies of London 1485–1640*. Malone Society Collections, 3. Oxford: Oxford University Press, 1954; with *Addenda*, Malone Society Collections, 5, 1959.

61 Wasson, John, ed. *Records of Early English Drama: Devon*. Toronto: University of Toronto Press, 1987.

See also 158 (York), *179*, *182* (Chester), *257* (Norwich), *252* (Norfolk and Suffolk).

5 EDITIONS, AND EDITORIAL ISSUES
Anthologies and collections

62 Bevington, David, ed. *Medieval Drama*. Boston: Houghton Mifflin, 1975.

63 Cawley, A.C., ed. *Everyman and Medieval Miracle Plays*. London: Dent, 1956.

64 Dodsley, Robert, ed. *A Select Collection of Old Plays*. 12 vols. London, 1744.

65 Farmer, John S., ed. *Early English Dramatists*. 13 vols. London: privately printed for subscribers, 1903–8.

66 Happé, Peter, ed. *English Mystery Plays*. Harmondsworth: Penguin Books, 1975.

67 Happé, Peter, ed. *Four Morality Plays*. Harmondsworth: Penguin Books, 1979.

68 Lester, G.A., ed. *Three Late Medieval Morality Plays*. London: Benn, 1981.

69 Young, Karl. *The Drama of the Medieval Church*. 2 vols. Oxford: Clarendon Press, 1933.

Cycle plays

70 Beadle, Richard, ed. *The York Plays*. London: Edward Arnold, 1982.

71 Beadle, Richard, and Pamela M. King, eds. *York Mystery Plays: a Selection in Modern Spelling*. Oxford: Clarendon Press, 1984.

72 Smith, Lucy Toulmin, ed. *York Plays*. Oxford, Clarendon Press, 1885.

73 Lumiansky, R.M., and David Mills, eds. *The Chester Mystery Cycle*. vol. I: Text (EETS, SS 3). vol. II: Commentary and Glossary (EETS, SS 9). Oxford: Oxford University Press, 1974, 1986.

74 Mills, David, ed. *The Chester Mystery Cycle: a New Edition with Modernised Spelling*. East Lansing: Colleagues Press, 1992.

75 England, George, ed. *The Towneley Plays*. With side-notes and introduction by Alfred W. Pollard (EETS, ES 71). London: Kegan Paul, Trench, Trübner & Co., 1897.

76 Cawley, A.C., ed. *The Wakefield Pageants in the Towneley Cycle*. Manchester: Manchester University Press, 1958.

77 Rose, Martial, ed. *The Wakefield Mystery Plays*. London: Evans Bros., 1961.

78 Spector, Stephen, ed. *The N-Town Play*. 2 vols (EETS, SS 11–12). Oxford: Oxford University Press, 1991.

79 Meredith, Peter, ed. *The Mary Play from the N. Town Manuscript*. London: Longman, 1987.
80 Meredith, Peter, ed. *The Passion Play from the N. Town Manuscript*. London: Longman, 1990.
81 Block, K.S., ed. *Ludus Coventriae, or the Plaie called Corpus Christi*. EETS, ES 120. Oxford: Oxford University Press, 1922.
82 Craig, Hardin, ed. *Two Coventry Corpus Christi Plays*. EETS, ES 87. Oxford: Oxford University Press, 2nd edn 1952.

Non-cycle plays, moralities, saints' plays, interludes

83 Eccles, Mark, ed. *The Macro Plays*. EETS 262. Oxford: Oxford University Press, 1969.
84 Baker, Donald C., John L. Murphy and Louis B. Hall Jr, eds. *The Late Medieval Religious Plays of Bodleian MSS Digby 133 and E Museo 160* (EETS 283). Oxford: Oxford University Press, 1982.
85 Davis, Norman, ed. *Non-cycle Plays and Fragments* (EETS, SS 1). Oxford: Oxford University Press, 1970.
86 Cooper, Geoffrey, and Christopher Wortham, eds. *Everyman*. Nedlands, W.A.: University of Western Australia Press, 1980.
87 Cawley, A.C., ed. *Everyman*. Manchester: Manchester University Press, 1961.
88 Nelson, Alan H., ed. *The Plays of Henry Medwall*. Cambridge: D.S. Brewer, 1980.
89 Lancashire, Ian, ed. *Two Tudor Interludes: the Interlude of Youth. Hick Scorner*. Manchester: Manchester University Press, 1980.
90 Neuss, Paula, ed. *John Skelton, Magnyfycence*. Manchester: Manchester University Press, 1980.
91 Axton, Richard, ed. *Three Rastell Plays*. Cambridge: D.S. Brewer, 1979.
92 Axton, Richard, and Peter Happé, eds. *The Plays of John Heywood*. Cambridge: D.S. Brewer, 1991.
93 Axton, Marie, ed. *Three Classical Tudor Interludes*. Cambridge: D.S. Brewer, 1982.
94 Happé, Peter, ed. *The Complete Plays of John Bale*. 2 vols. Cambridge: D.S. Brewer, 1985–6.
95 Hamer, Douglas, ed. *The Works of Sir David Lindsay of the Mount, 1490–1555*. Scottish Text Society, vols. I–II, VI, VIII. Edinburgh and London: William Blackwood, 1931–6.
96 Lyall, Roderick, ed. *Sir David Linsday of the Mount. Ane Satyre of the Thrie Estaitis*. Edinburgh: Canongate Publishing, 1989.

Cornish drama

97 Norris, Edwin, ed. *The Ancient Cornish Drama*. 2 vols. Oxford: Oxford University Press, 1859.
98 Neuss, Paula, ed. *The Creacion of the World: a Critical Edition and Translation*. New York and London: Garland, 1983.
99 S[tokes], W[hitley]. 'Cornica IV. The Fragments of a Drama in Add. Ch. 19,491, Mus. Brit.'. *Revue Celtique* 4 (1879–80): 258–62.
100 Stokes, Whitley, ed. *The Life of St Meriasek, Bishop and Confessor. A Cornish Drama*. London: Trübner, 1872.

Editorial issues

101 Bevington, David M. 'Drama Editing and its Relation to Recent Trends in Literary Criticism'. In *17*, 17–32.
102 Kahrl, Stanley J. 'Editing Texts for Dramatic Performance'. In *The Drama of Medieval Europe*, ed. Richard Rastall. Leeds: University of Leeds, Graduate Centre for Medieval Studies, 1975, 39–52.
103 Lancashire, Ian. 'Medieval Drama'. In *Editing Medieval Texts: English, French, and Latin written in England*, ed. A.G. Rigg. New York and London: Garland, 1977, 58–85.

104 Meredith, Peter. 'Scribes, Texts and Performance'. In *18*, 13–29.
105 Meredith, Peter. 'Stage Directions and the Edition of Early English Drama'. In *17*, 65–94.
106 Mills, David. 'Theories and Practices in the Editing of the Chester Cycle Play Manuscripts'. In *Manuscripts and Texts: Editorial Problems in Medieval English Literature*, ed. Derek Pearsall. Cambridge: D.S. Brewer, 1987, 110–121.
107 Mills, David. 'Modern Editions of Medieval English Plays'. In *20*, 65–79.
108 Parry, David. 'A Margin of Error: the Problems of Marginalia in *Castle of Perseverance*'. In *17*, 33–64.

6 FACSIMILES

109 Beadle, Richard, and Peter Meredith, eds. *The York Play: a Facsimile of British Library MS Additional 35290, together with a Facsimile of the Ordo Paginarum Section of the A/Y Memorandum Book, and a Note on the Music by Richard Rastall*. Leeds: University of Leeds, School of English, 1983.
110 Lumiansky, R.M., and David Mills, eds. *The Chester Mystery Cycle: a Facsimile of MS Bodley 175*. Leeds: University of Leeds, School of English, 1973.
111 Lumiansky, R.M., and David Mills, eds. *The Chester Mystery Cycle: a Reduced Facsimile of Huntington Library MS 2*. Leeds: University of Leeds, School of English, 1980.
112 Mills, David, ed. *The Chester Mystery Cycle: a Facsimile of British Library MS Harley 2124*. Leeds: University of Leeds, School of English, 1980.
113 Cawley, A.C., and Martin Stevens, eds. *The Towneley Cycle: a Facsimile of Huntington MS HM1*. Leeds: University of Leeds, School of English, 1976.
114 Meredith, Peter, and Stanley J. Kahrl, eds. *The N-Town Plays: a Facsimile of British Library MS Cotton Vespasian D.VIII*. Leeds: University of Leeds, School of English, 1977.
115 Bevington, David, ed. *The Macro Plays. The Castle of Perseverance, Wisdom, Mankind. A Facsimile Edition with Facing Transcription*. New York: Johnson Reprint Corporation, 1972.
116 Baker, Donald C., and J.L. Murphy, eds. *The Digby Plays: Facsimiles of the Plays in Bodley MSS Digby 133 and E Museo 160*. Leeds: University of Leeds, School of English, 1976.
117 Davis, Norman, ed. *Non-Cycle Plays and the Winchester Dialogues: Facsimiles of Plays and Fragments in Various Manuscripts*. Leeds: University of Leeds, School of English, 1979.
118 Farmer, John S., ed. *Tudor Facsimile Texts*. 143 vols. Amersham, 1907–14.

7 CONCORDANCES AND DICTIONARIES

119 Kinneavy, Gerald Byron. *A Concordance to the York Plays*. With a textual introduction by Richard Beadle. New York and London: Garland, 1986.
120 Pfleiderer, Jean D., and Michael J. Preston. *A Complete Concordance to The Chester Mystery Plays*. New York and London: Garland, 1981.
121 Preston, Michael J., and Jean D. Pfleiderer, *A KWIC Concordance to the Plays of the Wakefield Master*. New York and London: Garland, 1982.
122 Kinneavy, Gerald Byron. *A Concordance to the Towneley Plays*. New York and London: Garland, 1990.
123 Preston, Michael J., and Jean D. Pfleiderer. *A Concordance to the Ludus Coventriae or N-Town Plays*. New York and London: Garland, forthcoming.
124 Preston, Michael J., and Jean D. Pfleiderer. *A Concordance to the Non-Cycle Plays and Fragments*. vol. I: Plays from East Anglia. New York and London: Garland, forthcoming.

125 Dent, Robert W. *Proverbial Language in English Drama Exclusive of Shakespeare, 1495–1616: An Index*. Berkeley, Los Angeles and London: University of California Press, 1984.

126 Whiting, Bartlett Jere. *Proverbs, Sentences, and Proverbial Phrases from English Writings Mainly before 1500*. Cambridge, Mass.: Harvard University Press, 1968.

8 CYCLE PLAYS: GENERAL

127 Bills, Bing Duane. 'The "Suppression Theory" and the English Corpus Christi Plays: a Re-Evaluation'. *Theatre Journal* 32 (1980): 157–68.

128 Clopper, Lawrence M. 'Lay and Clerical Impact on Civic Religious Drama and Ceremony'. In *12*, 102–36.

129 Gardiner, Harold C. *Mysteries' End*. New Haven: Yale University Press, 1946.

130 Kolve, V.A. *The Play Called Corpus Christi*. Stanford: Stanford University Press, 1966.

131 Lepow, Lauren E. 'Middle English Elevation Prayers and the Corpus Christi Cycles'. *ELN* 17 (1979): 85–8.

132 Pearson, Lu Emily. 'Isolable Lyrics in the Mystery Plays'. *ELH* 3 (1936): 228–52.

133 Prosser, Eleanor. *Drama and Religion in the English Mystery Plays: a Re-Evaluation*. Stanford: Stanford University Press, 1961.

134 Robinson, J.W. *Studies in Fifteenth-Century Stagecraft*. Kalamazoo: Western Michigan University, Medieval Institute Publications, 1991.

135 Stevens, Martin. *Four Middle English Mystery Cycles*. Princeton: Princeton University Press, 1987.

136 Taylor, George Coffin. 'The Relation of the English Corpus Christi Play to the Middle English Religious Lyric'. *MP* 5 (1907): 1–38.

137 Wells, Henry W. 'Style in the English Mystery Plays'. *JEGP* 38 (1939): 496–524.

138 Woolf, Rosemary. *The English Mystery Plays*. London: Routledge and Kegan Paul, 1972.

9 THE YORK CYCLE

139 Beadle, Richard. 'The Origins of Abraham's Preamble in the York Play of *Abraham and Isaac*'. *Yearbook of English Studies* 11 (1981): 178–87.

140 Beadle, Richard. 'The Shipwrights' Craft'. In *18*, 50–61.

141 Beadle, Richard. 'The York Hosiers' Play of *Moses and Pharaoh*: a Middle English Dramatist at Work'. *Poetica* 19 (1984): 3–26.

142 Beadle, Richard. 'Poetry, Theology and Drama in the York *Creation and Fall of Lucifer*'. In *Religion in the Poetry and Drama of the Late Middle Ages in England*, ed. Piero Boitani and Anna Torti. Cambridge: D.S. Brewer, 1990, 213–27.

143 Beadle, Richard. 'The York Cycle: Texts, Performances, and the Bases for Critical Enquiry'. In *Medieval Literature: Texts and Interpretation*, ed. Tim William Machan (Binghamton, New York: Centre for Medieval and Early Renaissance Studies, 1991), 105–119.

144 Butterworth, Philip. 'The York Mercers' Pageant Vehicle: Wheels, Steering and Control'. *METh* 1 (1979): 72–81.

145 Cawley, A.C. 'The Sykes Manuscript of the York Scriveners' Play'. *LSE* 7–8 (1952): 45–80.

146 Collier, Richard J. *Poetry and Drama in the York Corpus Christi Play*. Hamden, Conn.: Archon, 1977.

147 Davidson, Clifford. *From Creation to Doom: the York Cycle of Mystery Plays*. New York: AMS Press, 1984.

148 Davidson, Clifford, and David E. O'Connor. *York Art: a Subject List of Extant and Lost Art, Including Items Relevant to Early Drama*. Kalamazoo: Western Michigan University, Medieval Institute Publications, 1978.

149 Dorrell, Margaret 'The Mayor of York and the Coronation Pageant'. *LSE* 5 (1971): 35–45.

150 Dorrell, Margaret. 'Two Studies of the York Corpus Christi Play'. *LSE* 6 (1972): 63–111.

151 Epp, Garret P.J. 'Passion, Pomp and Parody: Alliteration in the York Plays'. *METh* 11 (1989): 150–161.

152 Johnston, Alexandra F. 'The Procession and Play of Corpus Christi in York after 1426'. *LSE* 7 (1973–4): 55–62.

153 Johnston, Alexandra F. 'The Plays of the Religious Guilds of York: the Creed Play and the Paternoster Play'. *Speculum* 50 (1975): 55–90.

154 Johnston, Alexandra F. 'The York Corpus Christi Play: a Dramatic Structure based on Performance Practice'. In *The Theatre in the Middle Ages*, ed. H. Braet and others (Leuven: Leuven University Press, 1985), 362–73.

155 Johnston, Alexandra F. 'The *York* Cycle and the *Chester* Cycle: What Do the Records Tell Us?' In *17*, 121–43.

156 Johnston, Alexandra F., and Margaret Dorrell, 'The Doomsday Pageant of the York Mercers, 1433'. *LSE* 5 (1971): 29–34.

157 Johnston, Alexandra F., and Margaret Dorrell. 'The York Mercers and their Pageant of Doomsday, 1433–1526'. *LSE* 6 (1972): 10–35.

158 Johnston, Alexandra F., and Margaret Rogerson, eds. *Records of Early English Drama: York*. 2 vols. Toronto: University of Toronto Press, 1979.

159 Justice, Alan D. 'Trade Symbolism in the York Cycle'. *Theatre Journal* 31 (1979): 47–58.

160 Meredith, Peter. 'The Development of the York Mercers' Pageant Waggon'. *METh* 1 (1979): 5–18.

161 Meredith, Peter. 'The *Ordo Paginarum* and the Development of the York Tilemakers' Pageant'. *LSE* 11 (1980): 59–73.

162 Meredith, Peter. 'John Clerke's Hand in the York Register'. *LSE* 12 (1981): 245–71.

163 Meredith, Peter. 'The York Millers' Pageant and the Towneley *Processus Talentorum*'. *METh* 4 (1982): 104–14.

164 Mill, Anna J. 'The Stations of the York Corpus Christi Play'. *Yorkshire Archaeological Journal* 37 (1951): 493–500.

165 Rastall, Richard. 'The [York] Music'. In *109*, xli-xlviii.

166 Reese, Jesse Byers. 'Alliterative Verse in the York Cycle'. *SP* 48 (1951): 639–68.

167 Robinson, J.W. 'The Art of the York Realist'. *MP* 60 (1963): 241–51. Also in *21*, 230–44.

168 Robinson, J.W. 'A Commentary on the York Play of the Birth of Jesus'. *JEGP* 70 (1971): 241–55.

169 Rogerson, Margaret. 'The York Corpus Christi Play: Some Practical Details'. *LSE* 10 (1978): 97–106.

170 Twycross, Meg. '"Places to Hear the Play": Pageant Stations at York, 1398–1572'. *REED Newsletter* 2 (1978): 10–33.

171 Twycross, Meg. 'Playing *The Resurrection*'. In *Medieval Studies for J.A.W. Bennett*, ed. P.L. Heyworth. Oxford: Clarendon Press, 1982, 273–96.

172 Wall, Carolyn. 'York Pageant XLVI [now XLV] and its Music'. *Speculum* 46 (1971): 689–712.

173 Wallis, J.P.R. 'The Miracle Play of *Crucifixio Christi* in the York Cycle'. *MLR* 12 (1917): 494–5.

174 White, Eileen. 'Places for Hearing the Corpus Christi Play in York'. *METh* 9 (1987): 23–63.

175 Young, M. James, 'The York Pageant Wagon'. *Speech Monographs* 34 (1967): 1–20.

See also 383 (character), *413, 423* (staging), *6, 70* (further bibliography).

10 THE CHESTER CYCLE

176   Ashley, Kathleen M. 'Divine Power in the Chester Cycle and Later Medieval Thought'. *Journal of the History of Ideas* 39 (1978): 387–404.

177   Clopper, Lawrence M. 'The Staging of the Medieval Plays of Chester: a Response'. *TN* 28 (1974): 65–70.

178   Clopper, Lawrence M. 'The History and Development of the Chester Cycle'. *MP* 75 (1978): 219–46.

179   Clopper, Lawrence M., ed. *Records of Early English Drama: Chester*. Toronto: University of Toronto Press, 1979.

180   Clopper, Lawrence M. 'The Principle of Selection in the Chester Old Testament Plays'. *Chaucer Review* 13 (1979): 272–87.

181   Greg, W.W. *'The Trial and Flagellation' and Other Studies in the Chester Cycle*. Malone Society. Oxford: Oxford University Press, 1935.

182   Lumiansky, R.M., and David Mills. *The Chester Mystery Cycle: Essays and Documents*. Chapel Hill and London: University of North Carolina Press, 1983.

183   MacLean, Sally-Beth. *Chester Art: a Subject List of Extant and Lost Art, Including Items Relevant to Early Drama*. Kalamazoo: Western Michigan University, Medieval Institute Publications, 1982.

184   Marshall, John. 'Players of the Coopers' Pageant from the Chester Plays in 1572 and 1575'. *TN* 33 (1979): 18–23.

185   Marshall, John. ' "The Manner of these Playes": the Chester Pageant Carriages and the Places Where They Played'. In *188*, 17–48.

186   Meredith, Peter. ' "Make the Asse to Speake", or Staging the Chester Plays'. In *188*, 49–76.

187   Mills, David. 'The Stage Directions in the Manuscripts of the Chester Cycle'. *METh* 3 (1981): 45–51.

188   Mills, David, ed. *Staging the Chester Cycle*. Leeds Texts and Monographs, 9. Leeds: University of Leeds, School of English, 1985.

189   Rastall, Richard. 'Music in the [Chester] Cycle'. In *182*, 111–64.

190   Rastall, Richard. ' "Some Myrth to his Majestee": Music in the Chester Cycle'. In *188*, 77–99.

191   Salter, F.M. *Medieval Drama in Chester*. Toronto: University of Toronto Press, 1955.

192   Travis, Peter W. *Dramatic Design in the Chester Cycle*. Chicago and London, University of Chicago Press, 1982.

See also 426 (costume), 6, 73 (further bibliography).

11 THE TOWNELEY CYCLE

193   Brown, Carleton. 'The Towneley *Play of the Doctors* and the *Speculum Christiani*. *MLN* 31 (1916): 223–6.

194   Carey, Millicent. *The Wakefield Group in the Towneley Cycle*, Baltimore: The Johns Hopkins University Press, 1930.

195   Carpenter, Nan Cooke. 'Music in the *Secunda Pastorum*'. *Speculum* 26 (1951): 696–700. Also in *21*, 212–17.

196   Cawley, A.C. 'The Towneley *Processus Talentorum*: a Survey and Interpretation. *LSE* 17 (1986): 131–9.

197   Cawley, A.C., Jean Forrester and John Goodchild. 'References to the Corpus Christi Play in the Wakefield Burgess Court Rolls: the Originals Rediscovered'. *LSE* 19 (1988): 85–104.

198   Cawley, A.C., and Martin Stevens. 'The Towneley *Processus Talentorum*: Text and Commentary'. *LSE* 17 (1986): 105–30.

199   Diller, Hans-Jürgen. 'The Craftsmanship of the Wakefield Master'. *Anglia* 83 (1965): 271–88. Also in 21, 245–59.

200   Dunn, E. Catherine. 'Lyrical Form and the Prophetic Principle in the Towneley Plays'. *Medieval Studies* 23 (1961): 80–90.

201   Dunn, E. Catherine. 'The Literary Style of the Towneley Plays'. *American Benedictine Review* 20 (1969): 481–504.

202   Forrester, Jean, and A.C. Cawley. 'The Corpus Christi Play in Wakefield: a New Look at the Burgess Court Records'. *LSE* 7 (1974): 108–16.

203   Frampton, Mendel G. 'The Date of the Flourishing of the "Wakefield Master"'. *PMLA* 50 (1935): 631–60.

204   Frampton, Mendel G. 'The Date of the "Wakefield Master": Bibliographical Evidence'. *PMLA* 53 (1938): 86–117.

205   Frampton, Mendel G. 'Towneley XX, the *Conspiracio (et Capcio)*'. *PMLA* 58 (1943): 920–37.

206   Gardner, John. *The Construction of the Wakefield Cycle*. Carbondale and Edwardsville: Southern Illinois University Press, 1974.

207   Helterman, Jeffrey. *Symbolic Action in the Plays of the Wakefield Master*. Athens, Georgia: University of Georgia Press, 1981.

208   Meyers, Walter E. *A Figure Given: Typology in the Wakefield Plays*. Pittsburgh: Duquesne University Press, 1970.

209   Mills, David. ' "The Towneley Plays" or "The Towneley Cycle"?' *LSE* (1986): 93–104.

210   Palmer, Barbara D. ' "Towneley Plays" or "Wakefield Cycle" Revisited'. *CD* (1988): 318–48.

211   Ross, L.J. 'Symbol and Structure in the *Secunda Pastorum*'. *CD* 1 (1967–8): 122–43. Also in 21, 177–211.

212   Stevens, Martin. 'The Staging of the Wakefield Plays'. *RORD* 11 (1968): 115–28.

213   Stevens, Martin. 'The Missing Parts of the Towneley Cycle'. *Speculum* 45 (1970): 254–65.

214   Stevens, Martin. 'The Manuscript of the *Towneley Plays*: its History and Editions'. *Papers of the Bibliographical Society of America* 67 (1973): 231–44.

215   Stevens, Martin. 'Language as Theme in the Wakefield Plays'. *Speculum* 52 (1977): 100–17.

216   Stevens, Martin. 'Did the Wakefield Master Write a Nine-Line Stanza?' *CD* 15 (1981): 99–119.

217   Wann, Louis. 'A New Examination of the Manuscript of the Towneley Plays'. *PMLA* 43 (1928): 137–52.

218   Watt, Homer A. 'The Dramatic Unity of the "Secunda Pastorum"'. In *Essays and Studies in Honor of Carleton Brown*. New York: New York University Press, 1940, 158–66.

See also 395, 396 (character), 6, 76 (further bibliography).

12   THE N-TOWN PLAYS

219   Ashley, Kathleen M. ' "Wyt" and "Wysdam" in the N-Town Cycle'. *PQ* 58 (1979): 121–35.

220   Cameron, Kenneth, and Stanley J. Kahrl. 'The N-Town Plays at Lincoln'. *TN* 20 (1965–6): 61–9.

221   Cameron, Kenneth, and Stanley J. Kahrl. 'Staging the N. Town Cycle'. *TN* 21 (1967): 122–38, 152–65.

222   Collins, Patrick J. *The N-Town Plays and Medieval Picture Cycles*. Kalamazoo: Western Michigan University, Medieval Institute Publications, 1979.

223   Fletcher, Alan J. 'Layers of Revision in the N-Town Marian Cycle'. *Neophilologus* 66 (1982): 469–78.

224 Fry, Timothy. 'The Unity of the Ludus Coventriae'. *SP* 48 (1951): 527–70.

225 Gauvin, Claude. *Un cycle du théâtre religieux Anglais au moyen âge: le jeu de la ville de N*. Paris: Éditions du CNRS, 1973.

226 Gay, Anne C. 'The "Stage" and Staging of the N-Town Plays'. *RORD* 10 (1967): 135–40.

227 Gibson, Gail McMurray. 'Bury St Edmunds, Lydgate, and the N-Town Cycle'. *Speculum* 56 (1981): 56–90.

228 Meredith, Peter. ' "Nolo mortem" and the *Ludus Coventriae* Play of the Woman Taken in Adultery'. *MÆ* 38 (1969): 38–54.

229 Meredith, Peter. 'A Reconsideration of Some Textual Problems in the N-Town Manuscript (BL MS Cotton Vespasian D viii)'. *LSE* 9 (1977): 35–50.

230 Plummer, J.F. 'The Logomachy of the N-Town Passion Play I'. *JEGP* 88 (1989): 311–31.

231 Poteet II, Daniel P. 'Time, Eternity, and Dramatic Form in *Ludus Coventriae* "Passion Play I" '. *CD* 8 (1975): 369–85. Also in *13*, 232–48.

232 Rose, Martial. 'The Staging of the Hegge Plays'. In *14*, 196–221.

233 Spector, Stephen. 'The Composition and Development of an Eclectic Manuscript: Cotton Vespasian D viii'. *LSE* 9 (1977): 62–83.

See also 6, 78 (further bibliography).

13 THE EAST ANGLIAN DRAMA

234 Baker, Donald C. 'When is a Text a Play? Reflections upon What Certain Late Medieval Dramatic Texts Can Tell Us'. In *12*, 20–41.

235 Beadle, Richard. 'The Medieval Drama of East Anglia: Studies in Dialect, Documentary Records and Stagecraft'. 2 vols., D.Phil. thesis, University of York, 1977.

236 Beadle, Richard. 'The East Anglian "Game Place": a Possibility for Further Research'. *REED Newsletter* 3 (1978): 2–4.

237 Beadle, Richard. 'Plays and Playing at Thetford and Nearby, 1498–1540'. *TN* 32 (1978): 4–11.

238 Beadle, Richard. 'Prolegomena to a Literary Geography of Later Medieval Norfolk'. In *Regionalism in Late Medieval Manuscripts and Texts*, ed. Felicity Riddy (Cambridge: D.S. Brewer, 1991), 89–105.

239 Beadle, Richard. 'Monk Thomas Hyngham's Hand in the Macro Manuscript'. Forthcoming.

240 Clark, Andrew. 'The Fifteenth Century Drama in Essex'. *Essex Review* 14 (1905): 104–10.

241 Clarke, R. Rainbird. *East Anglia*. London: Thames and Hudson, 1960.

242 Coldewey, John C. 'The Digby Plays and the Chelmsford Records'. *RORD* 18 (1975): 103–21.

243 Coldewey, John C. 'The Last Rise and Final Demise of Essex Town Drama'. *MLQ* 56 (1975): 239–60.

244 Coldewey, John C. 'That Enterprising Property Player: Semi-Professional Drama in Sixteenth-Century England'. *TN* 31 (1977): 5–12.

245 Coldewey, John C. 'Playing Companies at Aldeburgh 1566–1635'. Malone Society Collections, 9. Oxford: Oxford University Press, 1977 (for 1971).

246 Cutts, Cecilia. 'The Croxton Play: an Anti-Lollard Piece'. *MLQ* 5 (1944): 45–60.

247 Davis, Norman. 'The Language of the Pastons'. *Proceedings of the British Academy* 40 (1955): 119–44.

248 Dodd, Kenneth M. 'Another Elizabethan Theatre in the Round'. *Shakespeare Quarterly* 21 (1970): 125–56.

249 Dutka, JoAnna. 'Mystery Plays at Norwich: their Formation and Development'. *LSE* 10 (1975): 107–20.

250   Dutka, JoAnna. 'The Lost Dramatic Cycle of Norwich and the Grocers' Play of The Fall of Man'. *RES* 35 (1984): 1–13.
251   Galloway, David, ed. *Records of Early English Drama: Norwich 1540–1642*. Toronto: University of Toronto Press, 1984.
252   Galloway, David, and John Wasson, eds. *Records of Plays and Players in Norfolk and Suffolk 1330–1642*. Malone Society Collections, 11. Oxford: Oxford University Press, 1980–1.
253   Gibson, Gail McMurray. *The Theater of Devotion. East Anglian Drama and Society in the Late Middle Ages*. Chicago and London: University of Chicago Press, 1989.
254   Heiatt, Constance B. 'A Case for *Duk Moraud* as a Play of the Miracles of the Virgin'. *Medieval Studies* 32 (1970): 345–51.
255   Homan, Richard L. 'Two Exempla: Analogues to the *Play of the Sacrament* and *Dux Moraud*'. *CD* 18 (1984): 241–51.
256   Homan, Richard L. 'Devotional Themes in the Violence and Humor of the *Play of the Sacrament*'. *CD* 20 (1986): 327–40.
257   MacCulloch, Diarmid. *Suffolk and the Tudors*. Oxford: Clarendon Press, 1986.
258   Maltman, Sr Nicholas. 'Meaning and Art in the Croxton *Play of the Sacrament. ELH* 41 (1974): 149–64.
259   Mepham, W.A. 'General Survey of Medieval Drama in Essex'. *Essex Review* 54 (1945): 52–8, 107–12, 139–42.
260   Mepham, W.A. 'Medieval Plays in the Sixteenth Century: Heybridge and Braintree'. *Essex Review* 55 (1946): 8–18.
261   Mepham, W.A. 'Municipal Drama in Maldon'. *Essex Review* 55 (1946): 34–41.
262   Mepham, W.A. 'Medieval Drama in Essex: Dunmow'. *Essex Review* 55 (1946): 57–65, 129–36.
263   Mepham, W.A. 'Chelmsford Plays of the Sixteenth Century'. *Essex Review* 56 (1947): 148–52, 171–8.
264   Nichols, Ann Eljenholm. 'The Croxton *Play of the Sacrament*: a Re-Reading'. *CD* 22 (1988): 117–37.
265   Pfleiderer, Jean D. 'The Community of Language in the East Anglian Drama'. Ph.D diss., University of Colorado, 1981.
266   Wright, Robert R. 'Community Theatre in Late Medieval East Anglia'. *TN* 28 (1974): 24–39.
267   Wright, Robert R. 'The Medieval Theatre in Some Essex Towns: Dunmow, Chelmsford, Maldon, Heybridge and Braintree'. *Essex Journal* 9 (1974–5): 110–20.

14   THE CORNISH DRAMA

268   Bakere, Janet A. *The Cornish Ordinalia: a Critical Study*. Cardiff: University of Wales Press, 1980.
269   Crawford, T.D. 'The Composition of the Cornish *Ordinalia*'. *Old Cornwall* 9 (1979–85): 145–53.
270   Crawford, T.D. 'Stanza Forms and Social Status in *Beunans Meriasek*'. *Old Cornwall* 9 (1979–85): 431–9, 485–92.
271   Cross, Sally Joyce. 'Torturers and Tricksters in the Cornish *Ordinalia*'. *NM* 84 (1983): 448–53.
272   Denny, Neville. 'Arena Staging and Dramatic Quality in the Cornish Passion Play'. In *14*, 124–53.
273   Doble, Gilbert H. *St Meriadoc, Bishop and Confessor*. Truro: Netherton and Worth, 1935.
274   Ellis, P. Beresford. *The Cornish Language and its Literature*. London and Boston: Routledge and Kegan Paul, 1974.

275 Fowler, David C. 'The Date of the Cornish *Ordinalia*'. *Medieval Studies* 23 (1961): 91–125.

276 Fudge, Crysten. Aspects of Form in the Cornish *Ordinalia*. *Old Cornwall* 8 (1973–9): 457–64, 491–8.

277 Fudge, Crysten. *The Life of Cornish*. Redruth: Truran, 1982.

278 Harris, Markham, ed. *The Cornish Ordinalia. A Medieval Dramatic Trilogy*. Washington: Catholic University of America, 1969.

279 Harris, Markham, ed. *The Life of Meriasek. A Medieval Cornish Miracle Play*. Washington: Catholic University of America, 1977.

280 Holman, Treve. 'Cornish Plays and Playing Places'. *TN* 4 (1949–50): 52–4.

281 Jenner, Henry. *A History of the Cornish Language*. London: Nutt, 1904.

282 Jenner, Henry. 'The Cornish Drama, I and II'. *Celtic Review* 3 (1906–7): 360–75; 4 (1907–8): 41–68.

283 Long, F.R. 'New Light on the Mystery Plays of Cornwall'. *Old Cornwall* 7 (1972): 458–9.

284 Longsworth, Robert. *The Cornish Ordinalia, Religion and Dramaturgy*. Cambridge, Mass.: Harvard University Press, 1967.

285 Marx, C.W. 'The Problem of the Doctrine of the Redemption in the ME Mystery Plays and the Cornish *Ordinalia*'. *MÆ* 54 (1985): 20–32.

286 Meyer, R.T. 'The Liturgical Background of Medieval Cornish Drama'. *Trivium* 3 (1968): 48–58.

287 Meyer, R.T. 'The Middle Cornish Play *Beunans Meriasek*'. *CD* 3 (1969): 54–64.

288 Murdoch, Brian O. *The Recapitulated Fall*. Amsterdam: Rodopi, 1974.

289 Murdoch, Brian O. 'The Breton *Creation ar bet*'. *Zeitschrift für Celtische Philologie* 35 (1977): 157–79.

290 Murdoch, Brian O. 'The Holy Hostage: *de filio mulieris* in the Middle Cornish Play *Beunans Meriasek*'. *MÆ* 58 (1989): 258–75.

291 Murdoch, Brian O. '*Pascon agan Arluth*: the Literary Position of the Cornish Poem of the Passion'. *Studi Medievali* 22 (1981): 822–36.

292 Murdoch, Brian O. 'Creation, Fall and After in the Cornish *Gwreans an Bys*'. *Studi Medievali* 29 (1988): 685–705.

292a Murdoch, Brian O. *Cornish Literature*. Cambridge: D.S. Brewer, 1993.

293 Murdoch, Brian O. 'The Place-Names in the Cornish *Passio Christi*'. *Bulletin of the Board of Celtic Studies* (forthcoming).

294 Nance, R. Morton. 'The Plen an Gwary or Cornish Playing Place'. *Journal of the Royal Institution of Cornwall* 24 (1935): 191–211.

295 Nance, R. Morton. 'A Cornish Poem Restored'. *Old Cornwall* 4 (1943–51): 368–71.

296 Nance, R. Morton, and A.S.D. Smith, eds. *The Cornish Ordinalia*, ed. G. Sandercock. 3 vols. N.p.: Kesva an Tavas Kernewek/Cornish Language Board, 1982–9.

297 Neuss, Paula, 'Memorial Reconstruction in a Cornish Miracle Play'. *CD* 5 (1971): 129–37.

298 Neuss, Paula. 'The Staging of the "Creacion of the World"'. *TN* 33 (1979): 116–25. Also in *16*, 189–200.

299 Stokes, Whitley. 'The Passion, a Middle Cornish Poem'. *Transactions of the Philological Society* (1860–1): 1–100.

300 Thomas, Charles. *Christian Antiquities of Camborne*. St Austell: Warne, 1967.

301 Wellworth, George E. 'Methods of Production in the Medieval Cornish Drama'. *Speech Monographs* 24 (1957): 212–28.

302 Whetter, James. *The History of Glasney College*. Padstow: Tabb House, 1988.

See also 7 (bibliography)

15 THE MORALITY PLAYS AND EARLY INTERLUDES
General Studies

303 Bevington, David. *From Mankind to Marlowe: Growth of Structure in the Popular Drama of Tudor England.* Cambridge, Mass.: Harvard University Press, 1962.

304 Craik, T.W. *The Tudor Interlude.* Leicester: Leicester University Press, 1958.

305 Davenport, W.A. *Fifteenth-Century English Drama. The Early Moral Plays and their Literary Relations.* Cambridge: D.S. Brewer, 1982.

306 Fichte, Joerg O. 'The Presentation of Sin as Verbal Action in the Moral Interludes'. *Anglia* 103 (1985): 26–47.

307 Happé, Peter. ' "The Vice" and the Popular Theatre, 1547–80'. In *Poetry and Drama 1570–1700: Essays in Honour of Harold F. Brooks*, ed. Antony Coleman and Antony Hammond (London: Methuen, 1981), 13–31.

308 Jones, Marion. 'Early Moral Plays and the Earliest Secular Drama'. In *19*, 213–91.

309 Kelley, Michael R. *Flamboyant Drama: a Study of The Castle of Perseverance, Mankind and Wisdom.* Carbondale: Southern Illinois University Press, 1979.

310 Pettitt, Thomas. 'Tudor Interludes and the Winter Revels'. *METh* 6 (1984): 16–27.

311 Potter, Robert. *The English Morality Play.* London: Routledge and Kegan Paul, 1975.

312 Spivack, Bernard. *Shakespeare and the Allegory of Evil.* New York and London: Columbia University Press, 1958.

313 Wasson, John. 'The Morality Play: Ancestor of Elizabethan Drama?'. *CD* 13 (1979): 210–21. Also in *13*, 316–27.

314 Westfall, Suzanne R. *Patrons and Performance: Early Tudor Household Revels.* Oxford: Clarendon Press, 1990.

The Castle of Perseverance

315 Belsey, Catherine. 'The Stage Plan of *The Castle of Perseverance*'. *TN* 28 (1974): 124–32.

316 Cornelius, Roberta D. *The Figurative Castle* (Bryn Mawr, Pa.: Bryn Mawr University Press, 1930).

317 Forstater, Arthur, and Joseph L. Baird. ' "Walking and Wending": Mankind's Opening Speech'. *TN* 26 (1971–2): 60–4.

318 McCutchan, J. Wilson. 'Covetousness in *The Castle of Perseverance*'. *University of Virginia Studies* 4 (1951): 175–91.

319 Proudfoot, Richard. 'The Virtue of Perseverance'. In *18*, 92–109.

320 Riggio, Milla C. 'The Allegory of Feudal Acquisition in *The Castle of Perseverance*'. In *Allegory, Myth and Symbol*, ed. Morton W. Bloomfield. Cambridge, Mass.: Harvard University Press, 1981, 187–208.

321 Schell, Edgar T. 'On the Imitation of Life's Pilgrimage in *The Castle of Perseverance*'. *JEGP* 67 (1968): 235–48. Also in *21*, 279–91.

Wisdom

322 Bevington, David C. ' "Blake and Wyght, fowll and fayer": Stage Picture in *Wisdom Who Is Christ*'. *CD* 19 (1985): 136–50. Also in *329*, 18–38.

323 Gatch, Milton McC. 'Mysticism and Satire in the Morality of *Wisdom*'. *PQ* 53 (1974): 342–62.

324 Gibson, Gail McMurray. 'The Play of *Wisdom* and the Abbey of St Edmund'. *CD* 19 (1985): 117–35. Also in *329*, 39–66.

325 Happé, Peter. Review of *Wisdom. RORD* 24 (1981): 196–7.

326 Hill, Eugene D. 'The Trinitarian Allegory of the Moral Play of *Wisdom*'. *MP* 73 (1975–6): 121–35.

327 Riehle, Wolfgang. 'English Mysticism and the Morality Play *Wisdom Who is Christ*'. In *The Medieval Mystical Tradition in England*, ed. Marian Glasscoe. Exeter: University of Exeter, 1986, 202–15.

328 Riggio, Milla C. 'The Staging of *Wisdom*'. *RORD* 27 (1984): 167–78. Also in *330*, 1–17.
329 Riggio, Milla C. *The Play of Wisdom: its Text and Contexts*. New York: AMS Press, 1988.
330 Riggio, Milla C., ed. *The 'Wisdom' Symposium*. New York: AMS Press, 1986.

Mankind

331 Ashley, Kathleen M. 'Titivillus and the Battle of Words in *Mankind*'. *Annuale Medievale* 16 (1975): 128–50.
332 Denny, Neville. 'Aspects of the Staging of *Mankind*'. *MÆ* 43 (1974): 252–63.
333 Heap, Carl. 'On Performing *Mankind*'. *METh* 4 (1982): 93–103.
334 Neuss, Paula. 'Active and Idle Language: Dramatic Images in *Mankind*'. In *14*, 41–68.
335 Pettitt, Thomas. '*Mankind*: an English Fastnachtspiel?'. In *Festive Drama*, ed. Meg Twycross. Cambridge: Boydell and Brewer, forthcoming.
336 Smart, W.K. 'Mankind and the Mumming Plays'. *MLN* 32 (1917): 21–5.

Everyman

337 Conley, John. 'The Doctrine of Friendship in *Everyman*'. *Speculum* 44 (1969): 374–82.
338 Cowling, Douglas. 'The Angels' Song in *Everyman*'. *N&Q* 233 (1988): 301–3.
339 Kolve, V.A. '*Everyman* and the Parable of the Talents'. In *21*, 316–40.
340 Ryan, Lawrence V. 'Doctrine and Dramatic Structure in *Everyman*'. *Speculum* 32 (1957): 722–35.
341 Van Laan, Thomas F. '*Everyman*. A Structural Analysis'. *PMLA* 78 (1963): 465–75.

The Pride of Life

342 Mackenzie, W. Roy. 'The Debate Over the Soul in *The Pride of Life*'. *Washington University Studies* 9 (1921): 263–74.
See also under '*Folk Drama*', *Character, Staging, Music and Iconography*; 3, 5 (further bibliography).

16 SAINTS' PLAYS
General Studies

343 Davidson, Clifford, ed. *The Saint Play in Medieval Europe*. Kalamazoo: Western Michigan University, Medieval Institute Publications, 1986.
344 Davidson, Clifford. 'The Middle English Saint Play and its Iconography'. In *343*, 31–122.
345 Gerould, Gordon Hall. *Saints' Legends*. Boston and New York: n.p., 1916.
346 Grantley, Darryll. 'Producing Miracles'. In *18*, 78–91.
347 Happé, Peter. 'The Protestant Adaptation of the Saint Play'. In *343*, 205–40.
348 Jeffrey, David L. 'English Saints' Plays'. In *14*, 69–89.
349 Muir, Lynette R. 'The Saint Play in Medieval France'. In *343*, 123–80.
350 Villar, Mary del. 'Some Approaches to the Medieval English Saints' Play'. *RORD* 15–16 (1972–3): 83–91.
351 Wasson, John. 'The Secular Saint Plays of the Elizabethan Era'. In *343*, 241–60.
352 Wickham, Glynne. 'The Staging of Saint Plays in England'. In *The Medieval Drama*, ed. Sandro Sticca. Albany: State University of New York Press, 1972, 99–119.

Mary Magdalen

353 Coletti, Theresa. 'The Design of the Digby Play of *Mary Magdalene*'. *SP* 76 (1979): 313–33.
354 Grantley, Darryll. 'The Source of the Digby *Mary Magdalen*'. *N&Q* 229 (1984): 457–9.
355 Jones, Mary K.I. 'Pilgrimage from Text to Theater. A Study of the Staging of the Digby *Mary Magdalen*'. Ph.D. diss., University of Colorado, Boulder, 1977.

356 Maltman, Sr Nicholas. 'Light in and on the Digby *Mary Magdalene*'. In *Saints, Scholars and Heroes: Studies in Medieval Culture in Honour of Charles W. Jones*, 2 vols. ed. Margaret H. King and Wesley M. Stevens. Collegeville, Minn.: Hill Monastic Manuscript Library, 1979, vol. I, 257–80.

357 Velz, John W. 'Sovereignty in the Digby *Mary Magdalene*'. CD (1968): 32–43.

St Paul

358 Pentzell, Raymond J. 'The Medieval Theatre in the Street'. *Theatre Survey* 14 (1973): 1–21.

359 Villar, Mary del. 'The Staging of *The Conversion of St Paul*'. TN 25 (1970–1): 64–8.
See also 270, 273, 287, 290 (*St Meriasek*) and 84 (further bibliography)

17 'FOLK DRAMA'

360 Axton, Richard. 'Popular Modes in the Earliest Plays'. In *14*, 13–39.

361 Axton, Richard. 'Folk Play in Tudor Interludes'. In *English Drama: Forms and Development*, ed. Marie Axton and Raymond Williams. Cambridge: Cambridge University Press, 1977, 1–23.

362 Baskervill, Charles Read. 'Dramatic Aspects of Medieval Folk Festivals in England'. *SP* 17 (1920): 19–87.

363 Brody, Alan. *The English Mummers and their Plays*. London: Routledge and Kegan Paul, 1970.

364 Brown, Arthur. 'Folklore Elements in the Medieval Drama'. *Folklore* 63 (1952): 65–78.

365 Burson, A.C. 'Model and Text in Folk Drama'. *Journal of American Folklore* 93 (1980): 305–16.

366 Cawte, E.C., Alex Helm and N. Peacock. *English Ritual Drama: a Geographical Index*. London: The Folk-Lore Society, 1967.

367 Chambers, E.K. *The English Folk Play*. Oxford: Clarendon Press, 1933.

368 Dietrich, Julia C. 'Folk Drama Scholarship: the State of the Art'. *RORD* 19 (1976): 15–32.

369 Green, A.E. 'Popular Drama and the Mummers' Play'. In *Performance and Politics in Popular Drama*, ed. D. Bradby, L. James and B. Sharratt. Cambridge: Cambridge University Press, 1980, 139–66.

370 Green, Thomas A. 'Folk Drama'. *Journal of American Folklore* 94 (1981): 421–32.

371 Happé, Peter. 'The Vice and the Folk-drama'. *Folklore* 75 (1964): 161–93.

372 Laroque, François. *Shakespeare's Festive World: Elizabethan Seasonal Entertainment and the Professional Stage*. Cambridge: Cambridge University Press, 1991.

373 Mills, David. 'Drama and Folk Ritual'. In *19*, 122–51.

374 Parker, Roscoe E. 'Some Records of the "Somyr Play"'. In *Studies in Honor of John C. Hodges and Alvin Thaler*, ed. Richard B. Davis and John L. Lievesay. Knoxville: University of Tennessee Press, 1961, 19–26.

375 Pettitt, Thomas. 'Early English Traditional Drama: Approaches and Perspectives'. *RORD* 25 (1982): 1–30.

376 Pettitt, Thomas. 'English Folk Drama and the Early German *Fastnachtspiele*'. *Renaissance Drama* 13 (1982): 1–34.

377 Pettitt, Thomas. 'Here Comes I, Jack Straw'. *Folklore* 95 (1984): 3–20.

378 Renwick, R. de V. 'The Mummers' Play and *The Old Wives' Tale*'. *Journal of American Folklore* 94 (1981): 433–55.

379 Tiddy, R.J.E. *The Mummers' Play*. Oxford: Oxford University Press, 1923. Repr. Chicheley: Paul P.B. Minet, 1972.

380 Weimann, Robert. *Shakespeare and the Popular Tradition in the Theatre*, ed. and transl. by Robert Schwarz. Baltimore: The Johns Hopkins University Press, 1978.

381   Wiles, David, ed. *The Early Plays of Robin Hood*. Cambridge: D.S. Brewer, 1981. *See also* 9 (further bibliography).

18   CHARACTER

382   Auerbach, Erich. *Mimesis: the Representation of Reality in Western Literature*. Trans. Willard R. Trask. Princeton: Princeton University Press, 1953, 143–73.

383   Brawer, Robert A. 'The Characterization of Pilate in the York Cycle Play'. *SP* 69 (1972): 289–303.

384   Carpenter, Sarah. 'Morality Play Characters'. *METh* 5 (1983): 18–28.

385   Clopper, Lawrence M. 'Tyrants and Villains: Characterization in the Passion Sequence of the English Cycle Plays'. *MLQ* 41 (1980): 3–20.

386   Cushman, Lysander W. *The Devil and the Vice in the English Dramatic Literature before Shakespeare*. Halle: Niemeyer, 1900.

387   Davenport, Tony [W.A.]. 'Lusty Fresche Galaunts'. In *18*, 111-25.

388   Kantrowitz, Joanne S. 'Allegory'. In *16*, 144–51.

389   Mills, David. 'Characterization and the English Mystery Plays: a Critical Prologue'. *METh* 5 (1983): 5–17.

390   Parker, Roscoe E. 'The Reputation of Herod in Early English Literature'. *Speculum* 8 (1933): 59–67.

391   Schmitt, Natalie Crohn. 'The Idea of a Person in Medieval Morality Plays'. *CD* 12 (1978): 23–34. Also in *13*, 304–15.

392   Skey, Miriam. 'Herod the Great in Medieval European Drama'. *CD* 13 (1979): 330–64.

393   Staines, David. 'To Out-Herod Herod: the Development of a Dramatic Character'. *CD* 10 (1976): 29–53. Also in *13*, 207–31.

394   Vinter, Donna S. 'Didactic Characterization: the Towneley *Abraham*'. *CD* 14 (1980): 117–36. Also in *13*, 71–89.

395   Walter, H. *The Devil in English Literature*. Bern: Franke, 1978.

396   Williams, Arnold. *The Characterization of Pilate in the Towneley Plays*. East Lansing: Michigan State College Press, 1950.

19   STAGING: ACTORS, ACTING, COSTUMES, PROPS, SPECIAL EFFECTS ETC.

397   Anglo, Sydney. *Spectacle, Pageantry, and Early Tudor Policy*. Oxford: Clarendon Press, 1969.

398   Bergeron, David M. 'Medieval Drama and Tudor-Stuart Civic Pageantry'. *Journal of Medieval and Renaissance Studies* 2 (1972): 279–93.

399   Butterworth, Philip. ' "Gunnepowdyr, fyre and thondyr"'. *METh* 7 (1985): 68–76.

400   Cawley, A.C. 'The Staging of Medieval Drama'. In *19*, 1–66.

401   Cowen, Janet. ' "Heven and Erthe in Lytil Space"'. In *18*, 62–77.

402   Happé, Peter, 'Properties and Costumes in the Plays of John Bale'. *METh* 2 (1980): 55–65.

403   Happé, Peter, and others. 'Thoughts and "Transvestism" by Divers Hands'. *METh* 5 (1983): 110–22.

404   Hosley, Richard. 'Three Kinds of Outdoor Theatre before Shakespeare'. *Theatre Survey* 12 (1971): 1–33.

405   Kahrl, Stanley J. 'Medieval Staging and Performance'. In *12*, 219–37.

406   King, Pamela M. 'Spatial Semantics and the Medieval Theatre'. In *Themes in Drama*, vol. IX: *The Theatrical Space*, ed. James Redmond. Cambridge: Cambridge University Press, 1987, 45–58.

407   Kipling, Gordon. *The Triumph of Honour: Burgundian Origins of the Elizabethan Renaissance*. Leiden: Leiden University Press, 1977.

408 Kipling, Gordon. 'Triumphal Drama: Form in English Civic Pageantry'. *Renaissance Drama* 8 (1977): 37–56.

409 Meredith, Peter, and John E. Tailby, eds. *The Staging of Religious Drama in Europe in the Later Middle Ages: Texts and Documents in English Translation.* Kalamazoo: Western Michigan University, Medieval Institute Publications, 1983.

410 Mill, Anna J. 'Representations of Lyndsay's *Satyre of the Thrie Estatis*'. *PMLA* 47 (1932): 636–51.

411 Mills, David. 'Diagrams for Staging Plays, Early or Middle Fifteenth Century'. In *Local Maps and Plans from Medieval England*, ed. R.A. Skelton and P.D.A. Harvey. Oxford: Clarendon Press, 1986, 344–5.

412 Nagler, A.M. *The Medieval Religious Stage: Shapes and Phantoms.* New Haven and London: Yale University Press, 1976.

413 Nelson, Alan H. 'Principles of Professional Staging: York Cycle'. *MP* 67 (1970): 303–20.

414 Nelson, Alan H. 'Six-Wheeled Carts: an Underview'. *Technology and Culture* 13 (1972): 391–416.

415 Nelson, Alan H. 'Some Configurations of Staging in Medieval English Drama'. In *21*, 116–47.

416 Pederson, Steven I. *The Tournament Tradition and the Staging of 'The Castle of Perseverance'.* Ann Arbor: UMI Research Press, 1987.

417 Ragusa, Isa. 'Goethe's "Women's Parts Played by Men in the Roman Theatre"'. *METh* 6 (1984): 96–100.

418 Rastall, Richard. 'Female Roles in All-Male Casts'. *METh* 7 (1988): 25–51.

419 Robinson, J.W. 'Medieval English Acting'. *TN* 13 (1959): 83–8.

420 Schmitt, Natalie Crohn. 'Was there a Medieval Theatre in the Round? A Re-examination of the Evidence'. *TN* 23 (1968–9): 130–42; 24 (1969–70): 18–25. Also in *21*, 292–315.

421 Southern, Richard. *The Medieval Theatre in the Round.* London: Faber, 1957. 2nd edn 1975.

422 Southern, Richard. *The Staging of Plays before Shakespeare.* London: Faber, 1973.

423 Stevens, Martin. 'The York Cycle: from Procession to Play'. *LSE* 6 (1972): 37–61.

424 Twycross, Meg. '"Transvestism" in the Mystery Plays'. *METh* 5 (1983): 123–80.

425 Twycross, Meg. '"Apparell Comlye"'. In *18*, 30–48.

426 Twycross, Meg. 'The Chester Cycle Wardrobe'. In *188*, 100–23.

427 Twycross, Meg. 'Felsted of London: Silk-Dyer and Theatrical Entrepreneur'. *METh* 10 (1988): 4–16.

428 Twycross, Meg, and Sarah Carpenter. 'Masks in Medieval English Theatre'. *METh* 3 (1981): 7–44, 69–113.

429 Wasson, John. 'Professional Actors in the Middle Ages and Early Renaissance'. *Medieval and Renaissance Drama* 1 (1984): 1–11.

430 Wickham, Glynne. *Early English Stages, 1300–1660.* 3 vols. London: Routledge and Kegan Paul, 1959–81.

431 Wierum, Ann. '"Actors" and "Play Acting" in the Morality Tradition'. *Renaissance Drama* 3 (1970): 189–214.

432 Withington, Robert. *English Pageantry.* 2 vols. Cambridge, Mass.: Harvard University Press, 1918–20.

20 MUSIC AND DRAMA

433 Bowles, Edmund. 'The Role of Musical Instruments in Medieval Sacred Drama'. *Musical Quarterly* 45 (1959): 67–84.

434 Brainard, Ingrid. 'The Dance Manuals of the Late Middle Ages and Renaissance: a Survey'. *EDAM Newsletter* 6 (1984): 28–33.

435 Dutka, JoAnna. *Music in the English Mystery Plays*. Kalamazoo: Western Michigan University, Medieval Institute Publications, 1980.

436 Greene, Richard L. 'Carols in Tudor Drama'. In *Chaucer and Middle English Studies in Honor of Rossell Hope Robbins*, ed. Beryl Rowland. London: George Allen and Unwin, 1974, 357–65.

437 Happé, Peter. *Song in Morality Plays and Interludes*. Lancaster: Medieval English Theatre Monographs 1, 1991.

438 Harrison, Frank Ll. *Music in Medieval Britain*. London: Routledge and Kegan Paul, 1958.

439 Hoppin, Richard H. *Medieval Music*. New York: W.W. Norton & Co., 1978.

440 Long, John H., ed. *Music in English Renaissance Drama*. Lexington: University of Kentucky Press, 1968.

441 Moore, J.R. 'The Tradition of Angelic Singing in English Drama'. *JEGP* 22 (1923): 89–99.

442 Rastall, Richard. 'All hefne makyth melody'. In *18*, 1–12.

443 Rastall, Richard. 'Music in the Cycle Plays'. In *12*, 192–218.

444 Smoldon, William L. *The Music of the Medieval Church Dramas*. London and New York: Oxford University Press, 1980.

445 Stevens, John. 'Music in Medieval Drama'. *Proceedings of the Royal Musical Association* 84 (1958): 81–95.

446 Stevens, John. *Music and Poetry in the Early Tudor Court*. Cambridge: Cambridge University Press, 1961; repr. 1979.

447 Stevens, John. 'Medieval Drama'. In *The Grove Dictionary of Music and Musicians*, 6th edn, ed. Stanley Sadie, (London: Macmillan, 1980), vol. XII, 21–58.

448 Stevens, John. *Words and Music in the Middle Ages: Song, Narrative Dance and Drama, 1050–1350*. Cambridge: Cambridge University Press, 1986.

See also *165*, *172* (York), *189*, *190* (Chester), *338* (*Everyman*).

21 ART AND DRAMA

449 Anderson, M.D. *Drama and Imagery in English Medieval Churches*. Cambridge: Cambridge University Press, 1963.

450 Bevington, David, ed. *Homo, Memento Finis: The Iconography of Just Judgement in Medieval Art and Drama*. Kalamazoo: Western Michigan University, Medieval Institute Publications, 1985.

451 Cave, C.J.P. *Roof Bosses in Medieval Churches*. Cambridge: Cambridge University Press, 1948.

452 Davidson, Clifford. 'Early Drama, Art and Music [EDAM]: A New Project'. *RORD* 20 (1977): 91–4.

453 Davidson, Clifford. *Drama and Art: an Introduction to the Use of Evidence from the Visual Arts for the Study of Early Drama*. Kalamazoo: Western Michigan University, Medieval Institute Publications, 1977.

454 Davidson, Clifford. 'Iconography: Some Problems of Terminology in the Study of Drama and Theater of the Renaissance'. *RORD* 29 (1986–7): 7–14.

455 Davidson, Clifford. 'The Lost Coventry Drapers' Play in its Iconographic Context'. *LSE* 17 (1988): 141–58.

456 Davidson, Clifford. *Visualizing the Moral Life: Medieval Iconography and the Macro Morality Plays*. New York: AMS Press, 1989.

157 Didron, Adolphe N. *Christian Iconography; or, the History of Christian Art in the Middle Ages*. Transl. E.J. Millington. 2 vols. London: Henry G. Bohn, 1851–86.

458 Hassall, W.O., ed. *The Holkham Bible Picture Book*. London: Dropmore Press, 1954.

459 Hildburgh, W.L. 'English Alabaster Carvings as Records of Medieval English Drama'. *Archaeologia* 93 (1949): 51–101.

460 Hodnett, Edward. *English Woodcuts, 1480–1535*. Rev. edn. Oxford: Oxford University Press, 1973.

461 Mâle, Emile. *The Gothic Image: Religious Art in France of the Thirteenth Century*. Transl. D. Nussey. London: J.M. Dent and Sons, 1913; repr. London: Collins, 1961.

462 Nichols, Ann E. 'Costume in the Moralities: the Evidence of East Anglian Art'. *CD* 20 (1986–7): 305–14.

463 Pächt, Otto. *The Rise of Pictorial Narrative in Twelfth-Century England*. Oxford: Clarendon Press, 1962.

464 Panofsky, Erwin. *Studies in Iconography*. Oxford: Clarendon Press, 1939; repr. New York: Harper and Row, 1962.

465 Phillips, J.B. *The Reformation of Images: Destruction of Art in England, 1535–1660*. Berkeley and Los Angeles: University of California Press, 1973.

466 Ragusa, Isa. 'The Princeton Index of Christian Art'. *METh* 4 (1982): 56–60.

467 Réau, Louis. *Iconographie de l'Art Chrétien*. 3 vols. Paris: Presses Universitaires de France, 1955–9.

468 Salter, Elizabeth. 'The Annunciation to the Shepherds in Later Medieval Art and Drama'. In her *English and International: Studies in the Literature, Art and Patronage of Medieval England*, ed. Derek Pearsall and Nicolette Zeeman. Cambridge: Cambridge University Press, 1988, 272–92.

469 Schiller, Gertrud. *Iconography of Christian Art*. Transl. J. Seligman. 2 vols., Greenwich, Conn.: New York Graphic Society, 1971.

470 Sheingorn, Pamela. 'On Using Medieval Art in the Study of Medieval Drama: an Introduction to Methodology'. *RORD* 22 (1979): 101–9.

471 Twycross, Meg. 'Beyond the Picture Theory: Image and Activity in Medieval Drama'. *Word and Image* 4 (1988): 589–617.

See also *147* (York), *183* (Chester), *222*, *481* (N-Town), *253* (East Anglia).

22 MODERN PRODUCTIONS OF MEDIEVAL PLAYS
General Studies

472 Elliott, John R., Jr. *Playing God: Medieval Mysteries on the Modern Stage*. Toronto: University of Toronto Press, 1989.

473 Jellicoe, Ann. *Community Plays: How to Put Them On*. London: Methuen, 1987.

474 Jones, Derek. *The Making of The Mysteries*. London: Channel Four Television, 1985.

475 McGrath, John. *A Good Night Out. Popular Theatre: Audience, Class and Form*. London: Methuen, 1981.

476 Meredith, Peter. 'Original-staging Productions of English Medieval Plays: Ideals, Evidence and Practice'. In *Popular Drama in Northern Europe in the Later Middle Ages: a Symposium*, ed. Flemming G. Andersen and others. Odense: Odense University Press, 1988, 65–100.

477 Neuss, Paula. 'God and Embarrassment'. In *Themes in Drama*, vol V: *Drama and Religion*, ed. James Redmond. Cambridge: Cambridge University Press, 1983, 241–53.

Particular productions

478 Happé, Peter. 'Acting the York Mystery Plays: a Consideration of Modes'. *METh* 10 (1988): 112–16.

479 McKinnell, John. 'Producing the York Mary Plays'. *METh* 12 (1990): 101–23.

480 Carpenter, Sarah. 'Towneley Plays at Wakefield'. *METh* 2 (1980) 49–52.

481 Coletti, Theresa M. and Kathleen M. Ashley. 'The N-Town Passion at Toronto and Late Medieval Passion Iconography'. *RORD* 24 (1981): 181–92.

482 McKinnell, John. 'Staging the Digby *Mary Magdalen*'. *METh* 6 (1984): 126–52.

Videotapes of modern productions

483 *The Castle of Perseverance*, Toronto 1979. Poculi Ludique Societas of Toronto.

484 *The N-Town Passion Play*, Toronto 1981. Poculi Ludique Societas of Toronto.

485 *The Chester Purification and Doctors*, Joculatores Lancastriensis. Lancaster University Television 1983.

486 *Fulgens and Lucres*, Joculatores Lancastriensis. Lancaster University Television, 1984.

487 *The Mysteries*, National Theatre. Channel Four Television, 1985.

488 *The Assumption of the Virgin* (York, 1988), Durham Medieval Players, Flare Video, 1988.

489 *That Girl from Andros* (*Terence in English*), Joculatores Lancastriensis. Lancaster University Television, 1988.

490 *The York 'Doomsday'*, Joculatores Lancastriensis. Lancaster University Television, 1988.

GENERAL INDEX